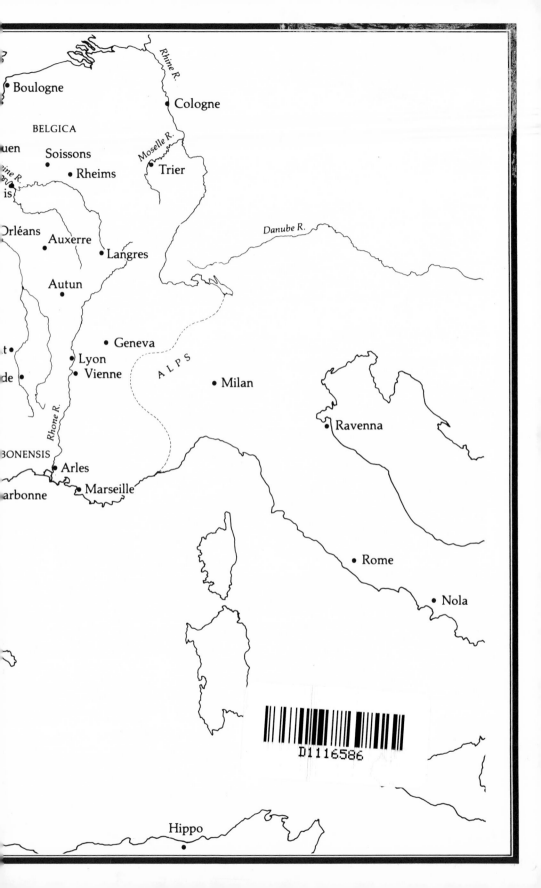

Boulogne

Cologne

BELGICA

uen

Soissons

Rheims

Trier

is

Orléans

Auxerre

Langres

Autun

Geneva

Lyon

Vienne

Milan

Ravenna

Rhone R.

BONENSIS

Arles

Marseille

arbonne

Rome

Nola

Hippo

Rhine R.

Moselle R.

Danube R.

ALPS

ine R.

D1116586

# THE TRANSFORMATION OF THE
# CLASSICAL HERITAGE

Peter Brown, General Editor

LEADERSHIP AND COMMUNITY
IN LATE ANTIQUE GAUL

RAYMOND VAN DAM

# Leadership and Community in Late Antique Gaul

UNIVERSITY OF CALIFORNIA PRESS
Berkeley · Los Angeles · London

DC
62
.V36
1985

University of California Press
Berkeley and Los Angeles, California

University of California Press, Ltd.
London, England

© 1985 by
The Regents of the University of California

Library of Congress Cataloging in Publication Data
Van Dam, Raymond.
   Leadership and community in late antique Gaul.
   Bibliography: p.
   Includes index.
   1. Gaul—58 B.C.–511 A.D.   2. Merovingians—History.
I. Title.
DC62.V36   1985      936.4      83-24321
ISBN 0-520-05162-9

Printed in the United States of America

1 2 3 4 5 6 7 8 9

*For three teachers, three friends:*

**BERT VANDER LEE**
**BOB OTTEN**
**DICK WHITTAKER**

# CONTENTS

# PREFACE

When Fortunatus set out to describe the life and miracles of St. Hilary, he was properly daunted by the task: it was, he wrote, like trying "to put one's finger on heaven." All historians know the feeling well, and they also know that their attempts to take the past into their own hands are greatly dependent upon the support and encouragement of others.

While researching and writing this book I have had the rare privilege of being associated with several outstanding academic institutions. I am especially grateful to King's College and Churchill College in the University of Cambridge, Stanford University, Dumbarton Oaks Center for Byzantine Studies, and now the University of Texas at Austin for financial support, library resources, and the time to work.

But I owe the most to friends: to Dick Whittaker, who supervised the dissertation that became parts of the first chapters of this book; to Peter Brown, who inspired my interest in Late Antiquity through his writings and now continues to encourage and enlighten me; to Dave Braund, Peter Garnsey, Richard Gordon, John Heath, Kent Kelley, Geoffrey Lloyd, Brent Shaw, and Ian Wood, for advice and criticism over the years; to Jody Maxmin and Aaron, for midnight phone calls; and to Doris Kretschmer, for assistance at the Press. A mere listing of names does not do justice to all they have taught me; and a simple acknowledgment of my gratitude can only hint at additional personal memories of intellectual inspiration and quiet laughter.

*—University of Texas at Austin*

# ABBREVIATIONS

| | |
|---|---|
| Budé | Collection des Universités de France publiée sous le patronage de l'Association Guillaume Budé (Paris). |
| *CChr. lat.* | *Corpus Christianorum*, series latina (Turnhout). |
| *Chron. Min.* | *Chronica minora*. Vols. I–III, edited by Th. Mommsen (= *MGH*, AA 9 [1892], 11 [1894], 13 [1898]). |
| *CIL* | *Corpus inscriptionum latinarum* (Berlin). |
| *CSEL* | *Corpus scriptorum ecclesiasticorum latinorum* (Vienna). |
| *DACL* | *Dictionnaire d'archéologie chrétienne et de liturgie* (Paris). |
| *DHGE* | *Dictionnaire d'histoire et de géographie ecclésiastiques* (Paris). |
| *DTC* | *Dictionnaire de théologie catholique* (Paris). |
| *FHG* | *Fragmenta historicorum graecorum*. Vol. IV, edited by C. Müller (Paris, 1851). |
| *GCS* | *Die grieschischen christlichen Schriftsteller der ersten Jahrhunderte* (Berlin). |
| *ILCV* | *Inscriptiones latinae christianae veteres*, edited by E. Diehl (Berlin, 1925–1931). |
| *ILS* | *Inscriptiones latinae selectae*, edited by H. Dessau (Berlin, 1892–1916). |
| LeBlant | E. LeBlant, ed. *Inscriptions chrétiennes de la Gaule antérieures au VIII<sup>e</sup> siècle*. 2 vols. (Paris, 1856–1865). |
| Loeb | Loeb Classical Library (Cambridge, Mass.). |
| *MGH* | *Monumenta Germaniae historica* (Berlin, Hannover, and Leipzig). |

AA   Auctores antiquissimi
SRM  Scriptores rerum merovingicarum
OCT  Oxford Classical Texts (Oxford).
PG   *Patrologia graeca* (Paris).
PL   *Patrologia latina* (Paris); and Supplementa, edited by A. Hamman (Paris, 1958–1974).
PLRE  *The prosopography of the later Roman Empire.* Vol. I, edited by A. H. M. Jones, J. R. Martindale, and J. Morris (Cambridge, 1971); Vol. II, edited by J. R. Martindale (Cambridge, 1980).
RE   *Paulys Real-Encyclopädie der classischen Altertumswissenschaft* (Stuttgart and Munich).
RIB  *The Roman inscriptions of Britain.* Vol. I, edited by R. G. Collingwood and R. P. Wright (Oxford, 1965).
SChr.  *Sources chrétiennes* (Paris).

# CHAPTER 1

# Introduction

This is a book about people, among them a Roman emperor who becomes very popular among the citizens of Gaul, even though he has virtually nothing in common with them and even finds their beer distasteful, and a Frankish king on his deathbed who gently chides the King of Heaven for allowing a fellow monarch to die in pain;[1] a village teacher in Spain who suddenly finds himself accused of being a Manichee and a magician, and a middle-aged professor at Bordeaux who is first invited to teach the young son of an emperor but is then promoted, a bit over his head, to the highest positions in the civil administration; an ex-soldier who lives like an uncivilized hermit but still becomes the most influential bishop of his time and, after his death, the most important saint of early medieval Gaul, and an educated Gallic nobleman who moves to the most popular resort area of Italy, but only in order to live as an ascetic near the shrine of his patron saint; a man who is stricken with paralysis for lacing his boots on a Sunday, and a woman who falls in love with her favorite saint.

In order to utilize these vignettes as more than anecdotes, however, this book has two main goals, which are complementary. One is to recast the historical problem of the transformation of the ancient classical world into the medieval Christian world as a less abstract and more immediately personal process by emphasizing the behavior and feelings of people; the other is to offer new interpretations of some conventional issues. Because discussion of this

1. Gregory of Tours *HF* IV.21. Perhaps King Chlothar was most annoyed because his fate was now in the hands of the same King of Heaven who had already seduced one of his wives into a convent: cf. Baudonivia *Vita Radegundis* II.4.

transformation is potentially endless, the boundaries of this book about Late Antiquity in Gaul are determined, first, by chronology and geography. Although before the middle of the third century most of Gaul beyond the southeastern corner of Narbonensis seems to have been peripheral to the affairs of the Roman Empire, thereafter barbarian pressure on the frontiers made these provinces a major concern of the imperial administration, a concern reflected by the literary sources. At the later end, a terminal date of 600 not only approximately coincides with the deaths of Gregory of Tours and his friend Fortunatus; it is also an appropriate point at which to conclude this study because the seventh century marks other significant changes in Gallic society and culture.[2] Geographically the emphasis is on Gaul from the Pyrenees to the Rhine, although literary material from Spain is often included, whereas southeastern Gaul is usually neglected, largely because Provence can be better considered in conjunction with northern Italy.

A second limitation on the subjects discussed in this book reflects an assessment about the topics that can contribute to our understanding of how people lived out this transformation and for which we have sufficient literary evidence. For many modern historians the fate of Gaul has come to encapsulate in miniature the fate of the Roman Empire in the West; Fustel de Coulanges, Dill, Lot, Bloch, Stroheker, Ewig, and Riché are a few of the outstanding historians of the ancient world who have been attracted to the study of late antique Gaul. Given their fine surveys I have decided not to write a narrative or descriptive history for either the period or the region, but rather to organize the material around topics that are often neglected, specifically, the role of local leaders and their sources of local authority, and the style of life in small communities. Because these two themes of leadership and community bring us closer to the underlying stable characteristics of traditional societies, they also seemed to me to have the poten-

2. Stroheker (1965) 275–308, is an excellent survey. As a brief selection from many other fine studies, see also Riché (1962) 232–3, 252–4, 271–4, for the breakdown of the old classical culture; Wallace-Hadrill (1971) 47–71, for new theories of European kingship; Wood (1977) 12–13, for a change in the pattern of royal succession; Claude (1964) 79, for the growing ascendancy of the aristocracy over the kings; Prinz (1965) 121–51, for the introduction of Irish monasticism; Duby (1974), for the expansion of the European economy; and below, Chapter 10, for a widening of the gap between written Latin and spoken languages and the fusion of the Roman, Frankish, and Burgundian aristocracies.

tial to help us better understand some of the more "superficial" problems about late antique Gaul, such as the transformation of the aristocracy with the appearance of an imperial court and then of an ecclesiastical hierarchy, and the rise and significance of relic cults. For in many cases the impact of the imperial court, the Christian church, and the barbarian kingdoms will resemble only so many coats of different-colored paint over characteristics of living in local communities, which remained remarkably durable throughout the period.

The second goal of this book is historiographical and arose out of my own uneasiness or frustration with other research on the period. As modern study of Late Antiquity expanded, it seemed to me that we were running the risks of turning the paths our predecessors had mapped out into ruts and of neglecting both new topics and alternative interpretations. In my own research I have therefore tried to define some new interpretations and new problems for further consideration.

One historiographical intention arose as a reaction to the conventional division of labor between secular and ecclesiastical history. In fact, the connection between the two must be preserved, because the mystery of the replacement of a pagan society by a predominately Christian one lies at the core of the transformation of the ancient world into the medieval world. Although virtually all scholars who work on late antique Gaul have had to consider this transformation, my purposes were, first, to make the connection explicit, and second, to evaluate it against a background of existing constraints and preconceptions about local leadership and communities.

Another historiographical intention was to modify the emphasis that previous research has placed on the behavior of either secular or ecclesiastical elites. The development of Christianity in Gallic society poses many problems, in part because our initial information in the fourth century makes Christianity appear already as a fully mature system of beliefs, in part too because the limited amount of information often prevents us from adequately evaluating such alternatives to orthodox Christianity as paganism and heresy. In contrast, the development of the aristocracy seems to offer a more coherent chronological progression from local men of authority to imperial magistrates to bishops. Hence its dynamism is often allowed to act as the organizing paradigm for the transformation of all aspects of Gallic society, and the intrigues of elites, whether secular or ecclesiastical, are allowed to substitute for discussion of the values that made aristocratic competition possible because they were shared with others.

Because our literary sources are so biased toward Gallic aristocracies, this book too cannot avoid discussion of them, but it also tries to put this top-heavy perspective into a wider context. An emphasis on the nature of life in small communities was therefore selected to complement the theme of local leadership. Virtually all the significant activities of elites took place in public, so that when Bishop Marcellus of Paris fought a huge serpent, "he won his triumph before the eyes of the citizens in a spiritual theater."[3] Rather than concentrating only on the feuds between aristocrats, I have tried also to bring the audience into the drama. For leadership cannot be understood in isolation from the communities that shaped it, and men of authority (including emperors and saints) cannot be isolated from their relationships with those dependent on them.

A third historiographical intention was to emphasize the difficulty of writing a smooth narrative for this period, even for the activities of elites, because our literary sources are so uneven in quality and quantity. Rather than trying to impose a chronicle-like narrative on the recorded events, I have concentrated on the specific incidents or people for which we have sufficient information and used them as paradigm cases, although without claiming that they necessarily represent the great turning points in the transformation of Gallic society. The Bagaudae were not responsible for bringing down the Roman Empire in Gaul, Priscillianism was not a major heresy in the history of Christianity, St. Martin did not single-handedly convert Gaul to Christianity, nor was his cult at Tours the only significant one in early Merovingian Gaul. Although I have tried to infer connections between disparate topics, times, and sources, I have also wanted to underline the limitations of an analysis based on these particular people and incidents.

These intentions were, however, preliminary to my primary purpose of interpreting the information at our disposal. Although I have gratefully drawn upon a long tradition of research offered by Roman and medieval historians, theologians, and patristic scholars, I have also found that its models of explanation were sometimes inadequate for understanding even the topics around

3. Fortunatus *Vita Marcelli* 46.

which they had first been constructed. In most cases I have therefore offered alternative or supplementary interpretations. In Part I
of the book I have discussed two closely related topics, the essentially stable local authority of Gallic aristocrats and the contrast
between the opinions of an "animating center" (usually an imperial court) and the realities of local authority on the periphery.
This discussion leads to a new interpretation of the Bagaudae,
who, although often described by modern historians as bandits or
peasants in revolt against the Roman Empire, instead demonstrate the emergence of local men of authority whenever the imperial administration failed or disappeared.

But a perspective that stresses the underlying continuity of local authority does not directly help us understand the transformation of many of these men into Christian bishops during later
centuries. After the disappearance of the Roman administration
during the fifth century we might have expected instead the reemergence of a series of local men of authority surrounded by
their dependent retainers and supporters. This expectation is
strengthened by Part II, which discusses life in the early Christian
communities of Gaul and Spain and emphasizes the highly restricted ideology that Christianity had to abandon if it was to
spread more widely. On the basis of an analysis of how educated
laymen and wealthy widows could not be easily accommodated
within the demands for conformity generated by small communities, and of how accusations of heresy or Manichaeism were
often used to deal with people who seemed out of place, I pro-
pose a new interpretation of the heresy of Priscillian and his supporters in terms of community dynamics.

These first two parts pose most concisely the element of paradox in the transformation of Gallic society. Often the entire process is taken for granted, as if it had been predetermined that
Gallic society would be totally Christianized and that local elites
could with apparent ease maintain their authority and prestige
throughout this long period. Yet it is obvious that both communities and aristocrats had first to revise their thinking before conversion to Christianity and the appearance of Gallic aristocrats as
bishops became possible. In Part III I discuss aspects of this wider,
but in many respects still improbable, fusion between Christianity and society during the later fourth and fifth centuries. Although concentrating on such familiar figures as Martin of Tours
and Sidonius of Clermont, I have offered different explanations of

the symbiosis of secular ideology with Christianity and of the rise of Christian relic cults to prominence.

In Part IV I discuss aspects of the new Christian society during the age of Gregory of Tours in the sixth century. This is the largest group of chapters, for the simple reason that we do not have information of this concentrated quality for earlier centuries. In order to conjure up a social order that is quite alien to our ways of thinking, I have investigated how a Christian perspective on society, as focused in particular on the shrine of St. Martin at Tours, offered a world view by means of which the aristocracy could continue to ensure its own locally prominent role and all people could articulate the values and conventions of their communities through the organization of sacred space and sacred time and through notions of illness and healing. The miracle stories of Gregory offer us many examples of people's behavior. Hence, unlike theological treatises, they also allow us to reconstruct the ordinary mental perceptions that made sense of these actions. Gregory and his contemporaries may have sincerely thought that relics were sacred and saints were holy on the basis of some divine objective criterion, but in fact, in these stories of miracles and the lives of saints we can see people at work on the making of holiness by using it to help them define authority, prestige, and meaning in their communities.

Discussing the material in this way produces, admittedly, an apparently lopsided account that accents social misfits, such as bandits, heretics, and prophets, as well as ideas of space, illness, and time. As I have already said, these topics are largely heuristic devices, ways of organizing familiar material into unfamiliar interpretations and of investigating themes about which our literary sources tend to be reticent. Yet, although study of this period of transformation is best confined to snapshots emphasizing the people and topics for which we have adequate information, we can still riffle through them to give the illusion of a motion picture illustrating a few major themes. For throughout this period the roles of local leaders and the pressures of living in small communities remained remarkably consistent. In short, the transformation of Gallic society during the period from 250 to 600 had a greater impact on the ways people thought about and articulated aspects of their society than on the ways they actually lived.

# I

# Local Authority
# and Central Administration

Emperors and bandits seem an unlikely combination in a book on the Roman Empire. Their conjunction in this part introduces, first, the relationship between late Roman Gaul and the rest of the empire, a relationship that depended largely on the presence or absence of emperors during periods of insecurity; and second, the nature of the authority exercised by local men of influence for small communities, whether their authority was seen as legitimate or not by the central administration. Because our literary sources described and evaluated behavior in the provinces from a dominant, imperial perspective, we could easily take over their prejudices and speak disparagingly of usurpers, bandits, and peasants in revolt. In fact, however, these conventional interpretations—both ancient and modern—are neither historically valid nor historiographically useful, because, as we will see, questions of legality were often of secondary (or no) importance for the inhabitants of Gaul, who were more concerned with security, generosity, and justice. At a local level people appealed for the assistance of whatever influential men were available, whether these were imperial magistrates, army officers, aristocratic landowners, or even bandits. At certain times during the late empire the authority of these various men overlapped, not just when aristocrats served in the imperial administration or when emperors employed even bandits in their service, but also when men with local authority adopted, or were invested by their supporters with, the trappings of imperial power. This discussion of local authority will furthermore provide a context for subsequent discussions about the rise of Christian bishops to prominence in Gallic society and about the merger between these bishops and the resident aristocracy; as we will see, changes in the distribution and functioning of authority could coexist with stability in local social structure and ideological values.

In these ways we can animate our scarce data and attempt to sidestep both the prejudices and the silences inherent in the literary sources. Not only did the imperial presence generate expectations and reactions that ancient writers often took for granted and thus did not mention, but local men of authority, even bandits, performed necessary functions that the condescending tone of the governing elites often obscured. Modern historians should not imagine these different types of leaders in terms of hierarchical levels of authority, as if an effective chain of command radiated down from the emperor, because powerful constraints restricted the exercise of authority in ancient societies. The emperors may have presided over the central administration and been honored in the imperial cult, but these institutions served as much to isolate them as to transmit their will; at a local level, authority may have been justified by the appropriate symbols of legitimacy, but it was best guaranteed by physical presence. Local leaders were present; the emperor and his magistrates, in most places, were not.

CHAPTER 2

# Emperors and Bandits
# in Roman Gaul

## Emperors and the Aristocracy

"Because of your presence the barbarians were afraid to cross the Rhine."[1] With these words a Gallic orator speaking before the emperor Constantine at Trier in 313 summed up what the "presence" of an emperor meant for the provinces of Gaul during the later Roman Empire. Other contemporary Gallic orators also celebrated the "restoration" of the empire after the confusion of the third century, and in their panegyrics they echoed the optimistic slogans engraved on coins and monuments.[2] According to them, the Roman world was once again an "undivided heritage."[3]

In fact, the establishment of a legitimate imperial court in Gaul in the later third century did benefit the Gallic provinces in many ways. Not only did the imperial court provide security (even if occasionally ineffective) against the pressures of barbarian settlers and invaders,[4] it also offered immediate access to the generos-

---

Galletier (1949–1955) is a fine edition with French translation, which numbers the panegyrics in chronological order. References here to the panegyrics follow his enumeration, although parentheses enclose the number of the panegyric in the manuscript sequence, the arrangement used in the edition of R. A. B. Mynors, *XII Panegyrici latini* (OCT, 1964). In addition to the introductory discussions by Galletier in his edition, MacCormack (1975) (substantially repeated in *Rev. étud. augustiniennes* 22 [1976] 29–77) is an excellent survey of prose panegyrics and their role in late antique society.

    1. *Pan. lat.* IX(12).22.3.

    2. *Pan. lat.* II(10).1.5, 3.1.

    3. *Pan. lat.* III(11).6.3; in contrast, see IV(8).10.1.

    4. A constant theme in the panegyrics: cf. II(10).7.7, and X(4).38.3. For campaigns against the Germans under the Tetrarchy, see Kolendo (1970), and Barnes (1976).

ity of the emperor. Trier, for instance, which became the seat of the imperial court in Gaul, received significant financial support from the emperors for new building projects.[5] Because of the nature of the surviving panegyrics Autun provides another, better-documented example of the new relationship between emperors and Gallic cities.

During the winter of 269/70 Autun had been besieged and sacked, probably by one of the local leaders and his supporters who were competing for power in Gaul. The city was in chaos, and many families either were forced to leave or simply deserted the ruins.[6] During the 290s Autun began to revive when the emperor Constantius brought in British craftsmen to help rebuild and encouraged the settlement of barbarians in the area.[7] The emperor also restored the municipal school by providing financial assistance and by appointing a new director. In 310 an orator invited Constantius' son Constantine, by then an emperor himself, to visit Autun, so that he might display his own generosity by restoring more buildings.[8] When Constantine visited the next year, another orator described his arrival into the city. "All men, all ages, rushed together from the fields so that they might see in person the man they had gladly hoped would visit them. . . . Without prompting you deigned to invite us to approach your divinity, to speak to us and to ask us what we desired. . . . As we lay prostrate at your feet you spoke most generously and had us stand up."[9] Constantine, according to this orator, was moved to tears, and as a result of his visit Autun received instantaneous relief from the difficulties it was facing in complying with the demands of the new tax assessments.

Individuals likewise benefited from the proximity of an imperial court. One orator, presumably a professor at a Gallic school, delivered a panegyric before the emperor Maximian, who then promoted him into the imperial bureaucracy;[10] another orator, who had once held office in the imperial bureaucracy, boldly recommended to the emperor his own five sons as well as his stu-

5. *Pan. lat.* VII(6).22.5–7, with Wightman (1970) 58–70, 98–123. For imperial generosity to Rheims, see *ILS* 703.
6. *Pan. lat.* VIII(5).4.4; cf. below, p. 304 for the family of Ausonius.
7. *Pan. lat.* IV(8).9.3, 21.2; V(9).4.3; and the survey of Buckley (1981).
8. *Pan. lat.* VII(6).22.     9. *Pan. lat.* VIII(5).8–9.
10. *Pan. lat.* IV(8).1.4–5.

dents, some of whom were already serving in the provincial administration.[11]

These panegyrics are our principal literary source of information about Gaul in the later third and early fourth centuries, and they can easily promote the impression that Gaul was then an integral, fully Romanized part of the empire. The orators consciously contributed to this impression by deliberately inserting their Gallic history into the mainstream of Roman history. One orator, for instance, claimed that the citizens of Autun had been "brothers" of the Romans even before the conquest by Julius Caesar three centuries earlier, and that they had assisted in the conversion of the more barbarian peoples of Gaul such as the Celts and the Belgians into true Romans.[12] In fact, these panegyrics occasionally present us with the strange spectacle of a provincial Gallic orator conceding that the present Roman emperor (admittedly a provincial himself) might not understand allusions to ancient Roman history.[13]

The primary purpose of these ceremonies and panegyrics was to sustain the illusion of a unified empire. Everywhere emperors went a similar language of authority was used to greet and address them. Not only were the ceremonies celebrating their arrivals at cities orchestrated according to the same score,[14] but the panegyrics addressed to emperors carefully followed the appropriate rules for composition. With this homogeneity of imperial idiom, emperors and their subjects could feel themselves part of a single empire, which was in turn a reflection on earth of a cosmic and divine harmony. In the dialogue between emperors and subjects these ceremonies and panegyrics helped create a consensus in which the emperor was morally justified in the demands he made upon cities and individuals, while in return they could expect him to show generosity; as we have seen, these expectations were often fulfilled.[15]

Once an imperial court was resident in Trier, Gaul seems to have become not merely an integral but a central part of the empire, one of the atomic nuclei of this political, moral, and cosmic

11. *Pan. lat.* VII(6).23.1–2.
12. *Pan. lat.* VIII(5).3.     13. *Pan. lat.* II(10).8.1–2.
14. On the ceremony of *adventus*, see MacCormack (1972), and (1981) 17–89.
15. Burdeau (1964) is an excellent discussion of the ideology of consensus; see also MacCormack (1975) 154–9, and (1981) 272–3.

harmony. Trier and the Rhine frontier had become a source from which flowed imperial authority, imperial patronage, and imperial generosity, simply because of the actual physical presence of the emperors: "Royal progresses . . . locate the society's center and affirm its connection with transcendent things by stamping a territory with ritual signs of dominance. When kings journey around the countryside, . . . they mark it, like some wolf or tiger spreading his scent through his territory, as almost physically part of them."[16] One Gallic orator of the early fourth century would have agreed with this statement by a modern anthropologist; for him, the new buildings in Gaul were not simply gifts of the emperor's presence, they also marked out his footprints.[17]

During Late Antiquity these footprints of Roman civilization were found everywhere in Gaul, not least on the roads "through whose entire length the name of Caesar shows bright on very old milestones."[18] Yet these footprints have also partially obliterated from our view the archaic, pre-Roman features that survived in Gallic society. Although third-century Gauls wished for the presence of an emperor, and although the emperor dispensed many benefits and tried to defend the frontiers, the establishment of an imperial court still represented a fundamental intrusion upon the basic structure of Gallic society. In the traditional fabric of provincial society the activities of an emperor, his court, his administrators, and his troops were as disruptive as they were beneficial.[19] Thus Autun, as we have seen, may have been able to request a tax remission directly from the emperor, but the imposition of that tax was indicative of the more intense centralization of authority in the empire during the later third century; the shortage of available manpower and the improper evaluation of the city's resources were a direct result of "the harshness of a new census."[20]

In the same manner the presence of an imperial court interfered in the competition over prestige and authority inherent

16. C. Geertz (1977) 153.
17. *Pan. lat.* VII(6).22.5–6, "circa tua . . . vestigia."
18. Sidonius *Carm.* XXIV.6–7.
19. Cf. MacIntyre (1973/74) 429: "Any book on enemies of the Roman order ought to include a chapter on emperors and a chapter on armies." For the powerful impact that the occupation by Roman legions had on northern Gaul and Germany, see Wells (1976); and for an example of disruption by the imperial court, see *Expositio totius mundi et gentium* 58.
20. *Pan. lat.* VIII(5).5.4.

among the local Gallic aristocracies. Because the emperor controlled appointments to virtually all positions in the imperial administration, as well as grants of senatorial status,[21] the problem for remote provincials was to make themselves known to him. But once known, anyone, and not only the most prominent or influential men, might benefit from imperial patronage. In this respect the promotion of an orator such as Eumenius can be seen as going against the grain of traditional Gallic society. As a professor cloistered in a school, never speaking at official occasions, Eumenius was not the kind of man likely to lead an embassy outside his province to the emperor. But the increased demand for skilled people in the expanded bureaucracy of the later third century affected his life too. He was selected by the emperor Constantius to become a top civil servant and then director of a school; he had to make a public, although very nervous, speech before a provincial governor; and he became wealthy enough to consider donating his entire salary toward the restoration of the schools of Autun.[22] In contrast, many professors never attained enough wealth even to consider acting as such generous patrons; most of them probably "enriched" their native cities only with their eloquence.[23] Now, however, the establishment of a court in northern Gaul had considerably reduced the distance between Autun and access to imperial patronage, and even self-effacing professors volunteered to lead embassies to the imperial court.[24]

In this perspective the establishment of an imperial court at Trier represented both a veneer over and a potential disruption within the organization of traditional Gallic society. In terms of social structure, the fundamental characteristics of the hierarchy of personal relationships and the exercise of authority in Gallic society, both before the conquest by Julius Caesar and within the Roman Empire, were its essentially "medieval" features.[25] From the point of view of social organization, medieval society is always earlier than we think. Briefly and schematically, even within

21. Millar (1977) 275–8, 479–90.
22. Galletier (1949–1955) I, 103–6, and Van Sickle (1934).
23. Ausonius *prof.* 6.16–19. In fact, none of the professors mentioned by Ausonius were civic benefactors.
24. *Pan. lat.* VIII(5).1.2–3.
25. Lewuillon (1975) 563: "La société gauloise doit être comparée plutôt avec une société médiévale, qu'avec une société antique classique." See also Wightman (1978), for an argument stressing "modified continuity" in Gallic social structure.

the Roman Empire the organization of Gallic society had emphasized "small local tyrannies,"[26] consisting of men with local authority who were surrounded by a group of subordinate retainers, and the bulk of the population, which was in some form of
personal dependence upon these leaders. Ultimately the power
of local aristocrats and the dependent relationships of the rest of
the population resulted, in most cases, from control over or ownership of the land,[27] but the adhesive holding this structure together was the exercise of informal patronage. And although
there was much mobility into and within these aristocracies as
new families replaced old ones, as new economic classes may
have appeared,[28] and as the barbarians were later assimilated,
nevertheless the essential ideology of local aristocracies and their
relationship to the rest of the population remained fairly constant.[29] External factors did not seem to threaten them. The imposition of an imperial administration, the creation of priesthoods
in the imperial cult,[30] the growth of municipal institutions,[31] or the
expansion of schools and the rise of literary culture did not necessarily lead, as in other traditional societies, to a plurality of elites,
because the old land-controlling aristocracies were usually able to
manipulate these potentially differentiating factors to their own
advantage and even to incorporate them into their own self-image.
Until the middle of the third century the local aristocracies of
Gaul, in particular those beyond Narbonensis, seem to have preserved their local influence in benign isolation from the Roman
Empire.[32] During the centuries discussed in the early chapters of
this book, however, the special circumstances of the barbarian in-

26. Lewuillon (1975) 544.
27. Whittaker (1980); see also Percival (1969), and Wightman (1975a).
28. Among many others arguing for the rise of a trading class or a Gallic
bourgeoisie under the Roman Empire, see Drinkwater (1978) and (1981); but this
may prove to be a misleading model for analysis: see Finley (1973) 57–60, and
MacMullen (1974) 49–51, 97–100.
29. The work of Stroheker is fundamental, especially (1948) and, on Spanish
senators, (1965) 54–87.
30. Fishwick (1978); note also Hopkins (1978) 210: "One of the main functions of these celebrations [of the imperial cult] was that they confirmed the
prominence of local leaders."
31. Especially in "Provençal" Narbonensis (Syme [1958] 451–64), although
even there the indigenous culture and society persisted under Roman rule: see
the excellent survey of Barruol (1976).
32. On the basis of the tables in P. Lambrechts, *La composition du sénat romain
de l'accession au throne d'Hadrien à la mort de Commode (117–192)* (Antwerp, 1936)
183–7, in the second century about 3.6 percent of known senators with known

vasions and the consequent presence of an imperial court allow us to investigate more thoroughly the nature of local authority, as Gallic aristocrats acted as brokers prepared to assist their supporters in dealing with the central administration, as leaders designated to protect the inhabitants from barbarians, or simply as local lords who effectively removed their dependents from any wider authority. Without making any claims about the presence of feudal (or even prefeudal) institutions during this late Roman period, we can already begin to detect some of the identifying characteristics of later medieval feudal society, among them regional fragmentation and the diffusion of authority at the expense of the central administration.[33]

Despite the hypnotic attraction of the imperial court and its viewpoints, it is important to keep in mind the persistence of these localized hierarchical networks in Gallic society. From the late third century to the late fourth century, the period when an emperor was usually resident in northern Gaul, this local authority was obscured beneath the presence of the imperial court, but it became prominent again with the retreat of the emperor and his court, armies, and administrators. In the later fifth century we will see a Gallic aristocrat leading his private army to help the Byzantine emperor in the East,[34] much like a medieval lord going on a crusade. But such behavior not only presaged medieval lordship; it also reasserted the local aristocratic authority and influence that had always been important in traditional Gallic society.

A good comparison can be made with the survival of indigenous languages. Celtic (or Gallic) was still used in Gaul during the imperial period, just as other native languages survived in other western provinces,[35] even though Latin had become the language

---

origins were from Gaul (primarily Narbonensis); on the basis of the information in G. Barbieri, *L'albo senatorio da Settimio Severo a Carino (193–285)* (Rome, 1952) 432–73, in the third century about 1.6 percent of known senators with known origins were from Gaul. Also note Colin (1954) 228: "Il semble que plus d'un sénateur, dont la famille était d'origine gauloise, se trouvait déjà à demi italien avant de siéger au Sénat."

33. On varieties of patronage and central authority, see Blok (1969), and Gellner (1977) 3.

34. *Vita S. Danielis Stylitae* 60–63 (ed. H. Delehaye, *Les saints stylites* [Brussels and Paris, 1923] 58–63).

35. For the survival of Celtic, see Schmidt (1980), and MacMullen (1966b). Other aspects of Celtic culture also persisted: see Hatt (1965) and Horne (1981), for religion; Duval (1963), for architecture; and MacMullen (1965), for a general survey.

of administration and (along with Greek) the language of culture. In the same way local authority survived beneath the imposition of imperial authority; and when that imperial authority disappeared, local authority emerged again, and even borrowed from the idiom of imperial authority. In fact, as we will see, in some instances the reappearance of the traditional structure of local authority coincided with the reemergence of native Celtic terms to describe relationships of dependence; in medieval society men will be not Roman clients, but vassals of their lords.[36]

An emphasis on structural continuity should not be seen as unique to Gallic society. Not only was the prominent, and persistent, local authority of regional aristocracies found in other provinces of the Roman Empire,[37] it was also characteristic of the periphery of many empires that covered much territory but also had an undermanned administration, poor communication, slow transportation, and no prevailing "national" ideology. But given the bias in our early sources toward the activities and the preferences of the central administration, how are we to investigate the nature and functions of secular local leadership? One solution is to consider the activities of men labeled by the sources as bandits.

## Bandits and Local Leadership

In the Roman Empire bandits seem to have been everywhere—a ubiquity not unnoticed by men living in the ancient world. Looking back almost three centuries, one early third-century historian wrote that "pirates always used to harass people sailing the seas, just as bandits harassed people living on land; and there was never a time when such activities were not known, nor will they cease so long as human nature remains the same."[38] Like this ancient historian, modern historians have usually evaluated banditry as a form of opposition to the established order and as a manifestation of increasing social chaos; its appearance is often cited as an example of how powerless the cities were to control it, or its supposedly increased incidence in the later empire is taken as both proof for and a result of the "crisis" of the third century.[39]

36. Marc Bloch (1961) 155–6.
37. Whittaker (1978) stresses the essential continuity of North African society before and under Roman rule.
38. Dio XXXVI.20.1.
39. E.g. Rostovtzeff (1957) 738–9, and MacMullen (1967) 192–7. For important reviews of the latter, see O. Murray, *J. Roman Studies* 59 (1969) 261–5, and MacIntyre (1973/74).

Treating banditry in this way, however, misleads us into making false presumptions, as we end up echoing the restricted and indignant viewpoint of men frustrated by their inability to control the course of events. In many respects banditry was a term of cultural insularity by means of which a social and power elite encompassed some people while excluding others; hence, although Roman jurists produced a fairly precise definition of official "enemies" and even gave examples of them, bandits, in contrast, were defined simply as "the others" in legal constitutions.[40] Banditry may have been "the reverse of Greco-Roman legality,"[41] but its presence also indicates one limitation on the central administration's control over certain areas or people nominally included within its geographical boundaries, and interpretations of banditry that start only from its status as a form of illegal or deviant behavior tend too quickly to classify it as resistance or even a form of protest movement against an imperial administration that had no effective authority in peripheral regions.

We already have several studies that collect and discuss the available information about banditry in the Roman Empire.[42] In order to evaluate the interaction between imperial center and local periphery in late antique Gaul, let us briefly consider some general points that will also be specifically applicable to an interpretation of the Bagaudae in the next chapter. First, thievery, poaching, rustling, smuggling, and extortion were always ways available for people to supplement their livelihoods; hence, many people could qualify as bandits. But some were more susceptible than others to being labeled as such, among them men who were marginal to society to begin with. Shepherds and herdsmen are good examples, because they led transient lives and spent much of their time in the mountains, which were notorious as hideouts for bandits and as likely spots in which people could be ambushed. Hence, shepherds were often simply labeled bandits: according to one early fifth-century imperial constitution, "If anyone allows

40. *Digest* XLIX.15.24, L.16.118.
41. Y. Garlon, *War in the ancient world* (English trans., London, 1975) 31–37.
42. Flam-Zuckermann (1970) is the best survey and discussion; for lists of references, see E. deRuggiero and G. Barbieri, "Latrones," in *Dizionario epigrafico di antichità romane* IV (Rome, 1947) 460–6; M. Hengel, *Die Zeloten* (Leiden and Cologne, 1961) 26–35; MacMullen (1967) 255–68; and, from the opposite perspective, O. Hirschfeld, "Die Sicherheitspolizei im römischen Kaiserreich," in his *Kleine Schriften* (Berlin, 1913) 576–612. E. Durkheim, *The rules of sociological method* (English trans., Chicago, 1938) 64–75, is a fundamental discussion of deviance in society.

his children to be brought up by shepherds, he will appear to support a gang of bandits."[43] The belittling combination of shepherds and bandits became a concise definition of cultural and social inferiority; thus in contemporary epitomes of Roman history these men represented how the Romans themselves had lived centuries earlier, before they built cities and became civilized.[44]

Second, among people who were geographically, socially, or culturally marginal to the mainstream of Roman civilization, it was possible for men to become prominent as alternative leaders and to acquire respect for themselves and their supporters. Among shepherds, for instance, a man might start out by running a "protection racket" and dispensing his own form of justice, and then rise within the Roman army.[45] Other men found their suport among ex-soldiers, either veterans or deserters. For Gaul a good example is Maternus, an ex-soldier who in the 180s formed a band of deserters, which was active apparently in both Gaul and Spain. At first he plundered small villages and estates; as more men joined him, he began to attack large cities and release prisoners. Although modern scholarship disagrees about the precise significance, and even historicity, of Maternus,[46] the salient points about his career are first, his function as an alternative (even though illegal) leader, and second, his apparent elevation to the status of a "social bandit," a man who had acquired, in addition, the support of the local population. For Maternus also displayed some of the characteristics associated with Robin Hood figures: righting wrongs by releasing prisoners, redistributing wealth by using booty as a reward, connivance with local magistrates (whom the emperor Commodus finally accused of "negligence"), immunity from imperial opposition until betrayed, even aspirations of imperial authority for himself.[47]

43. CTh IX.31.1; for other dismissive observations, see Firmicus Maternus Mathesis III.5.23, VIII.6.4–6, and Gregory of Tours VP 9.1. Shepherds in the ancient world deserve more study; in general see Grenier (1905), Skydsgaard (1974), and Frayn (1974) 13–15, as well as M. Gongora, "Vagabondage et société pastorale en Amérique latine (spécialement au Chili central)," Annales: é.s.c. 21 (1966) 159–77, for modern comparative material.

44. Eutropius I.1, 3; for context, see Momigliano (1963b) 85–86.

45. For instance, the early career of Maximinus Thrax: see Syme (1971) 179–93, and Loriot (1975) 666–88, 782–3. In particular, note SHA Maxim. 2.2, "saepe tamen iustus."

46. Alföldy (1971) is overly sceptical about the account by Herodian.

47. Herodian I.10, with SHA Pesc. Nig. 3.3–4 (which may be an authentic piece of information: see Barnes [1978] 51). On social banditry, Hobsbawm (1959)

Maternus' career demonstrates not the disintegration of Gallic society under the empire, but rather one of the forms that leadership could assume among people who were marginal to the central administration, as well as the fuzziness of the distinction between legitimate and illegitimate authority at a local level. References to bandits, therefore, allow us to glimpse aspects of local leadership that were usually limited by the one-sided perspective of our literary sources. Although ancient writers may have described the activities of bandits only because they offended their sensibilities about the proper working of the central administration, modern historians ought to seize the opportunity to investigate the functions of leaders with local authority. In particular, social bandits and their supporters were often only extreme versions of more conventional local leaders and their dependents, atypical in their social composition, methods, and aims, but characteristic in their roles and needs.[48] Admittedly, few people were as remote from mainstream society as shepherds or deserters; but many inhabitants of Gaul were culturally and socially depressed, and most, including local elites, had been geographically isolated from an imperial court. Similarly, few local leaders acted like strong-arm outlaws. But because leaders such as local landowners played roles similar to those of social bandits, the publicized activities of bandits can remind us of the many local aristocrats who neither served in the administrative or military bureaucracies nor appeared in the extant literary sources, but did provide security and justice for their clientele.

Such a reminder has special significance for our perspective on Gaul under the empire. Gaul was a region noted for its local dynasts, tribal chieftains, and large landowners, and the presence of influential men with local support marked the stable underlying context into which an emperor and his court were introduced during the later third century. The earlier relative indifference between local aristocrats and a remote imperial court was then complemented with other relationships. Sometimes local leaders manipulated the court to their own advantage by acting as brokers between the local population and imperial administrators; sometimes

---

and (1969) are outstanding, as are the essays in D. Hay et al., *Albion's fatal tree: Crime and society in eighteenth-century England* (Harmondsworth, 1975). Many of the same characteristics of social banditry also appear in the career of Bullas Felix, for which see Dio (Xiph.) LXXVI.10, SHA *Sev.* 18.6.

48. See Lewin (1979) 139, on Brazilian social bandits as typical patron figures.

local patronage supplemented official imperial authority, either because local aristocrats became friendly with imperial magistrates or because they themselves served in administrative positions; but at other times local men of authority might substitute for the imperial administration, even take over some of the idiom of imperial authority in order to ensure their own prominence, and thereby also run the risk of being viewed as bandits or usurpers.[49]

During the later empire the fluctuations in this uneasy relationship between the imperial court and these local aristocrats and leaders provided much of the apparent dynamism in the transformation of late Roman society in Gaul, as we will see in the next chapter about the Bagaudae. But before going on to discuss the "crisis" of the third century, let us note briefly two points that will become significant later. First, along with the changing relationship between imperial court and local aristocracies, the perspective of our extant literary sources changes; in fact, the origin of the literary sources also changes, because with the promotion to wider prominence of these already locally influential men we have the survival of literature written by Gallic provincials in which they evaluated their own membership and role in the empire. Second, a study of banditry also suggests, in passing, the appearance of one type of local leadership whose authority was not necessarily based on control of the land or on holding magistracies. In later chapters we will see the rise of other local leaders who were usually not, at least initially, members of the landed aristocracies, but who sometimes did establish themselves through open violence. In this case too, the emergence of these Christian bishops is to be understood in terms of the functions of leaders and the social needs of communities.

## The Presence of the Emperor

The usual interpretation of the fifty years between the death of Severus Alexander in 235 and the accession of Diocletian in 284 is in terms of a catastrophic crisis with political, military, economic, and intellectual consequences.[50] This depressing interpretation of

49. For examples of the manipulation of legal distinctions by the ruling elite, see SHA *Quad. Tyr.* 2, and MacMullen (1963). Note also S. N. Eisenstadt, *The political systems of empires* (New York, 1963) 175–83, for a generalized discussion of the role of aristocracies in centralized polities.

50. See especially Rostovtzeff (1957) Chap. X–XI.

the third century is apparently supported by the gloomy statements of contemporaries[51] as well as by archaeological findings in
Gaul and Spain, which show an increase in the construction of
fortifications.[52] Yet the attribution of the modern concept of crisis
has long been overdue for reappraisal, and especially since recent
studies have stressed instead that in intellectual and economic activities at local levels there was no drastic cleavage during the
third century. Although the veneer of a central administration
and its centralized economy may have temporarily disappeared,
local society and local economies, although disrupted, did not
collapse.[53]

It is possible to view the political confusion of the third century
within a similar perspective of local continuity. In the ancient world
the imposition of an imperial administration over a large territory
was a difficult task, especially in the face of passive resistance due
to slowness of communication, problematic geographical features,
and local networks of influence and authority: "The great historical empires at the height of their power are, as political systems,
atypical. For a sociological study of political structure there is
nothing abnormal in periods of chaos or disintegration."[54] Hence,
in addition to viewing the quick succession of usurpers as an
indication of instability in the third-century imperial administration, we can treat them as a conspicuous reemergence of traditional forms of authority in which local leaders provided protection and dispensed justice for their supporters. The contrast with
the earlier empire was that now some of these local leaders either
themselves assumed the trappings of imperial authority, or at
least were seen as a challenge to the existing emperors.

By the later third century, part of the idiom of imperial authority involved the presence of the emperor. In the panegyrics
extant from this period this theme was common: the presence of
the emperor led directly to security and generosity.[55] But the imperial presence blended two contrasting notions: just as the ceremonies and panegyrics celebrating an imperial arrival focused on

51. Alföldy (1973) and (1974); MacMullen (1976) 1–23, is now a necessary
corrective.
52. Although Rebuffat (1974) argues that city fortifications can be taken as an
indication of increasing wealth rather than as a sign of insecurity or crisis; for
Gaul and Britain see the similar arguments of Blagg (1981) 183–5.
53. See especially Brown (1972) 74–93; Whittaker (1976); and Hopkins (1980).
54. Southall (1967) 150.
55. *Pan. lat.* VII(6).8.1, 22.5–6.

the one specific event while simultaneously placing it into the timeless context of a lasting ideal of imperial behavior, so the presence of emperors entailed both actual physical presence and universal omnipresence. According to one panegyrist, the confrontation between the emperors Diocletian and Maximian during the winter of 290/91 was in fact a meeting of two deities: the emperors had only to reach the summit of the Alps for their bright glow to radiate over all Italy.[56]

Given that during much of the early imperial period only one or two emperors reigned at a time, most people in the empire had always had to be content simply with this glow from the emperor's omnipresence,[57] which could be ensured either through his images and icons or through his cult. Imperial images, for instance, could guarantee the decisions of magistrates or ensure asylum for fugitives, just as the celebration of the imperial cult provided reassurance of the imperial presence.[58] Yet images and cults never fully measured up to the actual physical presence of an emperor. In a tract written possibly in 335 or 336 during his exile at Trier, Bishop Athanasius of Alexandria stressed the negative consequences of the emperor's absence. In his discussion of the incarnation of the Son of God, he introduced comparisons to the imperial presence, claiming that a king or an emperor (or even God in heaven), in order not to lose control of his realm, must remind his subjects of himself through messages, personal representatives, and, if necessary, his own presence; otherwise, Athanasius wrote, usurpers might take advantage of his absence: "But when the real king comes forth and is revealed, then the deceitful revolutionaries are refuted by his presence, while the citizens, seeing the real king, abandon those who formerly deceived them."[59]

Because of this emphasis on the physical presence or absence of the emperor, the powerful tendency to fragment into smaller

56. Pan. lat. III(11).10.4–5, 11.4.

57. Although one panegyrist claimed that Maximian had a "split personality": Pan. lat. II(10).5.3.

58. Setton (1941) 196–211, and Hopkins (1978).

59. Athanasius de incarnatione 13, 55 (ed. and trans. R. W. Thomson, Athanasius, Contra gentes and De incarnatione [Oxford, 1971]). Nor did the problem disappear. For medieval kings, note Marc Bloch (1961) 62: "It would have been impossible to govern the state from inside a palace: to control a country, there was no other means than to ride through it incessantly in all directions. The kings of the first feudal age positively killed themselves by travel." For God, note Salvian de gub. Dei II.2: divine rule and justice were contingent on God's "presence."

local units reasserted itself during periods of disruption. During the later third century an imbalance in the interplay between such factors as barbarian pressure on the frontiers, the effectiveness of the Roman army, and the adequacy of the agricultural base for taxation led to a breakdown of the social equilibrium.[60] Another aspect of this breakdown involved the relationship between center and periphery, which in turn focused on the presence of the emperor. Previously, imperial images, the imperial cult, or imperial administrators had been sufficient to make the imperial presence felt in Gaul, but in different, more difficult circumstances, people desired the actual physical presence of an emperor, even if of a usurping emperor. As Clifford Geertz writes, the "most flamboyant expressions [of royal charisma] tend to appear among people at some distance from the center, indeed often enough at a rather enormous distance, who want very much to be closer."[61] Such a perspective does not discount the personal ambitions of individuals. Despite the ritual protests of new emperors about their lack of desire and ambition, hardly anyone became emperor against his will. On the other hand, not all ambitious men became emperors. Instead, local leaders were recognized as emperors because of the specific aspirations of other people; and although there were many potential catalysts in the creation of local emperors, from the later second century perhaps the most common precipitating factor was barbarian pressure on the frontiers, particularly when such pressure occurred simultaneously on more than one frontier.[62] Then especially the empire became too big for one emperor, and local leaders appeared as local emperors.

In sum, authority was neither conceived nor realized in impersonal terms; instead, the lexicon of imperial authority and particularly of imperial presence provided a mutually comprehensible vocabulary that enabled people to articulate any authority, no matter who exercised it. To talk about authority was to talk about emperors; hence, identification with imperial authority was a natural consequence of comparison with it. Just as men used whatever language was comprehensible in specific situations (for instance, speaking Celtic with the local peasants or preaching in simplified Latin),[63] so they used the vocabulary of imperial au-

60. Finley (1958).      61. C. Geertz (1977) 168.
62. Amit (1965).
63. Cf. Fournier (1955), for Gregory of Tours hearing and probably also speaking Celtic when necessary; and below, Chapter 10.

thority—the ceremonies, the panegyrics, and the ideology—to communicate their ideas about whatever authority—even local authority—was prominent; and conversely, just as the use of a formal language could maintain the illusion of a correspondingly formal setting, so the use of the imperial idiom, even by a usurper, might be able to evoke an appropriate imperial context. In this sense the emperor and his role in society were so identified with the ceremonies, the panegyrics, and the ideology of imperial authority, that they, and not his specific activities, came to be his vital essence. Seen from the periphery, therefore, the use of the imperial idiom by local usurpers was not necessarily an illegal seizure of imperial authority; it was rather an attempt to conjure up that imperial presence which in turn guaranteed security and generosity.

* * *

In order to investigate the transformation of Gaul from the ancient to the medieval world, it is important to keep in mind the resilient characteristics of Gallic society and their interaction with external forces. The "revolts" of the Bagaudae provide one example of the horizontal dialectic between center and periphery, and of the vertical dialectic between local leaders and the rest of the population. It is within this perspective of local influence that we can look, in the next chapter, at the Bagaudae in Spain and Gaul from the late third to the mid-fifth centuries; simply put, the Bagaudae appeared in peripheral geographical regions and at times of disruption, precisely where and when local leadership became most evident.

# CHAPTER 3

# The Bagaudae:
# Center and Periphery,
## A.D. 250–450

For many years the Bagaudae have had to bear the heavy burden of being cited as the classic example of peasant revolts, not just in late Roman Spain and Gaul but in the entire later Roman Empire. According to the traditional interpretation, the Bagaudae were peasants and slaves who imitated the barbarian strategy of small skirmishes in their attacks on large estates and even on cities, and whose aim was to set up an independent state separate from the Roman Empire in which former landlords would be reduced to slavery.[1] But as provocative as it has been, such an interpretation is no longer adequate, for several reasons: it deduces the social composition of the Bagaudae from the belittling epithets applied to them by the dominant elites; it uses random references to banditry without making clear that they have little, if any direct relevance to the Bagaudae; and by failing to appreciate distinctions between Bagaudae in late third-century Gaul, in early fifth-century Gaul, in the Alps about 407, and in northern Spain during the mid-fifth century, it glosses over discrepancies in geographical and social context.

Even more important is the failure to make explicit the overall perspective on the transitions and development of the Roman Empire into which this interpretation fits these peasant revolts. To

---

1. Thompson (1952a); all ancient references to the Bagaudae are conveniently printed in Czúth (1965). For the spelling, see Minor (1975), who concludes that *Bacauda* is a variant derived from *Bagauda*, for which there is an acceptable etymology from the Celtic *baga*, meaning "war," and the Celtic suffix *-aud*.

claim that "peasant revolts" against the Roman administration and against aristocratic landlords is the proper analytical term to use in this context is to imply both that the relationship between the central administration and local populations can best be understood in terms of a "conflict model" emphasizing assimilation or (more often) resistance, and that there was an implicit animosity between peasants and lords, as if from the peasants' point of view aristocratic lords were always an unfortunate and unnecessary imposition upon them. Both implications can, in turn, easily slip into larger negative judgments about the Roman Empire in which the significant terms evaluating social relationships become "oppression" and "exploitation." Not surprisingly, most subsequent discussions of the Bagaudae have come from Marxist-influenced historians who accept much of this traditional interpretation but who also put it into a historical context of explicit discontinuity by stressing the transition between different dominant modes of production, from an ancient society based on slave labor to feudal society.[2] But the result is to make the revolts of the Bagaudae explain too much. Although within a Marxist perspective that emphasizes intrinsic contradictions in late Roman society it is at least permissible to speculate about the possibility of additional revolts of Bagaudae (or of other peasants) not mentioned in our extant sources, other scholars too readily resort to the hypothetical insecurity caused by Bagaudae as a convenient explanation for the transfer of a city's site[3] or as an indication of increased anxiety in society.[4]

Another perspective on the transformation of late antique Gaul stresses instead, as we have seen, the continuities that link Roman society with medieval society. This perspective of continuity owes much to Marc Bloch, who argued in his history of rural France that medieval lords had as predecessors the masters of Gallo-Roman villas and even the village chieftains of ancient

2. Günther (1965) is a general, although not necessarily representative, survey; see also Engelmann (1956), Korsunski (1961), Szádeczky-Kardoss (1968), and Anderson (1974) 18–19.

3. On Lyon, see Audin (1952–1953) and (1953), with Drinkwater (1975), who instead stresses the intrinsic geographical disadvantages of the site. On the destruction of Autun, see LeGentilhomme (1943), and Galletier (1949–1955) I, 110–11. For speculation about Bagaudae in Britain, see Thompson (1956b), and Applebaum (1972) 32.

4. Rousselle (1976) 1104.

Gaul.[5] In such a model of structural continuity the basic organization of society, the relationships of authority and dependence between men, and the relationship of men to the land and the means of production remain essentially immune from the imposition of or changes in upper-level administration. But as Bloch also emphasized, this perspective of continuity does not deny modifications in the composition and ideology of the dominant elites due to the presence of imperial courts, the rise of Christianity, or the settlement of barbarian tribes. The point is rather that in the transformation of Gallic society, factors other than a change in the dominant mode of production—and this change is itself an arguable point, given that it rests upon the assumption that under the Roman Empire the dominant mode of production in Gaul had been slavery—were far more significant for influencing people's behavior.[6] Instead, as the previous chapter has stressed, people often appealed for assistance from men of local authority, who might in turn borrow from the lexicon of imperial authority. In this sense the Bagaudae represented not a revolutionary but rather a reformist social movement,[7] since their aim can also be seen as the imposition of greater, not lesser, ties of social dependence, and as a return to traditional ties of dependence that, however oppressive they may seem to us, still guaranteed security and assistance.

Another influential factor to keep in mind is the distinction in perspective between Roman and barbarian, which in many instances was equivalent to the distinction between freedom and slavery.[8] Some men dismissed activities in marginal and troubled areas by calling them barbarian, while the men actually living there would do everything possible to remain "free," and Roman.

Through a discussion of the various appearances of Bagaudae in late third-century Gaul and fifth-century Gaul and Spain, let us in this chapter highlight the functions performed by men of local authority during periods of disruption; an additional short study of the emperor Julian enables us to clarify the nature of the relationship between an emperor and the local inhabitants. A final brief section on the assimilation of the Bagaudae into Christian

5. Marc Bloch (1966) 76; Wallace-Hadrill (1962) 1–24, is another excellent survey.
6. Landsberger (1974) 32.    7. Hobsbawm (1959) 10–12.
8. Clearly seen by Burdeau (1964) 48–50.

hagiography points out the important role that Christian bishops began to fill in the fifth century, not only in acting as local patrons but also in influencing the outlook of society through their
writings.

\*          \*          \*

During the 250s both the Franks and the Alamanni crossed the
Rhine into the Belgian provinces and the Alps into northern Italy;
some even went as far as Spain and destroyed Tarragona. At the
same time the emperor Gallienus suddenly abandoned Gaul for
the East, leaving behind only his young son. To remedy this des-
perate situation (as later historians saw it)[9] Gallic emperors created a "Gallic Empire." Even though our sources for this period
are fragmentary, we can still detect the regional significance of
these local emperors: all had previously been military officers or
landowners, all owed their elevation to local support, and all, in
turn, attempted to defend their supporters.[10]

Postumus, who ruled from 260 to 268, had previously been a
military commander (or a governor), probably in one of the provinces along the Rhine; after the army proclaimed him emperor, he
immediately went with the troops who supported him to Cologne
and captured Gallienus' son, and he eventually also acquired support in Spain and Britain.[11] Along the Rhine frontier Postumus
was somewhat successful in improving the defenses by building
garrisons along internal roads; according to a later summary account, "By his power and by his firm control Postumus restored
provinces that had almost wasted away."[12] But during the reign of
Postumus we find other local uprisings too. Mainz, on the lower
Rhine, gave its support to Laelianus, whom Postumus eventually
defeated. Although our sources are confused, there is a hint that
Laelianus also attempted to improve the defenses of Gaul.[13] At
the end of Postumus' reign another emperor appeared, perhaps
for only a few days. This was a soldier named Marius, who had

9. Eutropius IX.9.1; cf. *Pan. lat.* IV(8).10.1.
10. For all the literary sources see Jankowski (1967), a provocative article
whose interpretation, however, goes too far in tracing a conflict between large
"feudal" landowners and the owners of estates based on slave labor; for chronology and other details see the appropriate entries in Barnes (1972).
11. Spain: *CIL* II.4919, 4943. Britain: *RIB* 820, 822, 2232, 2255, 2260.
12. Eutropius IX.9.1; cf. SHA *Trig. Tyr.* 5.4, and von Petrikovits (1971) 181.
13. Eutropius IX.9.1; Aurelius Victor *Caes.* 33.8; SHA *Trig. Tyr.* 5.4

originally been a blacksmith. As another man who came to prominence because of his huge strength he too, according to a (probably fictitious) speech attributed to him, wanted to strike fear into
the invading Alamanni: "May they think that the Romans are a
people made of iron."[14]

After the death of Postumus, Victorinus became emperor in
Gaul from 268 to 270. A military officer like Postumus, Victorinus
helped to improve fortifications of cities in Gaul, and he seems to
have gained some support in Britain.[15] He also may have been
connected to the local aristocracy, because after he was killed his
mother promoted the senator Tetricus, who many thought was
related to her, as the new emperor. Tetricus was already serving
as governor of Aquitania. With the support of troops he was proclaimed emperor at Bordeaux, although in 274 he surrendered to
the emperor Aurelian. During his years as emperor Tetricus was
said to have defended Gaul, and he too acquired some recognition in Britain and perhaps in Spain.[16]

These Gallic emperors demonstrate how, in periods of turmoil,
local men of authority assumed the imperial idiom of authority
with the support of troops and citizens. These leaders appeared
most often in cities along the lower Rhine, where there was probably most pressure from barbarian invasions. But it is important
to stress that although these men were known as Gallic emperors
and even acquired some support in Britain and Spain, they should
still be seen primarily as local leaders with limited influence. Under Postumus one city at least had turned to another man, Laelianus, and part of the army had supported Marius. During the
reign of Victorinus a series of inscriptions was set up in Spain and
southern Gaul in dedication to the emperor Claudius, who spent
most of his time on the Danube frontier.[17] And during the reign
of Tetricus the literary sources hint at military uprisings and
explicitly mention one provincial governor who turned troops
against him.[18] In short, the same need for security that con-

14. SHA *Trig. Tyr.* 8.11.
15. *RIB* 2241, 2251; and Schönberger (1969) 177–8.
16. Britain: *RIB* 1885, 2224–26; Spain: SHA *Claud.* 7.5. In a triumph later
celebrated by the emperor Aurelian, Tetricus appeared in "Gallic trousers" (SHA
*Aurelian* 34.2), which might suggest that he was a Gaul by birth.
17. Spain: *CIL* II.1872 (Baetica), 3619, 3737, 3833–34, 4505 (= *ILS* 568), 4879
(all from Tarraconensis). Narbonensis: *CIL* XII.1551, 2228 (= *ILS* 569).
18. Tetricus surrendered to Aurelian because he lost the support of the troops:
Eutropius IX.10, 13.1; Aurelius Victor *Caes.* 35.4–5; SHA *Trig. Tyr.* 24.2–3.

tributed to the recognition of local Gallic emperors also precipitated revolts against them.

Although after the surrender of Tetricus emperors began to
spend more time in Gaul and encouraged the construction of urban fortifications,[19] pressure on the frontiers continued. It is in
this context, in the early 280s, that Bagaudae first appeared in
Gaul. Our sources for these Bagaudae of the later third century
are only brief references in late epitomes and summaries of Roman history, and none mentioned where the Bagaudae were active. These later historians called the Bagaudae "farmers," "countryfolk," "rural bandits," and "shepherds," terms that do not help
determine either geographical provenance or social status.[20] The
description of these people as shepherds might have some value,
because there was a wool industry in the north of Gaul, especially
in the Belgian provinces;[21] and it is perhaps also relevant to note,
first, that Carausius, who served with the emperor Maximian
when he was sent against the Bagaudae by Diocletian, was later
stationed at Boulogne, and second, that in the fifth century Bagaudae were active in Armorica, a large area including most of
western and central Gaul.[22]

More significantly, however, these Bagaudae were placed in
the same line of usurpers as the Gallic emperors. In the late fourth
century a Greek translation of a Latin epitome elaborated on the
Bagaudae by describing them as "native usurpers."[23] Our sources
name two commanders of the Bagaudae, Amandus and Aelianus;
for Amandus we even have some coins on which he was styled
"Augustus."[24] One source hints that the Bagaudae had a cavalry,[25]

19. See von Petrikovits (1971) 181, 188, 190; and Schönberger (1969), for a
survey of fortifications along the Rhine frontier from the late third to the early
fifth centuries.

20. *Pan. lat.* II(10).4.3, *agricolae, arator, pastor, rusticus, vastator*; Eutropius
IX.20.3, *rusticani, agrestes*; Aurelius Victor *Caes.* 39.7, *agrestes ac latrones*; with
MacMullen (1974) 30–32, on the social prejudice of such terms. Note especially
Aurelius Victor *Caes.* 39.17: the Bagaudae may have been *agrestes*, but the em-
peror Maximian was *semiagrestis*!

21. *Edictum Diocletiani* 19.38, 44, 66, 72; 22.21 (ed. Lauffer [1971] 154–9,
166–7), for clothing from Cambrai, Trier, Amiens, Bourges; *Notitia Dignitatum
Occ.* 11.54–59, for *procuratores gynaeciorum* in Gaul, in particular the Belgian
provinces.

22. Below, pp. 36–48.

23. Paeanius *Versio graeca* . . . *Eutropii* IX.20.3 (*MGH AA* 2, p. 163).

24. *The Roman imperial coinage*, vol. V.2, ed. P. H. Webb (London, 1933) 595.

25. *Pan. lat.* II(10).4.3.

but if it is correct that shepherds joined them, then this is perhaps simply recognition that some of the Bagaudae rode horses.

Like the Gallic emperors, Amandus, Aelianus, and the Bagaudae whom they led also acquired local support. Although one tradition claimed that Amandus and Aelianus had called these men Bagaudae and another that they had called themselves Bagaudae,[26] still another tradition insisted that they had received their name from local inhabitants: "The emperor Diocletian learned that in Gaul, after a band of countryfolk and bandits whom the inhabitants called Bagaudae had been formed, Aelianus and Amandus were destroying estates far and wide, and controlling many cities."[27] The name takes on added force if indeed it was derived from the Celtic word for "war"; in that case these men had been designated as local warriors fighting on behalf of the local population. Hence, along with the reemergence of traditional patterns of authority, a Celtic title was applied to these men.[28] It is significant to note too that, as in the case of bandits who acquired local support, it was necessary for a commander and troops to be sent in from outside the area to defeat the Bagaudae.[29]

In this interpretation the Bagaudae become men rallying around local leaders out of a need for security. If these Bagaudae were in fact active in central or northern Gaul, regions in which literary and archaeological evidence attests the existence of large and medium-sized estates,[30] then perhaps Amandus and Aelianus were local landowners, and perhaps the descriptions of their supporters as farmers and shepherds were more accurate than their derogatory overtones suggest. The threats motivating these men

26. Orosius VII.25.2; Eutropius IX.20.3; and Eusebius/Jerome *Chron.* s.a. 287/88 (*GCS* 47, p. 225).

27. Aurelius Victor *Caes.* 39.17.

28. Szádeczky-Kardoss (1968) col. 347, and above, p. 25 n. 1. For another native name for local bandits, see Sidonius *Ep.* VI.4.1.

29. Above, p. 18; below, p. 54, for the Theban Legion; and see Hobsbawm (1969) 90, on collusion between local magistrates and bandits.

30. See Agache (1975), for estates in northern Gaul; N. K. Chadwick (1965) 249, 254, for Brittany; and below, p. 42, for central Gaul. The fate of large villas as units of production during the third century might also be relevant to the appearance of Bagaudae, but archaeology produces contradictory results for different regions: e.g. villas were abandoned in northern Gaul (Reece [1981]) and in western Gaul (Galliou [1981] 274), but survived in central Gaul (Buckley [1981] 299). Since the location of the third-century Bagaudae is uncertain, the economic implications of these archaeological results cannot be applied to an interpretation of the Bagaudae.

to support Amandus and Aelianus are also obscure; depending on the location of the Bagaudae, barbarian raiding parties along the Rhine or pirate raids along the coast are both possibilities.[31]

After Maximian defeated the Bagaudae he left Carausius in charge of raising a fleet to be stationed at Boulogne, with the task of pacifying the Frankish and Saxon pirates.[32] But by the standards of the emperor Maximian, Carausius was too successful, because after defeating the barbarian pirates he kept the booty for himself and his supporters and eventually was recognized as emperor.[33] For several years he then controlled Britain and northern Gaul, until he was assassinated by his lieutenant Allectus, who in turn was defeated by a general of the emperor Constantius in 296.

Significantly enough, although he served initially as an admiral over a Roman fleet, Carausius was a native of a coastal region just north of Boulogne[34] and can therefore be seen as another man of local authority who became a local emperor. In a panegyric delivered before Constantius in 297, we can detect a trace of the local support given to Carausius. After he had been put in charge of operations in northern Gaul, Carausius quickly built ships and trained crews; but Constantius—otherwise noted for his swiftness—did not launch his final invasion of Britain until three years after regaining control of Boulogne, perhaps because he had first to subdue local resistance.[35] This panegyric also illustrates the contrasting perspectives people held on local emperors. Although both Carausius and Allectus improved the fortifications in Britain and northern Gaul, and although Carausius seems to have become a legendary local figure,[36] in this panegyric before a legitimate emperor the orator denounced both these men as pirates and bandits.[37] In another panegyric delivered a few years later, the orator claimed that Constantius had saved the Batavians from Carausius, "their own foster son," and had forced the Franks who helped Carausius to become "Roman people" instead. In this ora-

31. Cf. SHA *Quad. Tyr.* 15.1 for Germans burning the Roman fleet on the Rhine.

32. Eutropius IX.21, and Aurelius Victor *Caes.* 39.20. Almost a century later the identical problem still existed: Ammianus Marcellinus XXVII.8.5–6.

33. Aurelius Victor *Caes.* 39.21. This booty may have been used to recruit barbarian mercenaries or to pay off the barbarians: cf. *Pan. lat.* IV(8).12.1.

34. Aurelius Victor *Caes.* 39.20.

35. Gricourt (1967) 244–5, using *Pan. lat.* IV(8).6.1, 12; also Casey (1977).

36. Seston (1946) 82–85; below, p. 39 n. 72.

37. *Pan. lat.* IV(8).12.1.

tion, then, Carausius was described as a barbarian supported by other barbarians, and so the war against him had not been a civil war but rather a struggle between Romans and barbarians.[38]

For the fourth century we have no extant references to Bagaudae in Gaul, which indicates more than a peculiarity about the nature of our sources.[39] Already during the late third century emperors had begun to spend more time in Gaul. Aurelian and Probus conducted campaigns along the Rhine; the emperor Carus sent his son Carinus to Gaul as Caesar in 283; Diocletian, shortly after his accession, sent Maximian to Gaul; and finally, within the Tetrarchy, the Caesar in the West was Constantius, whom one historian described as an emperor "born to bring the provinces of Gaul back to Roman laws."[40] Thus one difference between the mid-third century and the fourth century was the location of an imperial court at Trier. In contrast to the situation during most of the third century, now a legitimate emperor was present in Gaul.

Another difference, perhaps more significant, was in how men of local authority in central, western, and northern Gaul were utilized within the imperial administration. Although they still ran the risk of being seen as interfering nuisances to the central administration, these wealthy landowners and local leaders could now also become imperial magistrates, provincial governors, or praetorian prefects.[41] But is worth stressing again that these local leaders did not now decide to enter a remote bureaucracy; instead, because of pressure on the Rhine frontier, an imperial court had come to them. For a significant period during the fourth century, Gallic aristocrats could become authentic Romans by participating in the imperial administration. Thus at the end of the century one who had been very successful boasted of how he had transcended his provincial origins: "Bordeaux is my native city, but Rome surpasses all native cities."[42] Yet the local authority and prestige of these men remained constant, and when in the later fourth century the imperial administration retreated from Trier to

38. *Pan. lat.* VII(6).5.3, with Gricourt (1967) 245–7, derived from Seston (1946) 110–11.
39. Cf. Thompson (1952b) 34, speculating about *de rebus bellicis* 2.2–3.
40. SHA *Carus* 18.3, considered authentic information by Barnes (1978) 77–78. See also Barnes (1982) 47–87, for the residences and journeys of emperors during the late third and early fourth centuries.
41. [Aurelius Victor] *Epit.* 35.7, for Tetricus' promotion from emperor in Gaul to governor in Italy.
42. Ausonius *ord. urb. nob.* 20.39.

the south coast of Gaul and then to Italy, these local aristocrats again provided direction and leadership for Gallic society. Significantly enough, as we will see, Bagaudae also reappeared.

*     *     *

Not only are our extant sources usually reticent about the activities of local leaders (except when they were seen as usurpers or bandits), they also do not say much about the relationship between the local population and the emperors who resided in Gaul during the fourth century. One exception, however, is Julian, who went to Gaul late in 355 and left early in 361.[43] His career not only illustrates the attachment that could arise between an emperor and local residents, but also helps us understand why, in the absence of a legitimate emperor, the army and people might invest the imperial ideology on a local leader. As Julian was a foreigner in Gaul without any local personal connections, his popularity arose largely from his success as a leader who fulfilled what was expected of an emperor.

When Julian set out for Gaul in the winter of 355, the Rhine frontier was under pressure again from the Franks, Alamanni, and Saxons, and recently Cologne had been overrun. Julian took with him no new troops, having only a small bodyguard,[44] nor was he in sole command of the legions in Gaul, because the senior emperor Constantius had carefully appointed a prefect, military commanders, and even personal attendants who were to be directly responsible to himself. According to Julian's account, Constantius had sent him to Gaul not as another emperor, but as someone who was merely bringing the insignia and the image of the only emperor, Constantius; Julian went to Gaul "with no authority except to wear the uniform."[45] In addition, Julian did not have much in common with the Gauls. He was a true southerner in the land of the north, a short, swarthy man[46] among fair-haired

43. On Julian in Gaul, see C. Jullian, *Histoire de la Gaule* VII (Paris, 1926) 181–233, and Bidez (1930) 123–99. Athanassiadi-Fowden (1981) 52–78, is an excellent account of Julian's thinking during this period.

44. Ammianus Marcellinus XV.8.18. On Julian's own description this bodyguard composed of Christians was more equipped for praying than for fighting: Zosimus III.3.2 = Julian, frag. 5 (Loeb *Julian* III, p. 298).

45. Julian *Ep. ad Athen.* 278A; Libanius *Orat.* XVIII.42.

46. Ammianus Marcellinus XVII.11.1, for Julian mocked as "an ape in purple," and XXV.4.22; cf. Julian *Misopogon* 339B–C, for Julian preferring to compare himself to a shaggy lion.

giants.[47] He was a "little Greekling," as his soldiers called him,[48] who probably spoke Latin with an accent[49] and who was unfamiliar with Gallic beer—he thought it smelled like a goat![50] When Julian set out from Italy, then, he was neither a supreme commander bringing an army of liberation nor a man for whom Gallic society had a natural affinity.

Yet when Julian approached Vienne he was received with great honor as "the man who had been hoped for." The citizens saluted him as a "legitimate emperor," and one blind woman, hearing the shouts about "Iulianus Caesar," prophesied that he would restore the temple of the gods; we can well wonder whether this triumphant arrival of Julian at Vienne was somehow influenced by a myth about the return of Julius Caesar.[51]

Julian's campaigns in northern Gaul turned out to be uncannily successful, and he became very popular with the army. Before battles he stressed the significance of his presence, and during the fighting soldiers had only to recognize the proximity of his insignia to recover their courage.[52] For the presence of Julian meant the replacement of mere imperial images with a "living icon"; hence, when it was once rumored that he had been killed, a potential riot was avoided only when soldiers "were admitted into the council chamber and saw Julian shining in his imperial dress."[53]

Another significant consequence of the imperial presence was Julian's authority to preside over judicial cases, decide rates of taxation, and, very simply, solve problems. During the fourth century, men who served in the imperial administration were often appointed to govern regions in which they already had great private influence, usually as large landowners;[54] the effect of this merger of private and public authority was to reduce the al-

47. Ammianus Marcellinus XV.12.1.
48. Ammianus Marcellinus XVII.9.3.
49. Consentius *de barbarismis et metaplasmis*, p. 394 Keil, for differences in pronunciation between Gauls and Greeks; Ammianus Marcellinus XVI.5.7, and Thompson (1944), for Julian's knowledge of Latin.
50. Julian *Epigram* 1 (Loeb *Julian* III, p. 304); contrast Ammianus Marcellinus XV.12.4.
51. Ammianus Marcellinus XV.8.21–22; cf. Weinstock (1971) 407–9, for earlier cults of Julius Caesar in Gaul. Julian had apparently studied some of Caesar's writings: cf. *Paneg. Euseb.* 124B, and *Ep.* 8 (Loeb), 414C–D.
52. E.g. Ammianus Marcellinus XVI.12, a description of the battle of Strasbourg partially based on accounts of men who fought in it.
53. Ammianus Marcellinus XX.4.22.
54. For the pattern, see Arnheim (1972) 155–9, and Matthews (1975) 23–31.

ternative sources of authority available to people living in those regions. But now Julian was available to hear complaints and accusations against the "thieves" in the imperial administration[55] and to make the system of taxation more predictable and equitable. In short, an emperor offered both military security and a fair administration; as one of his panegyrists insisted, "Julian spends every summer in camp and every winter in the court room; so the years are divided, with the result that he is either conquering the enemy or restoring the laws to the citizens."[56]

Julian's success as a Gallic emperor also allowed him to recognize and use other locally prominent men, even some whose talents were unusual. Charietto, for instance, was a vigilante who had made his reputation by defending Trier with his gang of bandits. Julian supported him, and Charietto eventually became a military commander along the Rhine.[57] Without the recognition offered by the emperor, however, Charietto and his supporters might have been condemned as bandits; and in the absence of a legitimate emperor, men such as Charietto (but not Charietto himself, because he was a German) could perhaps have become local emperors in the same way that others had in the later third century and still others would do again in the early fifth century after the retreat of the imperial court from northern Gaul.

*     *     *

In the first half of the fifth century our sources again mention Bagaudae in Gaul, as well as in the Alps and in nothern Spain. The references to these Bagaudae are, again, fragmentary and brief. Although modern historians have assumed that the Gallic Bagaudae were active in Armorica, which at this time included the provinces of Aquitania I and II, and Lugdunensis II, III, and IV (Senonia),[58] in fact only one combination of sources explicitly connects Bagaudae and events in Armorica. Hence, although we have more information to provide historical context, the inherent

55. Julian's own description of Constantius' magistrates: *Ep.* 4 (Loeb), 385B–D; cf. Claudius Mamertinus *Pan. lat.* XI(3).4.2.

56. Claudius Mamertinus *Pan. lat.* XI(3).4.6–7; for the propaganda of this panegyric, see Blockley (1972).

57. Zosimus III.7; Eunapius, frag. 11 (*FHG* IV, p. 17); Ammianus Marcellinus XVII.10.5, XXVII.1.2.

58. Although many scholars define Armorica as the region between the mouths of the Seine and Loire rivers, a more expansive definition that includes much of central Gaul can be based on *Notitia Dignitatum Occ.* 37.24–29.

vagueness of the label "Bagaudae" is compounded by uncertainty about which events are relevant to their activities.

Because most references to Bagaudae during the early fifth century present them as apparent opponents either to the Roman administration or to local aristocrats, the usual way of interpreting these events in central and northern Gaul has been in terms of a peasant revolt against a parasitical Roman bureaucracy and oppressive landowners, which happened in conjunction with the barbarian invasions.[59] Such an interpretation can be maintained, however, only within the most doctrinaire perspective. For the "crisis" of the early fifth century in Gaul was similar to the "crisis" of the later third century, involving another breakdown of the social equilibrium—which by now included the presence of an imperial court, army, and administration—and another appeal for the assistance of local men of authority. In other words, these revolts of Bagaudae again indicate discontent, although not with the basic structure of Gallic society, which allowed local elites (among them the emperor, when he was there) to function as patrons and lords, but rather with the inability of the imperial administration to provide protection and security.

Due to pressure from barbarian tribes, the Roman administration was retreating from northern and central Gaul, where previously it had maintained troops and magistrates. Already by the early fifth century the seat of the praetorian prefect of the Gauls was transferred from Trier to Arles.[60] In 418 the emperor Honorius attempted to establish a provincial assembly at Arles that magistrates, landowners, and city councillors were expected to attend. Defining the scope of this assembly as only the southeastern provinces of Gaul marked a telling limitation on the imperial court's own perception of its influence; according to the constitution of Honorius, special concessions were made even for the governors of the western provinces of Novempopulana and Aquitania II: "These provinces are situated far away."[61]

Corresponding with this new limited perspective on the extent of Roman administration was the imperial policy of encouraging

59. E.g. Szádeczky-Kardoss (1968) col. 354.
60. Palanque (1934), repeated in (1973), dates the transfer to 395, although Chastagnol (1973) dates it to 407. For context, see Courcelle (1964) 79–114, 143–81.
61. Text in *Epist. Arelatenses* 8. Bruguière (1974) 122–39, discusses the activities of the assembly; Matthews (1975) 334–6, is excellent on the context.

or simply allowing the settlement of barbarians. Shortly after the invasion of 406/7, during which a number of tribes had swept across the Rhine, the Burgundians were settled on the west bank of the Rhine in the province of Germania II, north of Coblenz. At about the same time one band of Alans under King Goar was settled in northeastern Gaul in the provinces of Belgica I and II.[62] In 418 the Visigoths were recalled from Spain and allowed to settle in southwestern Gaul, primarily in the province of Aquitania II.[63] During the 430s the Burgundians attempted to expand into the Belgian provinces; although many were massacred by a Roman general, the survivors were allowed to settle in 443 in Sapaudia in eastern Gaul.[64] In 440 a group of Alans under King Sambida was settled in the territory of Valence in southern Gaul,[65] and in 442 another group of Alans under King Goar was settled around and to the north of Orléans. Thus, during the first half of the fifth century, scattered bands of barbarians had begun to replace the Roman administration in much of Gaul (with the exception of the southeast).

During the early fifth century the disrupting factors in Gallic society were therefore the retreat of the imperial administration and the presence of barbarian settlements, which in turn led, again, to the enhancement of local leadership as well as the appearance of usurping emperors in outlying regions. Already in 406 a man named Marcus had been installed as emperor by soldiers in Britain, although after a short time they replaced him with Gratian, who was a municipal magistrate.[66] But the army subsequently replaced Gratian with a low-ranking soldier named Constantine III, who then won support also in Gaul. According to a later historian, these men had been invested as emperors because of fear of the barbarians who had invaded Gaul during that winter.[67]

Presumably what the people and the troops in Britain and northern Gaul wanted was an emperor who would be present. In 392 the usurping emperor Eugenius had campaigned along the

62. Bachrach (1967), with his map at p. 480.

63. Thompson (1956a), with the necessary corrections in Bachrach (1969).

64. *Chron. Gall. a. 452* s.a. 443 (*Chron. Min.* I, p. 660); and Duprac (1959), with his map at p. 383.

65. *Chron. Gall. a. 452* s.a. 440 (p. 660).

66. Orosius VII.40.4. Stevens (1957) is still an important discussion.

67. Zosimus VI.3.1; cf. Jerome *Ep.* 123.15, for Belgian cities besieged by barbarians.

Rhine, and in 396 the emperor Honorius and his general Stilicho had visited the Rhine frontier,[68] but in the early fifth century the imperial court, then in Italy, was preoccupied with more immediate threats from Goths. The Rhine frontier had become of lesser importance.

Yet "hope in his name"[69] also played an important role in the investment of Constantine III. Almost a century earlier one Gallic orator had insisted to Constantine the Great that "we in Gaul are protected not by the floods of the Rhine but rather by the terror of your name."[70] In the early fifth century the Rhine frontier had collapsed. All that remained were memories of the house of Constantine the Great, whose dynasty had had an intimate relationship with Britain and Gaul. The elevation of Constantine III may therefore have been an attempt to revive that dynasty and that favored relationship, which seemed all the more possible because the sons of Constantine III were named Constans and Julian.[71] The remark of an early fourth-century panegyrist to a son of Constantine the Great was applicable again: "Rome expects from you as much as you promise in your name."[72]

Even Constantine III was not entirely effective, however, because by taking his troops into southern Gaul and then into Spain he left Britain and northern Gaul without any means of defense. In 409, possibly because of threats from the Burgundians settled on the lower Rhine or from an attack by the Saxons,[73] the inhabitants of both Britain and Armorica "freed their cities from the barbarians." Although he was writing about a century later, the historian Zosimus further claimed that Britain and Armorica were no longer subservient to Roman laws because they had revolted from Roman rule, expelled the Roman magistrates, and set up their own government in isolation. On the basis of this elaboration some modern historians have argued that Zosimus was describ-

---

68. Eugenius: Sulpicius Alexander, *apud* Gregory of Tours, *HF* II.9; *ILS* 790. Honorius: Symmachus *Ep.* IV.28; Claudian *de cons. Stil.* I.188–245, and *de IV cons. Hon.* 439–59.

69. Orosius VII.40.4.

70. *Pan. lat.* VII(6).11.1; cf. 16.9.

71. Orosius VII.40.7, and Olympiodorus, frag. 12 (*FHG* IV, p. 59); cf. *Pan. lat.* VII(6).9, for the dynastic association.

72. *Pan. lat.* X(4).37.5. Gratian and Marcus may also have been reminiscent of previous emperors, such as Gratian and (Marcus) Carausius: see Stevens (1957) 320–1.

73. *Chron. Gall. a. 452* s.a. 408 (*Chron. Min.* I, p. 654), for a Saxon attack.

ing a secessionist movement from Roman rule.[74] This interpretation is unlikely, for two reasons. First, inhabitants of these regions still believed they were Romans. The cities of Britain apparently appealed for assistance to the imperial court in Italy, because in 410 the emperor Honorius responded by instructing them to defend themselves.[75] And during the 420s the province of Lugdunensis IV, located in Armorica, was still paying taxes to the Roman government.[76]

Second, other passages in his history indicate that Zosimus seems to have viewed this revolt not in political but in cultural terms: "living according to Roman laws" implied a cultural transition, a way for even barbarians to become acceptable. In the late third century, for instance, the emperor Probus had settled a band of defeated Basternae in Thrace, who "continued to live according to Roman laws"; likewise, in the later fourth century Roman soldiers told Danubian barbarians who misbehaved that "such things are not done by men wishing to live according to Roman laws."[77] Thus when Zosimus narrated how Britain and Armorica were living on their own, he exposed his cultural prejudices; to him, regions whose inhabitants were trying to defend themselves had regressed and become barbarian again.

Spain provides a comparable contemporary example of local resistance led by men with imperial associations. In the early fifth century the people of northern Spain also defended themselves against barbarians and against the usurper Constantine III. According to the Spanish historian Orosius, two wealthy young brothers of noble birth attempted to garrison the Pyrenees. When Constantine III sent troops against them, they were forced to use, in addition to the Roman cohorts in Spain, an army raised from the "domestic slaves and farmers" on their own estates. But these brothers and their makeshift army were defeated by one of the sons of Constantine III, who then replaced this "private garrison" with his own Gallic and British troops.[78]

It is important to note that these brothers were relatives of the reigning emperors and hence members of the family of Theodo-

74. Zosimus VI.5.3; for this interpretation see Thompson (1956b) and (1977).
75. Zosimus VI.10.2.
76. Constantius *Vita Germani* 7.
77. Zosimus I.71.1, IV.30.4.
78. Orosius VII.40.8, "privato praesidio," and Zosimus VI.5.1; for the imperial troops, see below, p. 51 n. 136. Note also Sidonius *Ep.* III.3.7, for another "public army collected by private financing."

sius the Great.[79] While under pressure from barbarians and from a man who was seen as a usurper, the people of northern Spain turned to members of the Theodosian family, in much the same way as the people of Britain and Gaul had supported men who were reminiscent of the family of Constantine the Great. But unlike other usurpers in Gaul and Spain, these local dynasts were not denounced by contemporaries as "tyrants," as Orosius made quite clear.[80] As a result, even though these brothers raised an army of slaves and farmers, they have also been spared being called by modern historians the leaders of a peasant revolt.

The contrast between Romans and barbarians is evident also in a reference by Rutilius Namatianus to the activities of Exuperantius in Armorica shortly before 417. Because Rutilius wrote that Exuperantius, after "renewing the laws and restoring liberty, did not allow men to be the slaves of their own servants," the conventional interpretation has been that peasants had revolted against their masters.[81] Such a social reversal is difficult to place in this context; the ideology for it was absent even in utopian thought, and perhaps the only precedent was the reversal of roles during the celebration of the Saturnalia, at which, because it was a festive ritual, the traditional roles were in fact being reinforced.[82] Instead, these people in Armorica probably had no vision of striving toward a totally different social order, and wanted only to remain "traditional," that is, to remain Roman and "free," even if that meant increasing their dependence on local aristocrats. Rather than eliminating local leaders, whether landlords or emperors, they wanted them simply to function better. In this instance it was the reappearance of barbarians that disrupted these people's lives, because even in this allusive reference we can see how Rutilius, like Zosimus, evaluated activities in outlying regions within a cultural perspective. In describing the actions of Exuperantius, Rutilius wrote that "the shores of Armorica were learn-

---

79. Zosimus VI.1.1, 4.1; Sozomen IX.11.4. Their estates were perhaps in the vicinity of Palencia (cf. Orosius VII.40.8), which was near the native city of Theodosius (cf. Zosimus IV.24.4).

80. Orosius VII.40.5–6.

81. Rutilius Namatianus *de reditu suo* I.213–16. For this interpretation, see Thompson (1952a) 19; Szádeczky-Kardoss (1968) col. 350; and, most recently, G. E. M. de Ste. Croix, *The class struggle in the ancient Greek world* (London, 1981) 478: "A clear indication of the class war which had been taking place in northwest Gaul." Alan Cameron (1967) argues for 417 as the date of Rutilius' voyage.

82. In general, see Finley (1975); and for the later Roman Empire, Hahn (1962).

ing to love *postliminium pacis* [the return of peace]." *Postliminium* is
a significant choice of words, since it refers to the legal process restoring to Roman territory a Roman citizen or his property that
had been seized by people legally declared to have been enemies.[83] Thus, Rutilius is describing how Exuperantius restored to
"freedom" an area that had previously been under the control of
barbarian enemies, not of bandits or rebellious peasants.

At this time Exuperantius probably held no imperial magistracy and was acting in a purely private capacity as a local land-
owner.[84] The movements of the Visigoths and a band of Alans provide a possible context for actions against barbarians. Although by
413 the Visigoths under Athaulf had captured Narbonne, Toulouse, and Bordeaux, the imperial court at Ravenna was able to
force them to move to Spain; as they left, they sacked Bordeaux
and then besieged Bazas. For a while a band of Alans supported
their siege. Hence, during precisely the years in which Rutilius
placed the activities of Exuperantius, the Visigoths and some
Alans marched through Aquitania II and the south of Gaul.[85] Exuperantius was himself from the region of Poitiers, in Aquitania II,
an area where there were many other large estates,[86] and so it is
likely that his "restoration of liberty" to Armorica in some way resulted from his resistance to the barbarians in the region.

Even the writings of a Christian such as Salvian illustrate how
differing perspectives influenced the application and meaning
of the cultural distinction between Romans and barbarians, who
were no longer adequately distinguished by a frontier. Salvian was
from a wealthy family, perhaps from Trier; but like many others he
fled before the barbarians south to a monastery in Provence and
eventually became a priest at Marseille. Sometime during the 440s
he wrote a long tract about the "government of God,"[87] which was
his attempt to come to terms with what must have been an obvious
dilemma for Christians: how was it that the barbarians, who were
pagans or heretics,[88] were conquering the Romans who, as good

83. Cf. *Digest* XLIX.15.24, with Berger (1953) 639.
84. Stroheker (1948) no. 141, and *PLRE* II, p. 448, for his career.
85. Courcelle (1964) 90–104; and below, p. 150.
86. Prosper Tiro *Epit.* s.a. 424 (*Chron. Min.* I, p. 470), for Exuperantius' origin; Paulinus of Nola *Carm.* X.249, for an estate of Ausonius; and Ausonius *Ep.*
5.35–36, for the association between Armorica and Poitiers.
87. Salvian *de gub. Dei* VI.72–76, for the destruction of Trier; Lagarrigue
(1971–1975) I, 11–15, for the date of composition.
88. *de gub. Dei* IV.61, 67; V.5.

Christians, should have had God on their side? In other words, Salvian was attempting to resolve a paradox in his, and presumably others', understanding of the Providence of God: evil men seemed to flourish, while good men perished.[89] From recent events people could conclude that, like the Roman emperors, God had withdrawn his beneficent "presence" from Gaul.[90]

Salvian's explanation put the blame squarely on the misbehavior of powerful aristocrats and magistrates.[91] Officials in the central administration were cheating the local population,[92] while large landholders continued to pass the burden of taxation onto small landholders.[93] According to Salvian, this fiscal extortion was forcing almost everyone to drastic measures. Yet it is important to stress that many in this predicament were not simply poor peasants, since he also claimed that educated men from good families were fleeing to the barbarians.[94] Presumably these men were councillors in their respective cities, but with smaller landholdings and little influence; if so, then forcing them to flee or to sell out was yet another contributing factor to the demise of this curial class in the later empire.[95] In addition, men with a legal status slightly lower than city councillors were feeling the pinch of taxation and considering abandoning their small fields.[96]

According to Salvian, these people wanted only to live within the *libertas Romana*. But few options now enabled them to go on living as free Romans.[97] One was to seek the protection and assistance of "great men." Although such an appeal need not have unfortunate consequences, Salvian insisted that the great men were misusing their positions, because while some men acquired the protection of powerful patrons, on their death their land went into the possession of these patrons, who could then sell it as their own—and often did. For men who had lost their land, an-

89. *de gub. Dei* I.1, IV.54.
90. *de gub. Dei* II.2–5.
91. *de gub. Dei* III.41, IV.60–64. See Courcelle (1964) 146–55, and Cleland (1970), although both eventually ask the irrelevant question whether this was deliberate propaganda against Rome.
92. *de gub. Dei* IV.21, for extortion by prefects, and Sidonius *Ep.* II.1.3, by vicars. Note the proverb quoted in Sidonius *Ep.* III.6.3: "A good year should be judged by the greatness not of its harvests but of the governing powers."
93. *de gub. Dei* IV.31, V.25, 29–30, 35.
94. *de gub. Dei* V.21, 23.        95. Jones (1964) 737–57.
96. *de gub. Dei* V.27, 38, on *humiliores*.
97. Cf. Salvian *Ep.* 1.6, for a widow at Cologne too poor to stay and too poor to leave.

other option was to become tenants of larger landowners, even though this often meant being treated like "slaves."[98]

But by becoming "men without property," Salvian claimed, they had also lost their "right of liberty."[99] Another way men lost their Roman liberty was by going off to live among the barbarians.[100] This decision was difficult for people to contemplate, not least because of repulsive cultural differences: "And although they differ from those to whom they flee in regard to religion and language, although they are put off by the stench of barbarian bodies and clothes, . . . they still prefer to endure an unfamiliar life among the barbarians than savage injustice among the Romans. So they migrate either to the Goths or to the Bagaudae or to the other conquering barbarians."[101]

Salvian gave no indication where these "migrations" were taking place, and it is likely that he was only acknowledging that many people were accepting the barbarians as their new neighbors or masters. We cannot therefore presume to know exactly where in Gaul (or Spain)[102] he was referring to, and least of all in the case of the Bagaudae. Nor did he describe the Bagaudae as peasants in revolt; in fact, his discussion of them was developed only in the context of those well-born and educated men who were fleeing. More important, however, is to note that Salvian classified the Bagaudae with the barbarians.[103] Like people who sought the protection of powerful men and thereby lost their "right of liberty," so the Bagaudae and men who fled to the barbarians forfeited their liberty as well as "the dignity of the Roman name": "Those whom we compel to be outside the law we call rebels or corrupt men."[104] Men who were outside the Roman administration, even if for reasons not of their own choosing, were denigrated by the central elites as rebels, barbarians, or Bagaudae.

With these observations Salvian illustrates that the distinction between Romans and barbarian rebels had become largely a reflection of how the central administration viewed its shrinking world.[105] Perspective determined how people evaluated the fur-

98. *de gub. Dei* V.38–45.
99. *de gub. Dei* V.44, "ius libertatis amittant."
100. *de gub. Dei* V.22; cf. Orosius VII.41.7, for a similar observation.
101. *de gub. Dei* V.21–22. For one example, see *Chron. Gall. a. 452* s.a. 448 (*Chron. Min.* I, p. 662).
102. *de gub. Dei* V.23.      103. *de gub. Dei* V.26.      104. *de gub. Dei* V.24.
105. Brown (1972) 52–62, on prejudice and intolerance toward barbarians. For the comparatively more limited ideological ambitions of the barbarians, see Brown (1972) 315–16, and Thompson (1966) 110.

ther development of these early seigneurial institutions: from the center the trend seemed pernicious because it hampered central authority, while from the periphery of northern and central Gaul it seemed necessary in order to compensate for the absence of an emperor and his troops. And while Salvian was not critical of the enhanced prominence of local landowning aristocracies in itself, he did severely censure the specific aristocrats who appeared to overlook their new responsibility of providing security. Presumably others, like Salvian, could also see how some local patrons acted like "bandits";[106] and this too may have been one contributing factor to another significant phenomenon of the time, appeals for assistance to other men of local authority, such as Christian bishops.

Germanus of Auxerre offers one example of the expanded role of bishops. In the middle 430s, when Auxerre faced an unusually high tax assessment, Germanus agreed to travel to Arles and appeal to the praetorian prefect.[107] With this particular arbitrary tax assessment we can probably link the revolt of Tibatto and the Bagaudae in "remote Gaul," an area near Auxerre, in the late 430s. According to the account in one Gallic chronicle, this revolt was supported by almost all the *servitia* of Gaul.[108] *Servitia* here probably referred to anyone in a subordinate status, and so this revolt would have corresponded closely with Salvian's contemporary analysis. Even though the references are brief, it seems that the citizens of Auxerre, because of their surprise at an unexpected tax assessment, first requested the intercession of Bishop Germanus and then of Tibatto, who may have been a local aristocrat.[109] In return, others saw them only as Bagaudae in revolt. In this case, after Germanus successfully obtained a tax remission for the city, it was still "rich men" who took most advantage of it.[110] A few years later, however, these large landowners may themselves have been among the people asking for the help of the bishop.

In the 440s Germanus again responded to a request for assis-

---

106. *de gub. Dei* IV.30–31, V.18.

107. Constantius *Vita Germani* 19, 24.

108. *Chron. Gall. a. 452* s.a. 435, 437 (*Chron. Min.* I, p. 660), with Marc Bloch (1961) 149–50, on *servitium.*

109. Barnes (1974).

110. *de gub. Dei* V.35, for a "recent" reduction in taxes from which the rich alone benefitted; and Thompson (1957) 135–6, for the connection between this tax reduction mentioned by Salvian and the one obtained by Germanus.

tance from a delegation from Armorica. Since the last time Germanus had journeyed to Arles, a band of Alans under King Goar had been settled near Auxerre by the Roman general Aetius. But in contrast to the other barbarian tribes, the Alans were often not settled according to the arrangement of *hospitalitas*, whereby Roman landowners shared their estates with barbarian settlers.[111] Instead, the Alans simply confiscated this land. Naturally enough, as one of the Gallic chronicles recorded, this forced settlement led to hostility between the Alans and the resident landowners.[112] Although Germanus forced Goar to come to terms, the bishop also agreed to travel to the imperial court at Ravenna in 445 to ask for an indulgence. During his absence, the people of Armorica, under the leadership of Tibatto, again revolted.[113]

Eventually Tibatto was killed and Armorica was pacified by Aetius. Even though the conflict had been between Alans and the local landowners who had been displaced, an orator who celebrated the success of Aetius evaluated the episode only as another example of mastery over barbarian tribes. Like the barbarians on the Rhine and in southwestern Gaul, the "bandits" of Armorica had been tamed and were now growing grain.[114]

This long discussion has repeatedly stressed discrepancies in people's perspectives and the influence these different viewpoints had in turn on the way men acted or wrote. Many provincials could not understand why the barbarians were victorious, why the Roman administration no longer provided defense, why tax assessments were apparently unfair, or why a Roman general allowed barbarians to settle among them. Yet others considered some of the Gallic provinces as peripheral or unimportant, or labeled as Bagaudae people who only tried to defend themselves or who objected to the misuse of patronage. These discrepancies are concisely illustrated in an early fifth-century play, in which an old man named Querolus reveals to his household god, the *Lar familiaris*, what would make him a happy man.[115]

111. Lot (1928) 1010 n. 4.

112. *Chron. Gall. a. 452* s.a. 442 (*Chron. Min.* I, p. 660).

113. Constantius *Vita Germani* 28, 40; the reference to Tibatto is the only one that explicitly links the Bagaudae with Armorica. For the chronology, cf. below, p. 142 n. 2.

114. Merobaudes *Paneg.* II, with Clover (1971) 41–59, for a detailed discussion.

115. *Querolus* or *Aulularia* pp. 16–17 Peiper; for discussion and bibliography, see M. Schuster, *RE* XXIV (1963) col. 869–72.

Q.:   If you can, Lar familiaris, bring it about that I might be both a private citizen and a powerful man.

L.f.:   What kind of power do you want?

Q.:   I want to be able to rob those who don't owe me anything and kill the others—I want to be able to rob and kill even my neighbors!

L.f.:   You're looking for brigandage, not power; I don't know how I can get that for you. Wait, I know: you've just about got what you want. Go and live beside the Loire River.

Q.:   What happens there?

L.f.:   There men live by the common law of nations,[116] with no fraud. Capital sentences are pronounced under an oak tree and recorded on bones. There countryfolk give speeches and private citizens pronounce judgment—you can do anything you want! If you are a rich man, you will be called *patus*, as they say in our Greek.[117]

Q.:   But I'm not a rich man, and I don't want to use an oak tree. I don't like these forest laws.

L.f.:   Then look for something easier and more honorable if you can't live by these laws.

This colloquial exchange reveals how some people, presumably the governing elites, viewed life in central Gaul during the early fifth century. Because the old man in the comedy wanted to have power without holding an imperial magistracy or losing his status as a private citizen, the Lar proposed that he go live in Armorica along the Loire River, where private citizens did exercise authority. The audience for the play might have taken the remark as a joke, but it did accurately reflect a society in which private citizens, especially large landowners and bishops, were men of authority. Yet it is also significant to note that the society described by the Lar had a definite structure. It emphasized justice, even if of a peculiarly backwoods type, which was not part of the old man's dream of wanton robbing and killing, and it gave precedence to wealthy men, which again the old man did not appreciate.

Even in remote areas where the central administration had told people to fend for themselves, inhabitants continued to think of themselves as Romans. In 410 the emperor Honorius had written to the cities in Britain and suggested that they defend themselves;

116. *Ius gentium* is a problematic phrase; for a good discussion, see H. F. Jolowicz and B. Nicholas, *Historical introduction to the study of Roman law*, 3rd ed. (Cambridge, 1972) 102–7.

117. *Patus* may be a corruption of παχύς, "rich" (cf. Sulpicius Severus *Dial.* I.27, II.1.4, for knowledge of Greek in Gaul), or it may be a Celtic word meaning "master" (cf. Whatmough [1970] 1337). If the latter is correct, then this is another example of the reappearance of Celtic terms to describe a traditional relationship of patronage.

this letter effectively marked the end of Roman administration, and sub-Roman Britain quickly went back to a pre-Roman condition in which local leaders tried to provide security for their communities.[118] Yet throughout at least the first half of the fifth century the people of Britain still apparently thought themselves to be subservient to the emperor, and in 446 they again appealed to the Roman general Aetius for assistance against invading barbarians.[119] Armorica too still considered itself Roman. In 451 Armoricans were among the "Romans" whom Aetius led against the Huns of Attila.[120] Such collaboration is inexplicable for modern historians who interpret the history of central and northern Gaul during the first half of the fifth century in terms of revolts against the Roman Empire.[121] But, as we have seen, throughout the early fifth century the people of Armorica wanted the Roman Empire to stay; they "revolted" to remain Romans.

*   *   *

Our information about Gaul during the first half of the fifth century is less fragmentary than for the other northwestern provinces, and it has been possible to present a plausible context for the references to Bagaudae. We also have references to Bagaudae in the Alps and in northern Spain during the early fifth century that can be considered together, because they illustrate not only the survival of traditional lifestyles but also the restricted impact of the Roman Empire in areas with mountainous and difficult terrain.

The Alps were an obvious barrier protecting Italy on the north and the west; there they were called "the walls of Italy."[122] These mountains posed a severe obstacle to invading armies, offered hideouts for bandits, and even allowed the local men of authority who controlled particular passes to become wealthy by charging tolls.[123] In the early fifth century Bagaudae appeared in the Alps.

In 407 a general and his army preparing to retreat to Italy from

118. Procopius Bell. Vand. I.2.38, and Sawyer (1978) 76–91.
119. Gildas de excidio et conquestu Britanniae 20 (Chron. Min. III, p. 36).
120. Sidonius Carm. VII.547–9, and Jordanes Getica 36.191.
121. Thompson (1948) 140, and (1952a) 20.
122. Isidore of Seville Etymologiae XIV.8.18 (PL 82.523); cf. Paul the Deacon, Hist. Langobardorum II.9 (MGH, SRLangobardicarum, p. 77).
123. SHA Quad. Tyr. 12–13, for the noble bandit Proculus; Sulpicius Severus Vita Martini 5, for St. Martin's experiences; Zosimus IV.42, for Maximus' difficulties in crossing the Alps with an army.

southern Gaul found their way through the Alps blocked by Bagaudae, who allowed them to proceed only after they had handed over their booty.[124] These Bagaudae were surely no more than local inhabitants who were taking advantage of the difficult terrain to extort tribute from an army that had recently plundered a town. Perhaps these Bagaudae were augmented by soldiers who had deserted[125] or by refugees displaced by the invasions, but it is unlikely that they can be fitted into any overall interpretation of "rebellious peasants and shepherds in the Alpine region."[126] Instead, in a period when Roman domination in outlying regions was declining, these people revived a traditional livelihood, which was seen by others as banditry and extortion.[127]

Because mountains have always been intractable to the great empires of the past, Roman domination in the Alps was correspondingly tenuous. Imperial administrations were confined by both vertical and horizontal frontiers, as Fernand Braudel argues: "The mountains are as a rule a world apart from civilizations, which are an urban and lowland achievement. Their history is to have none, to remain almost always on the fringe of the great waves of civilization, even the longest and most persistent, which may spread over great distances in the horizontal plain but are powerless to move vertically when faced with an obstacle of a few hundred metres."[128] Hence, although emperors tried to establish colonies in the Alps, such "urbanization" was highly artificial, and by the fourth and early fifth centuries all that survived in the Alps were the original Celtic settlements.[129] A comparable area was Isauria, a region of mountains in the south of Asia Minor that, in the fourth century at least, Roman legions tried to make into an enclave by surrounding it with a virtual frontier defense system. Isauria was noted most of all for its bandits and its mountain lions; since the Romans could hardly pacify the region, they attempted instead simply to isolate it.[130]

124. Zosimus VI.2.5–6.
125. Cf. *CTh* VII.18.1 (a. 365), for deserters in the Alps.
126. Thompson (1956a) 73; cf. Szádeczky-Kardoss (1968) col. 349, based on Czúth and Szádeczky-Kardoss (1959).
127. van Berchem (1956b), for pre-Roman and medieval evidence.
128. Braudel (1972) 34.
129. van Berchem (1955).
130. *Expositio totius mundi et gentium* 45, and the illustration in *Notitia Dignitatum* Or. 29.5, for mountain lions. In general, see Rougé (1966), and Dagron (1978) 113–23.

In the province of Tarraconensis in northern Spain was another natural enclave along the Ebro River. This valley was bounded on the north and south by mountains and on the east and west by roads giving access to central and southern Spain; through the valley ran another road linking the cities on the Mediterranean coast with the cities in northern Spain on the Atlantic coast.[131] Although the Pyrenees may once have sheltered boorish "mountain men," under the empire the valley had come to be dominated by estates and ranches and was noted in particular for its hams.[132] By the later empire the development of a villa economy had put the Ebro valley firmly into a Mediterranean context, and had even led to the importation of its classical culture and ethos. The mosaics now being uncovered by Spanish archaeologists in these Roman villas still portray figures from Greek mythology or local grandees enjoying their magnificent hunts—precisely the heritage and behavior characteristic of civilized aristocratic life throughout the Mediterranean world.[133]

During the fourth century the aristocracy of northern Spain presumably lived in a fashion similar to that of the better-known aristocracy of southern Gaul, and hence the Ebro valley served as a welcome retreat for Gallic aristocrats on the run from their pasts, among them an accused adulterer[134] and Paulinus of Nola as he worked out the implications of his conversion to Christianity. Although his old mentor Ausonius failed to understand the attractions of Spain, Paulinus insisted upon the charms of such cities as Saragossa, Barcelona, and Tarragona, as well as the prosperity of the fields. In reply to Ausonius' hint that he was now living in the mountains among bandits and barbarians, Paulinus insisted that the Ebro valley was in fact comparable to southern Gaul and had even provided him with a wife.[135]

Throughout the first half of the fifth century this enclave of aristocratic families along the Ebro River remained uniquely isolated from barbarian invaders. When Constans, a son of the emperor Constantine III, withdrew from Spain in 408 after defeating

131. Strabo III.4.9–10; see Dupré (1973).
132. Strabo III.4.8, 11, for pigs, and *Edictum Diocletiani* 4.8 (ed. Lauffer [1971] 104–5), for Cerritanean hams.
133. For these mosaics see Fernández de Avilés (1945); Balil (1960) and (1966).
134. Ausonius *prof.* 23.4–5.
135. Ausonius *Ep.* 29, and Paulinus of Nola *Carm.* X; see Etienne (1966), for the limitations of Ausonius' knowledge of Spain.

the relatives of Theodosius, he left behind a replacement garrison of Gallic and British troops. These troops were probably stationed at the western end of Tarraconensis, approximately where the private army of the relatives of Theodosius had been active,[136] and when in and after 409 barbarians pushed through the Pyrenees, presumably these troops deflected them toward the west and the south and prevented them from entering the Ebro valley. Instead, the valley seems to have become autonomous in a rough-and-ready way, even producing its own emperor and later acting as a safe haven for a Roman general.[137]

Furthermore, when the barbarians finally settled in Spain, the various tribes "allotted" to themselves different regions, including almost all of Spain except Tarraconensis.[138] In 415 part of Tarraconensis was temporarily occupied by Visigoths, who had been forced to leave Gaul, although in 418 they were called back and allowed to settle in Aquitania. But even these Visigoths seem not to have gone up the Ebro valley; their excursions through Spain had taken them on a circuit down the east coast to Baetica and Lusitania, and then back through the center of Spain along the western edge of the Pyrenees to Aquitania. For the next few decades much of what we know about Tarraconensis comes from some confusing references to Bagaudae; since these references are obviously laconic, it would be unwise to read too much into them.[139] What we can stress, however, is that throughout most of the fifth century the Ebro valley remained an isolated stronghold of aristocrats who sometimes themselves led the opposition to the barbarians and sometimes were assisted by Roman troops or allies.

Whoever these Bagaudae were, their activities should be associated with the movements of the Sueves, who threatened to take over all of Spain after the departure of the Vandals; for if the Sueves intended to expand over the entire peninsula from their original settlement in the northwest of Spain, then Araceli (per-

---

136. For the location of army units in early fifth-century northern Spain, see *Notitia Dignitatum Occ.* 42.19, 26–32, and *de laude Pampilone epistola*, ed. Lacarra (1945) 268–9; for discussion, see Demougeot (1956) and, especially, Arce (1980).

137. For the usurper Maximus, see Sozomen IX.13.1; Frigeridus, *apud* Gregory of Tours *HF* II.9; Olympiodorus, frag. 16 (*FHG* IV, p. 60); and Orosius VII.42.5. For the general Castinus, see Hydatius *Chron.* 77 (*Chron. Min.* II, p. 20).

138. Hydatius *Chron.* 49 (p. 18).

139. Cf. Thompson (1952a) 16–17, and Szádeczky-Kardoss (1968) col. 352–3, based on Czúth and Szádeczky-Kardoss (1958). For an extended discussion of the end of Roman Spain, see Thompson (1976–1979).

haps modern Arbizu) at the western end of the Ebro valley would have been one of the first towns to feel the pressure. In this case it is unclear whether the Bagaudae whom the Spanish chronicler Hydatius placed at Araceli opposed or supported the Sueves, but either way, two Roman generals were sent to Tarraconensis in the early 440s to defeat them. Similarly, in 446 another general was sent from Italy, this time to force the Sueves out of southern Spain.[140] A few years later Bagaudae were apparently collaborating with the Sueves. In 449 a man named Basilius led Bagaudae against "allies" (presumably Visigoths) at Tarazona, and then assisted the Sueves when they sacked Saragossa and Lerida.[141] These raids threatened the center of the Ebro valley, and this time the imperial court in Italy eventually sent Visigoths against both Bagaudae and Sueves.[142]

In the later fourth century, during the reign of the Spanish emperor Theodosius, Spanish aristocrats had served at the imperial court and in the central administration. In addition, the patronage they had received from the imperial family, the appearance in their cities of Christian cults dedicated to saints from both Rome and Spain, and their own need to preserve a cultural contrast between themselves and barbarians had motivated these aristocrats to develop an ideology allowing them to be both Spaniards and "Romans."[143] But by the fifth century Spanish aristocrats seem to have retired again to their estates, serving neither in the Roman administration nor at the courts of barbarian kings.[144] The preceding discussion has suggested that we can perhaps see in the Ebro valley an enclave of aristocratic landowners that continued to survive in self-imposed isolation throughout most of the fifth century. So when the emperor Majorian traveled to the western provinces in 460, he could visit Saragossa, in the center of this "Roman" valley.[145] In 465 a letter to Pope Hilarus still mentioned

140. Hydatius *Chron.* 125, 128, 134 (p. 24).

141. Hydatius *Chron.* 141–2 (p. 25); note that Isidore of Seville *Hist. Sueb.* 87 (*Chron. Min.* II, p. 301), a passage derived from Hydatius (see *Chron. Min.* II, p. 244), claimed that the Sueves were assisted, not by Basilius, but by Goths. Basilius has been variously identified as a Roman general, a Gothic chieftain, or a Suevic general: see Tranoy (1974) II, 87–88.

142. Hydatius *Chron.* 158, 170, 172–3 (pp. 27–28).

143. Fontaine (1976b) has an excellent discussion of these points.

144. See Stroheker (1965) 75–87, and his excellent survey stressing this contrast in (1972–1974).

145. Hydatius *Chron.* 200 (p. 319, and *Chron. Caesaraugust.* s.a. 460 (*Chron. Min.* II, p. 222).

the aristocrats and landowners from a number of cities along the Ebro River, including Tarazona and Calahorra.[146] And it was these local aristocrats who had apparently fought hardest to maintain themselves as Romans. During the late 460s the Visigoths under King Euric began to expand permanently into Spain; but even then, in order to gain control over Tarraconensis, the Visigoths had first to defeat a resistance led by the "nobles" of the province.[147]

\* \* \*

The preceding discussion of the Bagaudae during the fifth century has emphasized two main points: first, the reemergence of a substratum of local leadership, and second, the importance of evaluating prejudices and perspectives when interpreting references to bandits and Bagaudae. Rebellions and usurpations were an indication of confusion and barbarian pressure, although not necessarily of hostility to the Roman Empire. That regions or individuals were prepared to support local emperors indicates attitudes favoring the presence of the Roman Empire, when the alternative would have been local or regional separatism or barbarian rule. What were seen from the center as "revolts" often represented attempts by local citizens to revive a Roman administration that was abandoning them.

In conclusion, since Christianity will now become the dominant topic of this book, let us briefly consider the connection between it and the Bagaudae. In folklore, bandits have frequently been linked with Christianity. Robin Hood's band of outlaws, for example, included a friar; Jesse James was thought of as a teetotaling Baptist who sang in a church choir.[148] Although often incorrect, these associations nevertheless invested outlaws with an aura of morality and even legitimacy and allowed them one acceptable link with conventional society. But although the Bagaudae were "warriors," they did not in their own time become "warriors for Christ";[149] only later would they enter Christian hagiographical traditions as true orthodox martyrs.

By the middle of the fifth century the Bagaudae were already

146. Hilarus *Ep.* 16.1 (ed. Thiel [1867] 165–6).
147. Isidore of Seville *Hist. Goth.* 34 (*Chron. Min.* II, p. 281); cf. *Chron. Gall. a. 511* 651–2 (*Chron. Min.* I, pp. 664–5).
148. Steckmesser (1966).
149. As did happen with the Circumcellions in North Africa: see Augustine *Ep.* 88.8, and Frend (1952) 172–7.

implicitly linked with specifically Christian forms of heroism. In the 440s Salvian had described the Bagaudae as men who were being forced to become barbarians when all they wanted was to remain Romans: "They fled to the enemy so that they would not perish under the burden of persecution by the state."[150] Thus, men who became Bagaudae did so because they were being "persecuted" by Roman magistrates, and in the eyes of Christians these men were morally justified in fleeing because even among barbarians they were preserving true Roman attitudes. Also during the 440s, Bishop Eucher of Lyon wrote an account of the illustrious members of the Theban Legion who had been executed by the emperor Maximian for refusing to fight against Christians in Gaul at the end of the third century.[151] Although Eucher never identified these rebellious Christians as Bagaudae, contemporary fifth-century historians were repeating earlier traditions that Maximian had been sent to Gaul to subdue Bagaudae, while at the same time in northern and western Gaul "revolts" were occurring that other writers thought had involved Bagaudae again. Hence, whatever the Bagaudae may have been in the later third century, Christians of the fifth century remembered only the tradition of dissent and resistance to an unfair and persecuting emperor. Not surprisingly, in much later medieval hagiography the Bagaudae who had opposed the ungodly Maximian were themselves associated with Christianity, and their leaders were described as "believers in the Christian faith."[152] By the later Middle Ages the original significance of the third-century Bagaudae had been lost, and their resistance illustrated only a simple religious dichotomy, according to which the Christian soldiers of the Theban Legion had refused to assist the pagan emperor Maximian against the Christian Bagaudae.

Despite the complexity of these later hagiographical traditions, the outright distortion of the historical Bagaudae and the substitution of a new perspective have important implications. First,

150. *de gub. Dei* V.21.
151. Eucher *Passio Acaunensium martyrum* 4. See Dupraz (1961) 62, for the date of composition, and Jullian (1920a), on the historical problems connected with this legion.
152. See *Passio SS. Mauritii et Thebaeorum* 1–2 (*Acta Sanctorum* Sept. VI, p. 345), dated to the ninth century or earlier by van Berchem (1956a) 21; and *Vita S. Baboleni*, in M. Bouquet, ed., *Recueil des historiens des Gaules et de la France* III (Paris, 1869) 568–9, with P. Sejourné, *DHGE* VI (1932) 24–27, and Jullian (1920b).

Christian bishops seem to have taken the lead in establishing this new interpretation. Not only had Bishop Germanus of Auxerre, for example, represented the interests of his community against both the imperial administration and local large landowners, he had also founded a chapel at Auxerre in honor of the martyrs of the Theban Legion who had (supposedly) identified themselves with the rebellious Christians of Gaul.[153] On one of his journeys Germanus had passed through Lyon,[154] where Bishop Eucher later laid the foundation for a reinterpretation of the Bagaudae of the late third century. Hence, although the contrast between bishops and oppressive landowners must not be drawn too sharply,[155] the emergence of bishops as local leaders in the fifth century seems to coincide with sympathy for favorable traditions about the Bagaudae.

Second, this reinterpretation of the Bagaudae also highlights the reciprocal influence between different cultural levels in late antique and medieval society.[156] The extant fourth- and fifth-century histories, chronicles, and panegyrics had always associated the Bagaudae with bandits, farmers, and even barbarians; but these later saints' lives, the most popular literature of their time, described them as true believers, even as Christian martyrs. Instead of being dismissed as marginal to Roman civilization, the Bagaudae were eventually integrated into the very center of a new Christian society.

Yet, third, there is nothing that can be taken for granted about the transformation, not of Bagaudae into Christian martyrs, but rather of Gaul into a Christian society in which bishops and hagiography were so prominent. With the reemergence of local aristocrats in sub-Roman Gaul of the fifth century, legends of the Bagaudae might well have been absorbed into their secular traditions in the same way that the Robin Hood ballads became part of the literary culture of the English gentry.[157] Instead, the result was the

153. Although the information about this foundation comes from late ninth-century sources: *Gesta pont. Autissiodorensium* 7 (ed. Duru [1850–1863] I, 318), and Heiric of Auxerre *Miracula S. Germani* I.37 (ed. Duru [1850–1863] II, 132–3).

154. Constantius *Vita Germani* 23.

155. *de gub. Dei* V.19–20, 52–55, for bishops as part of the problem for poor people; but note also that in Spain some sixth- and seventh-century bishops were named Bacauda: A. Lambert, *DHGE* VI (1932) 42–44.

156. Le Goff (1980) 153–8.

157. For this debate, see Hilton (1976) 221–72, and Maddicott (1978).

rise of bishops and of a Christian society, which is all the more surprising when we consider, in the next group of chapters, the limited and hardly comprehensive form of Christianity available in fourth-century Gaul.

# II

# Christian Society in
# Fourth-Century Gaul and Spain

The pattern of interaction between Christianity and society in late antique Gaul differed from that in other regions of the empire. In Asia Minor, for instance, the early strength of Christianity in provincial cities was enhanced by the foundation of Constantinople and the consequent promotion of local municipal elites;[1] in Italy the resident pagan senatorial aristocracy, which already had a proud tradition of imperial service, was challenged in the fourth century by men backed by the patronage of Christian emperors. In Gaul under the early empire, in contrast, we find only local aristocracies living in apparent isolation and few Christians living outside southern Gaul. During the fourth century, therefore, the expansion of Christianity in Gaul accompanied the expectations generated by the presence of an imperial court, while in the fifth century, as we will see in Part III, Christianity rose to prominence without having to contend with an imperial administration.

In historiographical terms, Christian sermons, tracts, and letters finally allow us to glimpse the nature of life in small cities. With these writings we can supplement the self-consciously "classical" literature produced by educated elites and investigate the ordinary shared beliefs that enabled men of Late Antiquity (including elites)[2] to live in their communities. On the assumption that Gaul and Spain formed a culturally homogeneous whole,[3] we

1. Jones (1963).
2. In other words, cultural stratification and social stratification did not necessarily coincide; Momigliano (1972), and Brown (1981) 12–22, are perceptive discussions of learned and popular beliefs in Late Antiquity.
3. Fontaine (1974) is an implicit demonstration of the homogeneity of the region that one chronicler called "Spanogallia" and "Hispanogalia": *Chron. a. 354* (*Chron. Min.* I, pp. 98–99).

can integrate the scattered Christian literature from that region with a limited amount of comparative material from other western provinces in order to construct a general impression of these small communities in which Christian doctrine and liturgy performed important social functions and in which Christian bishops became local men of authority. In the next chapter we will look at aspects of these small communities that will be relevant to an interpretation of Priscillianism in Chapter 5, although keeping in mind that in fact many of these aspects are characteristic of small communities in most traditional societies. The introductory discussion in the next chapter will emphasize, first, the nature of Christian leadership and the public pressures that ensured that people behaved correctly and conformed to community values; second, the self-limiting restrictions inherent in a Christian outlook that could barely accommodate some types of people; and third, the way in which Christian communities ensured their purity and bishops their authority through the use of accusations of heresy. Since this general discussion is also an introduction to the role of Christianity in late antique Gaul, it occasionally anticipates subsequent chapters that discuss in greater detail the conversion of Gallic society during the later fourth and fifth centuries.

# CHAPTER 4

# The Christian Society
# of Late Roman Gaul and Spain

## Urban Christian Communities

The arrival of relics at Rouen in the late fourth or early fifth century offered Bishop Victricius the opportunity to deliver a sermon: "Behold how great a part of the heavenly army has thought it worthwhile to visit our city."[1] Throughout his sermon the bishop addressed these relics as saints who were being greeted by the entire Christian community, which Victricius seemed to represent as the entire town. And he called upon the people to celebrate not only the presence of the saints, but also the construction of a new church for them.

One way of looking at the festival celebrating the translation of relics is to compare it with an *adventus* ceremony, which normally celebrated the arrival of an emperor or the imperial images at a city.[2] Even though the citizens of Rouen may never have seen an imperial arrival, Victricius probably had in his younger days when he had served as a soldier, and also, perhaps, when he visited Rome in 403.[3] Thus it is not surprising that many elements in his description of the arrival of these holy relics corresponded with aspects of an imperial arrival. At Rouen the relics arrived under the escort of other bishops, much as a delegation of notable

---

1. Victricius *de laude sanctorum* 1; on Victricius see Griffe (1964–1966) I, 306–10.

2. Above, pp. 10–11, and Gussone (1976). On the "Trier Ivory," which illustrates the *adventus* of relics, see the recent debate between Spain (1977), Holum and Vikan (1979), W. Weber (1979), and Wortley (1980).

3. Paulinus of Nola *Ep.* 18.7, 37.1. At the end of 403 the emperor Honorius also visited Rome: Claudian *VI cons. Honorii*, esp. 523–639.

citizens would have gone to meet an emperor and to accompany him into the city. In the presence of the relics citizens made requests, although not for tax remissions but for forgiveness from sins; like good kings and emperors, saints showed impartiality—a quality apparently lacking in local magistrates.[4]

But Victricius also stressed the profound differences in significance between these similar celebrations. "If one of the emperors were to visit our city today, every street would happily be covered with garlands, women would fill the rooftops, and a wave of people would surge from the city gates. . . . People of every age would sing of honor and of war, and they would marvel at the flaming splendor of the emperor's cloak and at the imperial purple. . . . But now, instead of the royal cloak there is right here the garment of eternal light. Here is the purple, . . . here are diadems decorated with the splendid gems [of different Christian virtues]."[5] By now a new meaning had obviously been attached to a traditional ceremony. Once the presence of an emperor had led to improvements in local fortifications; now the presence of saints was sufficient protection against attacks by demons, and the remission of sins by these saints meant that people were no longer threatened by battles.[6] But the most significant difference was that these saints had come to Rouen to stay. Even an emperor, when he was present on a particular frontier, could be in only one city at a time, and the best that emperors had supplied for Rouen had been merely a resident military commander.[7] With the arrival of these relics, however, Rouen had its own permanent garrison of "divine troops," and for it the citizens of Rouen were building a "palace," which was the new church whose construction Victricius mentioned at the end of the sermon.[8]

Yet, despite the superficial aspects of continuity in their external trappings and of discontinuity in their context and application, these ceremonies of arrival were essentially idiomatic rituals that highlighted the men who had authority in communities and that precipitated consensus around those men and the values they

4. *de laude sanctorum* 5, 8, 12; contrast Ammianus Marcellinus XVI.5.14.
5. *de laude sanctorum* 12.
6. *de laude sanctorum* 6; cf. Paulinus of Nola, *Ep.* 31.1.
7. *Notitia Galliarum* 2.1, and *Notitia Dignitatum Occ.* 37.13, 21.
8. *de laude sanctorum* 12. Note that because Christianity did not take over the corresponding ceremony of imperial departure (on which see Koeppel [1969]), there was no clear procedure in the Middle Ages for transferring relics, which often circulated instead by ritual "theft": see Geary (1978).

represented. Previously these ceremonies had spotlighted the benefits an emperor could grant upon his arrival as well as the support given to the emperor in return, and thus during the ceremony the emperor acted and was seen by others as an almost divine figure. In 357 the emperor Constantius had entered Rome in a magnificent parade. But during the procession Constantius himself had stood motionless in his golden carriage: "As if his neck were in a vise he kept the gaze of his eyes straight ahead and turned his face neither to the right nor to the left. Like a human statue he neither nodded when the wheel jolted, nor was he ever seen to spit, or to wipe or rub his face or nose, or to move his hands about."[9] By the later fourth century, however, what had been strictly an imperial ceremony was also being used in a clearly Christian context to focus on the leadership of bishops and saints and on the values of Christian communities.

This last statement only raises further difficulties, however, because the sermon of Victricius has, typically, plunged us into the middle of the process. Secular concerns were not erased by new-fashioned religious preoccupations; instead, this reformulation of traditional ceremonies implies the previous existence of Christian leaders and communities that now only took over secular idioms of authority and consensus to articulate and validate their increasing prominence. This and the next chapter therefore attempt to look behind this "transposed rhetoric" of the literary sources at Christianity before it was "contaminated" by secular perspectives.

Most obviously, Christian leaders were men of spiritual power whose greatest victories were won over demons. In a Christian perspective, not only were demons the true barbarians, even in a city such as Trier near the Rhine frontier,[10] but any unfamiliar or threatening behavior was attributed to demonic motivation.[11] In the long run this emphasis on demons transformed society itself as well as the nature of leadership, because men who were able to find demons and force them to reveal their true selves had tapped into a new source of authority. Such a man was Martin of Tours who, according to his admirer Sulpicius Severus, not only detected the devil in whatever disguise he used, but also rendered

---

9. Ammianus Marcellinus XVI.10.9–10. Constantius' particular self-control was all the more impressive in Rome, where the techniques of spitting had become a mark of distinction: Ammianus Marcellinus XXVII.3.5.

10. Sulpicius Severus *Vita Martini* 18.1–2.

11. *Vita Martini* 6.1–2, 12.

him powerless.[12] In addition, Martin and other Christian leaders like him were able to perform spectacular deeds by means of their *virtus*, their "power"; Martin, for instance, brought a dead person back to life, converted many regions to Christianity, destroyed pagan temples, and checked raging fires.[13] Yet we should not interpret this *virtus* as an innate attribute of these men; they themselves may have insisted that it was a gift from God,[14] but in fact it was a quality assigned to them by their audience and thus was indicative of the ties between leaders and Christian communities. Men thought to possess divine power were seen by their supporters as links between the sacred world and ordinary life, as witnesses who displayed in their human form such divine characteristics as impassiveness and imperturbability. As a result, the behavior that the emperor Constantius had exhibited when making his formal entrance at Rome was eventually also expected of a bishop such as Martin: "No one ever saw him angry or disturbed or grieving or laughing. He was always one and the same; displaying on his face a divine joy he seemed beyond the nature of man."[15] In bishops people saw men who were "similar to God."[16]

But ordinary Christians were not merely passive in the face of this divine power, because they, as the community, had largely created the values summed up in their leaders. Hence we must not overlook the importance of those moments at which ordinary Christians came "in touch" with their leaders, moments that crystallized around the celebration of the sacraments and the exposition of the Scriptures.

Participation in the ritual of mass emphasized most firmly this interaction between congregations and their bishops. Because during this period in Gaul people were still expected to bring offerings, the sacrifice by a bishop at the altar was also their sacrifice, and by visualizing the presiding bishop to be clothed in purple and jewels like an emperor, they were also sharing in his

---

12. *Vita Martini* 17.5–7, 21.1. The significance of the career of Martin is elaborated in Chapter 6.

13. *Vita Martini* 7, 13.9, 14.

14. *Vita Martini* 16.5.

15. *Vita Martini* 27.1, "extra naturam hominis."

16. *de septem ordinibus ecclesiae* 7 (PL 30.158). This anonymous tract may have been written in Gaul during the late fourth or early fifth century (see Morin [1928b], and Griffe [1956]), or in Spain during the early seventh century (see Reynolds [1970]).

"gifts of divine favor." [17] In return, ordinary believers had the opportunity to receive that "honey-sweet food" of the Eucharist and so to taste, if only for a moment, the same sweetness that refreshed saints in heaven. [18]

To prepare themselves for these moments of intense participation, Christians were expected to rely on a close and continual reading of the Scriptures. The ideal was to imitate a man such as Jerome, whom a pilgrim described to his friends back in Gaul: "Always he is totally involved in reading and in his books, and he rests neither day nor night." [19] The practice of *lectio divina*, "reading the Scriptures," was a preparation of the soul for its journey to God; it brought the divine order near, not least because people could hold the Scriptures in their hands. But although both the Scriptures and a room were available in churches for those who wished to read, many people were illiterate, and even those who could read might have difficulty interpreting and understanding sacred books. As in a secular education, so in reading the Scriptures it was necessary to have a teacher, for "even a literate needs to be guided through the learning to be won from books; an independent approach to the written word is fraught with mystical dangers." As a result, "the role of the teacher as the mediator of knowledge is given pre-eminent importance. He adds personal charisma to book-learning, in a combination of oral and literate modes of communication." [20] The need for teachers again emphasizes the relationship between leaders and congregations, because usually these exegetes were the local bishops; as Jerome wrote, a bishop was to be a *doctor* just like the professors of classical learning, [21] teaching his congregation through sermons as well as in smaller study groups. [22] One important quality in good bishops was their ability to answer questions arising from the Scriptures. Martin provided an exemplary model: "How sharp

---

17. Sulpicius Severus *Dial.* III.10.6, with Dix (1945) 12–15, and Jungmann (1952–1958) II, 276–7, for the offertory procession. Du Boulay (1974) 57–63, provides modern comparative material on the expression of village identity through the celebration of Christian liturgy.

18. See the inscription of Pectorius found at Autun, discussed in Quasten (1950) 173–5; and Gregory of Tours *HF* VII.1, for the *odor suavitatis* that eliminated appetite and thirst in heaven.

19. Sulpicius Severus *Dial.* I.9.5; in general see Gorce (1925).

20. Goody (1968) 13.

21. Jerome *adv. Iovinianum* I.35; cf., e.g., Ausonius *prof.* 4.6.

22. Council of Saragossa a. 380, Can. 1 (*PL* 84.315).

and capable, how quick and ready he was in resolving the problems of the Scriptures!"[23]

One of the few surviving fourth-century sermons from Spain and Gaul reveals how a bishop put his congregation at ease by confronting their anxieties. In the middle of the fourth century Bishop Potamius of Lisbon discussed the death and resurrection of Lazarus, a topic not without relevance to his congregation.[24] Of all the ideas associated with death, Potamius chose to stress the "black horror" of putrefaction of the body, imagery that grotesquely emphasized the transience of earthly life as contrasted with the permanence of a divine life that was detached from the usual mundane processes.[25] After he had described the decay of Lazarus' body in macabre detail, his entire congregation would also have been aroused to fever pitch: "Behold, in the midst of these events Jesus Christ, the Savior of the human race, is said to have wept!" But Potamius was able to conclude his sermon by describing how, after his body had been restored, Lazarus recognized his parents, ate some bread, and went home. In this way the bishop had reaffirmed the simple values of the community in the face of the horrors of death.

\*      \*      \*

Although bishops' main source of power was spiritual and although they were seen as the human embodiments of divine virtues, their authority still had to take more practical forms that linked them with other Christians. Like other cult leaders bishops presided over festivals and the celebration of the sacraments and interpreted the appropriate sacred writings. But festivals, sacraments, and sacred books also defined proper behavior; hence, in addition to offering alternative notions about leadership and authority in communities, a Christian perspective on the means of access to holiness and moral purity also created new social regulations—or rather, it reinterpreted in Christian terms the pressures toward correct behavior and correct beliefs characteristic of most ancient and modern small communities. In other words, Christian exhortations that seem to us to be only pietistic homilies were

---

23. *Vita Martini* 25.6.
24. *de Lazaro* (*PL* 8.1411–15, and ed. A. Wilmart, *J. Theol. Studies* 19 [1918] 298–304).
25. Huizinga (1924) 138–51.

also reinforcement for some of the constraints inherent in the very structure of small communities.

In Gaul and Spain many towns had a population of only a few thousand, and some of only a few hundred;[26] hence, even if everyone was a member of the church, Christian communities were small and members were well known to each other. These towns were also very cramped, enough so to make one Gallic aristocrat long to leave Bordeaux and return to his country estate, where he had more privacy and peace of mind.[27] In such small communities rumor and innuendo had become effective means of controlling people's behavior, and a man who misbehaved was hardly able to conceal the fact; as Victricius wrote, "A good conscience presents nothing that rumor might harm or the slightest suspicion vex." Similarly, Gallic councils repeatedly stressed that men and women should avoid any compromising situations from which gossip might arise.[28]

In these small communities appearances became very important. Victricius emphasized how, at the festival marking the arrival of holy relics, no one had come out dressed in purple finery with pearls and gold bracelets. Although at a ceremony celebrating the arrival of an emperor everyone did attend in their most spectacular attire, in the case of the arrival of relics, to dress as a suppliant was a mark of conformity to the demands of the Christian community as well as an expression of contrition for past sins.[29] For people's lives as Christians, in fact their entire lives in an urban setting, were public. Debates between rival religious leaders were staged before huge crowds in the town baths or in the church. Confessions were public too, "before the eyes" of local bishops. Similarly, the celebration of sacraments such as the Eucharist implied a public affirmation of participants' purity and acquiescence. Jerome, for instance, was critical of people who took communion on the same day as they had had sexual inter-

26. For the size of towns see Griffe (1964–1966) III, 5–11, and Pounds (1969); for the area enclosed by town walls see Butler (1959); and for a possible decrease in population during Late Antiquity, see Boussard (1948). MacMullen (1974) is a full collection of comparative material from all regions of the Roman Empire except Gaul and Spain.

27. Ausonius *Ep.* 6.19–34.

28. *de laude sanctorum* 3; and Council of Tours a. 461, Can. 3; Council of Agde a. 506, Can. 28; Council of Orléans a. 538, Can. 4.

29. *de laude sanctorum* 3.

course; as he wrote in another context, "Whenever I have been angry or have had evil thoughts in my mind . . . , I do not dare to enter the churches of the martyrs; in body and mind I tremble all over."[30] In this context even the overworked distinction between light and dark takes on a significance beyond that of a theological metaphor for good and evil, because a man could be considered pure and innocent only when he appeared in public before his fellow Christians: "Crime looks for hiding places but innocence seeks out the public eye."[31] While the lack of privacy ensured public conformity, the application of religious sanctions was a similar attempt to guarantee that people's internal dispositions corresponded with their visibly correct behavior.

For people who had not completely integrated themselves with the demands of community life and the ethical constraints of Christianity, only a limited number of options was available. Although landowners might try to avoid some of the pressures of town life by staying on their estates, they still felt the need to participate in the important Christian festivals in order to avoid suspicion. One aristocrat, for instance, who begrudgingly attended Easter services in Bordeaux, wanted only to leave again: "In the first days after holy Easter I long to visit my estate."[32]

Christians who lived in or near cities, however, had fewer options for avoiding their obligations; according to a canon of an early fourth-century Spanish council, "If someone who is situated in a town does not go to the church for three Sundays, . . . he seems to have sinned."[33] One way of escaping these obligations was simply to run away, as becomes apparent from a series of injunctions issued by another Spanish council against people who, during the season of Lent, avoided attendance at church by fleeing to the mountains or by hiding away in country villas.[34] But leaving was not always a viable choice because mobility was limited,[35] and it furthermore implied that people who were considered impure by communities also perceived themselves as such. Thus another alternative was the use of violence. Sometimes this

30. Jerome, *contra Vigilantium* 12; cf. *Ep.* 48.15.
31. *de laude sanctorum* 11, with H. Chadwick (1972) for the early Christian belief in the potency of the night.
32. Ausonius *Ep.* 4.9–10, 6.17–18.
33. Council of Elvira, Can. 21 (*PL* 84.304).
34. Council of Saragossa a. 380, Can. 2, 4 (*PL* 84.315–16).
35. Gaudemet (1958) 369–70, for letters of introduction from bishops, and Sidonius *Ep.* VI.8, for an example.

compulsion took a subtle form; as we will see in a later section of this chapter, by accusing a man of being a heretic or a Manichee a community gave him the choices of leaving town or of confessing and then being accepted back. But perhaps more often even the niceties of an accusation were eliminated, and "troublemakers" were simply run out of town. At Rome, for example, Jerome mentioned that people bitterly complained about Christians who were living as excessive ascetics: "Why has that detestable race of monks not yet been run out of the city, or pelted with stones, or thrown in the river?"[36] Before he became bishop of Tours, Martin himself had been expelled from several towns by Arians. When he returned to Pannonia to visit his family, he was whipped in public and then run out of town; when he tried to found a monastery at Milan he was insulted and expelled. Afterwards he simply secluded himself for a time as a monk on a deserted island.[37]

The pressures and demands of life in these small communities are clearly apparent in a letter written by Bishop Severus of Minorca in 417 in which he described the conversion of the entire island to Christianity.[38] Although in the early fifth century most regions of the western empire had been disrupted by barbarians, Minorca maintained its seclusion. Here the most pressing problems men faced still arose, not from barbarian invasions, but from feuds and hostilities between the various small ethnic or religious communities sharing the island.[39] In this illuminating letter we have a description of one such feud in which the inhabitants of a Christian town took it upon themselves to invade and forcibly convert a Jewish town.

Previously Jews and Christians had divided the island, each community segregated into its own small village and each with its own religious leader. But the arrival of relics of St. Stephen at the Jewish town encouraged the few Christians there to assert them-

36. Jerome *Ep.* 39.6.
37. *Vita Martini* 6.4. Bialor (1968) shows how people in a small village could resolve their rivalries by "love" at Easter, by arbitration or civil suits, by ignoring each other, or by physical violence.
38. *Epistola de Iudaeis*, cited by column number in *PL* 20.731–46. Although Blumenkranz (1960) 76 n. 34, 283–4, argues that the letter was not written until the seventh century, his scepticism is rightly discounted by Baer (1961) 381–2 n. 2. Both the incident and Severus' letter have now acquired independent confirmation in a recently published letter sent from Consentius, a theologian living in the Balearic Islands, to Augustine in 419: see *Ep.* 12*.13–15 (ed. J. Divjak, *CSEL* 88 [1981] 78–79). Hunt (1982) offers commentary on the letter of Severus.
39. Closa Farres (1978) discusses this ethnic mixture.

selves: "They appealed to the protection of their [new] patron, St. Stephen."[40] And when reinforcements arrived from the Christian town led by Bishop Severus, the conflict rapidly grew out of hand; after both sides pelted each other with stones, the Christians burned down the Jewish synagogue. Some Jews may initially have fled into the mountains, but eventually all 540 of them converted to Christianity (a fine indication, by the way, of the small size of these towns); in other words, the new condition for returning to the village was conformity to a different cult as well as, presumably, recognition of Bishop Severus as their new leader.

This incident exposes the pressures of conformity within small communities, the use of physical violence against people who did not fit, and, significantly, how Christian communities had come to identify themselves with urban life and civilized values. Severus himself provided an explicit example of this new contrast between the urban character of Christianity and the allegedly uncivilized, rustic nature of paganism, heresy, or, as in this case, Judaism. Even after they decided to return to their village two of the Jews who had taken refuge in the hills remained lost, totally confused by the narrow paths. Finally they called on the name of Christ: "And then they rushed along the path which . . . brought them back to the town."[41]

The conversion of the Jews on Minorca also had a predictable ending. The new Christian converts built a church to replace their ruined synagogue, much as at Rouen a few years earlier the Christians had built a new church for their recently acquired relics. Presumably these new churches were built inside the walls of their cities, a fact that illustrates again the increasing identification of Christianity with urban society and urban values. For the walls of cities had always held a special significance in the thinking of late antique men, to the extent that cities could be designated simply as "walls."[42] Now, in the later fourth and early fifth centuries, Christian churches were being built inside these city walls,[43] and people who did not fit into Christian communities were excluded outside them.

In reaction to M. Rostovtzeff's powerful thesis of the antago-

40. *Ep. de Iudaeis* 733–4.
41. *Ep. de Iudaeis* 740–1.
42. E.g. Ausonius, *ord. urb. nob.* 10.7.
43. For other examples see Griffe (1964–1966) III, 21–30, with the modifications of C. Pietri (1976).

## ITEM CHARGED

| | |
|---|---|
| Patron: | Ken S. Sawyer |
| P.Barcode: | |

2 9 9 6 7 0 0 0 4 4 0 9 6

| | |
|---|---|
| P.Group: | LSTC/MTS faculty |
| Due Date: | 5/20/2015  07:00 PM |
| Title: | Leadership and community in late antique Gaul / Raymond Van Dam. |
| Author: | Van Dam, Raymond |
| CallNo.: | DC62 .V36 1985 |
| Enum.: | |
| Chron.: | |
| Copy: | 1 |
| I.Barcode: | |

3 9 9 6 7 0 0 1 7 0 2 6 3 3

nism between town and country in the later empire, scholars have stressed instead the clear economic and social links between the two.[44] Yet we cannot overlook that men of Late Antiquity recognized a cultural distinction between urban society and life in the countryside and that the boundary between these two "cultural zones" was marked most obviously by city walls, "solid walls four-square, which raise lofty towers so high that their tops pierce the soaring clouds."[45] In Late Antiquity the additional distinction between orthodoxy and heresy would be imposed on this existing cultural prejudice with the result that in some imperial constitutions, as we will see, one penalty against heretics was expulsion outside the city walls. Eventually this intransigent attitude would cause even more problems when Christian churches were faced with the task of absorbing the barbarians who settled among them in Gaul and Spain.[46] Yet this attitude still died hard. In a Spanish manuscript from the tenth century we find an illustration of the city of Toledo showing the city's walls and towers with armed men standing behind them. Staring out at us with wide eyes, these men could feel secure knowing that they were inside, and everyone else was outside, the walls of their city.[47]

## Rhetoricians, Women, and Christianity

Although Christianity spread comparatively late into the northwestern provinces of the Roman Empire, throughout previous centuries its supporters elsewhere had more and more elaborately defined its theology and organization, and by the fourth century Christianity offered itself both as a specific ideology that reflected and defined the way its adherents could understand and articulate their place in society[48] and as a formal institutional structure that specified the proper relationships between clergy and laity, Christians and non-Christians. For us the problem of "conversion" can therefore focus upon how easily and how readily the church was to accommodate and integrate people from these more

44. Momigliano (1966b), and Bowersock (1973).
45. Ausonius *ord. urb. nob.* 20.13–14, describing the walls of Bordeaux; and MacMullen (1974) 28–56, on cultural snobbery and economic symbiosis.
46. Meslin (1964).
47. Illustration in Rice (1965) 183, plate 24, with the corrected references in Pijoán (1954) 503–14.
48. C. Geertz (1975b) is an outstanding discussion of religion with great relevance for the historian of Late Antiquity.

remote provinces into its ideology and structure, which were already rather fully defined.

Previous research on conversion in the later Roman Empire has inevitably concentrated on its effects on specific individuals.[49] Yet in studies stressing individual experiences we tend to forget that conversion is a dual process: not only did individuals change their orientations by joining a new social group, but, conversely, that group then acquired new members, all with their own aspirations and backgrounds, and it somehow had to integrate them into its structure and ideology. Groups that practiced discrimination faced no problems because only certain types of people could join in the first place. But for an organization such as the Catholic church, which preached both uniform orthodoxy and the possibility of universal membership, the ambiguities that inevitably appeared required resolution to prevent the formation of splinter groups.[50]

In the fourth century probably the most spectacular example of such structural and ideological inadequacies arose from the conversion of the emperor, because the Catholic church then faced the sticky problem of accommodating an emperor who was both God's viceregent on earth and yet, as a layman, technically subordinate to Christian bishops. Many of the higher-level conflicts between church and state should thus be seen in terms of the problems that any social group has faced with the admission of new, and sometimes unexpected, categories of people.[51] On a more local level, however, let us consider two other types of people who might cause problems by their admission into Christian communities during the fourth century, that is, well-educated men and wealthy but unmarried women; both examples are selected for their applicability to the next chapter about Priscillianism.

*     *     *

In addition to promotion within the hierarchies of the church, the army, and the imperial administration, a successful academic career was one way of enhancing social status, and rhetoricians

49. E.g. Nock (1933); see now the remarks of S. C. Humphreys, *Anthropology and the Greeks* (London, 1978), 20–21.

50. Fundamental on tensions within social groups are Simmel (1955), and, in general, R. K. Merton, *Social theory and social structure*, rev. ed. (New York, 1957).

51. Williams (1951) is an important discussion of the theological aspects of the "conflict between Church and State"; Marc Bloch (1961) 380–1, shows that

and professors from southern Gaul supply some of the best examples of upward social mobility.[52] As a Roman senator wrote to
the Gallic rhetorician Ausonius, "Advancement toward obtaining
administrative positions is often promoted by literary skills." Ausonius himself was living proof; not only did he become consul in
379, he also obtained important posts for his relatives and friends.[53]
Other Gallic professors also succeeded in obtaining imperial magistracies; one rhetorician at Narbonne, for example, was appointed
to be governor of a Spanish province when his former pupil became Caesar in 335.[54]

These examples are important for demonstrating social mobility in the fourth century. They also reveal a general expectation,
especially among rhetoricians themselves, that educated men
would rise in status and obtain perhaps a high imperial appointment, a lucrative professorship at Rome or Constantinople, or at
least a respectable position in their native cities.[55] The success of
Gallic rhetoricians in fulfilling this expectation reached its peak
during the fourth century, largely because an emperor and his
court were resident in Gaul. But this tradition of success and
heightened expectations made the "failures" all the more em-
phatic. One rhetorician, poet, and advocate from Bordeaux who
delivered a panegyric on the emperor Julian in 363, for example,
had the opportunity to obtain an imperial post, but he refused,
and Ausonius thought it significant enough to comment how his
love of learning made him avoid "ambition."[56]

Another example is the family of the rhetorician Attius Tiro
Delphidius, whose members illustrate both the reality and the expectation of upward social mobility among educated men. Delphidius' grandfather had been a local pagan priest in Armorica,
who in his old age had become a Latin grammarian at Bordeaux.[57]
His son rose further in the academic world by becoming a professor of rhetoric, first at Bordeaux and then at Rome, and thus
effectively transformed this priestly family from central Gaul into

---

medieval kings posed similar problems for the church. The application of new
approaches may prove to be helpful in the debate over the role of the emperors
and kings in the church: see, e.g., Leach (1972).

52. Hopkins (1961).
53. Symmachus *Ep.* I. 20; cf. below, p. 304.
54. Ausonius *prof.* 17.
55. Marrou (1965) 446–8, and Alföldi (1952) 106–21.
56. Ausonius *prof.* 2.11–14.
57. Ausonius *prof.* 10.22–30.

a respectable academic family.[58] His son Delphidius tried, in turn, to make his career in the political world of the middle fourth century. After beginning as a poet and rhetorician at Bordeaux, he served as an advocate and eventually obtained palatine offices— but under the usurper Procopius, and after Procopius fell, only the intercession of his father enabled him to resume a career as a rhetorician.[59] Significantly, Ausonius claimed explicitly that Delphidius never achieved his potential: "Having wandered through all the titles of honor, Delphidius deserved more than he obtained."[60]

Some of the outstanding church fathers of the fourth century had also started out with the intention of making a career on the basis of their educations. After studying at Rome for about ten years, Jerome went in the later 360s to Trier, probably with the hope of entering a career at the imperial court or in the central administration.[61] Augustine, whose father had had to scrimp to find the money for him to complete his education, became a teacher of rhetoric at Carthage. In 383 he went to Rome, in part because friends promised him higher earnings and greater honors; a year later the prefect of the city appointed him professor of rhetoric at Milan.[62]

Both men, however, converted to Christianity, and in Spain and Gaul—regions especially famous for their schools[63]—Christian communities began to receive similarly educated and articulate men who anticipated a rising future for themselves in secular society, but who also may not have fulfilled all their ambitions.

Only a few options were available for integrating educated men into Christian communities, however. First, such men could become exegetes of the Scriptures. As we have seen in the previous section, a teacher was necessary to guide study of the Scriptures: no one could attain perfection without one.[64] Even men already educated in the classical heritage might need teachers for understanding the Bible; thus, one fifth-century rhetorician found

58. Ausonius *prof.* 4, and Jerome *Chron.* s.a. 336.
59. Ausonius *prof.* 5; Jerome *Chron.* s.a. 355; and Ammianus Marcellinus XVIII.1.4. Green (1978) 23, and Booth (1978) 236–9, present the arguments that Delphidius supported Procopius.
60. Ausonius *prof.* 5.29–30.
61. Cavallera (1922) I, 17–19. For the debate whether Jerome and one of his friends became *agentes in rebus*, see Courcelle (1968) 181–7, and Kelly (1975) 30.
62. Brown (1967) 65–72.
63. *Expositio totius mundi et gentium* 59.
64. Jerome *Ep.* 50.2, 53.6.

his verse paraphrase of Genesis being praised for its piety, but still dismissed as "lightweight": "No one had taught him the divine Scriptures."[65] In most cases these teachers were the bishops, as one insisted in a self-serving argument: "A bishop of God is to fill his congregation with the spirit and teach them literary culture."[66] But sometimes bishops were unable to carry out their duties, and often some of the instructions of catechumens was delegated to other men. In both cases educated men would have filled a need.

One alternative Christian communities could therefore choose was to patronize learned men as teachers, as happened with Jerome after he returned to Rome.[67] Another common option was to co-opt these men into the clergy; this happened to Augustine when he returned to Africa. Another possibility was for these men to become monks and live in the "asylum" of a secluded monastery. And still another alternative was simply to expect these men to be content as laymen living under the jurisdiction of the bishop and his clergy. Indeed, with some late Roman aristocrats, we cannot be sure whether they actually were Christians;[68] neither bishops nor educated laymen seem to have been confident about their roles, and so the less said, the better.

Given these options, it is also possible to see that rivalries and tensions might arise. When a man was co-opted into the clergy, for instance, he was not expected immediately to reach the top and become bishop, but instead to go through the normal sequence of offices. Unique cases such as the rise of Ambrose—who held the successive church offices on successive days until, inside of a week, he became bishop—remained exceptional occurrences.[69] Perhaps the most ambiguous relationship between the church and educated men arose with regard to exegetes. Such teachers had no official standing; at Rome, Jerome flourished because he had papal support, but when Pope Damasus died, Jerome had to leave Rome in the same style that heretics often had to leave cities, under a cloud of abusive accusations.[70] These

65. Gennadius *de scriptor. eccles.* 60, on Claudius Marius Victor.

66. Agroecius of Sens *de orthographia*, p. 113 Keil.

67. Cavallera (1922) I, 75–120, and Kelly (1975) 80–115.

68. Note the endless debate over whether Ausonius was a Christian: see Langlois (1969).

69. Paulinus of Milan *Vita Ambrosii* 9 (*PL* 14.30).

70. Babut (1909) 78 n. 2, for the accusations. In Gaul a generation later, men still had to go out of their way to insist that Jerome was a Catholic, not a heretic: Sulpicius Severus *Dial.* I.9.5.

teachers furthermore competed among themselves. Again Jerome is the best example, because throughout his writings he was constantly critical of rival teachers, including men who were not even teaching in Rome.

Thus, even if the presence of educated men might lead to rivalries, Christian communities had some options for accommodating them, largely because communities were eager to use their talents. But Christian communities had few alternatives to offer with regard to wealthy women, particularly if these women were unmarried and therefore without the derivative status of husbands. In fact, we often hear about these women in connection with heresies or unorthodox teachers; Jerome, typically, claimed that all heresies were somehow derived from "little women loaded down by sins."[71] But however much more accommodating toward independent women heretical sects may have been, Catholic communities were also interested in having them as members.

One good example was Theodora, a widow who lived in Spain during the later fourth century. In her case we can see the transition in her status, because we have one letter from Jerome written to her husband and another written shortly thereafter to Theodora in condolence on his recent death. In his first letter Jerome praised Theodora only in passing for assisting her husband and thereby transforming herself into "a man instead of a woman."[72] A year later he was still extolling the merits of her husband, this time as an opponent to "savage heresies."[73] Although Theodora seems to have done nothing in her own right, Jerome was quite aware of her new status as a wealthy widow. The heresy that her husband had opposed had allegedly had special appeal for wealthy women, and Jerome now hoped to keep Theodora pure in body and spirit. Thus he entrusted her safekeeping to a blind monk; Theodora had already made her exodus from this world, from "Egypt," and this monk rather than some heretical teacher would help her through the desert to the promised land.[74]

71. Jerome *Ep.* 133.4.

72. Jerome *Ep.* 71.3. Although *Ep.* 71 makes it clear that Lucinus and Theodora lived in Spain, the fact that they lived in Baetica is stated only in the superscription to *Ep.* 71, for which the manuscript readings are not definitive: see *CSEL* 55, p. 1.

73. Jerome *Ep.* 75.3, referring probably to Priscillianism.

74. Jerome *Ep.* 76.3.

In the early fifth century Jerome exchanged some letters on biblical exegesis with Hedibia, who probably lived at Bordeaux and whose ancestors included the rhetorician Delphidius as well as some women who had once supported the "Manichee" Priscillian.[75] Hedibia was apparently a widow, because Jerome's first response was to a question about how a widow who is left without any children ought to live. In response to another question on a text about the Kingdom of God, Jerome rejected as myth any sort of millennial interpretation and wrote instead about the "kingdom of the church." To a question on the time of the sending of the Holy Spirit, he sneered at "Montanus and those madwomen of his." And in another reply Jerome criticized people who wished, in their explanation of a particularly obscure passage, to accept the interpretation of Manichaeism. Surely Jerome was aware of Hedibia's family and its previous involvement with heresy, but more significantly, he advised this woman to remain in the Catholic church even though she seemed more interested in fanatical and rigorous sects.

The Catholic church's attitude toward women, however, made it difficult to integrate independent and wealthy widows into congregations. The New Testament offered some suggestions, but these instructions had been written for poor widows who might become wards of the church. Nor, obviously, were women allowed into the ecclesiastical hierarchy; like dumb ornaments there for the adornment of congregations, they were to be silent.[76] In the spiritual warfare against demons, women were expected only to seek shelter inside the fortifications of churches, not to man the front lines as soldiers.[77] Eve, the tempting seductress, had provided the common image of women for early Christian writers; not until the later fourth century did they develop the contrasting image of the holy Virgin Mary, the "gateway" through which Christ had entered the world.[78]

Like Roman society in general, Catholic Christianity was a "man's world," and women with differentiating characteristics had to be thought of as men in order to resolve the apparent con-

75. Jerome *Ep.* 120, praef.
76. de Labriolle (1911), and H. Leclercq, *DACL* XV (1953) 3007–26.
77. Sulpicius Severus *Dial.* II.11.6–7; cf. II.12.8, for a virgin who properly concealed herself even from St. Martin.
78. Fortunatus *Carm.* XI.1.17, "per portam virginis," and Vogt (1974) 161–4.

tradiction between their gender and their prominence. Thus an aunt of Ausonius who had studied medicine but also remained a virgin was given a masculine cognomen to replace her feminine name.[79] Actual physical mutation was another means of eliminating this ambiguity, but it was obviously such a rare occurrence that mutants ended up on display at Rome.[80] Instead, Christian women became "men" by adopting a life of chastity and asceticism. In the fifth century a bishop could give no better advice to one young girl than that she "act like a man"; so she did, by remaining a virgin.[81] Similarly, after one widow achieved fame within the Catholic church as a benefactor, Paulinus of Nola wondered whether she was only a woman.[82] By remaining chaste, women could even achieve one of the most venerated statuses within the church: in the early fifth century, for instance, Jerome wrote to a young girl who had talked herself out of marriage only a few days before her wedding and told her that "the preservation of your chastity involves its very own martyrdom."[83]

From this brief survey we can see that Christian communities in the fourth century did not quite know what to do with women who were unmarried and therefore without the derivative status of a husband, but who were wealthy and therefore potentially influential. Some of these women set off on pilgrimages to the East. There they were treated with great deference, even by bishops, but at the same time they were belittled by opponents.[84] Other wealthy women could become, as was expected anyway, patrons of their local bishops and churches. In this case they also introduced the risk that their generosity and influence could unduly influence the process of ecclesiastical promotions; Damasus, for instance, was said to have been elected pope largely because he was a genuine "ladies' man."[85]

*    *    *

79. Ausonius *parent*. 6.
80. Ambrosiaster *Quaest*. 115.72 (*CSEL* 50, p. 343).
81. *Vita Genovefe virgine* 5, "viriliter age," and Kurth (1919) II, 94: "Il y a chez Geneviève une originalité d'allures et une virilité de tempérament."
82. Paulinus of Nola *Ep*. 29.6; cf. Palladius *Hist. lausiaca* 9, and Goldschmidt (1940) 104–5, for the confusion over the masculine and feminine forms of Mela-nia/us. See also Palladius *Hist. lausiaca* 41, for more "masculine women."
83. Jerome *Ep*. 130.5.3.
84. Jerome *Ep*. 54.13, referring probably either to Silvia of Aquitania (see Hunt [1972] 358–9) or to Poemenia (see Devos [1973] 117–20).
85. *Coll. Avell*. 1.9 (*CSEL* 35, p. 4), "matronarum auriscalpius." Damasus was also accused of adultery, but acquitted: see *Liber pontificalis* 39, and Hoepffner (1948).

It is essential to emphasize that these problems of integration were not unique to this one period in the history of the Catholic church, and that they were not peculiar to the structure and ideology of the church as distinct from other social groups. Women have always been difficult for many organizations to accept.[86] Throughout the early history of Christianity, women found readier acceptance and recognition in heretical sects such as Montanism, which first appeared in the late second century.[87] Yet in the fourth century Christianity had begun to spread among aristocratic women with wealth and influence; then the conflicts resulting from the structural and ideological inadequacies in the church became particularly acute. Nor did the church adequately solve these problems. In the early sixth century bishops in central Gaul were horrified to discover that priests in Brittany not only allowed women could be included within the generic term *homo*.[89] And we need only skim through later medieval history to note that neither said nor heard without a certain mental shuddering."[88] In 585 a Gallic bishop was still confused enough about his theology (or, more likely, his Latin vocabulary) as not to understand how women could be included within the generic term *homo*.[89] And we need only skim through later medieval history to note that women were still attracted to splinter religious groups and that the demands of women to participate fully in religious life eventually led to the foundation of female religious orders, although these were usually under the control of men.[90]

Similarly, educated men frequently posed a problem for the church, particularly when they remained outside the clergy. With their evident talents these men could be useful in Christian communities that needed teachers. Yet men with the knowledge, or merely the possession, of books might also be thought to have acquired special powers; hence, just as even emperors sometimes viewed them with suspicion, so Christian bishops often treated them as potential rivals. As a corollary, just as periods of political

86. See Levy (1957) 91–134, and Rosaldo (1974) 31–34.

87. See Vokes (1966).

88. *PL* Suppl. III.1256–7. Although the letter compares this despicable practice to an Eastern heresy, and likewise H. Chadwick (1976) 159, in a discussion of Council of Nîmes a. 394/396, Can. 2, suggests Greek influence for the ordination of female deacons in Gaul, N. K. Chadwick (1965) 274, suggests that the ministry of women here indicates the survival of an archaic Celtic institution.

89. Gregory of Tours *HF* VIII.20, with Kurth (1919) I, 161–7.

90. Cohn (1962), and Bolton (1973). Note Gregory of Tours *GC* 16, for a woman disguising herself as a man in order to enter a monastery.

uncertainty during the early empire had been accompanied by outbreaks of book burning,[91] so one of the penalties placed on heretics was the confiscation and burning of their books.

It is also important to stress that the integration of educated men and wealthy women into Christian communities did not always result in misunderstandings. But when problems did arise, although we can analyze them in terms of the structural and ideological inadequacies of small Christian communities, late antique men never did. Although the ambiguities were real enough to them, they often expressed these problems in terms that may strike us as irrelevant. In Christian communities one common idiom for articulating these ambiguities was the distinction between orthodoxy and a heresy such as Manichaeism.

## Accusations of Manichaeism

Historians have long considered that many heresies appearing in the Roman Empire during the fourth century arose from theological disagreements. In most cases genuine differences of opinion did exist, although this does not explain which side of any argument came to be regarded as Catholic orthodoxy and which as heresy; yet in other cases the genuine theological differences were ignored or minimized and replaced by the attribution of outrageously sordid activities to heretics. With less than adequate theological justification, some people were accused of being immoral heretics or, more specifically, of being Manichees.

The insights of contemporary social anthropology can help historians of Late Antiquity with the issue of orthodoxy and heresy. Modern anthropologists and social historians have shown how accusations of witchcraft work in communities by performing the integrative functions of reinforcing accepted social standards and of resolving latent tensions and conflicts by allowing them to be discussed openly, even if obliquely, on the mystical level of witchcraft accusations: "Beliefs in sorcery and witchcraft invariably have a social setting in the sense that they mediate, though they sometimes complicate, the living together of people in the ongoing process we call a society. They do this by providing a means of expressing tense social relationships."[92] With this perspective

91. Cramer (1945).
92. Marwick (1970) 293. Other useful studies include Marwick (1965); Turner (1967b); and Douglas (1970).

we can complement discussions of theology by considering how accusations of Manichaeism functioned in the same way as witchcraft accusations in other communities and how local animosities, not the dictates of imperial legislation, generated these accusations. Let us briefly examine, first, the legislation against the Manichees and the penalties placed on them; second, the negative stereotype of the Manichees and how they were seen as the evil antithesis of acceptable society; and third, the roles of bishops in making and judging these accusations and of Christian communities in reintegrating the men who had been accused.

\*     \*     \*

If the contents of imperial constitutions can be taken as an accurate indication of the motivations that went into issuing them, then the constant objection to the Manichees was against their communities.[93] In addition to restrictions on making wills and leaving legacies, the legislation was directed against the Manichees' organization: their leaders were punished, their homes and buildings were confiscated, and they were forbidden to form communities. In short, they were excluded from any participation in the focal point of Roman, and now also Christian, society, the city. In the constitutions against Manichees and other heretics, the standard refrain was for them to hand over their churches to the Catholics—and then get out of town.[94] "A fortified wall" like that surrounding an army camp was to mark the distance between Catholics and heretics,[95] and adherents of Manichaeism and other heresies had to forsake membership in cities and live in isolation, "outside human society."[96]

Yet it remains peculiar that Manichees should have been singled out in the imperial constitutions against heresies and that accusations of Manichaeism (as contrasted with other heresies) should have become so common and effective. Although by identifying the Manichees with their Persian origins some scholars have wanted to see in this legislation a form of national prejudice, such a view is now misleading, since it does not take account of the

---

93. Kaden (1953), for this legislation.
94. *CTh* XVI.5.6, "ab ipsis etiam urbium moenibus exterminato furore propelli iubeamus."
95. *CTh* XVI.5.14, "quasi vallo quodam ab humana communione."
96. *CTh* XVI.5.3.

fluctuating status of Manichaeism in the Persian Empire.[97] Nor is it adequate to claim that the "secret societies" of Manichees constituted a unique threat to the established order; in fact, all cults or religious movements, whatever their social or political intentions (if any at all), produce what can appear to be political action.[98] More significant is to note the close similarity between Manichaeism and Christianity, to the extent that Manichees even claimed to speak on behalf of a man who had considered himself another apostle of Jesus Christ.[99] In the Christian empire of the fourth century, this imperial legislation was therefore being used to suppress not an external enemy, but an internal rival. In this situation the differences that did exist were stressed all the more; the simple danger of confusion between Christians and Manichees seems to have enhanced the allegations until the image of the Manichee came to function as a powerful symbol of moral perversion and evil.

*  *  *

The fourth century presents us with a surprising proliferation of heresies. On the basis of the creeds issued by various councils, men could have the illusion of knowing exactly what constituted the *catholica fides*, "orthodox belief," an illusion reinforced at the end of the century by the production of magnificent handbooks listing hundreds of heresies.[100] Modern scholars may have occasional difficulties understanding the differences between orthodox and heretics, but late antique men had no hesitations. To one churchman of the early fifth century, heretics were like ostriches: they may have looked like birds, they may even have claimed to have the "wings of wisdom," but in fact they simply could not fly![101]

Some heresies arose from genuine theological differences and continued to be treated as such, even when Catholic writers insulted their supporters. Other heresies arose from deviant practices and, however humorous they may seem to us, they were still treated seriously by fourth-century churchmen. To sample the flavor of these heretical deviants (as they were seen by Catholics), we may note the Valesians, who thought that the way to

97. Seston (1946) 150–3; contrast Baynes (1948) 110; Brown (1972) 94–118; and, especially, Decret (1979).
98. Worsley (1968) 312.
99. Ries (1964).          100. McClure (1979).
101. Eucher of Lyon *Formulae* IV, s.v. *struthio* (*CSEL* 31, pp. 22–23).

serve God was by castrating both themselves and their guests; another group of heretics called "Peg-on-Nose," who insisted upon placing a finger over (or perhaps even in) the nose and mouth in order to practice a vow of silence, and the Circuitores in Africa, who in their zeal for martyrdom held up travelers on the road and demanded to be killed by them![102]

With Manichees, however, the emphasis was not always on strictly theological or practical differences: according to one imperial constitution, "Manichees have descended to the most vile depths of evil deeds."[103] What many Christians found so repulsive about the Manichees was not their doctrines, but all the immoralities associated with them. One bishop could barely contain his righteous anger: "Under the pretext of a Christian confession, Manichees, just like bandits, never cease to captivate many souls with their deceit and bestial immorality."[104] Given the prevalence of banditry in the Roman Empire, it is striking that Manichees were perhaps the only heretics to be compared with bandits. But the comparison with bandits was also often applied to demons, who were likely to waylay Christian travelers on their journeys through life.[105] The implication seems to be that Manichees, like evil spirits, were inherently dangerous.

Very simply, Manichees were used to represent an image of evilness, an image based in part on reprehensible moral behavior and in part on a strange appearance. The stereotype of Manichees came to include "secret and secluded assemblies," which, according to one imperial constitution, supposedly included funeral rites.[106] In irresponsible hands these secret meetings were exaggerated to lurid proportions, so that Jerome, with almost pornographic fascination, could hardly bring himself to describe the orgies of alleged Manichees in Spain: "They shut themselves up alone with silly women, and between intercourse and embraces they enchant them with suggestive quotations from Virgil."[107] The stereotype of Manichees also involved a distinctive appearance. Jerome described how some people at Rome, whenever they saw a woman who was "gloomy and pale," quickly labeled her as either a mourner, a monk, or a Manichee.[108] Since many Christians in Rome at this time were "killing themselves with fasting" as a

---

102. Augustine *de haeres.* 37, 63; and Filastrius *diver. heres.* 76(48), 85(57).
103. *CTh* XVI.5.65.     104. Filastrius *diver. heres.* 61(33).
105. Bartelink (1967).     106. *CTh* XVI.5.7, with Abel (1966).
107. Jerome *Ep.* 133.3.4.     108. Jerome *Ep.* 22.13.3.

part of their spiritual regimen,[109] they were also susceptible to accusations of being "pale-faced" Manichees. At one point Jerome almost trapped himself in the absurdity of his own prejudices, and finally had to concede that, given the example of the apostle Paul, fasting did not always imply that people were Manichees.[110]

Pointing out that Manichees had come to represent an image of evilness is not to deny that there remained theological arguments against their teachings. But whenever genuine theological debate took place, the claims about the immoralities of the Manichees were either discarded or greatly subordinated. When Augustine debated the Manichee Fortunatus in 392, he was quickly challenged on those "falsely alleged evil deeds" with which Manichees were always abused. Augustine eventually conceded that at the meetings he had attended when he had been a Manichee many years earlier he had seen nothing immoral occur, but he also raised another possibility: since he had never been a Manichaean "Elect," he did not know what went on at their meetings. So the innuendo remained, even though Augustine and Fortunatus then argued only theology.[111]

Because Manichees had become representatives of all immoralities, they also functioned as powerful symbols against which people would rally. These same allegations were also used to denigrate usurpers such as Magnentius in the 350s, who had supposedly permitted nocturnal sacrifices and their inevitable result, criminal licentiousness.[112] By associating the possession of heretical books with the crime of magic, imperial constitutions further enhanced the potency of accusations of Manichaeism.[113] Just as magicians learned from books the secret lore that enabled them to perform scandalous rites and to make drugs such as love philtres and poisons, so other people might find in books the justification, or perhaps even the initial suggestion, for immoral behavior. In the late fourth century Augustine learned about Manichees in Gaul who were literally acting out their belief that through the intercourse of males and females they could unite their respective "portions of God": "When they were asked on the authority of

109. Cf. Jerome *Ep.* 39.6.
110. Jerome *Ep.* 71.6.
111. Augustine *contra Fortunatum* 1, 3. Decret (1970) 39–50, is an excellent discussion of this debate.
112. *CTh* XVI.10.5.
113. *CTh* XVI.5.34.

which writing they did this, they confessed that it was from their *Thesaurus.*" Augustine proposed an easy solution: "So let them throw away their books if they detest the crime they are forced to perform."[114] Like heretics, magicians could avoid expulsion from cities only if they were prepared to accept the Catholic faith and burn their books "before the eyes of the bishops."[115]

The confusion of Manichaeism, heresy, magic, and immorality is often baffling, and probably as much for men of Late Antiquity as for modern historians. The addition of an accusation of magic clarified the situation in some respects, because it was easier to produce specific magical books or instruments than to demonstrate alleged immorality or doctrinal deviation.[116] But in other respects this confusion only points out the arbitrary capriciousness of such accusations. As in other traditional societies, magic in the later Roman Empire could be either good or bad, a distinction presumably based on whether it was helpful or harmful. Although some imperial constitutions did use this distinction, it could also be easily manipulated, so that one suspicious emperor was prepared to execute as a traitor even someone who used an "old wives' charm."[117]

The notion of immorality was also arbitrary. Although one bishop praised women who had saved themselves from being forced into compromising behavior by Manichees, he was also puzzled that no one could, or would, reveal who the men had been, and he could only worry that perhaps in their merriment everyone had been pleased when the lights went out.[118] A stereotype based on personal appearance was likewise open to manipulation. Thus Jerome seems to contradict himself by insisting that true Christians were "pale-faced and dressed in black," as contrasted with heretics, who were the "beautiful people."[119] Writing in Gaul in the late fourth century, Sulpicius Severus complained bitterly that some men were considered heretics simply on the

114. Augustine *de natura boni* 47 (*PL* 42.570); cf. below, p. 102 n. 69.
115. *CTh* IX.16.12, "sub oculis episcoporum."
116. Hence, perhaps, the use of accusations of magic in feuds between rivals in the imperial administration, between academics at Antioch, or during purges of the governing classes: see Libanius *Orat.* XVIII.131; Brown (1972) 119–46; and Funke (1967).
117. *CTh* IX.16.3, 9; and Ammianus Marcellinus XVI.8.2.
118. Augustine *de mor. Manich.* (II.) 19.70 (*PL* 32.1374–5).
119. Jerome *adv. Iovinianum* II.36. Jerome recommended to one young girl that she pick her friends on the basis of their complexions: *Ep.* 22.17.1.

basis of their complexion or clothing rather than because of their beliefs. One of the men most susceptible to such an adverse evaluation, as it happened, was the hero of Sulpicius' writings, Martin of Tours. For however saintly Martin may have been, his appearance was truly repulsive: once some animals were actually frightened off the road by Martin in his shaggy black garments and billowing cloak.[120]

From such confusion only men with authority could define what was acceptable, and in this sense the multiplication of heresies in the fourth century is one indication of the increasing authority given to Christianity, and in particular to its bishops. In a neat reversal the same allegations once made against the early Christians were now applied to heretics. The Manichees, in particular, had become the "bogeymen" of the late empire, providing a potent image of pale-faced moral degenerates that was created and applied primarily by Christian bishops and writers, but which was also a powerful symbol against which to rally people. The imperial administration was acquiescent in issuing constitutions against the Manichees and other heretics, thus making accusations of Manichaeism legally as well as morally effective. The Manichees themselves never had a chance; their predicament was now similar to that of the Christians during the early empire, and thus their name alone was sufficient to elicit horror and condemnation. In Spain the Christian teacher Priscillian, who was finally executed after being accused of Manichaeism and magic, made the most clairvoyant remark of all when he described how a bishop had overreacted in his vendetta by obtaining an imperial rescript against him: "There is no one who does not feel hatred when he hears about pseudobishops and Manichees."[121]

In the imagery of Late Antiquity, Manichees were compared with serpents and dragons, common symbols of fear and loathing.[122] Even in later centuries the imagery survived. In an eleventh-century manuscript containing the text of Augustine's debate with Faustus—a Manichaean teacher whom Augustine (then a Manichee himself) had known in Africa over a decade before he became a Christian bishop—there is an illustration showing both men brandishing books at each other. But, similar to the iconog-

120. Sulpicius Severus *Dial.* II.3.2, III.11.5.

121. Priscillian *Tract.* II.50 (*CSEL* 18, pp. 40–41); below, pp. 101–4.

122. Augustine *de Genesi contra Manichaeos* II.25.38 (*PL* 34.216–17), with Courcelle (1966).

raphy of St. Michael or St. George slaying the dragon, so here Augustine, anachronistically dressed as a bishop, has pinned Faustus to the ground by his bishop's crosier in the man's mouth.[123] The association of Manichees with dragons is still apparent, and the illustration also reveals that the man to overcome Manichees had almost always been the local Christian bishop.

\* \* \*

In the early 380s the emperors defined the true religion that they wished everyone to accept. Interestingly enough, the theological aspects of the definition were only secondary, because it rested primarily on the personal preferences of certain bishops.[124] Thus, although congregations were expected to inform on heretics in their midst, the final judgment was reserved for bishops, and in the drama surrounding accusations of Manichaeism they evaluated people's orthodoxy. The importance of bishops was a recurring characteristic of Christian opposition to Manichees: always Manichees were "found" or "exposed," and although there may have been civil trials, bishops played pivotal roles in these "discoveries." In Rome, pope after pope found Manichees and promptly exiled them.[125] In North Africa, Augustine informed another bishop that one of his sub-deacons was really a Manichee. But, Augustine added, "he has been exposed." When this poor man asked to be taken back, Augustine refused, claiming that he was horrified by the man's deceit: "I made sure that he was forcibly thrown out of the town."[126]

In North Africa, where real Manichaean communities existed, the evidence of Augustine reveals the form these hearings took. In 404 a Manichaean missionary named Felix wandered into Hippo, and although Augustine consented to hold a debate with him, the encounter soon became a public trial. Felix had to confess his helplessness before the enthroned Augustine: "I cannot do much against your power, because the bishop's position is wonderfully powerful, nor either against the laws of the emperor." Felix had entered this debate with Augustine only because the alternative offered him was to leave town, but after being badgered

123. Courcelle (1968) 514–15 and his plate XX.
124. *CTh* XVI.1.2–3.
125. *Liber pontificalis* 33, 40, 41, 51, 53, 54; and Valentinian III *Nov.* 18 (a. 445), with Ensslin (1937).
126. Augustine *Ep.* 236.

by Augustine on two separate days he suddenly decided to recant: "What do you want me to do?" Augustine replied that he wanted him to anathematize Mani; so Augustine first wrote out a formula of abjuration, and Felix then copied out his own version in the presence of the community.[127] In these hearings, then, local bishops not only judged the accusations, they could also forgive Manichees who confessed and readmit them to the community. The communities, in turn, in addition to hearing and evaluating these public confrontations, could later force repentant Manichees to continue to conform because of their need for testimonials from them.[128] A discussion of witch-cleansing provides a close parallel: "The moral pressure to confess is enormous. For the accused, the choice is between outlawry and reintegration into the community. Not surprisingly, most do what is wanted."[129]

During the fourth century Manichees had become potent symbols of the antithesis of the social ideal to which Christian communities aspired, an ideal that emphasized the spiritual leadership of bishops and conformity of behavior and belief within congregations. But we have also noted how this expected conformity and harmony were often illusions, since both the structure and the ideology of Christian communities were inadequate for integrating such people as educated laymen and wealthy widows. At this time, however, Catholic Christians were not prepared to rethink and change either structure or ideology; instead, people who did not fit were often condemned as heretics and treated as outcasts. By excluding certain people, these accusations of Manichaeism also reinforced the inner cohesiveness of communities and heightened the influence of bishops; in other words, this perspective, however limiting, was internally consistent and coherent.

Before going on to a specific application of these observations, let us recall that although virtually all our information is about small Christian communities, in fact many small communities operated in a similar fashion. Our study of late antique Gaul, however, is handicapped by our lack of adequate information about the functions of pagan cults and the earlier development of Christianity, when the roles were reversed and Christians were per-

---

127. Augustine *contra Felicem* I. 12, II.22, with Decret (1970) 71–89, 328–31.
128. See the "Commonitorium quomodo sit agendum cum Manichaeis qui convertuntur" (*PL* 42.1153–6, and *CSEL* 25.2, pp. 979–82), and the "Forma epistolae quam dat episcopus conversis" (*PL* 65.28–30).
129. Willis (1970) 130.

secuted for nonconformity. Christianity may have been new, but the nature of small communities and the role of a religious cult in developing mechanisms for ensuring conformity were not. Much of the evidence for the application of accusations of Manichaeism has come from North Africa, where there were Manichaean communities. But accusations of Manichaeism were also used against such people as Priscillian and his supporters in Spain and Gaul who, in addition to proclaiming their own orthodox opposition to Manichaeism, came from regions of the empire where no Manichaean communities existed. In this case in particular it becomes apparent that accusations of Manichaeism can usefully be seen as beliefs and forms of positive action that helped men to cope with the constraints of their small Christian communities.

# CHAPTER 5

# The Heresy
# of Priscillianism

Although usually treated primarily as a theological heresy, Priscillianism also illuminates the nature of life in small communities.[1] Priscillian himself was prominent in Spain already in the late 370s, because the Council of Saragossa in 380 discussed him and his supporters.[2] But the early 380s marked the height of the controversy, as well as the period for which we have the most information. The main opposition to Priscillian and his supporters came from the Catholic bishops of Merida and Ossonuba; both sides solicited imperial rescripts and bribed officials, and eventually some Priscillianists traveled from Spain through southern Gaul to Italy in an attempt to see Pope Damasus at Rome or Bishop Ambrose at Milan. Eventually the accusations of Manichaeism and magic made by the Catholic bishops against Priscillian and his support-

1. In general, see Vollmann (1965), for bibliography, review of earlier research and a list of sources, and Domínguez del Val (1967) 22–27, for Priscillianism in the fifth and sixth centuries.
2. The eight canons of this council pose a paradox. Sulpicius Severus *Chron.* II.47.1–3, stated that the council condemned Priscillian and his supporters; Priscillian *Tract.* II.42, 48–49, 53 (pp. 35, 39–40, 42), insisted that the council did not even accuse him and his supporters. Most scholars implicitly resolve this paradox by simply using the canons as an accurate description of Priscillianist activities or of Priscillian's methods as a religious leader. But even if this resolution is correct, or even if the canons were merely used against Priscillian and his supporters, we are no closer to understanding his "heresy," because we are still left with the fundamental questions of by whom and by what criteria it was decided whether any given belief or behavior was orthodox or heretical. It is easy enough to find orthodox parallels for most of the behavior mentioned in the canons (e.g. Can. 2, 4, with Gregory of Tours *HF* I.34)—which merely demonstrates that orthodoxy and heresy are socially determined concepts. Hence the discussion in this chapter will not use these canons as an integral part of the argument.

ers were effective. At a council held at Bordeaux in 384 one of the bishops who had supported Priscillian was defrocked; at Trier in 385, under the jurisdiction of the usurper Maximus, Priscillian and some of his supporters were executed on charges of magical and obscene behavior. Priscillianism, however, did not die with its founder, because it retreated into the province of Galicia in the rugged highlands of northwestern Spain. Throughout the fifth century we find scattered references to Priscillianism, usually still associated with Galicia; in the sixth century the evidence becomes even more fragmentary until finally at the councils of Braga in 561 and 572 Priscillianism was apparently anathematized into oblivion.

Although the basic narrative framework can be accepted without hesitation, the interpretation of Priscillianism raises essential questions. One has been over the authorship of eleven tracts discovered and then published by G. Schepss in 1889.[3] Most scholars have agreed that these tracts, or at least the first three, were written by Priscillian or a close supporter,[4] and for convenience Priscillian will here be considered the author. We also have other writings that are anonymous and difficult to date, but that have been variously described as "Priscillianist" or "anti-Priscillianist." Such pigeonholing not only assumes that anonymous writings can be classified on the basis of internal characteristics alone,[5] it also presupposes a consistent distinction between heresy and orthodoxy. In fact, another problem that has challenged scholars has been whether Priscillian and Priscillianism were orthodox or heretical.

Prior to the discovery of actual writings by Priscillian this problem did not exist, because most modern scholars repeated the opinions of late antique writers, who had been virtually unanimous in their execration of Priscillian and his teachings. But after the publication of the *Tractatus* in which Priscillian openly condemned all heresies and insisted upon his adherence to the Catholic faith, the problem of his heresy became acute. Although now with occasional misgivings, scholars generally still accept the

3. The reprinted edition in *PL* Suppl. II includes additional textual annotations, and indicates the page numbers of the original *CSEL* edition, which are here given in parentheses.

4. Sáinz Rodríguez (1964) 654; Vollmann (1974) col. 490, 552–9; and H. Chadwick (1976) 47–51, 62–69.

5. Vollmann (1965) 70–83, gives a list of Priscillianist and anti-Priscillianist writings, although he does not make clear how arbitrary many of these attributions are; see instead the judicious remarks of H. Chadwick (1976) 100–10.

judgment of Late Antiquity, and by looking hard enough they can
find in the *Tractatus* statements that deviated from orthodoxy.[6]

In one sense it has seemed that this problem about the orthodoxy or heresy of Priscillian must be open to a proper solution.
The fourth century especially was a "prophetic time," and Christians of the era following the conversion of Constantine thought
they were only too aware of where history was leading. Under the
influence of their sense of direction modern scholars have also
concluded that orthodoxy represented an "ultimate concern" in
the development of Christian doctrine[7] and that heresy was a deliberate distortion of that true faith, a deviation based primarily
on foreign, external influences. Scholars have therefore attempted
to identify the Egyptian teachings that opponents claimed were
the source for Priscillian's thought. Yet such source analysis alone
does not help us understand Priscillianism as a social phenomenon, and not simply because the notion of "Egypt" had become a
commonplace image for any life of sin as contrasted with truly orthodox behavior.[8] Even if we could accurately pin down the origins of Priscillianist beliefs,[9] we would still not be any closer to
comprehending how they functioned in fourth-century Spanish
and Gallic society.

As a counterweight to these problems over the diffusion of foreign beliefs, Priscillianism has also been interpreted, like other
heresies of the fourth century, as an expression of indigenous social and economic discontent. One argument claims that Priscillianism was a sect of rigorism that was prevalent in the countryside, while the Catholic opposition came from the cities, where
the authority of bishops coincided with the authority of the central administration. Church and state therefore worked together
to suppress this heretical form of ascetic Christianity that also
served as a revolutionary ideology for the rural masses.[10]

This interpretation of Priscillianism as a manifestation of social
discontent closely duplicated a powerful interpretation of the contemporary heresy of Donatism in North Africa; but although that

6. d'Alès (1936) 78–117, and G. Bardy, *DTC* XIII (1936) 399.
7. Drewery (1972) 264.
8. E.g. [Bachiarius] *Ep.* 1 (*PL* Suppl. I.1037), on which letter see Morin
(1928a); and cf. above, p. 74.
9. For orientals in Gaul and Spain, see Albertini (1912), and García y Bellido
(1959).
10. Barbero de Aguilera (1963) 5–25, explicitly based on Frend (1952), on
whom see Markus (1972).

approach to Donatism has generated a negative response, this similar interpretation of Priscillianism has received a favorable reaction.[11] The thesis has, however, little historical support. Some supporters of Priscillian were bishops and clerics themselves, and their adherence marks Priscillianism as an urban phenomenon. Although the sect eventually became prominent in the under-civilized province of Galicia, this says nothing either about the origins of the movement or about the status of Priscillian and his supporters. An opposite perspective is in fact more persuasive. Not only did Priscillian's early supporters include local elites such as rhetoricians or their widows, but the usurping emperor Maximus was criticized by a Gallic panegyrist for using this religious feud as a pretext for confiscating these people's fortunes.[12]

More recent studies of Priscillianism have shifted their emphasis again to religious factors. One argues that Priscillian, as an educated Christian, formed a "school" or ascetic community whose teaching was based both on the Bible and on apocryphal books, and that he thereby conflicted with the ecclesiastical hierarchy. Another study reinforces this conclusion by claiming that the use of the apocryphal Acts lay behind some of Priscillian's unorthodox assertions.[13] Yet both interpretations remain somewhat forced in their attempts to pinpoint a specific factor or two that made Priscillian and his supporters into heretics. There is no evidence that Priscillian was challenging the Catholic clergy, that he founded a school, or that he established a sect (whatever may have happened after his execution). An emphasis on the theological background to his thought, even though it does show his acquaintance with noncanonical literature, does not provide sufficient motivation for opposition to him, simply because many of his teachings were also similar to orthodox doctrines. Attempts to resolve theological problems tend only to obscure the paradoxes that are vital for historical understanding.

The fundamental inadequacy of strictly religious interpretations is the use of a theological distinction between orthodoxy and heresy as a tool for historical analysis.[14] The accusations of

11. E.g. Blázquez (1974) 502.

12. R. Etienne, in *Les empereurs romains d'Espagne* (Madrid, 1965) 267; cf. Sulpicius Severus *Dial.* III.11.10–11.

13. Vollmann (1974) esp. col. 494–5, and H. Chadwick (1976) 99; the latter was reviewed in *J. Roman Studies* 68 (1978) 199–201.

14. Gager (1975) 79: "In dealing with a religious movement like early Christianity, where we confront diversity and disharmony from the very first, any effort

Manichaeism make it appear as if the issue revolves around an external problem, that is, around the importation of bizarre beliefs. In fact it was an internal problem generated by the rivalries appearing when a religious organization for which books were central acquired educated men as members. In this perspective it is important to recall the more mundane factors, which an anthropologist stresses: "If we remember that it is a practical interest in living and not an academic interest in metaphysics which has produced these beliefs, their whole significance alters."[15] Since one feature of fourth-century Christianity is the number of heretical sects with similar rigorous attitudes that appeared in scattered parts of the empire, we need more than a model based on regional peculiarities of economic or social structure; these sects arose out of paradoxes common to the Catholic church and its role in society.[16] Yet to see how men responded and lived, we need to examine small local communities as closely as possible. In this chapter let us investigate, first, the types of people who supported Priscillian and the nature of the message that appealed to them; and second, the types of people who opposed Priscillian and the accusations they used to deal with him and his supporters. In the affair of Priscillian we are offered a unique insight not into a simple ecclesiastical squabble, but rather into the role of cults in small communities characterized by petty intrigue, jealousy, and sudden brawls.

*     *     *

Priscillian and many of the men mentioned by name who were associated with him were apparently well educated but still only laymen within the church. If indeed he was the author of the *Tractatus*, then Priscillian seems to have tried to minimize the background of himself and his supporters: "Even though it is not proper to boast of what we have been, still we have not been placed in such an obscure position in this world nor are we called so unwise that the faith of Christ and the knowledge of belief could bring death rather than salvation to us."[17] Other writers,

---

to single out one point of view as more authentic than others will necessarily compromise a thoroughly historical orientation. Such an approach may be justified in an ecclesiastical or theological setting, but it will not find, nor should it seek, any historical justification."

15. Douglas (1966) 108.
16. Frend (1961), and Brown (1972) 237–59.
17. *Tract.* I.2 (p. 4).

however, described Priscillian as an extraordinary figure, well born, intelligent, highly educated (presumably in the schools of Gaul or Spain), and thus a man quite capable of writing these small tracts.[18] Yet in the Christian church Priscillian was only a layman when he was (perhaps) condemned by the Council of Saragossa in 380; only later was he consecrated bishop of Avila (in Lusitania).[19] Other men associated with Priscillian came from similar backgrounds, although we know fewer details about them. Helpidius, a rhetorician who had instructed Priscillian and who was also prominent enough to have been condemned at the Council of Saragossa, was only a layman.[20] Latronianus, from Spain, a man admitted to have been a learned poet comparable to the past masters, was also a layman.[21] Other prominent supporters included Tiberianus, from Baetica, who wrote an apologetic tract, and Asarbus, a coauthor of this tract.[22]

The observation that Priscillian and some of his prominent supporters were educated laymen can be misleading in two ways, however. First, we cannot assume that educated men always elicited such strong opposition as we will find in this instance. Paulinus of Nola, for example, had once been taught at Bordeaux by the famous professor Ausonius, but later became an influential layman living in Campania. Although his life in many respects parallels that of Priscillian,[23] Paulinus eventually became a respected bishop in Italy. Second, we should not impose on this dispute any simple tension between heretical laymen and Catholic clergy, because among the supporters of Priscillian we also find bishops and other clerics.

Some bishops apparently supported Priscillian from the beginning, while others later defected to join him. Among the original "corrupted" bishops were Instantius and Salvianus who, accord-

---

18. Sulpicius Severus Chron. II.46.1–4, and Jerome de vir. illus. 121. Priscillian's teachers were said to have included Agape and Marcus, on whom see U. Rouzies, DHGE I (1912) 877, and DeClercq (1957).

19. Sulpicius Severus Chron. II.47.4.

20. Sulpicius Severus Chron. II.46.2, 47.2, and Jerome Ep. 133.4.3.

21. Jerome de vir. illus. 122, and Hydatius Chron. 16 (Chron. Min. II, p. 15).

22. Jerome de vir. illus. 123, and Priscillian Tract. I.1 (p. 3), with A. Lambert, DHGE IV (1930) 871.

23. See Babut (1910), who suggests that Paulinus may even have been a supporter of Priscillian, and Fontaine (1974) 271–8, who insists on the profound differences between the two. Both views are distorting because they are overly schematic and do not allow for ambiguities; more balanced discussions include Fabre (1949) 107–16, and Lienhard (1977) 52–57.

ing to one source, formed a "conspiracy" with Priscillian.[24] All three were said to have been condemned at the Council of Saragossa in 380, and all three subsequently traveled to Italy. One bishop who defected in support of Priscillian was Hyginus of Cordoba, who had first referred the problem of Priscillian to Bishop Hydatius of Merida. Later, Hyginus restored contact with Priscillian and his supporters, and even acted as an arbitrator for them; thus, the Council of Saragossa excommunicated him, and Hydatius labeled him a heretic.[25] Another supporter was Symposius, a bishop who attended the Council of Saragossa and who along with Hyginus acted as an arbitrator in the dispute between Priscillian and his accuser Hydatius. If, as many scholars assume, this Symposius is to be identified with the Symphosius who recanted Priscillianism at the Council of Toledo in 400, then he later became a leader of the Priscillianists when they retreated into Galicia after the execution of Priscillian.[26] Other supporters included Bishop Vegetinus, who also condemned Priscillian at the Council of Toledo, and some clerics and a deacon.[27]

Hence Priscillian and his supporters did not necessarily pose a challenge to the clergy, especially as they insisted that they themselves were "Catholics."[28] As far as possible they appealed their grievances within the institutions of the church, and even complained to Pope Damasus that their opponents were treating them unfairly. There is furthermore no hint that Priscillian or any of his lay supporters were openly intent upon becoming bishops or that they founded their own churches.

Instead, Priscillian and the other educated men who supported him were all "charismatic" figures. This is not meant to imply that they had some innate extraordinary quality, because although in the later empire we find many eccentric and striking personalities, not all became leaders. Some, such as the Egyptian hermit who came to Rome wearing only a loincloth and tried to persuade an ascetic woman to walk naked through the streets,[29] seem to

24. Sulpicius Severus *Chron.* II.46.7.
25. Sulpicius Severus *Chron.* II.46.8, 47.3, and Priscillian *Tract.* II.48, 51, (pp. 40–41).
26. This identification is probably confirmed by Council of Toledo a. 400, "Exemplar professionum," ed. H. Chadwick (1976) 236, although there is no explicit evidence that Symposius was bishop of Astorga; cf. below, p. 109 n. 100.
27. "Exemplar," ed. H. Chadwick (1976) 237, and Sulpicius Severus *Chron.* II.51.2, 4.
28. *Tract.* II.52 (p. 42).
29. Palladius *Hist. lausiaca* 37.

have been ignored. Others remained within the orthodox pale; but still others were condemned as heretics. For whether any of these men became successful leaders depended largely on the relevance and appeal of their message. "Charisma . . . sociologically viewed, is a social relationship, not an attribute of individual personality or a mystical quality. . . . The leader is followed because he embodies values in which the followers have an 'interest.' "[30] In this sense the writings of Priscillian articulated not just the doctrines of a few educated men, but also the desires and aspirations of the people who joined them.

Perhaps the outstanding impression received from a reading of the *Tractatus* is the continual emphasis on orthodoxy, or agreement with the Catholic faith; in fact, one of the purposes for which Priscillian wished to see Pope Damasus was to reveal to him "the Catholic faith according to which we live,"[31] because it would vindicate his orthodoxy. In a letter to Damasus, Priscillian first gave as his *fides* a basically orthodox confession and then proceeded to condemn in great detail almost every known heresy.[32] Like other Christians of the time, Priscillian had a clear conception of the boundary between Catholics and heretics and even though he professed hesitation at offending Christian sensibility by actually mentioning all these heresies, he eagerly set to the task of refuting them.[33]

In addition to the delineation of hard boundaries, his Catholic faith also offered a perspective on life; for Priscillian, life was an *iter*, a road or a journey. Thus he could write that by ascending into heaven Christ had "mapped out a road for those coming to him"; and in accepting the creed of the Catholic faith Christians too could begin to travel on this "road of renewed grace." In their struggle against heresy they had become the guardians of this "road of the creed."[34]

A single road: the contrast could hardly be more pointed with the claim of a pagan contemporary that there were many ways to

30. Worsley (1968) 288.
31. *Tract.* II.51–52, 53 (pp. 41–42); cf. I.36 (p. 30).
32. Tract. II.44–45 (pp. 36–37).
33. E.g. *Tract.* I.6 (p. 7), II.46–47 (p. 38). Note that like professional heresy-hunters such as Filastrius of Brescia, Priscillian too refuted heresies from times long past: cf. Marrou (1966).
34. *Tract.* I.2, 3–4 (pp. 4, 6), II.45 (p. 37). The concept of life as an *iter* is so pervasive and important that it was mentioned in the first sentence of both of Priscillian's apologetic tracts, I.1 (p. 3), and II.41 (p. 34).

the truth.[35] Equally clearly, with his concept of life as a journey involving a constant struggle, Priscillian was echoing a "Christianity of despair" that would find its major champion in Augustine.[36] No longer could people see life in terms of an "ascent," the Platonic notion previously used to interpret the writings of St. Paul; by becoming a Christian a man was merely taking the first step in a lifelong journey that was sure to be tiring. An early fifth-century monk knew how to characterize such an ascetic journey: it was like the wanderings of the Israelites in the desert before they finally reached the promised land. And in a world where traveling, especially over land, was indeed wearisome, such a comparison took on great significance; another bishop stressed to his congregation that only saints could travel without suffering any fatigue.[37]

Since the journey along this road implied a clean break with secular concerns, Priscillian also emphasized the rebirth people found in baptism. Not only were they redeemed from their past, "from that empty way of life based on ancestral tradition"; they could even be "repaired" through baptism:[38] "We wholly dedicated ourselves to God and claimed that anyone who loved someone else more than God could not be his disciple."[39] Yet, although not discouraging people from abandoning their families to take up a quest for spiritual perfection, neither did he withhold the hope of forgiveness from married couples who were prepared to observe chastity; by rejecting secular activities they too could share in "the light of the Lord."[40]

The distinctive message of Priscillian in the *Tractatus* can easily be lost in his obscure style and in his indiscriminately excessive use of citations: the pages of his writings were "dyed and colored" through with biblical references, as one later Catholic writer found to his horror.[41] In fact, his message was an influential one, in part because it was based on the authority of books. Not only had Priscillian offered one possible interpretation of the Bible and of whatever was useful from apocryphal books, he had also in-

35. Symmachus *Rel.* 3.10.
36. Brown (1967) 151–2.
37. Eucher of Lyon *de laude heremi* 8–16, and Victricius of Rouen *de laude sanctorum* 9.
38. *Tract.* I.2, 17, 31 (pp. 5, 15–16, 26), II.41–42 (pp. 34–35).
39. *Tract.* II.42 (p. 35).
40. *Tract.* I.16 (p. 15), II.43 (p. 36).
41. Vincentius of Lérins *Comm.* 25.

vited his supporters to participate in the task of interpreting these holy books: "We understand the riddles of these sayings and the interpretations of the parables."[42] Furthermore, his was a message with immediate implications for people's lives, because another theme was an emphasis on *nostra vita*, how people lived. For Priscillian and his supporters the Catholic faith was more than an abstract theology against which people might measure heresy and orthodoxy; it was also "the Catholic faith in which we live."[43]

Living out the demands of these teachings, however, led to a single-mindedness that provides a context for understanding some of the events in the clash between Priscillian's supporters and Catholics. After Bishop Hydatius returned to Merida from the Council of Saragossa, one of his own priests made an unspecified charge against him. Some of his clerics then apparently appealed to Priscillian, not wanting to risk consorting with anyone who might be morally tainted; as Priscillian wrote, "Many of his clerics segregate themselves and insist that they will communicate only with a pure bishop." But when Priscillian and his supporters went to Merida to hear the confession of these dissenting clerics, a mob prevented them from entering the church, and then ran them out of town.[44] The pressures of small Christian communities were here apparent: some people could not take the chance of associating with an impure bishop, while others rallied around their local bishop against the intrusion of "outsiders."

This intensity is also apparent during the journey made by Priscillian and some of his supporters to Italy, probably in 381. After they had been outlawed in Spain by an imperial rescript, they decided to appeal either to Pope Damasus, who had only recently been designated by an imperial constitution as one of the arbitrators of Catholic faith, or to Bishop Ambrose, who had weighty influence at the court of the emperor Gratian.[45] On the journey to Italy Priscillian and his supporters appeared in the towns of southern Gaul like the itinerant monks of the Middle Ages. At Eauze they were warmly received, but at Bordeaux they were expelled. Along the way the journey probably came to re-

---

42. *Tract.* I.7 (p. 8); cf. *Tract.* III, on the apocryphal books, and H. Chadwick (1976) 77–86, 98–99.

43. *Tract.* II.42, 48 (pp. 35, 40).

44. *Tract.* II.48–49 (pp. 39–40).

45. On Damasus, see *CTh* XVI.1.2; on Ambrose, see Matthews (1975) 186–97.

semble one of the pilgrimages to Rome that were so common at the time, and in Aquitania, according to one source, a number of women joined them.[46]

The beliefs and the behavior of the people who supported Priscillian should not surprise us, because in the later empire many self-conscious Christians were attempting to live distinctive lives. Jerome had outlined this goal to one young girl at Rome: "Learn a holy arrogance, know that you are better than those others."[47] But in this quest for perfection it was necessary, as we have seen, to have a teacher, and men such as Priscillian were qualified to fill this role: "Leadership still has to be comprehended as the meeting of social wants in potential followers in a given situation of unsatisfied aspirations. From this standpoint, all leadership, whatever the empirical facts, is primarily symbolic and relational, and only secondarily personal."[48] It is not surprising either that even before the execution of Priscillian there seems to have been a multiple leadership consisting of both bishops and educated laymen;[49] both types of men could serve equally well as guides for people determined to live uncontaminated lives.

Already before his execution Priscillian can be considered primarily as a symbolic figure. In him, and in other teachers like him, some Christians found the embodiment of their desires. To a certain extent we can see this symbolic significance in the description of Priscillian given by Sulpicius Severus. According to him, although Priscillian was capable of living as an extreme ascetic, he was also a magician, deceptive and overly proud of his knowledge of "unholy things."[50] This description of Priscillian was closely modeled after the description of Catiline given by Sallust centuries earlier in his monograph on the conspiracy, and it was written at a time when comparison with Catiline was still considered an insult.[51] By describing Priscillian in this way, Sulpicius seems to

46. Sulpicius Severus *Chron.* II.48.2–3, with Bardy (1949).

47. Jerome *Ep.* 22.16.

48. Worsley (1968) 293.

49. Although contemporaries claimed that Priscillian alone was the "instigator of all evils" (Sulpicius Severus *Chron.* II.47.4), by arguing that Instantius was the author of the *Tractatus*, Morin (1913) effectively shows that there were other leaders besides Priscillian.

50. Sulpicius Severus *Chron.* II.46.4–5, with Fontaine (1975).

51. Ausonius *Ep.* 22.61; Ammianus Marcellinus XXV.3.13; Sidonius *Ep.* II.1.1. A third- or fourth-century statuette of a teacher on which were inscribed the first words of Cicero's *In Catilinam* I, shows that this was a common topic in Gallic schools: see Passelac (1972).

have considered him as another destructive force in the social order. Yet we can also sense more, because it was precisely these
unique qualities that made Priscillian an attractive man whom others could acknowledge as capable of mediating on their behalf between this world and the divine order. Favorable or unfavorable
evaluations depended on the circumstances and prejudices of the
audience; in a similar fashion other Christian bishops were alleged by their opponents to have been only "magicians."[52]

Seen in this context, neither the people nor the beliefs involved
in this "heresy" were necessarily peculiar, because while some
bishops and their congregations considered Priscillian and other
educated men like him to be beneficial teachers, others felt threatened by their presence. The essential motivation behind Priscillian and his supporters was not a point of doctrine, either in the
sense that they had been influenced by foreign ideas or that they
objected to Catholic theology; rather, it was an attitude of moral
regeneration emphasizing homogeneity and equality. As such, it
could claim precedents from the early apostlic church, which had
in fact been more concerned with ethics and the idea of community than with the development of sophisticated theology or of a
precise hierarchy of authority; but in the later fourth century
when the Christian church had already elaborated a more complex structure and ideology, it would be perceived as opposition
to orthodoxy. However innocent in itself, an insistence on moral
regeneration could hardly fail to be misjudged as a threat to others who now found their prestige and satisfaction elsewhere; and
their instinctive reaction was to resort either to outright violence
or to the mechanism of accusation and confession that could resolve and heal tensions in communities.

\* \* \*

Catholic bishops offered the most articulate opposition to Priscillian and his supporters. Among the twelve bishops at the Council of Saragossa in 380, at least two were from Aquitania.[53] One,
Bishop Delphinus of Bordeaux, remained in opposition. In 381 he
mobilized the citizens of Bordeaux to expel Priscillian and his supporters as they were traveling through southern Gaul on their

52. H. Chadwick (1976) 52 n. 5; contrast Thomas (1971) 318–32, on the interplay between magic, religion, and holiness.
53. Sulpicius Severus *Chron.* II.47.1, with H. Chadwick (1976) 12–13.

way to Italy, and in 384 a council at Bordeaux voted to defrock one bishop who had supported Priscillian.[54] Another Gallic bishop who opposed Priscillianism was Britannius of Trier, potentially a powerful adversary because his see was also the seat of the imperial court.[55]

The principal opponents, however, were bishops Hydatius of Merida and Ithacius of Ossonuba. As we saw earlier, Priscillian had complained to Pope Damasus because Hydatius had obtained an imperial rescript for use against him. Ithacius, although at one point forced to flee to Trier, eventually won the support of the usurper Maximus, and when Priscillian finally appeared before the imperial court, Ithacius initially acted as prosecutor. These two bishops furthermore circulated, and probably also formulated, the accusations made against Priscillian and his supporters.

One accusation was that his supporters included many women, which led to immoral and scandalous behavior. Part of this accusation was in fact correct, because some women, among them a wealthy widow, did support Priscillian. On their journey through southern Gaul, after Bordeaux refused to admit them, Priscillian and his supporters were allowed to stay on the estate of Euchrotia, widow of the rhetorician Attius Tiro Delphidius. She and her daughter Procula accompanied Priscillian to Italy, and eventually, after the trial at Trier, Euchrotia was executed along with him. Procula was alleged to have been the mistress of Priscillian, although that is all we know of her.[56] Another supporter was Urbica, perhaps also a member of an academic family at Bordeaux, who was stoned to death because of the "obstinacy of her impiousness."[57] Although the allegiance of these women presumably indicates the attractiveness of Priscillian's leadership, uncompromising Catholic writers instead emphasized the apparent scandals. Women from respectable families were desirable members for Catholic churches, as we have seen in the previous chapter, but when they supported a "heretical" teacher, they were belittled as the source of all evils.

54. Sulpicius Severus Chron. II.48.2, 49.7–8.
55. Sulpicius Severus Chron. II.49.2, 4.
56. Sulpicius Severus Chron. II.48.2–3, 51.3; Pacatus Pan. lat. XII(2).29.2; Jerome Ep. 75.3.
57. Prosper Tiro Epit. s.a. 385 (Chron. Min. I, p. 462). This Urbica may have belonged to the family of Urbicus, a grammarian and poet at Bordeaux (Ausonius prof. 21.10–28, and Etienne [1962] 269), or she may have been an in-law of Ausonius himself (cf. Ausonius parent. 22.30, and Green [1978] 22).

Jerome even argued that Priscillian, like other heretics, had been influenced by women "spun around by every doctrinal breeze": "In Spain a blind woman led a blind man straight into a pit."[58]

Even more prominent were the related accusations of practicing magic and being Manichees. Bishop Ithacius apparently accused Priscillian of making incantations over fruit and offerings to the sun and moon[59] and insisted that the doctrines of Priscillian were obscene and magical, taught to him by an Egyptian magician.[60] In Jerome's tidy summary, Priscillian had become a bishop from being a magician.[61] Bishop Hydatius obtained from the emperor Gratian a rescript against Manichees and pseudobishops that could be used to evict Priscillian and his supporters from their churches and cities; he also circulated apocryphal writings that he claimed had been produced by Priscillian or his supporters.[62]

Although most later Catholic writers simply treated these allegations as facts and argued that for such heretics even execution by civil magistrates had been an appropriate penalty, the significant point is that at the time, bishops who opposed Priscillian and his supporters accused them of being Manichees and accompanied their accusations with the usual charges of magic and moral perversions. We have seen that such accusations can often be best understood not in literal terms as an accurate description of these men, but rather in functional terms. This approach is reinforced when we consider, first, that on the basis of his own denial Priscillian was not a Manichee at all. In reply to the accusation of magic, Priscillian wrote that magicians "ought to be persecuted with a sword" and even executed if necessary.[63] He similarly condemned the Manichees: "Let him be anathema who does not condemn Mani and his works, teachings, and instructions." Priscillian was particularly critical of the moral perversions of the

58. Jerome *Ep.* 133.4.

59. *Tract.* I.27–28 (pp. 23–24).

60. Isidore of Seville *de vir. illus.* 15 (*PL* 83.1092). The accusation was repeated by Sulpicius Severus *Chron.* II.46.2, and Jerome *Comm. in Isaiam proph.* XVII (*PL* 24.622–3), although Jerome is also obviously confused: see E. Amann, *DTC* IX (1926) 1960–3.

61. Jerome *Ep.* 133.4.3.

62. *Tract.* II.50, 52 (pp. 40–41), and Sulpicius Severus *Chron.* II.47.6–7. Note also Filastrius *diver. heres.* 61(33), 84(56), presumably based on the information Hydatius sent to the imperial court in north Italy.

63. *Tract.* I.28 (p. 24).

Manichees and of their magical practices: "We totally condemn the Manichees not just as heretics but as idolaters and magicians, servants of the sun and moon."[64]

Additional support for a functional perspective is provided by the recognition that in late antique Gaul and Spain there were no true Manichees. Although scholars have claimed that Manichaeism spread to Spain and Gaul in the fourth century, the sole proof has always been the affair of Priscillian;[65] whereas in fact Christians in Gaul and Spain were familiar with only the image of Manichaeism. In the late fourth century a Spanish bishop wrote a tract against Manichees and other heretics,[66] and a Spaniard inquired about one aspect of the Manichaean heresy.[67] A poem by a Spanish writer described the Manichaean belief in an insubstantial God, which was similarly mentioned by a Gallic monk in the early fifth century.[68] Also in the early fifth century Augustine, writing about Manichees in Gaul who had confessed at a public trial, probably referred to the trial of Priscillian at Trier.[69] In 414 Orosius, a priest from Galicia, described to Augustine how Priscillianists were worse than Manichees.[70] The monk Bachiarius, who scholars think came from Galicia in the late fourth or early fifth century, may have mentioned Manichees in the East.[71] Before 419, as part of the feuding between cities over ecclesiastical primacy in

64. *Tract.* I.26 (p. 22), II.47 (p. 39).

65. de Stoop (1909) 89–102, cites only Priscillianism; Puech (1949) 64, and Widengren (1965) 117–18, give no evidence.

66. Gennadius *de scriptor. eccles.* 14, with H. Chadwick (1976) 12, 172, 220, for possible identification.

67. Jerome *Ep.* 71.6; above, p. 82.

68. Prudentius *apotheosis* 956–8, and Vincentius of Lérins *Comm.* 14.

69. Augustine *de natura boni* 47 (*PL* 42.570), with the discussion in Courcelle (1968) 218, 228–9, and H. Chadwick (1976) 206–7. Note that in 415 Augustine claimed that at the time he was writing his *De libero arbitrio* in 387–391 he had not yet heard of Priscillianism (*Ep.* 166.7, *PL* 33.723). But by the early fifth century, because some of his own writings against Manichees were circulating in Spain (although not read by Orosius: *ad Orosium* 1, *PL* 42.669), he may have indirectly contributed to the development of the stereotype of Priscillianism.

70. Orosius *Commonitorium de errore Priscillianistarum et Origenistarum* 2 (*CSEL* 18, p. 153), whose source was apparently Bishop Ithacius: see H. Chadwick (1976) 203–6.

71. Bachiarius *Fides* 2 (ed. Madoz [1941] 465), although the clause is missing in some manuscripts. Our only information about Bachiarius is in Gennadius *de scriptor. eccles.* 24, but by comparing his *Fides* with Priscillian *Tract.* I, scholars have assigned him a provenance in Galicia: see Duhr (1928); A. Lambert, *DHGE* VI (1932) 58–68; and H. Chadwick (1976) 167–9, who is too confident about this attribution.

southern Gaul, the bishop of Valence was accused of Manichaeism by his clergy and even condemned at a Gallic council.[72] From
the later fifth and early sixth centuries we have a few passing references to Manichees by Gallic writers,[73] a formulaic abjuration of
Manichaeism,[74] and some secondhand references to Manichaeism
in sermons by Caesarius of Arles.[75] The only Manichee that Gregory of Tours knew of in the late sixth century was Pontius Pi-
late[76]—proof, if it were still needed, that the image of Manichaeism had been a stereotype that did not correspond to any historical
reality.

This evidence is listed to show that, excepting the vague references to Manichaean doctrines, it is all negative, in the form of
allegations and denials. Unlike North Africa, where there were
genuine Manichees, in late Roman Spain and Gaul only the image and the accompanying accusations of Manichaeism were in
circulation.

In North Africa, when a man was accused of being a Manichee
or proclaimed that he was one, the procedure was straightforward: after being tried before bishops or given a chance to debate,
he had either to leave town or to repent and beg reconciliation.
But in the affair of Priscillian, what had begun, and should have
been resolved, as a series of local animosities instead became en-
meshed in a wider political context. Hydatius had refused to meet
Priscillian and his supporters when they had come to Merida to
see him, and instead appealed to the emperor Gratian. Priscillian
and his supporters refused to accept the judgment of the bishops
who opposed them, and so declined to leave town or to repent.
Instead they tried to appeal to Pope Damasus and Ambrose, and
then solicited civil patronage for themselves. At the Council of
Bordeaux in 384 Instantius, one of the bishops who had sup-

72. Bonifatius I *Ep.* 3.1 (*PL* 20.757), with Duchesne (1894–1915) I, 109–10.

73. Faustus of Riez *de gratia*, prol. 1.5; [Gennadius of Marseille] *Liber eccles. dogmatum* 4, 21, 33, 42; Julianus Pomerius *de vita contemplativa* II.24.1–2; and Avitus *Ep.* 4, referring to the correspondence between Faustus of Riez and Paulinus of Bordeaux (see Faustus of Riez *Ep.* 4–5, *CSEL* 21, pp. 181–95).

74. *PL* 65.23–26, from a manuscript found at Lyon; for discussion, see Chatillon (1954a) and (1954b), and Ries (1957, 1959).

75. Caesarius of Arles *Serm.* 59.2, 5, 83.7, 101.1, 4, 114.1, 2, 125.1, 3, 127.1;
most of these references were derived or directly excerpted from works of
Augustine.

76. Gregory of Tours *HF* I.24. See also Grondijs (1952), for what he claims to
be a seventh-century Manichaean church in Spain.

ported Priscillian, seems to have recanted, but Priscillian appealed for a hearing before the usurping emperor Maximus.[77]

At the imperial court he and his supporters had no chance of success. Priscillian was accused and convicted of "magic," a basic allegation that was elaborated with three more specific accusations: that he had studied obscene doctrines, that he had organized nocturnal covens of immoral women, and that he had been accustomed to pray while naked. Before a civil court, then, the primary accusation was of magic, which was normal because accusations of heresy and Manichaeism were usually left to episcopal jurisdiction.[78] Priscillian and some of his supporters were executed and others were sent into exile; according to Sulpicius, these were men "most unworthy of the light of day."[79]

But when Maximus wrote to Siricius, the new pope in Rome, he emphasized how he had suppressed Manichees immediately upon his arrival in Gaul.[80] Maximus was trying to win support for his new regime and therefore stressed his opposition to Manichaeism before Siricius, who would himself later "find" Manichees in Rome. Interestingly enough, because of this propaganda, Maximus at least spared himself some subsequent vilification. Although he would be accused of surrounding himself with bishops who were sycophants and executioners, of sanctioning the execution of the wife of a famous rhetorician, and of being a mere bandit,[81] he was not accused of condoning immoralities, a charge made some thirty years earlier against Magnentius, another usurper in Gaul.

By mobilizing the evidence in this less explicit way, we can see how accusations of Manichaeism were supposed to function as a mechanism to resolve ambiguities within the structure and ideology of small Christian communities. In this case, however, the mechanism failed, and Priscillian and some of his supporters were executed. This final tragic result seems to have imposed a peculiar perspective of hindsight on the affair, because the actions leading to it have had to be explained and justified ever since. In

77. See Girardet (1974), for the legal and ecclesiastical problems connected with the trial; and H. Chadwick (1976) 111-32, who is particularly perceptive on the wider politics and imperial intrigues.

78. Sulpicius Severus Chron. II.50.8, with Suys (1925).

79. Sulpicius Severus Chron. II.51.5.

80. Coll. Avell. 40.4 (CSEL 35, p. 91).

81. Pacatus Pan. lat. XII(2).29.2–3; Ausonius ord. urb. nob. 9.9; Ambrose Ep. 24.12; and Palanque (1965) 255.

his first reference to Priscillian, written in 392, Jerome was unsure what to make of him: "Today Priscillian is accused by some of the Gnostic heresy . . . , while others defend him and say that he did not think as they argue."[82] But as the years went by, Jerome became harsher and more definitive in his condemnation of Priscillian, and other writers, equally far away geographically and even more removed chronologically, were just as certain about their judgments.

Although from a slightly different angle, this uneasiness is also apparent in the writings of a contemporary, Sulpicius Severus. One noticeable aspect of his narrative is that he did not mention the accusation of Manichaeism. Other writers described the heresy of Priscillian as a form of Manichaean beliefs, perhaps mixed with Gnostic teachings; Sulpicius described it only as "that notorious heresy of Gnostics."[83] Priscillian insisted that the rescript of Gratian had been directed against Manichees; Sulpicius claimed that it was used against Gnostics. Yet Gnosticism was hardly a pressing problem in the fourth century, and nowhere was it mentioned in any of the extant imperial constitutions about heresies. Certainly there were theological similarities between Gnosticism and Manichaeism, and in some parts of the empire, such as North Africa, Manichaean communities seem simply to have replaced Gnostic communities.[84] But since there were no true Manichees to hide in late antique Gaul and Spain, it is likely that Sulpicius was instead protecting other men from accusations of Manichaeism.

One man who was susceptible to such an accusation was Martin of Tours. Martin had gone to Trier and attempted to convince the usurper Maximus that he should not sentence anyone to death and that the affair could be best handled by episcopal jurisdiction. As a result, Martin too came under suspicion. "Ithacius was so silly that he accused all men, however holy, who had a desire for reading or the intention of struggling by fasts with being supporters of Priscillian"; and in fact Ithacius was almost successful in having Martin condemned as a heretic.[85] After the executions Martin returned to Trier, and this time he begged Maximus not to send

---

82. Jerome *de vir. illus.* 121.
83. Sulpicius Severus *Chron.* II.46.1; cf. Prosper Tiro *Epit.* s.a. 379 (*Chron. Min.* I, p. 460).
84. Frend (1953).
85. Sulpicius Severus *Chron.* II.50.3, *Dial.* III.12.2.

armed officers to Spain to search for more heretics; he also refused to communicate with the bishops who had opposed Priscillian, who claimed in turn that Martin was acting as the "avenger"
of Priscillian.[86]

In his narrative Sulpicius was hostile toward and even cynical
about the bishops who had opposed both Priscillian and Martin.
According to him, Bishop Ithacius was in no way a "holy man";[87]
yet, as we have seen, Priscillian and his supporters were caught
up in the pursuit of holiness, absorbed in reading the Bible and
living correctly in this world. In many ways Priscillian and Martin
resembled each other, even being opposed by the same bishops;
so in this curiously roundabout way of speaking about Gnostics,
Sulpicius was probably protecting Martin of Tours.[88] The ambiguity in such accusations becomes apparent again, because Priscillian and his supporters eventually succumbed to accusations of
Manichaeism and magic, while Martin was never directly accused.
As long as men such as Martin retained the support of their communities, they were seen as Christian leaders rather than as heretics or social deviants.

*     *     *

The preceding discussion of Priscillian and his supporters has
suggested that a context of community dynamics can help us redefine some of the conventional theological problems over orthodoxy and heresy. These notions about heretics and Manichees
were beliefs held in such a way that they enabled people and
communities to act in the face of the tensions and implicit rivalries
that had been generated by the structural and ideological inadequacies of their own religious system. Although the discussion
has, to this point, concentrated on the affair of Priscillian before
his trial at Trier, it is worthwhile to consider a few aspects of the
subsequent history of Priscillianism, in part to trace out the development of some themes already considered, but also to emphasize the significance of the execution of Priscillian.

The trial at Trier did not end the conflicts within the Christian

86. *Dial*. III.11–12.1; cf. Gregory of Tours *HF* I.46, *VJ* 4.
87. Sulpicius Severus *Chron*. II.50.2.
88. Jerome *Ep*. 22.13, had pointed out that a strange appearance and a pale
complexion were sufficient to mark a person as a Manichee, and Martin's appearance was certainly, terrifyingly, strange; significantly enough, Sulpicius was
familiar with this letter of Jerome (see *Dial*. I.9.2).

churches in Gaul and Spain, largely because the bishops who had opposed Priscillian and his supporters were disgraced for having let the affair lead to executions imposed by secular magistrates. Although Bishop Hydatius quickly resigned from his see, Ithacius survived longer as a bishop, and after the execution of Priscillian he and the bishops who had supported him enjoyed the protection of Maximus. But both Martin, when he returned to Trier to urge Maximus to be lenient toward the former supporters of Gratian, and Ambrose, when he traveled to Trier on an embassy representing the legitimate imperial court at Milan,[89] refused to associate with these bishops. Eventually Ithacius was defrocked and went into exile, where he tried to defend himself one last time by writing an *Apology*, which unfortunately no longer survives.

In contrast, Priscillian, who had been considered a "holy man" by his supporters before his execution, afterwards could justifiably be considered a martyr.[90] In the first centuries of its existence the Christian church had glorified the concept of martyrdom to the extent that it may have been an important factor in the outbreaks of persecution against the Christians. Martyrdom was seen as the absolute and perhaps only total imitation of Christ, ensuring perfect union with him.[91] Yet martyrdom had usually been achieved at the hands of opponents such as civil magistrates, and after the conversion of Constantine the antagonism between orthodox Christians and secular magistrates had supposedly come to an end. The notion of martyrdom thus was subtly redefined. Most commonly, the life of asceticism was considered a martyrdom; or sometimes influential men in the church were seen as "living martyrs."[92] In the fourth century, as the veneration of relics and the shrines of martyrs became significant, Christians even mistakenly honored as martyrs any men who had been executed by civil authorities.[93] But now Priscillian and some of his supporters had become martyrs in the classic manner: like so many of the early martyrs whose *Acta* still survive, they had been tried for their beliefs before a civil court and then executed.

89. Sulpicius Severus *Chron.* II.51, *Dial.* III.11.2–3; Ambrose *Ep.* 24.12.
90. Sulpicius Severus *Chron.* II.51.7–8.
91. See de Ste. Croix (1974) 234–7, and, in general, Frend (1965) 79–103.
92. Paulinus of Nola *Ep.* 18.9, in a description of Victricius of Rouen: "martyrem vivum."
93. Sulpicius Severus *Vita Martini* 11; and Ammianus Marcellinus XXVII. 7.5, with Marrou (1951/52).

Thus it is understandable that a man who had been a prominent religious leader while alive would have been seen as a genuine martyr after his execution, because martyrdom, although in one sense an apparent failure, was still the most impressive proof of a person's holiness.[94] Priscillian and some of his supporters were entered on the lists of martyrs, and their exploits were apparently commemorated during church services.[95] At the Council of Toledo in 400, one bishop from Galicia claimed in his own defense that he had ceased reading the names of these alleged heretics during the liturgy. But another bishop refused to back down and instead supported his clergy, "who, on their own initiative and without being asked, shouted that Priscillian was Catholic and a holy martyr; finally the bishop himself claimed that Priscillian had been Catholic and had been persecuted by other bishops."[96]

It must be emphasized that we have no evidence prior to the execution of Priscillian at Trier for the formation of a new sect separate from the Catholic church. Once Priscillian had become a genuine martyr, however, some Christians were prepared to separate themselves or be excommunicated from the Catholic churches because of their devotion to his memory. But again, we must not too hastily see in these people the formation of a sect or a movement, with all that those terms imply about organization and aims. Despite the obvious problem of limited information, we find little indication of any "Priscillianist church" in Spain or Gaul; instead, let us briefly consider three incidents which demonstrate how Priscillianism became, like Manichaeism, a stereotyped image of evils and immoralities. In fact, in some respects Priscillianism seems to have replaced Manichaeism in Spain and southern Gaul as a homebred idiom of heresy with which people articulated unacceptable aspects of their communities.

The first example takes us to the province of Galicia in the remote northwest of the Spanish peninsula, which Hydatius, a bishop from the area, called "the very end of the world."[97] This

94. Worsley (1968) 289.

95. Note Augustine *contra mendacium* 9: when Priscillianists *lie* in order to present themselves as Catholics, they criticize "Priscillianistarum falsa martyria." Note also Petrus de Natalibus *Catalogus sanctorum* II.42, XI.89, for some scrambled references to Priscillian and Latronianus, with de Gaiffier (1976), on this medieval martyrology, and (1954), for liturgical readings from hagiography.

96. Council of Toledo a. 400, "Exemplar," ed. H. Chadwick (1976) 237–8.

97. Hydatius *Chron.* praef.1, 7 (*Chron. Min.* II, pp. 13–14). In general, see Broughton (1959) and (1965), as well as Meslin (1969), for the church's own lack of success at taming the region.

region of Spain had always been the most difficult for the Romans to conquer and control. The province was rugged, mountainous country, as desirable for its gold mines as it was intractable because of its excessive tribal warfare and brigandage; although the Romans had first entered Spain in the late third century B.C., they did not conquer "the end of the world" until the reign of Augustus. Despite the assertion of Strabo that the presence of the Romans had a civilizing effect on the native tribes,[98] the region never advanced far beyond a society of small villages and tribal networks, and it became even more isolated from the Roman Empire when the Sueves settled there in the early fifth century. Catholic bishops such as Hydatius claimed that heresy now also contributed to the unruliness of the province; according to him, "The heresy of the Priscillianists invaded Galicia"—with the obviously dismissive implication that these heretics were similar to all the other invading barbarians.[99]

In 400 a council of nineteen bishops met at Toledo, all of whom were opposed to the followers and the heresy of Priscillianism. Other bishops also attended, among them Dictinius and Symphosius, but only in order to condemn Priscillianism and then be accepted back into Catholic communion.[100] Yet it is significant that the formula of abjuration that these men recited was apparently written out for them, in the same way that Augustine later wrote out a formula for Felix, the Manichaean missionary whom he had defeated in debate. Symphosius, for instance, first agreed with

98. Strabo III.3.8.

99. Hydatius *Chron.* 16 (p. 15), as well as the even harsher assessment of Orosius *Commonitorium* 1 (*CSEL* 18, p. 152), followed by Augustine *Ep.* 166.2, and Consentius, *apud* Augustine *Ep.* 11*.1 (*CSEL* 88, p. 52). Note also Prosper Tiro *Epit.* s.a. 379 (*Chron. Min.* I, p. 460), who described Priscillian as "episcopus de Callaecia"; since his episcopal see, Avila, was in Lusitania and not Galicia, this phrase has been taken by some as a reference to Priscillian's place of birth: see Torres (1949) 383.

100. Hydatius *Chron.* 31 (p. 16), and Council of Toledo a. 400, "Exemplar," ed. H. Chadwick (1976) 234–9. Many scholars have assumed that this Symphosius was bishop of Astorga, probably because he seems to act like the metropolitan bishop, but his see is nowhere explicitly stated. Hydatius, *Chron.* 101 (p. 22), also mentions another Bishop Symphosius who was an ambassador from the Sueves in 433; and intrinsically it seems wiser to identify this Symphosius of 433 with the Symphosius of 400, since Hydatius himself does not distinguish between them (cf. *Chron. Min.* III, p. 625). But most scholars identify the Symposius at the Council of Saragossa in 380 with the Symphosius at the Council of Toledo in 400, and make the Symphosius of 433 another bishop: see Tranoy (1974) II, 68; Claude (1978) 669–70 no. 77; and above, p. 94.

the anathemas that had been recited to him and then read out a full condemnation of what were alleged to be Priscillianist teachings.[101]

Other bishops followed the lead of Symphosius, although some, along with their clergy, refused and continued to insist that Priscillian had been a martyr. But it is also significant that this theological controversy was now intertwined with an argument about the ordination of bishops. Contrary to the explicit decree of Ambrose, Symphosius had ordained Dictinius as a bishop. These two also confessed that, because they had the support of the people of Galicia, they had ordained bishops in other sees.[102] Nor, apparently, did they fill only empty sees, because in one case Priscillianists claiming to act on behalf of the Catholic faith had expelled a bishop from his city.[103] Now, however, the condition for remaining a cleric was acquiescence to the decrees of this council: "If they do not subscribe to the form that we send them, they are not to retain the churches they possess." The other bishops were to be vigilant in order to prevent men who had been excommunicated from gathering women together or reading apocryphal books that had been condemned.[104] If these bishops were to have their way, then never again would teachers like Priscillian acquire any influence.

In this example we can see how, by the early fifth century, accusations of Priscillianism had become part of the religious vocabulary that men used to enunciate and resolve personal rivalries and feuds over ecclesiastical priorities in Spain and in southern Gaul.[105] The formal procedures following from accusations of Manichaeism were now also activated by accusations of Priscillianism. Yet a fundamental ambiguity was also part of this inheritance, not least because, as we saw with accusations of Manichaeism, accusations of Priscillianism could be applied rather indiscriminately. Another incident narrated in a wonderfully vivid

101. "Exemplar," ed. H. Chadwick (1976) 235–6. Priscillian did use *innascibilis* once (*Tract.* VI.99, p. 74), but not in an unorthodox manner: see Vollmann (1974) col. 545–6, and H. Chadwick (1976) 88–89.

102. "Exemplar," ed. H. Chadwick (1976) 237. There is no explicit evidence that Dictinius was either the son of Symphosius or bishop of Astorga after him.

103. Hydatius *Chron.* 31 (p. 16).

104. "Exemplar," ed. H. Chadwick (1976) 238–9. For conflicts over ordinations, see also Innocent I *Ep.* 3.

105. Note Zosimus *Ep.* 4.3, for allegations of Priscillianism in 417 as part of the feud between Arles and Marseille.

letter to Augustine emphatically demonstrates how careful we must be in distinguishing between Priscillianists and Catholics on theological grounds alone.

In 420 Consentius, a budding theologian living in the Balearic Islands, wrote to Augustine, in part to ask his advice, but even more to describe his success at ferreting out heretics in the lower Ebro River valley of northern Spain.[106] In the previous year he had instructed a monk at Tarragona named Fronto to insinuate himself into the confidence of an old woman and learn from her the names of other heretics. Fronto was successful, and eventually made a public accusation against Severus, a priest at Huesca who had acquired some allegedly magical books. But his zeal, in this case, almost backfired. Not only was Severus related to Count Asterius, who came to Tarragona with his retinue to hear the case, he was also supported by local bishops who carefully orchestrated the citizens into threatening Fronto with stonings and beatings. Eventually Fronto left for Arles, before coming to tell Consentius about his exploits.[107]

Augustine, upon reading the account, took Consentius seriously enough to write a long rebuttal, not against heresies, but rather against lying. He could overlook Consentius' rather undiplomatic suggestion that he encourage a more heavy-handed response in Spain than he had in Africa against the Donatists, but he could not countenance the fraudulent maneuver of exposing heretics through deceit. Priscillianists may have thought that lies were justified to conceal their religion, but Catholics were not to imitate their lead.[108]

In addition to its role in generating another tract by Augustine, the incident has wider historical implications. First, many motifs characteristic of life in small communities reappear, such as a rivalry between a monk and his supporters (including, in the end, bishops), and a priest and his supporters; charges involving books of magic; and the threat of potential crowd violence. In this

106. See Consentius, *apud* Augustine *Ep.* 12*.4 (*CSEL* 88, p. 72), for the Balearics as his home. About 410 Augustine and Consentius had also exchanged letters over the nature of the Trinity (Augustine *Epp.* 119–20), but neither had mentioned Priscillianism. Now both did, presumably because Orosius, who visited Augustine in 414 and the Balearics in 416, had enlightened them.

107. Consentius, *apud* Augustine *Ep.* 11* (ed. J. Divjak, *CSEL* 88 [1981] 51–70).

108. Augustine *contra mendacium* 25, 35, referring to the *Libra* of Dictinius that had provided biblical justification for circumstantial lying.

case even the appeal to an imperial magistrate only reinforced the local context, because the count was a relative of one defendant, and brought his court to Tarragona.[109] Second, the men this time accused of heresy were Catholic clerics, who were obviously furiously insulted by this blemish on their reputations. But third, although in his testimony Fronto had referred to his opponents only as heretics, Consentius, in contrast, elaborated on the account by describing them as Priscillianists. Fronto, who was uncertain of the strength of his opponents, preferred to make his charges a bit vague; but meddling outsiders such as Consentius simply glossed the controversy in terms of Priscillianism.

The third incident returns us to Galicia and points out again that accusations of Priscillianism are more illuminating in terms of the way men thought about the distribution of authority and prestige in their communities than in terms of the development of doctrine and theology. In the middle of the fifth century, when Bishop Turibius of Astorga returned to his see and found that he was no longer completely in control of doctrine there, he immediately urged the congregation not to read any of the apocryphal books that Manichees and Priscillianists used (although in the process he carefully named and described each forbidden book!).[110] Next, predictably enough, he proceeded to "find" Manichees who, he claimed, had been in hiding for many years,[111] and then appealed for the support of other bishops, including Pope Leo at Rome. In 447 Turibius sent Leo a letter, a pamphlet of advice, and another pamphlet of allegations against his opponents; in return he received a long letter condemning all Priscillianist beliefs. Significantly, however, Leo knew nothing about the Priscillianists beyond what Turibius had written to him, and his listing of their doctrines was simply a recapitulation of that information.[112] Leo was also more interested in telling Turibius about what he had recently done in Rome, where he too was "finding" Manichees. Priscillianists and Manichees were all alike to him: "But in their accursed mysteries . . . there is in short one crime, the same perversity and immorality. And this immorality, even though I blush to talk about it, was still hunted down with the most careful in-

109. Although cf. *Ep.* 11*.24 (p. 68), for a hint that the bishops of southern Gaul might refer the matter to the emperor.

110. Turibius *Ep.*, 2, 4 (*PL* 54.693–4).

111. Hydatius *Chron.* 130 (p. 24).

112. Leo I *Ep.* 15, praef., dated to 447. In general, see Vollmann (1965) 139–75.

vestigations and discovered by the confession of the Manichees who were caught, and I brought it to the public notice."[113] With the sanction of Leo, Turibius could convene a council and take action even against other bishops who, as he himself had admitted to Leo, nevertheless called themselves Catholics.[114]

In each of these three examples, it is significant that "catholics" were being threatened, either by "Priscillianists" who had expelled them from their sees, by a monk who, probably rightly, accused them of heresy and perjury, or by a bishop who insisted they were in fact Priscillianists in disguise. In other words, we are still dealing with intrigues between individuals who were carefully promoting themselves and belittling their opponents, rather than with disputes between competing sects. We can also see how accusations of Priscillianism cluster precisely in the times and regions in which Christian communities were facing uncommon situations. Often these accusations were associated with conflicts over the authority of bishops in Galicia, an area that had barely been controlled by Roman legions, and that was now, in the fifth century, occupied by barbarians, whose presence was an additional complicating factor for the church administration. Hence, although in Rome Pope Leo had been all too able, and willing, to use imperial legislation in his purge of Manichees, when he replied to Bishop Turibius he bemoaned the settlement of the Sueves because it made enforcement of imperial constitutions impossible in Galicia.[115] In Tarraconensis local feuds were presumably enhanced by the threat of Visigoths, who had only recently evacuated the region;[116] on the Balearics the newly acquired relics of St. Stephen had completely disrupted local communities in favor of the Christians. And in southern Gaul accusations of Manichaeism and Priscillianism seem to have been related to the

113. Leo I *Ep.* 15.16; cf. Prosper Tiro *Epit.* s.a. 443 (*Chron. Min.* I, p. 479), with Gaudemet (1958) 619, for Leo's own activities in Rome.

114. Leo I *Ep.* 15.17, although probably no council ever met: see Barbero de Aguilera (1963) 38.

115. Leo I *Ep.* 15, praef.; contrast *Ep.* 7.1, for Rome. For the imperial sanctions against Priscillianism, see *CTh* XVI.5.40, 43, and *Constitutiones Sirmondianae* 12 (ed. Th. Mommsen and P. Krueger [Berlin, 1905] 916–17).

116. In fact, the sacrilegious books of Severus first appeared because barbarians had confiscated and then tried to sell them at Lerida: see Consentius, *apud* Augustine, *Ep.* 11*.2 (p. 53); and above, p. 51, for the Visigoths in Tarraconensis. Count Asterius was now preparing a campaign against the Vandals in Galicia: *Ep.* 11*.12 (p. 60), and Hydatius *Chron.* 74 (p. 20).

confusion arising from shifting civil and ecclesiastical administrative boundaries.

Although the correspondence between Bishop Turibius and Pope Leo raises difficult problems over the accuracy of its description of Priscillianism, not least because Turibius went out of his way to associate the heresy with virtually all previous heresies, it still became the canonical definition of Priscillianism, and later authors and councils simply referred either to the correspondence itself or to statements derived from it.[117] Like the *Malleus Maleficarum*, the fifteenth-century encyclopedia of demonology that advertised witchcraft all over Europe, so the letters of Turibius and Leo continued to propagate the image of Priscillianism as a perverse compilation of Manichaean doctrines. But we have also seen how the affair of Priscillian and his supporters pointedly illustrates the limitations inherent in Christianity during the later fourth century. These shortcomings, in turn, make it difficult to understand how Christianity could ever have become so influential in fifth-century Gaul, and in particular among its aristocracy.

117. E.g. Montanus of Toledo *Ep.* 1.8 (*PL* 65.54); note also Council of Braga a. 561, praef. (*PL* 84.562–3).

# III

# The Assimilation of
# Christianity and Society

At the end of the fourth century Sulpicius Severus and his mother-in-law began to expand their monastic settlement in southern Gaul. Between two new churches they built a new baptistery, a place where "a man achieves a happy death and birth, dying to things earthly and being born to things eternal."[1] In this baptistery Sulpicius placed the portraits of two men who had gone through just such a death and rebirth: Martin of Tours and Paulinus of Nola. As we will see, Martin had profoundly influenced Sulpicius' life by converting him from a civil career to monasticism; in return, Sulpicius kept the memory of St. Martin alive through his writings. "In you," Paulinus of Nola wrote to Sulpicius, "St. Martin still breathes."[2] Paulinus had been a friend of Sulpicius for over a decade, ever since they had both converted to a more ascetic form of Christianity. Both men came from prominent Gallic families, both had received fine educations in the schools of southern Gaul, and both, upon their conversions, had gone to live in monastic communities. When Paulinus learned that Sulpicius had honored him along with Martin, he was both pleased and chagrined: "What is the relationship between serpents and doves—a proper comparison of myself with Martin?" At Sulpicius' request he composed some verses to accompany the portraits, stressing in them that, just as St. Martin exemplified a life of holiness, so he, Paulinus, was a model for repentant sinners.[3]

1. Paulinus of Nola *Ep.* 32.5.
2. *Ep.* 27.3.      3. *Ep.* 32.2–3.

But the implications of the juxtaposition of these two portraits go further than their obvious significance for catechumens waiting to be baptized. Although Martin had been, in almost every possible way, an "outsider" to Gallic society, his career demonstrates how Christian communities and their leaders appropriated the ideology and relationships of secular society. As a result, Christianity became more appealing to local aristocrats, who had continued to maintain their local prominence by the traditional means of control over the land, illustrious ancestry, education in the classical heritage, and service in the central administration. Seen from the opposite perspective local aristocrats now became desirable members in Christian communities that required leadership. Paulinus of Nola is one example of an "insider" to Gallic society who ostensibly discarded these traditional perquisites in order to become a convert, a monk, and finally a bishop in Italy. Elsewhere in Gaul we begin to see the same transformation as local aristocrats, whether they first had a civil career or not, entered the ecclesiastical hierarchy.

It is easy to take this transformation for granted, because not only has the "Christianization" of Gallic society long been a favorite topic of research, the "aristocratization" of the Gallic church during the fifth century has also been well explored. In fact, however, the implications of the previous chapters ought to make us hesitate. First, the discussion of heresy has suggested the inability of Christian communities easily to absorb such people as, in particular, men educated in the classical heritage—as many local aristocrats would have been. Second, the discussion of local authority has suggested that in any case these aristocrats did not need the sanction of Christianity to maintain their local prominence; as we have seen, they had been quite successful in performing outside, alongside, or inside even the central administration to their own advantage. The rise of Christianity to its dominating position in early medieval Gallic society therefore involves at least two simultaneous and interacting processes: first, the accommodation of Christian attitudes to secular ideology, and second, a disruption in the conventional exercise of local authority and a consequent redefinition of the options available to local aristocrats.

Neither process can be reduced to a continuous narrative, in part because of unevenness in the quality and quantity of the literary sources, and in part because the available literature of this period concentrates so greatly on specific individuals. In contrast to previous chapters, in which our extant literary sources often viewed and evaluated events in Gaul from the outside, subsequent chapters are largely derived from Gauls writing about their heroes or, with perhaps more distortion, about themselves. The following three chapters therefore use the careers of four well-known men as paradigm cases in order to discuss the appropriation of secular idioms of authority by Christian communities, the assimilation of local aristocrats into the ecclesiastical hierarchy, and the rise of Christian relic cults as both the administration and the ideal of the western Roman Empire waned in the later fifth century. Here we can sense the appearance of a Christian, medieval Gaul, even if it still firmly retained many similarities to and memories of a pagan, Roman Gaul.

# CHAPTER 6

# Martin of Tours
# and the Conversion
# of Gaul

When Sulpicius Severus sat down in the middle 390s to write his *Vita* of Martin, who was then bishop of Tours and still very much alive, he had already come under his spell. Somehow this was no ordinary man; in fact, Sulpicius sometimes wondered whether he was a mere mortal, since much of his behavior appeared to be "beyond the nature of man."[1] If the epic poet Homer himself were to reappear, he would be unable to describe the bishop's life: "To such an extent were all aspects of Martin so superior that they cannot be embodied in words."[2] Yet, faced with what he made out to be such a daunting task, Sulpicius somehow found the words and, in his "singing Gallic Latin,"[3] passed on to us what will always remain the fundamental evidence for any evaluation of Martin and his role in Gallic society.

Almost immediately after their appearance, however, his works were already the center of a controversy over what is now called "la question martinienne."[4] Essentially this problem concerns the "historical Martin," because Sulpicius' account was, and still is, vexingly peculiar. First of all, Martin had been presented as a "wonder-worker," a thaumaturge who impressed people with his

On Martin of Tours the work of J. Fontaine is outstanding; in addition to the articles mentioned below, see his introduction, edition, translation, and commentary for the *Vita Martini* and the *Epistolae* by Sulpicius Severus, in *SChr.* 133–135 (1967–1969). Valuable earlier work includes Griffe (1964–1966) I, 271–98; Delehaye (1920); and Jullian (1910), (1922), and (1922–1923). In this chapter, references to the writings of Sulpicius Severus (*VMart., Ep., Dial.*) omit his name.

1. *VMart.* 2.7, 27.1; *Dial.* II.2.7.    2. *VMart.* 26.3.    3. Dix (1945) 375.
4. Fontaine (1967–1969) I, 171–210.

power to perform miracles and his supernatural control over demons. In Sulpicius' day the issue was not whether the miracles
had actually occurred, but rather what their proper significance
was for Martin's authority. Critics scoffed at his self-professed
conversations with saints and demons, or claimed that his "ridiculous fantasies about visions" were in fact indications of senility.[5]
Sulpicius in reply was most indignant, and he insisted that neither he nor Martin had fabricated anything: "The demons have
always confessed the miraculous powers of Martin; do Christians
not believe them?"[6]

Another historiographical problem arises from the close association between Martin and St. Martin. Already at the time of his
death the two appear to have blended into each other, so that
Martin's funeral procession was both mourning for the dead Martin and exaltation for the St. Martin newly arrived in heaven. St.
Martin would continue the work that Martin had been performing as bishop, and in his new capacity as a patron in heaven he
would still assist people whenever they spoke about or prayed to
him.[7] But for modern historians the obvious question has been
whether Sulpicius' own writings are to be classified in this latter
genre of supplication, whether the *Vita* and the other writings
about Martin are to be considered as reliable historical evidence or
as apologetic propaganda. The claims of both the author and his
friends about the trustworthiness of the account have been offset
by the investigations of modern literary shcolars into Sulpicius'
rhetorical skills: short of using heroic verse, Homer himself could
probably have done no better.[8]

Because of these misgivings about Sulpicius' evidence for the
career of Martin, the creation of an appropriate setting for interpretation becomes all the more important. Yet the invention of
this context has also contributed to the ambiguity of Martin's role
in Gallic society. As we have seen, in the long run Christianity
could easily have remained a minority religion confined to specific regions or types of people. Many modern historians have
therefore forced Martin to carry a huge burden by making him
into a "missionary"[9] responsible for the conversion of the Gallic

5. *Dial.* II.13.7, III.15.4; cf. *Ep.* 1.
6. *Dial.* I.26.3–6, III.5.2–7, 6.1.        7. *Ep.* 2.8.
8. *Dial.* III.5.6, and Paulinus of Nola *Ep.* 11.11, 29.14; contrast Fontaine
(1967–1969) I, 61.
9. E.g. Griffe (1964–1966) I, 284: "un évêque missionnaire."

countryside, if not of all Gaul, even as, conversely, Martin's "missionary" zeal is used to explain his militant personality.

Resorting to the notion of mission work, however, has become merely a labor-saving device of modern historiography that ignores both the multiformity and the limited impact of early Christianity in Gaul. During the middle fourth century, for instance, the dominant Christian figure was Hilary, bishop of Poitiers. Yet it remains difficult to imagine how Hilary, an educated man who wrote extensive commentaries, had much in common with Martin, an uneducated monk who was notorious most of all for his unkempt appearance. A tramp like Martin, other bishops muttered at his consecration, did not deserve to become a bishop.[10] After the death of Martin we continue to be perplexed, because whereas the Christians keen enough to probe for evidence of Christianity on other continents were aristocrats,[11] pagan customs lingered far into the Middle Ages among the countryfolk whom Martin had supposedly converted by demolishing their shrines.[12]

The idea of the "conversion" of Gaul is thus far too blunt an analytical model with which to dissect the role of Martin and the transformation of Gallic society. Martin's rather outlandish techniques of evangelism ultimately become so significant that our interpretation can no longer keep him in focus, and so we blur such lesser, but no less distinctive, aspects of his personality as his pity for animals or the wit that seasoned his grave demeanor.[13] We also need a model of analysis more comprehensive than one stressing only conversion to Christianity. At the beginning of the *Vita* Sulpicius had insisted that myths about heroic warriors and Greek philosophers were of no benefit for readers;[14] in comparison, he presented Martin as a new kind of soldier and a new kind of teacher. In fact, in many respects Martin's chief competitors were not pagan priests in their strictly religious roles, but teachers and doctors, and one way Martin and his supporters consolidated his position was by using an idiom of authority previously reserved for such men as generals and emperors.

10. *VMart.* 9.3, with Fontaine (1968).
11. *Dial.* I.4.2.
12. E.g. Hubert (1977) 261–7, and Ropert (1976).
13. *VMart.* 27.1; *Dial.* II.9.6, 10.1; *Ep.* 3.7–8. Martin's personality becomes even more complex if we concede the influence of Eastern asceticism on his spiritual authority, or at least on Sulpicius' portrait of him: see Rousseau (1978) 143–65.
14. *VMart.* 1.3.

In other words, the important problem raised by the career of Martin is not the introduction of Christianity into pagan society, but rather the integration of an "outsider" such as Martin—a non-Gaul, a Christian, and an ascetic—into a society with preexisting expectations about leadership and community. The "conversion" of Gallic society hence marks changes in the distribution of authority and prestige, rather than a simple linear exchange of pagan for Christian beliefs. Because late antique men lacked the conceptual language to articulate in abstract terms the leadership and prominence of an anomalous, even bizarre, figure such as Martin, the use of conventional idioms of authority and influence, whether directly or in analogies, was necessary. Let us therefore investigate in turn the use of these traditional ideologies and relationships against a background, first, of the emperor and army in Gaul, and second, of the roles of doctors and teachers. In the process of assimilation both traditional pagan society and Christianity were challenged and modified; the final section of this chapter will briefly discuss how Christianity had finally to domesticate the career of Bishop Martin into the more acceptable image of St. Martin, and the next chapter will investigate how the application of traditional ideologies of authority to an "outsider" such as Martin eventually also made the episcopate a more attractive position for such "insiders" as Gallic aristocrats.

*   *   *

Early in 369 the Roman senator Symmachus traveled north to visit the court of the emperor Valentinian at Trier. Valentinian was a professional soldier whose father had risen within the ranks to become an officer and then a military governor, and who himself had served as an officer under the emperor Julian in Gaul before being proclaimed emperor. From 365 he had campaigned on the Rhine and Danube frontiers, and his vigorous actions there against the barbarians have earned him a reputation as the "last of the great military rulers of the Roman empire."[15] At Trier Symmachus delivered at least three panegyrics in honor of Valentinian and his young son Gratian, carefully keeping his feelings under control in each one. The emperor may have been brought up among the Illyrian snow and the African heat and so been used to hardship, but according to Symmachus, only his sense of duty kept Valenti-

15. Matthews (1975) 33, with references to Ammianus Marcellinus.

nian on the Rhine frontier: "Why have you taken up residence in that region in which the ruin of the entire state converges?"[16]

Beneath this rhetorical politeness runs a web of complicated prejudices. Valentinian was another of the Pannonian emperors who had come, since the third century, virtually to monopolize the rule of the empire. As we have seen, some of these emperors had developed close ties with the provinces of Gaul, and Valentinian's effectiveness on the Rhine and Danube frontiers gave him too a reputation for inspiring fear into the barbarians.[17] But Valentinian also clearly favored the military aristocracy and thus implicitly downgraded the old senatorial aristocracy of Rome of which Symmachus was a prominent member.[18]

During his year on the frontier Symmachus accompanied Valentinian on a minor campaign, and as a result received an honorary title of court attendance; he was thus one of the few senators from Rome to serve as a "soldier" at an imperial court.[19] His promotion did little to reduce his insecurity and resentment, however, because he still viewed the situation in terms of a contrast between military men and civilians, or between uncultured provincials and civilized senators at Rome who thought the empire in Gaul was on the verge of collapse. People in Gaul itself would have disagreed, since they perceived the presence of an emperor, his court, and his army as a guarantee of security and munificence; for them, "the imperial city of Trier, although near the Rhine, reposes unalarmed as if in the bosom of deep profound peace."[20] The image of northern Gaul conjured up by the Gallic professor and poet Ausonius, whom Symmachus had met in Trier, contrasted with the unflattering appraisal of Symmachus. In his poem honoring the Moselle River, Ausonius claimed that if a stranger from Italy were to arrive in this charming countryside, he would find a duplication of the pleasures to which he was accustomed. With its own imperial court, aristocracy, army, and even literary culture (in which Ausonius himself was training the

16. Symmachus *Orat.* I.15.
17. Ammianus Marcellinus XXX.7.6.
18. Symmachus *Orat.* I.23, and Jones (1964) 142–3. The isolation of Rome is clearly evident from the very few visits by emperors during the fourth century: see *Pan. lat.* X(4).38.6, and Barnes (1975).
19. *ILS* 2946. The closest most other Roman senators came was probably in the grand hunts that they equated with long military campaigns (Ammianus Marcellinus XXVIII.4.18).
20. Ausonius *ord. urb. nob.* 6.2–3.

young emperor Gratian), northern Gaul could defiantly compare itself to Rome.[21] Trier was now the "splendid abode of the emperors"; and therefore it had almost become Rome itself.[22]

Because the two men had initiated a friendship during his visit to Trier, Symmachus could try to ignore these differences of opinion, and he even obligingly ranked Ausonius' poem on the Moselle with the works of Virgil.[23] But Ausonius was also an imperial advisor, and underlying the early correspondence between the two was the additional implicit recognition that the Gallic provincial had immediate access to an imperial court that the Roman senator did not enjoy. For what rankled most with the old aristocracy at Rome was that with the emergence of Pannonians and other provincials as emperors, there was a corresponding elevation of local provincial aristocracies. Not only was the status of the military aristocracy enhanced under Valentinian, but supporters from Pannonia, as well as other provincials such as Gauls, came to dominate the imperial administration of the western empire.[24] It is within this context that we can situate the rise to prominence in Gaul of another military man from Pannonia: Martin of Tours.

Martin was a few years older than Valentinian, born in Pannonia although raised in northern Italy. As a young man he too had followed his father's profession and joined the army, in which he served for almost twenty-five years until 356. Then he came under the influence of Hilary of Poitiers, but after the bishop was sent into exile Martin became an itinerant monk, finally returning to Gaul with Hilary and founding a monastery outside Poitiers at Ligugé. From 371 until his death in 397 he was bishop of Tours.[25]

Martin remained a soldier throughout his life, however, and his background was particularly evident in the identification of his version of monastic Christianity with the Christian army. While Martin was serving in the Roman army, his virtues were so notable that "already then he was thought to be a monk and not a

21. Ausonius Mosella 345–8, 381–8.
22. Ammianus Marcellinus XV.11.9; and Vollmer and Rubenbauer (1926), for text and discussion of a (fourth-century?) epitaph describing Trier as "Belgica Roma."
23. Symmachus Ep. I.14.
24. Matthews (1975) 32–87.
25. See Delehaye (1920) 19–33, and Fontaine (1961), for the "long chronology" of Martin's life; and L. Pietri (1982), for a detailed discussion of the chronological references in Gregory of Tours.

soldier."[26] After he became a monk and then a militant bishop, he continued to see himself as a soldier, assisted now by angels armed with spears and shields "like celestial soldiers."[27] On his deathbed military language still came naturally to him: "I will serve beneath your standards, Lord, so long as you yourself will command."[28]

In this perspective Martin can be seen as yet another Pannonian who made his career in the fourth century as a military man in Gaul. As a soldier Martin always found the most support in the outlying provinces of the empire, particularly in Gaul. All we know about his tenure in the Roman army is that he served in northern Gaul at Amiens and Worms. As a veteran his one attempt at establishing himself and his version of monasticism in Italy ended in disaster. When he tried to found a monastery outside Milan he was run out of town, in part because of Arian opposition, but also, we may suspect, because there was no toleration for ex-soldiers such as Martin who refused to "retire" and become civilians again.[29] In Gaul, however, the use of military and imperial ideology to characterize Martin's version of Christianity found a strong response.

Because Tours was not a stronghold of Christianity during the fourth century,[30] it is surprising that the citizens wanted Martin to become their bishop, even if he was already known as a miracle-worker. In fact, with his election Tours acquired more than a mere bishop, because within his own sphere of influence Bishop Martin was the counterpart of a Pannonian emperor such as Valentinian. His arrival in Tours to become bishop, for instance, apparently resembled the arrival of an emperor. Since Tours was occasionally visited by prefects[31] and may have even welcomed a passing emperor, its citizens would have been familiar with the ceremonial used to celebrate the presence of powerful men. When Martin approached Tours, a huge crowd met him, shouting the kind of acclamations usually reserved for an emperor.[32] After he became bishop Martin demonstrated that he could resolve the ordinary problems people had with diseases, bad weather, and

26. *VMart.* 2.7.     27. *VMart.* 14.5.     28. *Ep.* 3.13.

29. *VMart.* 6.4. For other veterans, including former generals, becoming Christians in Gaul, see *Dial.* II.11; *ILCV* 61 = LeBlant I, no. 335, with L. Pietri (1970); and above, p. 59 for Bishop Victricius of Rouen.

30. Gregory of Tours *HF* I.48; cf. X.31.

31. *Dial.* I.25.6.

32. *VMart.* 9.2–3, with Fontaine (1967–1969) II, 645–52.

crop failure, as well as act like a powerful secular magistrate by successfully coping with barbarian invasions.[33]

Although Martin's role in the Christian community was defined by means of familiar ideologies of authority, because he was neither an emperor nor a general the conventional vocabulary took on additional significance. An excellent discussion of modern millenarian cults concisely summarizes this tension between custom and novelty: "A prophet delves into tradition for his initial sources of authority, provides new channels for tradition, and fills out these new channels with new assumptions, new rules."[34] In other words, the Christian community at Tours, which was familiar with the traditional military and imperial idioms of authority that had successfully ensured the stability of central Gaul during the fourth century, now used those same idioms to define the leadership of their new bishop, who as a veteran was also conversant with these forms of authority. In response, Martin, as both "emperor" or "general" and Christian bishop, was expected to protect people against their anxieties about barbarians as well as their concerns about demons. The weapons of the Roman army or of the local militia may not always have been successful against barbarian sorties, but at least Martin's weapons—prayer and the sign of the cross—were successful against demons.[35]

The use of secular idioms in a Christian context has a second implication, because by appropriating imperial ideology Martin made himself the equal of emperors.[36] Hence his behavior in the presence of emperors contrasted with that of other Gallic bishops who had used their religious authority to acquire access to the court and, once there, to enjoy a relationship with the emperor in which they sanctioned his activities in return for his support. We have already seen this relationship at work during the affair of Priscillian in the early 380s, when the emperor Maximus had been advised by a cabal of bishops who presumably also provided him with the justification for his war of usurpation against the emperor Gratian; in return, he protected them from any accusations of misbehavior in the way they had dealt with Priscillian and his

33. *VMart.* 18.1–2.
34. Burridge (1969) 47.
35. *VMart.* 4.5, 12.3, 13.8, 22.1; *Ep.* 1.15, 2.4. Note Fontaine (1967–1969) I, 161: "Il s'ensuit une véritable humanisation du monde surnaturel"—a statement that could be made equally well in reverse, because daily life was also "supernaturalized."
36. *Dial.* I.25.4.

supporters.[37] Sulpicius was bitterly critical of these submissive bishops in comparison with the proper behavior of Martin at the court of Maximus: "In Martin alone apostolic authority continued to assert itself."[38] The implication is clear: Martin's authority revived that of the original apostles, whose early church had been a small one struggling in the face of imperial hostility. In his dealings with emperors and their retinues, Martin always held himself aloof and compelled others to recognize his authority, once even waiting for Valentinian's throne to catch fire and thus force the emperor to rise and greet him.[39] Other bishops attended imperial banquets; Martin not only hesitated to attend, but also expressed misgivings about being served by Maximus' wife.[40]

Martin's perspective on Christianity therefore not only provided a model that renewed and redirected traditional ideologies of authority onto himself, it also challenged the position of Christian bishops who had adopted a more accommodating attitude toward civil authority. Martin saw Christianity as a military service of its own competing with the military and civil authorities; other bishops in Gaul, who had always been civilians, were instead prepared to coexist with the military and civil authorites. In Martin's perspective bishops could, and perhaps should, take over the functions of emperors and magistrates; in the alternative perspective, bishops only advised emperors. Not surprisingly, much of the opposition to him came from other bishops. Although Martin eventually decided to keep his distance by claiming that association with other bishops diminished his spiritual power,[41] his opponents in turn asserted that he had "defiled himself with his military actions"—an explicit comment on Martin's past but perhaps also an implicit evaluation of his idea of militant Christianity.[42]

This contrast in attitudes is also apparent in Sulpicius' account of an attempt by the Devil to tempt Martin by appearing in imperial purple robes and wearing a jewel-studded crown. Martin refused to accept him as Christ: "The Lord Jesus did not predict that he would come clothed in purple, with a glittering crown on his head. I will not believe that Christ has come unless he appears

---

37. *VMart.* 20.2–3; *Dial.* III.11.2.
38. *VMart.* 20.1.          39. *Dial.* II.5.5–10.
40. *VMart.* 20.3; *Dial.* II.6.3–7.          41. *Dial.* III.13.5–6.
42. *Dial.* III.15.4. For Sulpicius' own attempt to misrepresent Martin's military service, see Fontaine (1963b), and (1961) 208–22, esp. 211–17 on papal opposition to the ordination of veterans.

with that appearance and form in which he suffered, openly displaying the scars of his wounds from the cross."[43] Although this remark is an indication of Martin's apocalyptic thought,[44] his view of the millennium emphasized not the exultant, royal Jesus of the Second Coming, but rather the humiliated Jesus suffering on the cross. And indirectly, with his disavowal of an "imperial" Christ, Martin had refused to concede that the present Roman Empire, even though a Christian empire ruled by Christian emperors, could be a representation of the heavenly kingdom. In his perspective Christianity and its bishops could not yet claim victory and rest on their laurels. In contrast to other bishops, who sat on high thrones resembling imperial tribunals, Martin always presided in his church sitting on a low stool.[45]

\*     \*     \*

As we have seen in earlier chapters, an idiom of authority that highlighted the authority of emperors and generals was familiar in Gaul; and although borrowing it to articulate the position of Martin within his version of militant Christianity may have been unprecedented, its application did make intelligible both the authority of Martin and his relationship with others, whether civil magistrates or ordinary people. For Martin needed this explicit recognition of his leadership. Throughout his career he was as different from the Gauls as the emperor Julian had once been: he was a Pannonian, a veteran, one of the few early monks in Gaul, and he supposedly was no match for the voracious appetites of the Gauls either![46] Perhaps Martin's obvious status as an outsider was precisely what allowed, or even compelled, both him and the Christian community to adopt this conventional military and imperial idiom to define his role.

Martin's rise to prominence in Gallic society included, however, another dimension, because while bishop he was also seen by others as a doctor and a teacher. In late antique society doctors and teachers were commonly associated with each other and were found together in some families in Gaul. The father of Ausonius, for instance, had been a medical man with a Greek background,

43. *VMart.* 24.7; but in Merovingian Gaul the image of a suffering, humiliated Jesus was no longer popular (below, p. 247).
44. *Dial.* II.14.1–4, and Fontaine (1967–1969) I, 166–8.
45. *Dial.* II.1.3–4.
46. *Dial.* I.4, 8, 20, for the eating habits of Gauls.

while one of his aunts had been a midwife; Ausonius himself became a prominent professor at Bordeaux in the middle of the
fourth century.[47] Given the nature of ancient medicine, doctors
were also often associated or identified with local pagan priests,
because many cures involved the esoteric or divine knowledge
available only at shrines. Again, the same family could include
both pagan priests and teachers.[48] The influence of all these men
arose, in part, from the special knowledge to which they alone
had access in books or at shrines.[49] In order for laymen to benefit
from this knowledge, either a teacher or a priest was necessary. A
doctor was also required to communicate specialized medical
knowledge, such as that found in handbooks written in Greek.
Ausonius' father, for example, had acquired "the power to pro-
long men's lives by means of medicine and to make the Fates wait
their full time."[50]

From the late fourth century or early fifth century we have a
treatise of medical lore written by Marcellus, a Gaul probably
from Narbonne, who had served at the court of Theodosius.[51]
After his retirement he had returned to Gaul and compiled a hand-
book of miscellaneous medical lore gathered from local written
and oral sources and from the foreign traditions he had encoun-
tered during his civil career.[52] His book was an eclectic collection
of trivia, and in the preface to his sons Marcellus claimed that he
offered them his scholarship "so that it can demonstrate to you
cures and whatever else is necessary, without the assistance of a
doctor."

Such a claim can be misinterpreted, because Marcellus was not
intending that people read his book, find the appropriate remedies, and then treat themselves. Marcellus was very clear on this
point and carefully included, in both the preface and in the poem
at the conclusion, a warning against preparing these medicines
"without a doctor," since then something could too easily go

47. Above, p. 76, and below, p. 304.
48. Thevenot (1950), and above, pp. 71–72.
49. *Pan. lat.* VIII(5).5.3, for "praestantes scientia medici"—significantly, a
comparison with the emperor. Note also Ausonius *prof.* 26.1–6, for the special
skills of teachers.
50. Ausonius *parent.* 1.13–14.
51. Matthews (1971) 1083–7.
52. Marcellus *praef.*2 (p. 1 Helmreich), for his written and local sources; *de
medicamentis* 29.8, for a cure purchased from an African woman at Rome; and
Fleuriot (1974), for Celtic incantations.

wrong: "Take care lest you make a mistake, lest clumsy preparation by a healer turn what has been offered for relief into a death-
warrant; instead, use doctors . . . skilled by the greatest experience."[53] Rather than making his knowledge accessible to everyone
indiscriminately, Marcellus had handed it down to his sons, who
would first need another doctor to teach them to perform the procedures correctly before they could use these cures to benefit others. Marcellus' accumulated wisdom was to be kept strictly within
his family, and to be dispensed only by his sons.

This private knowledge derived from books and shrines had
important implications for the definition and distribution of authority. With their unique access to esoteric knowledge, men such
as teachers, doctors, and priests acquired positions of prominence
in local society and sometimes also in the imperial administration;
they were able to convert their special knowledge or skills into
forms of patronage, making other men dependent upon them.
Some helped people in legal cases; others promoted their students into the imperial administration.[54] Marcellus had been another product of the Gallic schools, and by transmitting this medical knowledge as an exclusive legacy to his sons, he clearly was
also attempting to ensure their continued prominence in local society, if not their promotion into imperial magistracies. Martin, in
contrast, was a different sort of teacher and doctor, because he
seems to have had little use for either books or shrines. Instead he
brought men's aspirations and desires to focus directly on himself
and, through himself, on the God he represented.[55]

Before Martin became bishop he was already given credit for
raising two men from the dead. According to the account of Sulpicius, Martin had not resorted to any shrines, potions, herbs, or
chants; he had merely prayed that "the power of the Lord" be successful. One of these men was later able to describe his brief encounter with death. He claimed that when he was led before the
tribunal in heaven, two angels had only to mention to the judge
that Martin was praying for this man for him to be led back to

53. de medicamentis, carmen 12–15 (p. 382 Helmreich); and cf. praef. 5 (p. 2 Helmreich).
54. Ausonius prof. 1.9–11, 2.15–18.
55. Rousselle (1976) is an important survey and interpretation of Martin's
role as a "doctor," although with too heavy an emphasis on psychological factors
such as psychosomatic diseases and anxieties and not enough concern for social
relationships.

life.[56] The implication was obvious: Martin had direct contact with divine power that was independent of either books or shrines. When he cured people, they concentrated directly on Martin himself; as the other man was being brought back to life, "his feeble eyes were on the face of Martin."[57]

Some of Martin's most notable—and outrageous—actions as bishop involved making this point explicit. Each time he found a place that was sanctified by a pagan cult, he exposed the falseness of the claim by insisting that, as on one occasion, "there is nothing religious in a tree trunk," and then replacing the discredited (and often demolished) shrine with a Christian foundation of his own.[58] As much as these foundations contributed to, for example, the geographical spread of churches or the growth of monasticism,[59] their further significance is that Martin replaced the communities organized around pagan shrines with different communities composed of new Christians or new monks, all of whom recognized his authority.

Martin had a similar atittude toward books. From the beginning, the Bible and supplementary writings had been central to the teaching of Christianity. Martin himself was not hostile to these books, because although an "illiterate man," he was reputed for his understanding of the Scriptures, and in the monasteries he founded he encouraged young monks to copy texts.[60] But Martin remains one of the more notable figures in the early church who have left no writings of their own. According to one of his disciples, Martin "detested the empty trappings of speech and ornaments of words."[61] His message was revealed not so much in his sayings or his writings as in his behavior; instead of teaching the Scriptures, Martin acted them out. Sulpicius emphasized this point in his writings about Martin: "Truly that disciple of Christ, by imitating the miracles performed by the Savior, showed Christ also working in him." Hence, to be sceptical of the miracles of Martin was also to disbelieve the teachings of the Scriptures: "He who does not believe that Martin accomplished such deeds, sim-

56. *VMart*. 7.6. For Martin himself as a "judge," see *Dial*. III.6.2; and for the later connection between healing and judgment, see below, pp. 272–274.

57. *VMart*. 8.3.     58. *VMart*. 13.2, 9.

59. Griffe (1961), and Stancliffe (1979).

60. *VMart*. 10.6, 25.6–8.

61. *Dial*. I.27.3, with Fontaine (1967–1969) I, 65: "Martin apparaît dans la *Vita* comme un homme qui parle très peu et qui agit sans cesse."

ply does not believe that Christ uttered such words."[62] Martin was a man of action and prayer; according to one scholar, whenever we see Martin, "he is in motion."[63] In contrast to the apparent rigidity of the written word and the fixity of shrines, Martin paid "house calls," taking his healing power with him and acting out the biblical teachings.

The miracles of Martin were thus not disruptions of the natural order, but demonstrations of the essential message of the Bible. A woman is healed after touching Martin's cloak: it was "just like the woman mentioned in the Gospel." Martin has conversations with various demons: such behavior was a fulfillment of the Scriptures.[64] Occasionally Martin did preach to people, but most often they responded to Christianity after one of his visible miracles. In this sense conversion was a result of "seeing" rather than of "hearing": "After seeing this miracle the man believed that Jesus was Lord."[65] Martin's miraculous displays of divine power were always associated with the preaching of the Bible, and as a result people thought that he had a direct connection to the divine world; one woman said to him, "We know that you are a friend of God."[66] And when people converted, it was not to Christianity but to "the God of Martin."[67]

Martin's career illustrates how new men could acquire authority, but within traditional structures and by means of conventional idioms. Martin did not criticize or compete directly with teachers and doctors; in fact, during one of his miracles, his cure for the eye disease of Paulinus of Nola, he perhaps used the techniques and implements of a traditional cure.[68] Similarly, although Martin visited the court of Valentinian at Trier while Ausonius was living there as tutor for Gratian, they apparently never met, or at least made no mention of each other, presumably because they had nothing in common. Instead, by minimizing or discrediting the sources from which doctors and teachers drew their authority, Martin was able to replace these men with himself and with others like him. The transformation did not consist in exchanging a religion organized around natural shrines for one focused on hu-

62. *Dial.* I.26.5, III.10.5.
63. Delehaye (1920) 101: "Il est en mouvement."
64. *Dial.* III.6.5, 9.3, and Fontaine (1967–1969) I, 163.
65. *VMart.* 17.4; cf. 14.7.        66. *Dial.* II.4.6; cf. III.9.2.
67. *VMart.* 14.7; cf. *Dial.* III.14.2.
68. *VMart.* 19.3–5, with Rousselle (1976) 1095–1100.

man agents,[69] but rather in replacing one group of influential men with another, although under the guise of conventional ideologies and personal relationships. Behind Martin's attacks on pagan shrines and his disregard for books we still sense continuity in the means by which men advertised and justified their local authority.

The use of traditional ideologies could perform many functions. In the case of Martin, they served to define and legitimate his position of prominence outside the Christian communities in which he was already a spiritual leader. Although Martin remained antagonistic to pagan society, through his appearance as an emperor, soldier, teacher, or doctor non-Christians were more easily able to recognize and concede his authority. One of Martin's "students," for instance, could therefore succinctly summarize his "conversion" in terms that were immediately comprehensible to himself and to others: "I left school and joined myself to the blessed man Martin"—by which he meant that he had acquired a new "teacher."[70]

Second, the use of traditional ideologies also made Christianity more acceptable and attractive in secular society. Within the next century, for instance, with the decline of the civil administration in Roman Gaul, municipal schools eventually disappeared and education survived largely in monastic and ecclesiastical schools. Churchmen became the new "teachers" in society at large, and "students" from these schools became highly desirable candidates as bishops.[71] This later development was possible only because of the activities of bishops such as Martin, who redirected the scope of traditional relationships without replacing them. Equally significantly, the position of bishops was put into proper perspective. Previously aristocrats had been accustomed to a tradition of service that allowed them to switch easily between office-holding and "retirement."[72] But holding an episcopal see was a lifetime position, and thus the aristocrats who became bishops in early medieval Gaul required the ideology of a lifetime service, such as that associated with emperors or teachers. And these local aristocrats lost nothing of their old status by joining the ecclesiastical

69. As Brown (1981) 124–6, argues.

70. *Dial.* I.26.8, II.1.1.

71. *VMart.* 10.9. See Prinz (1965) 59–62, on bishops produced by monasteries, in particular by Lérins; and Riché (1957), on municipal schools.

72. Matthews (1975) 9–12, on the ideology of *otium*; and Jones (1964) 377–90, for the rapid turnover in imperial magistracies.

hierarchy; in fact, they might even enhance it by acquiring a "military rank" that they could not obtain in secular society. In other words, this ideological symbiosis was a necessary prelude to the Christianization of Gallic society.

\*    \*    \*

The standing of Bishop Martin, however, seems to have been almost unique. Few other bishops in Gaul could imitate his example and, given the opposition to him from other bishops, perhaps even fewer wanted to follow his lead. It is important to keep in mind, first, that Martin represented only one possible type of fourth-century Gallic bishop, and second, that his career perhaps stood farther outside the mainstream of the development of Christianity in Gaul than modern historians usually care to admit. His cult, in contrast, was at the center: for the supreme irony is that books about St. Martin propagated his fame over the entire Mediterranean world, and his tomb at Tours became the most important shrine in early medieval Gaul. Since the cult of St. Martin will become central to our later discussion of sixth-century Gaul, it is important to investigate how its early development already indicated a distortion of Martin's own image of himself. Although during his lifetime Martin apparently initiated a prophetic movement involving the restoration of the pristine apostolic church,[73] after his death his defiance of the conventional forms of authority was gradually forgotten, and his cult was commemorated instead as legitimation for their survival and expansion.

Any historical account must consider the literary traditions about the life of Martin, the image of St. Martin, and the confusion between the two. Virtually all we know about the activities of Martin comes to us through the writings of Sulpicius Severus. Born into a respectable Gallic family, Sulpicius had become a prominent advocate and married into a consular family.[74] As a young man he had once made a pilgrimage to Tours in order to see Martin, already thinking too that the bishop's life might be an appropriate subject for his literary talents. Once he met Martin his hopes were confirmed: "I was overwhelmed by the authority of

73. *Dial.* II.5.2. On Martin's imitation of Old Testament prophets, see Fontaine (1963a); for the success of other fourth-century "prophets," see *VMart.* 23–24.3.

74. Paulinus of Nola *Ep.* 5.5; Gennadius *de scriptor. eccles.* 19, "vir genere et litteris nobilis."

the man."[75] In their conversations Martin urged him to abandon the allurements of the world, and for an educated man such as Sulpicius, a conversion of that nature largely entailed selling his estates and rejecting his literary training. Hence, Sulpicius' account of Martin was also an attempt to turn the old classical heritage on its head. By insisting that although literary works describing the pagan classical heroes might lead to eternal fame, only belief in Christianity led to eternal life,[76] Sulpicius seems to have been trying as much to convince himself of the truth of his new convictions as to make a statement about the intrinsic shallowness of classical literature.

Sulpicius also indicted himself, however, because his literary contrivances are in places so polished as to make readers suspicious of their historical accuracy. Throughout the Mediterranean world people were reading the *Vita* only a few years after it was written, and at Rome it became a best-seller.[77] According to Sulpicius, even Martin thought highly of the *Vita*, because in a dream he had seen the bishop gently smiling as he held out a copy in his hand.[78]

The smile was probably a bemused one, however, because it was precisely through the writings and attitudes of Martin's supporters that the bishop's apparent antagonism to secular society, for instance, was safely sanitized for further use within Gallic monasticism. Under the influence of Martin Sulpicius had founded his own monastery in southern Gaul. But this community, however strict its rules, resembled most of all an aristocratic spa, in which "learned men" spent their time in discussions similar to those they had once enjoyed on their estates. In contrast to the practice of Martin, these monks even allowed laymen who had been civil magistrates to listen to their discussions.[79]

The monasticism of Paulinus of Nola provides another example of how Martin's initiative was transformed after his death. Like his friend Sulpicius, Paulinus was an admirer of Martin. But Paulinus represented still another version of conversion to as-

75. *VMart.* 25.1, 3.
76. *VMart.* 1.4.
77. *Dial.* I.23.3–7. In Campania Paulinus of Nola "recited" it to his visitors (*Ep.* 29.14); and see Dekkers (1953) 203–4, for possible Greek translations.
78. *Ep.* 2.3.
79. *Dial.* III.1.7, 2.1, "viri sancti et diserti." with Fontaine (1967–1969) I, 137–9, and (1972). For Martin's contrasting attitude, see *Dial.* I.25.6–7.

ceticism, one that followed more closely the advice of Jerome than the example of Martin.[80] Martin had wanted to live his ascetic life in an isolated "desert," on an island or away from cities; Paulinus lived in a "garden."[81] Paulinus sold his possessions; Martin did not demand the same of his disciples.[82] Martin's aggressive asceticism led to active interference in pagan society; Paulinus was apparently little concerned about pagans or even other Christians who were not ascetics like himself. Paulinus provided a model of monasticism somewhere between the urban setting familiar to clergy and the isolation so dear to Martin, a rural monasticism that again closely resembled the traditional aristocratic ideal of the life of leisure.[83] Both men considered Christianity a lifetime commitment, but whereas Martin stressed that it involved full-time "military service," Paulinus was content to make it more of a full-time "retirement."

Paulinus' version of monasticism still, however, retained a military idiom, and in one of the first letters he wrote to Sulpicius he bluntly reminded him that he too was "a soldier of Christ."[84] Of course, some aspects of this fusion were not very appealing. Paulinus of Nola once found that the army stew prepared by another monk who had previously been a soldier was so repellent to his "senatorial fastidiousness" that it was the finest incentive to fasting he had ever tasted![85] More significantly, however attractive or distasteful this military ideology may have been to aristocrats such as Paulinus and Sulpicius, it too had been transformed into an emphasis, not on continual skirmishes, but on holding the frontiers: now monastic communities could be seen as simply "army camps of God."[86]

In short, the legacy of Martin transmitted to the early medieval church did not precisely reflect Martin's own image of himself. As with other prophetic movements the consolidation of the group after the death of the prophet was far more difficult than the initial formation of the community under the inspiration of the living prophet.[87] During the fifth and sixth centuries, although the

80. Rousselle-Esteve (1971); and see Prinz (1965) 88–94, for another contrast between "Rhone monasticism" and "Martinian monasticism."
81. Paulinus of Nola *Ep.* 11.14.
82. Cf. *Dial.* III.15.2, on Brictio.
83. Rousselle-Esteve (1971) 94: "un ascétisme champêtre."
84. *Ep.* 1.9.    85. Paulinus of Nola *Ep.* 23.6.
86. Hilary of Arles *Sermo de vita Honorati* 16, 20.
87. See Gager (1975) 67–76.

information still came from the writings of Sulpicius, the emphasis was less on Martin the iconoclastic innovator and prophet, but more on St. Martin the ascetic wonder-worker, monk, and bishop, known most of all for his acts of charity and his struggle with paganism; acting in the manner of Martin now meant healing lepers with a kiss.[88] In the church of St. Martin built at Tours in the later fifth century, Bishop Perpetuus had the walls covered with frescoes showing the miracles of Martin, which proved that he had been, and was still, a "doctor" with a genuine patent medicine for people.[89] Perhaps these frescoes displayed the same cycle of miracles that Bishop Gregory of Tours had painted on the walls of the cathedral at Tours a century later, a cycle stressing the charitable behavior and the militant antipaganism of Martin.[90] By comparison, Martin's more stridently apocalyptic prophecies about the end of the world came under quick criticism from contemporaries,[91] and in some cases, they disappeared from the manuscript traditions of the works of Sulpicius.[92]

Not only was the cult of St. Martin transmitted in books, it also focused on a holy shrine, the tomb of the saint located in the proper city, Tours, and at the exact spot that, according to later traditions, had been selected by divine intervention.[93] The result of both developments was to tie the cult of St. Martin to specific canonical writings and to specific shrines. Although over the next two centuries the cult was expanded and modified, the process was closely linked to the foundation of more shrines and to the composition of more books and poems, which were often revised versions of the writings of Sulpicius. In these ways the Christian church was able to stabilize its new prominence in Gallic society.

Another factor that modified the original intentions of Martin was the veneration for other shrines and relics that united such

88. *Vita [Patrum Iurensium] Romani* 15. Fontaine (1976) is a fine study of "the idea of Martin" through the early seventh century; Leclercq (1961) and Rosenwein (1978) discuss the image of St. Martin in medieval hagiography.

89. Paulinus of Périgueux *de orantibus* 23; cf. below, p. 168.

90. Fortunatus *Carm.* X.6.93–132. Note also Gregory of Tours *VM* 4.26, for St. Martin introducing himself in the sixth century as *miles Christi*.

91. Jerome *Comm. in Ezechielem* XI.36 (*PL* 25.339); cf. Gelasius(?), *Ep.* 42.8, "opuscula Posthumiani et Galli apocrypha" (ed. Thiel [1867] 467).

92. Delehaye (1920) 8–18. In their verse versions of Sulpicius' writings about Martin, neither Paulinus of Périgueux nor Fortunatus included *VMart.* 24.1–3 or *Dial.* II.14.1–4: see Chase (1932).

93. Gregory of Tours *HF* I.48, for the feud between Tours and Poitiers over the body of St. Martin.

men as Sulpicius and Paulinus of Nola.[94] Although the "pro-phetic" tendencies of Martin survived into later centuries and men continued to complain about religious cults that emphasized holy shrines, relics, and books, now this criticism was directed, not against paganism, but against Christian relic cults. In the early fifth century some of these complaints were expressed by a priest named Vigilantius, who was from southern Gaul (where he supposedly kept a tavern at the foot of the Pyrenees),[95] and who was (probably) an acquaintance of both Sulpicius Severus and Paulinus of Nola.[96] After returning from a pilgrimage to the East he began to criticize activities that were already common in Gaul, in particular the adoration of relics and the holy dust of martyrs; according to him, Christians who venerated relics were simply "ashmongers."[97] Given the provenance of Vigilantius his complaints may well have been directed against the recently expanded cult of St. Saturninus of Toulouse,[98] but the essential point is that they found a response among other people. Even some bishops supported him,[99] although others did not. Instead his opponents wrote to Jerome at Bethlehem, complaining that their parishes had been "stained" by proximity to Vigilantius.

Jerome wrote his response in one night, although the hastiness did not prevent him from producing yet another of his caustic, but sometimes silly, tracts: perhaps, he claimed, Vigilantius was worried that increased fasting and sobriety among the Gauls would ruin his tavern business![100] But most significantly, Jerome now represented a version of Christianity that located its meaning and authority in specific places, tangible objects, regulated ceremonies, and a limited number of holy books. Vigilantius had questioned all these assumptions about the authority of Christianity. Using an apocryphal book to support his arguments, he had claimed that the excessive veneration of shrines made it appear that martyrs and apostles were confined to their tombs and were therefore unable to pray for people in the presence of the Lord; that the Christian church had simply taken over pagan cere-

94. Paulinus of Nola *Ep.* 32.6–7.

95. Jerome *contra Vigilantium* 1, "caupo Calagurritanus"; later he became a priest at Barcelona: Gennadius *de scriptor. eccles.* 35.

96. If he can be identified with the courier Vigilantius mentioned in Paulinus of Nola *Ep.* 5.11.

97. Jerome *Ep.* 109.1.        98. Griffe (1964–1966) III, 226–30.

99. Jerome *contra Vigilantium* 2, *Ep.* 109.2.

100. *Contra Vigilantium* 13; cf. 4, where Jerome accuses Vigilantius of being a descendant of bandits.

monies in its veneration of relics; and that the churches dedicated to martyrs did not deserve such respect.[101] He also criticized the growth of a form of asceticism that preserved only diluted military overtones: "This is not to fight but to run away. Stand in the line of battle, put on your armor and resist your foes, so that after you conquer you may wear the crown."[102]

In his reply Jerome defined for his correspondents in Gaul a version of Christianity that was unlike the "prophetic" perspective of Vigilantius[103]—or of Martin. In it monasticism had become a way of elevating aristocratic retirement into Christian respectability, and true authority in the church was derived exclusively from relics, designated shrines, and canonical books. A churchman in the later fifth century left no room for argument: "The bodies of the saints and especially the relics of the blessed martyrs are to be honored as if they were the actual remains of Christ, and churches named after them are to be approached with a pious reverence and a faithful devotion, just as people approach the holy places belonging to the divine cult. If anyone thinks differently, he is to be considered a Vigilantian and not a Christian."[104] Such a "stabilized" Christianity had far-reaching consequences for the standing of its own priests, because when more information becomes again available we can see how the authority of bishops, the representatives of the power inherent in these shrines, relics, and books, has increased immeasurably. Without the recommendation of a bishop, for instance, a prophetess, no matter how useful her prophecies, might easily be stoned or drowned by her fellow citizens.[105] In the later sixth century "pseudoprophets" had even less chance of success. A man who arrived at Tours and then Paris carrying a cross, holy oil, and relics and tried to celebrate an alternative liturgy was locked up; a self-proclaimed miracle worker at Tours who claimed to have direct contact with St. Peter and St. Paul was promptly run out of town.[106] A man from Bourges who dressed in skins, began to prophesy the future, and finally claimed that he was Christ and a woman was his sister

101. *Contra Vigilantium* 4, 6–8, 10; note also Innocent I *Ep.* 6.13, dated to early 405, in which the pope tells Bishop Exsuperius of Toulouse which books are properly included in the Canon.

102. *Contra Vigilantium* 16.

103. Vigilantius supposedly wrote "secundam visionem Danielis": Gennadius *de scriptor. eccles.* 35.

104. [Gennadius of Marseille] *Liber eccles. dogmatum* 39, written c. 470/472.

105. *Vita Genovefe virgine* 12–13; cf. *Vita Hilarii* 17.

106. Gregory of Tours *HF* IX.6

Mary eventually acquired the support of over three thousand people, including some bishops, and began to announce his arrival in towns by sending ahead naked messagers. But one bishop was not impressed; he simply hired thugs who murdered "Christ" and tortured "Mary."[107] We can well wonder how much support there would have been in the fifth and sixth centuries for a Martin of Tours, yet another itinerant prophet who worked wonders, foretold the future, conversed with St. Peter and St. Paul,[108] dressed in shaggy clothes, and challenged holy (even if pagan) shrines.

The subsequently enhanced role of the church in society was, however, largely due to the fact that Martin, and perhaps other bishops and monks like him, seemed to dispense entirely with books and shrines. Eventually, however, the authority of these new leaders was conceptualized in terms of traditional relationships and ideologies, with the result that bishops and abbots could claim the authority and fill the functions of doctors, teachers, and even emperors. Sulpicius made this substitution explicit when he described Martin's funeral. This particular ceremony owed much to the ritual surrounding the arrival of an emperor into a city, as Sulpicius himself pointed out: "Let this spectacle be compared not with the pomp of a secular funeral but with that of a triumph."[109] As we have seen in earlier chapters, these imperial ceremonies essentially celebrated an emperor's presence in a specific place, even though at the same time they insisted that his power was not limited only to that spot. Martin's funeral ceremony had a slightly different implication. Whatever his significance for the development of Christianity in Gaul, in order for the church to consolidate its position after his death it could not permit a repeat performance. Hence the funeral ceremony for Martin also marked the arrival of St. Martin at Tours—where he had come to stay. In early Merovingian Gaul most of the personal appearances of St. Martin would be inside churches during the celebration of the liturgy, and people would rarely again see him "in motion." In this way Martin had been "put in his place," and it will be the cult of St. Martin, as it was filtered through specific books and focused around fixed shrines, that could be influential throughout early medieval Gaul.

107. HF X.25.        108. Dial. II.13.6.
109. Ep. 2.17, 3.18–21, with Antin (1964).

# CHAPTER 7

# The Transformation
# of the Aristocracy
# in the Fifth Century

Before Christianity could offer itself as a comprehensive system of beliefs that would be attractive to everyone, and in particular to local aristocrats, it had to expand its own limited structure and ideology. Although we saw in the previous chapter how a "prophetic" movement encouraged the employment of secular ideologies in a Christian context, the prophet himself had been an outsider to Gallic society. Martin had not been an aristocrat, and his position of authority had not been defined in terms of any specifically aristocratic values (except to the extent that local aristocrats may also have been doctors or teachers). On the other hand, once Christianity, and particularly its ecclesiastical hierarchy, took over some aspects of secular idioms, it became more appealing to local aristocrats who had lost other options for acquiring prestige. Eventually Christianity came to assimilate aristocratic values too, with the result that the conversion of the Gallic aristocracy in the fifth century can more properly be seen as the transformation of Christianity in order to conform with existing aristocratic structures of authority and ideologies of prestige.

Information about the relationship between Christianity and the Gallic aristocracy is fragmentary and disconnected during this period, and it illuminates only highlights of a long transition. In order to illustrate aspects of the two processes mentioned in the introduction to this group of chapters, let us concentrate on two well-documented careers. The first process is the expanded attractiveness of Christianity. Germanus of Auxerre is a good example of a local aristocrat who enhanced his own influence by becoming a bishop during the first half of the fifth century. His career, however, not only exemplified, but also contributed to the process, because his life, as presented in a subsequent *Vita*, provided a model for other local aristocrats. The second process is the contraction and redefinition of the options available to local aristocrats for maintaining their prestige and authority. Paulinus of Pella is a good example of a man who was stripped of his traditional bearings by the effects of both barbarian invasions and the withdrawal of the Roman administration. But although he did not have sufficient flexibility (or opportunity) to become a cleric, he did find in the Christian church satisfaction for his aristocratic dignity even as a layman.

*       *       *

Born in the later fourth century to a prominent family in Auxerre, Germanus was first educated in Gallic schools and then went to Rome to study law as a prelude to service within the imperial bureaucracy.[1] Because his career started in the very early fifth century before the contraction of the western empire took away many of the lower administrative posts in which men could begin their careers, he was able to become an advocate, make a successful marriage, serve as a military commander, and finally be promoted to a provincial governorship. Thus far Germanus had fulfilled most of the expected ideals of the Gallic aristocracy. But the next step of his career was, perhaps, unexpected, because (probably) in 415 he was suddenly acclaimed as bishop of his home town.[2]

Yet Germanus lost none of his local authority. Previously he had been an influential man because of his family connections,

1. The most important source is Constantius *Vita Germani* (hereafter in this chapter *VGerm.*); later literary sources about Germanus are conveniently collected in Duru (1850–1863). Levison (1904) is still an essential discussion, as is the collection of essays in *Saint Germain d'Auxerre et son temps* (Auxerre, 1950). For the family's local prominence, see *Gesta pont. Autissiod.* 7 (ed. Duru [1850–1863] I, 317–18), a list of the estates Germanus inherited from his father and gave to his church.

2. A length of thirty years for Germanus' episcopacy is given in a seventh- or eighth-century Gallic liturgy (quoted in Levison [1904] 150), and in the *Gesta pont. Autissiod.* 7. Thompson (1957) and Grosjean (1957) 180–5, date Germanus' death to 445 and hence his tenure as bishop to 415–445 (although Thompson [1977] 311 n. 35, withdraws his arguments for this chronology); Borius (1965) 78–79, prefers 418–448 as the dates for his episcopate; Mathisen (1981b) argues that Germanus died in 446.

his wealth, and his success within the imperial administration. Now his newly acquired spiritual powers allowed him to heal people, resolve feuds, even cure roosters.[3] Because Germanus was successful in his own community, others also requested his assistance. Once, in 429, Germanus and Bishop Lupus of Troyes (another local aristocrat who had become an ascetic bishop) traveled to Britain in response to an appeal for aid against Pelagianism.[4] But while they were there, Picts and Saxons attacked. Previously in times of crisis the people of Britain had appealed to the imperial court or, failing that, to a local magistrate or soldier; this time they appealed to the bishops. In this case they made a wise choice, because in his earlier secular career Germanus had been a general. Hence, his arrival offered much encouragement, and his presence, along with his strategy, ensured the success of the British army.

Germanus' authority also plainly extended beyond strictly ecclesiastical matters. During the middle 430s and again in 445 the citizens of Auxerre asked Germanus for assistance with tax assessments and barbarian settlements. On both journeys even imperial officials were eager to recognize the prominence of the bishop. In the first instance Germanus traveled to Arles to visit the prefect of the Gauls who, typically conscious of making friends with all the right people, wanted to become acquainted with "a man who was famous for his powers."[5] And in 445 Germanus visited the imperial court at Ravenna where the emperor, his mother, and the court officials all competed with each other to honor him.

In one sense the career of Germanus is therefore comparable to the careers of other Gallic aristocrats who had been successful in obtaining wider prestige and influence. His rhetorical training was now used in preaching and debating, and his legal knowledge qualified him to act as a judge and arbitrator.[6] Although a bishop, he was also a "general" for his monks,[7] and he had even commanded an army in Britain. Indeed, the final irony is that this

---

3. *VGerm.* 7–8, 10–11; for resolution of feuds, see Sidonius *Ep.* VI.4.

4. *VGerm.* 12, and Prosper Tiro *Epit.* s.a. 429 (*Chron. Min.* I, p. 472), with the discussions of Levison (1904) 118–29, and dePlinval (1950).

5. *VGerm.* 24.

6. As already noted by Constantius *VGerm.* 1. See also *Vita Hilarii* 14, and Heinzelmann (1976) 118–22, on the survival and importance of classical rhetoric in Christian preaching.

7. *VGerm.* 4, 9.

small-town bishop would die at Ravenna, presenting a petition before an imperial court that was going out of its way to honor him. No Gallic aristocrat could have asked for more.

One further notable characteristic of Germanus' authority was his willingness to travel and make himself accessible. Because they were ready to assist people on the spot, bishops expanded their influence far beyond their local communities. Germanus' trip to Britain, for example, provides a vivid contrast to the attitude of the imperial court, which, as we have seen, was inclined to abandon such outlying regions of the empire.[8] As a consequence, the imperial idiom of authority was now applied to bishops. At each city that Germanus visited, for instance, he was hailed in the same fashion that emperors had once been, as "a man who had been expected for a long time."[9] Similarly, just as once the emperors' "footprints" had been commemorated, so now the tracks of Germanus were marked with shrines.[10] This emphasis on the imperial nature of Germanus' presence led to another telling irony, in that the bishop's arrival was now received at Ravenna with pleasure by the imperial court.[11]

As an aristocrat whose career culminated with a bishopric, Germanus is an early forerunner of a medieval bishop. But as such his career also raises obvious historical problems. Not only do the motivations behind his move into an episcopal role elude us; but because most of our information about him comes from a *Vita* written a generation after his death—as well as shortly after the withdrawal of the Roman administration from Gaul—we might readily claim that the author, Constantius, was in fact describing only an ideal aristocratic bishop of the later fifth century and was not much concerned about the historical reliability of his account, and that he was more interested in teaching his audience what a bishop ought to be like in the later fifth century than in accurately narrating the events of Germanus' life.[12]

The circumstances leading to the composition and dissemina-

8. Germanus may have visited Britain again in the early 440s: cf. *VGerm.* 25–27, with Grosjean (1957) 174–80. See also Victricius *de laude sanctorum* 1, for his own visit to Britain.

9. *VGerm.* 35, "tandem diu expectatus excipitur"; and above, pp. 10, 35.

10. *VGerm.* 30; and above, p. 12.

11. *VGerm.* 35, "et adventus sui moras praevius accusabat affectus."

12. See Gessel (1970), who argues that the *Vita* is only homiletical preaching disguised as hagiography; also de Gaiffier (1970), for a sensitive discussion of hagiography and historiography.

tion of the *Vita* do indicate some ulterior motives. Although due to his celibacy Germanus had apparently contradicted aristocratic expectations by deliberately making himself into a man without a family, other men still wanted to be associated with his memory. Thus in the later fifth century the bishop of Lyon, a city once blessed by Germanus' presence, requested that his priest Constantius restore "the life of the holy bishop Germanus, which is shrouded in silence."[13] At first this *Vita* was kept within a small, local audience; then, at the insistence of the bishop of Auxerre, who had a vested interest in promoting the cult of one of his predecessors, it was circulated more widely.[14]

Of course, the motivations behind either the composition or the publication of a *Vita* need not affect the historicity of its contents. Yet is is also clear from the *Vita* itself that what Constantius wrote in his "unsophisticated style" was more than simply a narration of the life of a famous bishop; it was also another relic of Germanus. Constantius admitted that he was unable to record all the deeds and miracles of Germanus; hence, when a person read or heard the *Vita*, he would "see" through the little that was written down, and he would be impressed: "Just as when men gaze into the splendor of the sun, so that their eyes are dimmed . . . , so the weakness of my mind trembles before this huge surplus of praises and cannot cover them all in writing." The *Vita* may have narrated only selected highlights, but Constantius promised that they were adequate to advertise the divine powers of Germanus.[15]

In the West, "relics" such as this *Vita* would become the literary equivalents of Byzantine icons, in which, as the language that Constantius used made apparent, Christians could see through to another, divine existence. As we have noted with the supporters of Priscillian, the conception of daily life as a long, difficult journey was a common one, and Constantius used the idea by identifying Germanus' own life with an *iter*, an expedition that revealed the bishop's spiritual power as well as any of the journeys he had made on behalf of communities.[16] In this sense, then, Constantius has also turned the *Vita* into a homily, because the bishop's life-

13. Constantius *Ep. ad. Patientem* (*MGH*, SRM 7, p. 248), and *VGerm.* 23. Borius (1965) 44–46, dates the composition of the *Vita* to 475–480; on Constantius, see Levison (1904) 107–12, 142–3, and Bardy (1950).
14. Constantius *Ep. ad Censurium* (*MGH*, SRM 7, p. 249).
15. *VGerm.* praef., 46.
16. *VGerm.* 16, 20, 23.

long *iter* was also meant to provide inspiration. By looking into this *Vita*, Christians would be assured that, like Germanus, they too could find eternal peace at the end of their own "journeys."[17]

In short, this *Vita*, like most hagiography, already suggests the personal function of self-interest and the didactic purposes of instruction and edification that will become more apparent when we consider the cult of saints during the sixth century. Yet we still cannot simply dismiss its narrative as a later fabrication. First, because some aspects of Germanus' career were not necessarily those to which later fifth-century bishops wanted or were expected to aspire, the *Vita* may not have offered the most congenial model for the later church. Constantius had carefully emphasized that Germanus' spiritual power came from his asceticism. Once he became bishop, Germanus immediately transformed himself into an apparent "outsider" by setting aside his wealth, his wife, and his family, and by beginning a regimen of fasting that approached starvation.[18] According to the *Vita*, he became the "persecutor of his own body," and his life was now simply one long "death": "Among so many punishments, holy Germanus endured a long martyrdom." By means of these ascetic denials Germanus self-consciously turned himself into a mediator capable of channeling into daily life the security of a divine existence: "Although he dwelt in this world, he lived in a desert."[19] Given his ambiguous nature, it is not surprising that death did not change his role, or that his remains immediately became relics. After the imperial court had appropriated his cloak and his necklace reliquary, his body was sent back to Auxerre, where the citizens welcomed back "their very own patron."[20] Previously men had gone to Auxerre simply to look at Germanus; now they went there to worship, find sanctuary, or be healed at his shrine. In this sense Auxerre never lost its patron: "Although his body was buried, in his daily miracles and in his glory Germanus lives."[21]

17. *VGerm.* 41.
18. *VGerm.* 3, with Rousselle (1974), for a computation of the nutritional value of ascetic diets and their physcial consequences.
19. *VGerm.* 3–4, 6.
20. *VGerm.* 46. See also Gregory of Tours *HF* I.48, on St. Martin, and Heinzelmann (1976) 123–9, on the ideology of bishops as patrons.
21. *VGerm.* 46, "sepultus corpore, cotidianis miraculis vivit et gloria"; cf. *ILCV* 1117 = LeBlant II, no. 509, "hic positus vivit Concordius." For the cult of Germanus, see Gregory of Tours *HF* V.14, *GC* 40; Heiric of Auxerre *Miracula S. Germani* I.38–51 (ed. Duru [1850–1863] II, 133–9); and Louis (1950).

Thus Constantius' *Vita* seems in one respect to indicate the inability of Christianity to accommodate aristocratic values. Not yet, apparently, could men both be Christian bishops and live like secular aristocrats. Germanus may well have become, as did Martin of Tours, an influential man who could "loan out divine power";[22] but whereas Martin had had to integrate himself into Gallic society from the outside, Germanus felt compelled to dissociate himself from the inside of society. Neither model would have been very congenial to Gallic aristocrats who intended to keep authority away from foreigners such as Martin, but who also preferred not to trade in their conventional prerogatives as had Germanus.

The *Vita* could also be interpreted differently, however, because Constantius in addition stressed the dual functions of Germanus: only the bishop, for instance, could cross the Yonne River separating his monastery from Auxerre.[23] As a consequence Germanus had authority both before God and in the presence of imperial magistrates;[24] and if his asceticism had enhanced his spiritual power, it was also clear in the *Vita* that his secular authority depended largely upon such conventional attributes as rhetorical skills. And it was this modified interpretation of the *Vita*, which may have run counter to Germanus' own disposition as well as to Constantius' preferred perspective, that could be most attractive to Gallic aristocrats, as well as to other members of Christian communities. Thus in the later fifth century, for instance, a mere monk was belittled as a potential bishop because he could intercede successfully only with God.[25] Representation before both God and civil magistrates required, in addition, the skills still associated with local aristocrats.

A second argument that supports the trustworthiness of the *Vita* is that Germanus was not a unique example of the wider role bishops now played, and his actions did not provide the only precedent for the increasing authority of bishops. Elsewhere in Gaul other bishops asserted their authority either against or on behalf of the invading barbarians, especially in the middle of the century

22. *VGerm.* 4, "fenerator . . . virtutum."
23. *VGerm.* 6, "duplicem viam . . . instituens," 9, with the map in Borius (1965) 73. In the early fifth century such separation was common: see Lesne (1910) 81–83.
24. *VGerm.* 19, "et apud maiestatem divinam et inter mundi procellas."
25. Sidonius *Ep.* VII.9.9.

during "the time of the Huns."[26] When in 451 Attila and the Huns entered Gaul, one tradition recorded that Bishop Lupus protected Troyes by first conferring with Attila and then leading his congregation to safety in the hills.[27] According to another tradition Bishop Anianus of Orléans also protected his city from Attila. While the Huns were besieging the city walls, Anianus had the people pray until the Roman general Aetius arrived with his Visigothic reinforcements.[28] Another bishop, Aravatius of Tongres, even traveled to Rome to appeal for support against the Huns.[29] Other Gallic bishops who acted as ambassadors during this period include Orientius of Auch, who in the later 430s represented a Visigothic king before Roman generals, and Vivianus of Saintes, who forced another Visigothic king in the later 450s or early 460s to cancel a tax he had imposed on the city.[30]

In northwestern Spain the arrival of barbarians in 409 offered bishops there the similar opportunity of acting as brokers between them and Romans. In 431, when Sueves again did not honor their treaties, the inhabitants of Galicia sent a delegation led by Bishop Hydatius to the Roman general Aetius. Apparently their request was successful, because in the next year Aetius sent a count as an envoy to the Sueves. When this count left in 433, King Hemeric made another treaty with the Galicians, "with the assistance of bishops." Then Hemeric sent Bishop Symphosius as his envoy to the imperial court.[31]

These examples of bishops acting as protectors and ambassadors are admittedly selective ones, primarily as a result of the nature of the extant literary sources. Significantly, however, many of the cities mentioned were in regions that had become peripheral to the Roman administration by the mid-fifth century. The province of Galicia had been abandoned to the Sueves and Vandals; the lower Rhine was forgotten; Aquitania was settled by the Visigoths; and the central provinces of Lugdunensis II, III, and IV were first surrounded by Visigoths to the south and Alans, Franks, and

26. Gregory of Tours GC 71.

27. Vita Lupi 5–6. The composition of this Vita has been assigned to almost any time from the later fifth century on; for a customarily critical assessment of the reliability of the Vita, see B. Krusch, MGH, SRM 7, pp. 284–9.

28. Sidonius Ep. VIII.15, and Gregory of Tours HF II.7, with Loyen (1969).

29. Gregory of Tours HF II.5.

30. Vita Orientii 3; Vita Bibiani vel Viviani 4–6, with Lot (1929), and Courcelle (1964) 339–47.

31. Hydatius Chron. 96, 98, 100–1 (Chron. Min. II, p. 22).

Burgundians to the north and east, and then almost split in half by another settlement of Alans in 442. In these areas in particular bishops came to fill a more expanded role.

As we have seen in the life of Germanus, the authority of bishops in local affairs led on to their wider influence. In central Gaul and northwestern Spain, the transition may have been more easily accomplished because they had no competition. Imperial administrators had left or were ineffective, and more importantly, the old landed aristocracy had been reduced, either through deaths or because some had left to live elsewhere. One of the correspondents of Symmachus, for example, was a man named Protadius, who was probably a native of Trier, although he also owned an estate in southern Gaul. At the end of the fourth century, Protadius was interested in studying the early history of Roman Gaul and therefore requested books from Symmachus. But by 417 Protadius had settled in northern Italy, living near Pisa, where a small estate was his only compensation for his ancestral holdings.[32] Another Gallic aristocrat was likewise now living in Etruria, where he had fled after the capture of Toulouse.[33]

But at least these two were still alive. According to Salvian, in the 420s, after Trier had been sacked three times, only a few aristocrats survived. What particularly aroused Salvian's indignation, however, was that these aristocrats were acting like "madmen": "They have been demanding circus games from the emperors, as if that was the best cure for a destroyed city." The contrast with the behavior of bishops could hardly be greater, because according to Salvian these aristocrats were morally bankrupt, thinking that circus games, a public symbol of the old Roman grandeur, would be the solution for a devastated city.[34] In contrast, Germanus and other bishops like him were considered the best "remedies" for their towns. If other people in Gaul shared Salvian's outraged sensibilities, then they would naturally turn for assis-

---

32. Symmachus *Ep.* IV.18, 30; and Rutilius Namatianus *de reditu suo* I.551, with Stroheker (1948) no. 318.

33. Rutilius Namatianus *de reditu suo* I.495–6, with Stroheker (1948) no. 408.

34. Salvian *de gub. Dei* VI.85 This request may not have been as outrageous as Salvian claimed. Note *Pan. lat.* VII(6).22.5, in which the orator pointed out the huge circus theater at Trier as one "gift of the emperor's presence." Over a century later, when these aristocrats asked for new circus games at Trier, they may indirectly have been asking that an emperor come and revive the games in person—as in fact Majorian did at Arles in 461: see Sidonius *Ep.* I.11.10. For the transformation of Trier, see Ewig (1972).

tance to men such as bishops, who openly displayed their genuine concern.

Futhermore, the disintegration of the imperial administration and the settlement of barbarians who stood outside traditional ties of patronage had struck directly at some of the conventional prerogatives of local aristocrats. Some, such as Paulinus of Pella, had difficulty adapting. In the 450s, at the end of his life, Paulinus wrote a long autobiographical poem in which he set out not to commemorate his own splendid achievements, as famous Romans in the past had done, but rather to acknowledge how he had survived through the "long foreign journey" of his life with the aid of divine Providence.[35] In itself this introduction to his poem was an indication of how one Gallic aristocrat had changed his perspective. Instead of being concerned with handing on an account of his own eminence to his descendants, Paulinus passed his retirement in recalling for himself and for others his dependence on an almighty God.

Paulinus was born in 376 in the city of Pella, in Macedonia, where his father was vicar. Three years later the family returned to Bordeaux, where Paulinus met his grandfather Ausonius, who was consul that year. There Paulinus grew up as a typical son in an influential family, and he eventually married into another prominent family.[36] But when Paulinus was thirty his tranquil life was shattered. Not only did his father die, but more significantly, the barbarians crossed the Rhine into Gaul: "The enemy poured into the very bowels of the Roman kingdom."[37] The next decade was difficult for Paulinus and his family. When the Visigoths finally occupied Aquitania Paulinus seems to have received special respect, because not only did he not have to share his estate with a Goth, he also acquired a magistracy in the administration of a puppet emperor proclaimed by the king of the Visigoths. But after many of the Goths left for Spain, Paulinus was left with no protection, and he and his family had to abandon Bordeaux for Bazas. There they were besieged by both Goths and Alans, and only some private diplomacy by Paulinus saved the city. Looking back many years later Paulinus thought that this success had been the high point of his life, because thereafter he had lived at the

35. Paulinus of Pella *Eucharisticos* praef.1–2.
36. A typical background for a young Gallic aristocrat: cf. Hilary of Arles *Sermo de vita Honorati* 6, and Sidonius *Carm.* VII.171–206.
37. *Euch.* 235.

mercy of the barbarians. With his present life in ruins, he chose to remember only the past, "when my house was happy and prosperous . . . and when the display of my rank was very important, magnified and bolstered by deferential crowds of clients." To his own embarrassment he had to concede that once he had loved the life of an aristocrat.[38]

Paulinus' only consolation was his conversion to Christianity, because in 421 he had been baptized; at that moment, he later wrote, he had been happy again.[39] But the remainder of his life he described as an "eternal exile."[40] Most of his family died, and he moved to Marseille, in the one region of Gaul where, as another refugee put it, the Roman Empire was still alive.[41] When Paulinus wrote most of his poem in the early or middle 450s he had already lost possession of his townhouse and was living as "a penniless exile with no family." But by the time he published his poem in 459 his fortunes had changed.[42] In Aquitania a Goth who had presumably already occupied Paulinus' estate finally sent him some payment. Now, Paulinus claimed, he was able to avoid any further insult to his pride—a final concern that continued to mark him out as a conventional Gallic aristocrat.[43]

In Christianity, however, Paulinus had also been able to find enough of his traditional values to remain content for all these years of exile, because with the gradual accommodation of more groups of people the church itself had become the repository of true Roman culture. In his poem Paulinus reflected about the education he had received as a young boy; as he looked back, it was the old Roman "discipline" and, even more, "antiquarianism," that had been particularly beneficial for him and that still made his old age tolerable. Both attributes were significant in their evocation of that reverence for the past that had always been a significant component in Roman education and society.[44] Although Paulinus mentioned them primarily to lament their decline, he had become a more devout Christian specifically in order "to preserve that ancient custom that once had been maintained

---

38. *Euch.* 435–9.     39. *Euch.* 477.     40. *Euch.* 491–2.
41. Salvian *de gub. Dei* IV.30. See Prinz (1965) 47–58, for other Gauls fleeing to Provence, and Griffe (1964–1966) II, 28, and III, 341–4, for Marseille as a refugee center.
42. Moussy (1974) 17–18, for the dates.     43. *Euch.* 575–81.
44. *Euch.* 68–71, with Dürig (1952), on *disciplina*, and Stevens (1933) 14–18, on *vetustas*.

by the tradition of ancestors and that now our church safeguards and upholds."[45] Even the Roman past had been safely absorbed into the Christian church.

Of course, not all the great aristocratic families had fallen on such hard times as Paulinus and his family,[46] because the traditions and influence of the Gallic and Spanish aristocracies continued through the Middle Ages. The Ebro River valley in northern Spain seems, as we have seen, to have remained a bastion of local aristocrats at least until the permanent arrival of the Visigoths in the later 460s, and even in later fifth-century Galicia local aristocrats served as ambassadors to the court of the Visigothic king.[47] In northern and western Gaul the situation of the local aristocracy during the fifth century seems more complex, largely because we have more information concerning it. Although the withdrawal of the imperial court and administration led, as we have also seen, to the reemergence of traditional patterns of local authority, in which aristocrats organized and defended the residents of their regions, the establishment of barbarian kingdoms allowed aristocrats to exploit the courts of barbarian kings to their own advantage. Some served as advisers or legal experts; others acted as ambassadors for their communities before "kings dressed in skins" as well as before "emperors dressed in purple."[48] Still others used their familiarity with classical culture to establish links; the Gallic aristocrat Avitus, for instance, taught the poetry of Virgil to King Theodoric II, who later supported him as emperor.[49] Another Visigothic king in the early fifth century was supposed to have said that because his barbarians were too ill-mannered to obey laws, he had changed his mind about replacing the Roman Empire with a Gothic empire and now intended instead to restore the Roman name with his army.[50]

In central and southeastern Gaul, which were still nominally under direct imperial administration, the landowning aristocracy

45. *Euch.* 465–7.

46. Although cf. *Poema coniugis ad uxorem* 17–24 (*CSEL* 30, p. 344), and *Carmen de providentia Dei* 57–62, 903–24.

47. Hydatius *Chron.* 219, 229 (*Chron. Min.* II, p. 33). In general, see Stroheker (1965) 76–87.

48. Sidonius *Ep.* VII.9.19, with Wormald (1976) 222–4.

49. Sidonius *Carm.* VII.495–8; below, p. 159.

50. Orosius VII.43.3–8, for the well-known remark by Athaulf; and see Wallace-Hadrill (1962) 25–48, on the essential transience of the Visigothic settlement in southwestern Gaul.

remained even more prominent. Men such as Avitus, while still private citizens, continued to represent their native cities before imperial magistrates.[51] After 418 a provincial assembly for the aristocrats of southern Gaul met at Arles, and throughout the fifth century aristocrats from families in southern and central Gaul monopolized the higher offices of the praetorian prefecture of the Gauls.[52] The Gallic aristocracy also formed an alliance of interests with Aetius, the general who dominated the western empire until the middle of the fifth century, which may have led to the military policy of defending Gaul while acquiescing to the loss of Africa to the Vandals.[53] In central and southeastern Gaul in particular, which had always been more Romanized than the north and the west, many local aristocrats retained their traditional influence and prestige. Thus one aristocrat returned to southern Gaul in 417 and confidently proclaimed that a "renaissance" of Rome's glory was imminent.[54]

Yet within the themes of the present study the point is that these old aristocrats were no longer unchallenged as the only local leaders. Barbarians had to be taken into account in regions dominated by their settlements and garrisons, and Christian bishops were available to act as ambassadors to these barbarian settlers, who also posed a religious problem because most were either pagans or heretical Arians. The settlement of barbarians who needed to be integrated into society, the withdrawal of the imperial administration (with which local aristocrats were accustomed to act as brokers) the inability of some local aristocrats to adapt to changing circumstances, and the assimilation of Christian bishops into traditional relationships and idioms of authority all contributed, as we have seen, to the rise of new men—in this case, bishops—to act as additional local leaders. Hence another strategy the old aristocracy could adopt to preserve its prominence was to move "sideways" into the Christian church. During the fifth century not only did the old aristocracy begin to convert to Christianity, it also, by a process we might call "lateral mobility," merged into the new elite of the ecclesiastical hierarchy. In the same way that it had once essentially absorbed the threat posed

51. Sidonius *Carm.* VII.207–14, and Loyen (1942) 37–39.
52. Sundwall (1915), 8–20, with a list of the prefects, 23–24.
53. Moss (1973). See also Twyman (1970), for the alliance of Aetius and the Gallic aristocracy against the imperial court and the Italian aristocracy.
54. Rutilius Namatianus *de reditu suo* I.140, with Matthews (1975) 327–51.

by the presence of an imperial court and administration by turning them to its own advantage, so the aristocracy also began to
assimilate itself with this new ecclesiastical elite of bishops.

Other local aristocrats followed the lead of Germanus and
Lupus and also became bishops. Until about the middle of the
fifth century the bishops of Tours, for instance, do not seem to
have come from aristocratic backgrounds. Litorius, bishop in the
mid-fourth century, and Brictio, bishop for the first half of the
fifth century, were both merely citizens of Tours, while Martin
was a monk from Pannonia. After the death of Brictio, however,
during the last half of the fifth century a sequence of three bishops followed who were all described as descendants of a senatorial family, and who were furthermore all related to each other.[55]
Tours was thus an early example of what would later be a common phenomenon, a see dominated by a particular family.[56]

By now, becoming a Christian was no disadvantage for an aristocrat, and becoming a bishop had positive advantages. As we
have seen in the case of Germanus, an aristocrat who became a
bishop lost little of what he might have expected to do and become through holding imperial magistracies. Excepting whatever
asceticism he might adopt, he could go on acting in the same way
as his noble ancestors had done. In the early 470s, for instance,
one man's qualifications for being selected as bishop included his
own pedigree, his wife's pedigree, his education, his past service
as an ambassador, and his generosity in financing the construction of a church. Another local aristocrat who became a bishop
rightly observed that such a man was now competent to serve either in the secular administration or in the ecclesiastical hierarchy.[57] And once a man became bishop, he could continue to fi-
nance the construction of buildings and monuments, either with
his own wealth or from donations made to his church;[58] the difference, of course, was that now these public monuments were usually churches and shrines rather than theaters or halls. And if the
bishop became famous enough, he might have monuments built

---

55. Gregory of Tours HF X.31, and Stroheker (1948) nos. 135, 295, 411.
56. Wieruszowski (1922) esp. 50–60, and below, Chapter 10. Heinzelmann
(1975) is a discussion of northern Gaul with wider implications. In Spain this
transformation is more difficult to trace: see Stroheker (1965) 83.
57. Sidonius Ep. VII.9.16–24; cf. IV.25.2.
58. Marrou (1970).

in his own honor, or he might become an appropriate subject for laudatory poems.[59]

This movement by the secular aristocracy into the ecclesiastical hierarchy was possible because the church had absorbed particular idioms of authority and prestige that not only defined the role of these aristocratic bishops, but also offered them an ideology appropriate to the realities of their new lifetime service. Although, as we will see in the next chapter, it was still possible for aristocrats from central and southern Gaul to serve in the imperial administration, this service had to precede any ecclesiastical service, because once ordained, a man was not expected to slip back into "retirement." Conversely, the ecclesiastical hierarchy took over secular aristocratic attitudes too; as we will see in the next chapter, aristocrats could enjoy many aspects of a conventional retirement while serving as bishops. More significantly yet, already in the early fifth century it had been made explicit that aristocrats lost none of their wider social prerogatives and prestige by becoming bishops. Not only could they go on acting like their noble ancestors who had lived with the possibility of serving in the central administration, they could also go on thinking like them, because the Christian church began to use, and redefine, the distinctions of status previously acquired exclusively from holding civil magistracies.

Honoratus of Arles, for example, was a Gallic aristocrat who in the early fifth century first founded a monastery at Lérins (which also became another center for refugees), and then served as bishop of Arles for a few years in the later 420s.[60] According to his successor Hilary, although after his death Honoratus served as a patron in heaven by presenting people's petitions directly to God, this role was only a natural result of the patronage he had already wielded as a bishop.[61] Honoratus had furthermore retained all his original secular prestige even after becoming a monk and then a bishop, because as he belittled the significance of Honoratus' family connections Hilary presented an entirely new definition of

59. *VGerm.* 46, for roads repaired in honor of Bishop Germanus; *Vita Hilarii* 15, 23, for the verses of Edesius on Bishop Hilary.

60. Hilary of Arles *Sermo de vita Honorati* 4, for his aristocratic family. For Honoratus' possible origin in northern Gaul, see Heinzelmann (1976) 76, although deVogüé (1978) and Valentin (1977) 76–77, leave the question open.

61. *Sermo* 31, 35, 39.

"nobility." "We are all one in Christ, and the peak of nobility is to be reckoned among the sons of God. We are not capable of adding any glory to the dignity of our earthly family except by renouncing it; for in heaven no one is more glorious than he who has rejected the ancestry of his fathers and chooses to be enrolled only as a descendant of Christ."[62] Other late antique writers echoed these new definitions.[63] But already in this example we can detect a significant transformation within the society and culture of late Roman Gaul. Now local aristocrats, by becoming Christians, could even enhance their "nobility" and their "dignity"; the values of the old aristocracy had become characteristic also of the new aristocracy of churchmen.

62. *Sermo* 4.
63. Alan Cameron (1968), and Heinzelmann (1976) 200–11.

CHAPTER 8

# Sidonius and the Rise
# of Relic Cults

When Sidonius was born in Lyon in about 430, southern and central Gaul were experiencing yet another revival of Roman authority. Over a century earlier, after the barbarian invasions of the
third century, Gaul had recovered so successfully that its aristocracy would make important contributions to the imperial administration during the fourth century. Then Gaul had been drawn
into the Roman Empire because an imperial court had come to the
Rhine frontier and attracted local aristocrats to its service. Now,
after the "thunderstorms of war"[1] during the early fifth century,
southern and central Gaul seemed to have emerged from under
the clouds of another crisis, and aristocrats from these regions not
only dominated virtually all the remaining administrative positions in their provinces, they could also still hope to serve elsewhere in the empire.

Sidonius grew up in this relatively peaceful central Gaul among
men who had neither faced the setbacks of Paulinus of Pella nor
been tormented with the self-doubts and religious traumas of a
refugee such as Salvian. Writing when Sidonius was a boy, even
Salvian had conceded the beauty and fertility of Aquitania: there
landowners possessed "an image of Paradise." But in his typically

---

Stevens (1933) is still the best book on Sidonius and his world; Loyen (1942)
and (1943) provide much detailed scholarship; Rousseau (1976) is a perceptive
essay on Sidonius' attitudes toward the classical heritage, monasticism, and the
Roman Empire. For many readers a translation of Sidonius' writings is essential,
and fortunately two fine ones, with useful notes and discussion, are available:
W. B. Anderson et al. (Loeb, 1936–1965), and A. Loyen (Budé, 1960–1970). In
this chapter references to the writings of Sidonius omit his name.

1. *Carm.* VII.215–16.

self-righteous way Salvian had also claimed that because Aquitania had avoided the destruction of northern Gaul, it was all the
more susceptible to immoralities.[2] The young Sidonius had probably never suffered the same anxieties as Salvian. He was raised
in a Christian family, but one that had also realized the by-now
traditional hopes of success in the imperial administration. Both
his grandfather and his father had served as prefect of the Gauls;
as a teenager Sidonius had therefore been privileged to attend official ceremonies, and years later he still remembered how close to
a consul he had once been allowed to stand.[3] As a young man Sidonius was all too aware of the prestige inherent in his family and
of his own dreams to rise beyond his local origins. As he wrote to
a friend years later, "For a man with your family it is as important
to cultivate your reputation as your estate."[4]

Sidonius' entire life reflected this early insulation, because
even though he eventually became a Christian bishop, in many
respects he also continued to live as an old-fashioned aristocrat;
like one of his aged friends who tried to hide his wrinkles by
dressing like a young boy,[5] Sidonius too sometimes seems to us to
have been deluding himself, unable to adapt his outdated enthusiasm for the Roman Empire and the classical heritage in an increasingly barbarian and Christian society. In fact, the attitudes of
Sidonius, whose writings are a major source of information for
later fifth-century Gaul, illustrate again the complexity and ambivalence of the times; the two important processes discussed in
the two previous chapters—the disruption of traditional aristocratic leadership and the translation of bishops' spiritual power
into more familiar, even if secular, idioms of authority—were mutually influential, but without necessarily becoming intertwined.
In the first section of this chapter let us briefly consider some of
the attitudes of Sidonius, in part to illustrate the coexistence (perhaps even confusion) of values; in part to review some of the traditional means by which local aristocrats had enhanced and advertised their prominence, specifically, service in the imperial
administration and knowledge of classical culture; and in part

2. Salvian *de gub. Dei* VII.8, 16–25. The Auvergne too had received refugees
from the aristocracy of northern Gaul during the fifth century: see Prinz (1965)
48.
3. *Ep.* VIII.6.5, with Stroheker (1948) nos. 20, 358.
4. *Ep.* I.6.3.
5. *Ep.* IV.13.

too, to show that even these factors now took on new meanings. The second section provides a counterpoint, since we also need to account for the expansion during this period of the Christian relic cults that would be so influential in the sixth century. Significantly, Sidonius himself provided little evidence relating to relic cults and the Christian idiom of holiness; as the final section shows, his hopes still lay in a classical and Roman past.

*     *     *

As one of the last Gauls to serve at an imperial court, Sidonius seems to sum up the positive attitudes toward the Roman Empire that Gallic aristocrats had developed since the later third century. He himself first acquired wider prominence on the basis of two qualities that had long been distinguishing criteria among the Gallic aristocracy, that is, family connections and rhetorical skills. In 455 the emperor at Rome had appointed a prominent aristocrat from the Auvergne named Avitus as general for Gaul, a move clearly intended to eliminate pressure from Avitus' friend King Theodoric II and his Visigoths. A few months later, when the emperor was killed at Rome, King Theodoric and other Gallic aristocrats urged Avitus to become emperor. Avitus agreed, and later in 455 he entered Italy.

Along with him went his son-in-law Sidonius, already appointed to a junior position in the imperial civil service. At the time, Sidonius was so pleased with his own success that he conveniently did not mention how other Gauls also seized this opportunity to serve at the imperial court of another emperor with intimate ties to Gaul.[6] At Rome, however, more honors awaited Sidonius. On the first day of 456 Avitus became the first consul from Gaul in thirty-five years.[7] To celebrate the occasion the young Sidonius was selected to deliver a panegyric. In it he clearly formulated the concern Gauls continued to feel for the Roman Empire in the middle of the fifth century. For over a generation Gallic aristocrats had considered themselves increasingly abandoned, left to control their own provinces to be sure, but still cut off from immediate access to an imperial court; to them, the empire seemed

---

6. E.g. Consentius of Narbonne (Stroheker [1948] no. 96); see also Mathisen (1979c) and (1981a).

7. Unless we accept the arguments of Twyman (1970), that Opilio, consul in 453 (*PLRE* II, p. 807), was also a Gaul.

to be turning into a mere "shadow" of its former self.[8] But now, in contrast to the end of the third century when an imperial court had eliminated the regimes of Gallic usurpers by moving to the Rhine frontier, Gallic aristocrats had seized the initiative to move their own imperial court to Rome. According to Sidonius, the revitalization of the Roman Empire was their goal: "The world, they say, lies captive in the captive city of Rome; the emperor is dead, and now the empire has its head here"—that is, in Gaul. More precisely, the Auvergne was now "the sole hope for the world," especially since Rome, in contrast, had had "weak knees": with these words Sidonius clearly revealed the raw sentiments of an inexperienced young man. He concluded his oration by having Jupiter present Avitus as the new emperor for Rome: "Behold, an older emperor will bring back youth to a Rome which [previous] child-emperors have made old."[9] As a result of the success of this oration Sidonius looked as though he himself would be one of the leading young men who would rejuvenate the empire, even more so after a statue of him was placed alongside those of other distinguished verse panegyrists in the Forum of Trajan.[10]

Within a few months, however, Avitus had been discredited as emperor, forced to flee to Gaul, and eventually defeated by Majorian, who became emperor in the West. Throughout this setback, as well as during a revolt of an obscure nature at Lyon, Sidonius retained his faith in the Roman Empire. A few years later when he spoke before Majorian, who with his army had besieged Lyon, he insisted upon the beneficial aspects of the presence of the emperor, even one who had assisted in the overthrow (and possibly death) of his father-in-law: "You come and bring with you all restoration."[11] Almost a decade later he traveled to Rome, and in 468 delivered another panegyric in honor of the emperor Anthemius' consulship. As a result of this oration, the emperor made him prefect of Rome; and when Sidonius finally left Rome a year later, he was even more pleased with himself, because having received the title of patrician he could feel that he had indeed raised the status of his family.[12] In ancestral tradition, rhetorical skills and service

8. *Carm.* VII.533, 540–1.
9. *Carm.* VII.148, 545, 556–8, 597–8.
10. *Carm.* VIII.7–10; *Ep.* IX.16.3, lines 21–28.
11. *Carm.* V.584–5. On the revolt at Lyon see Max (1979), and (although very speculative) Mathisen (1979b).
12. *Ep.* V.16.4.

in the central administration or at the imperial court were still potent ways of enhancing his own and his family's reputations.

The obvious blots on Sidonius' optimistic perspective, however, were the increasing power of the Visigothic and Burgundian kingdoms in Gaul and, still more disconcerting, the fact that the emperor in Italy was prepared to cede Gallic cities to them in order to ensure their loyalties. Such a policy, Sidonius thought, only deprived "men of noble birth," such as himself and his Gallic friends, of the possibility of serving in a Roman administration.[13] This trend was accelerated with the accession of Euric in 466. The new king of the Visigoths intended to assert his own independence; as a later historian observed, "Euric's object was to rule Gaul in his own right."[14] Some Gallic aristocrats may have made common cause with Euric, but Sidonius never wavered,[15] especially after he became bishop of Clermont (probably) in 470. By then Clermont alone remained outside Visigothic hegemony over Gaul south of the Loire River and west of the Rhone River. Supported by Bishop Sidonius, the city tried to survive on its own; but its resistance was in the end ineffective, not so much against the Visigoths as against the imperial court in Italy. In 475 the current emperor decided that the security of "the boundaries of the Italian empire" took precedence, and so exchanged with Euric control of the Auvergne for possession of Provence.[16]

Even Sidonius, finally, was disillusioned, and he complained bitterly to one of the Provençal bishops who had negotiated the treaty.[17] Much of his earlier optimism about the Roman Empire was now lost. Twenty years earlier, when he had first gone to Rome, he had recommended it to a Gallic friend as "the head of the universe, the mother-city of liberty."[18] In 474 he could still congratulate a friend upon becoming prefect of Rome, thereby surpassing his ancestors,[19] and he was even more pleased when his brother-in-law Ecdicius (a son of Avitus) was appointed general and patrician, as if in readiness for an invasion from Italy

13. *Ep.* III.8.2.
14. Jordanes *Getica* 45.237; contrast *Carm.* XXIII.70–71, for Sidonius' earlier hope that the king of the Visigoths (then Theodoric) might instead become "the pillar and savior of the Roman race."
15. *Ep.* I.7, for the conspiracy of Arvandus. Note Stevens (1933) 106, on Sidonius' reaction: "Loyalty to the imperial idea was still strong."
16. Ennodius *Vita Epiphani* 80, "Italici fines imperii."
17. *Ep.* VII.7.2–5.        18. *Ep.* I.6.2.        19. *Ep.* VIII.7.3.

against the Visigoths.[20] Instead, in the next year Ecdicius was recalled to Italy and stripped of his command. When Sidonius learned of this insult to his brother-in-law he could only urge him to come home to the Auvergne: "Be quick to withdraw your attendance from the dangerous intimacy of emperors, because the most experienced observers well compare their friendship to the nature of flames, which illuminate what is a little way off but consume that which comes within their reach."[21]

Sidonius' warning was unnecessary, because by 476 almost all the western empire, including Italy, was ruled by barbarian kings. But the significant consequence was the effect on the self-image of Sidonius, one of whose ideals had been crushed by the cold behavior of a Roman emperor. Although only in his early forties, Sidonius was ready to dismiss his earlier accomplishments as the "first heat of my youth."[22] No longer could Gallic aristocrats even hope to acquire influence through service in an imperial administration; instead, they had to learn to promote themselves without the possible advantages resulting from acting as brokers with the imperial court or from acquiring imperial titles of status.[23]

Sidonius had already begun to look for other definitions of prestige. One was in the ecclesiastical hierarchy; as he once wrote, "Beyond question the humblest ecclesiastic ranks above the most exalted secular dignity."[24] As a bishop himself he could use such a remark to his own advantage, even if he had not openly aspired to hold a see.[25] But also as a bishop Sidonius could continue studiously to maintain activities associated with the traditional life of aristocratic leisure. Although he gave up writing poetry, he composed sermons that, despite his own exaggerated modesty, were still excellent examples of classical rhetoric.[26] And (fortunately for modern historians), he continued to write letters, thus preserving

20. *Ep.* V.16.4.
21. *Ep.* III.3.9, although A. Loyen, Budé edition II (1970) 86–89, 222 n. 14, dates the letter earlier and has *reges* refer to Burgundian kings, not Roman emperors.
22. *Ep.* IX.16.3, line 42.
23. See Chastagnol (1978), for the exclusion of Gauls (with the exception of those in Provence during the early sixth century when it was associated with the Ostrogoth kingdom in Italy) from the traditional titles of senatorial rank after 476.
24. *Ep.* VII.12.4.
25. *Ep.* VI.1.5.
26. *Ep.* IX.3.5, for the applause given to a Christian preacher; VII.9.5–25, for an oration of Sidonius.

those bonds of friendship that were such a self-conscious characteristic of the late antique aristocracy.[27]

A second means by which Sidonius maintained his identity and standing was through literary culture, which, even though it could no longer advertise men for promotion into the imperial administration, now served to define a new "nobility" of its own: "Now that the old degrees of official rank are swept away, the only token of nobility will henceforth be a knowledge of letters."[28] The literary culture of Sidonius requires some explanation, in part because it illustrates a facet of the Gallic aristocracy that had been characteristic already for generations, in part too because its functions changed in different situations, as we can see here and will see again in the sixth century. Because of the archaic qualities of his literary culture, and even more because of his highly mannered and apparently artificial Latin, Sidonius is often censured by modern critics. While his world swirled around him Sidonius supposedly "whiled away the hours with no lack of witty and humorous conversation"—a phrase of Sidonius himself that one critic seized upon as "an epigram for his life as well as his writings."[29] Another modern critic claimed that the use of archaic literary forms and language by Sidonius and his contemporaries was merely a futile attempt to resuscitate a dead culture, comparable to painting rouge on an embalmed mummy.[30] The fact that one of Sidonius' own correspondents had to write to Sidonius' son and ask for assistance in understanding his father's Latin seems only to enhance these negative evaluations of Sidonius' antiquarian literary culture.[31]

Such criticism overlooks both the context and the role of this literary antiquarianism. In one sense a writer such as Sidonius could hardly fail to appear as an anachronism, because by the later fifth century the public schools for which Gaul had been famous during the later Roman Empire had begun to decline, and genuine literary ability was concentrated more and more narrowly among an elite. The more limited availability of education seems, especially to us, to have led to the appearance of a literary

27. Note especially *Ep.* IV.2.2: a friend complains that Sidonius has broken "the laws of friendship" by not writing.
28. *Ep.* VIII.2.2.
29. *Ep.* II.9.9, with Loyen (1943) 44, and (1956).
30. Lot (1931) 128: "une momie peinturlurée."
31. Ruricius of Limoges *Ep.* II.26 (*CSEL* 21, pp. 410–11).

culture cut off from reality; as in other traditional societies, such as China, for example, "extremely low literacy . . . abetted the tendency towards preciosity, antiquarianism, and other forms of literary exclusiveness which characterize inbred scholarship in general."[32]

In the eyes of the literary elite, however, Sidonius and some of his contemporaries had in fact risen above the limitations of their society by consciously reviving the classical heritage.[33] In dedicating his volumes on the nature of the soul to Sidonius, the priest Claudianus Mamertus called him a "renewer of that old eloquence";[34] Sidonius returned the compliment: "In this treatise [of Claudianus] one finds words that are new because they are old; even the language of antique literature would justly fall from favor by comparison with it."[35] According to him, Claudianus was a genuine Platonic philosopher, even though disguised by a monastic habit.[36]

For these men the recovery of Gaul in the fifth century had involved more than revived aspirations of service at an imperial court; it also included a deliberate renaissance of the classical heritage and its traditional forms and language. As Gaul seemed to slip away from Roman society into a barbarian world, such a renaissance became a measured attempt by aristocrats—many of them churchmen like Sidonius and some of his friends—to preserve a continuity with a fixed reference point in the past, to ensure a final link to a stable and glorious heritage in the midst of their present novel circumstances. Some of them composed poetry;[37] others wrote declamations that were "as smooth as crystal" and "as sweet as Greek honey";[38] one bishop even wrote a treatise on the correct grammar, spelling, and vocabulary of Latin.[39] Sidonius' friends who preserved the purity of their culture therefore

32. De Francis (1950) 8; cf. Riché (1962) 87: "Cette culture . . . est le privilege de l'aristocratie."
33. Cf. Claudianus Mamertus *Ep. ad Sapaudum* (*CSEL* 11, p. 204), on the literary prowess of Sapaudus.
34. Claudianus Mamertus *de statu animae*, praef., "veteris reparator eloquentiae." For Sidonius' influence on later Latin poetry, see Faral (1946).
35. *Ep.* IV.3.3.
36. *Ep.* IV.11.
37. In addition to the obvious examples, note Hilary of Arles *Versus fontis ardentis*: mentioned in *Vita Hilarii* 14, one stanza quoted by Gregory of Tours *de cursu stellarum* 14.
38. *Ep.* IX.7.3, and Claudianus Mamertus *Ep. ad Sapaudum* (*CSEL* 11, p. 205).
39. Agroecius of Sens *de orthographia*.

deserved compliments. One such man was a count of Trier who, although he now lived in an area of the Rhine dominated by barbarians, still spoke a Latin free of "barbarisms."[40]

As we read Sidonius it is hard to avoid the suspicion that he was a man surviving only on strong doses of nostalgia, that his usefulness for modern historians is primarily to recapitulate earlier attitudes and opinions. For him, both the Roman Empire and the classical heritage seem to have had a past, but no future; they could only be revived and imitated. But such observations, however accurate in themselves, do not account for the usefulness of these ideals for men trying to live with bewildering changes. A revival of the classical heritage, for instance, was not only an attempt to create a common language and a self-consciously elite culture with which to differentiate Gallic aristocrats, whether lay or clerical, from their new barbarian rulers; its traditions could also be used to integrate barbarians into Gallic society, even those whose "cold hearts" had never been "thawed" by philosophy.[41] In 476, perhaps as part of his plea to be allowed to return to Clermont from exile, Sidonius wrote a poem extolling the might of King Euric. These verses were among the few exceptions to Sidonius' resolve that he would cease writing poetry upon becoming a bishop, and in them he accepted Euric as a representative of Gallic interests, much as twenty years earlier he had eulogized the emperor Avitus. Euric was cast as a lord surveying a "conquered world," and to his court even Romans now came as suppliants.[42] Despite the rancid butter in their hair,[43] the barbarians had not had a devastating impact on classical culture after all. The friend to whom Sidonius sent this poem about Euric, for instance, was a Gallic aristocrat who had become a confidant of the king. Now, according to Sidonius, his friend could be both an outstanding Latin poet and orator and, simultaneously, a "citizen" in the Visigothic kingdom.[44]

\*     \*     \*

Concurrent with the collapse of the secular ideal of the Roman Empire it is possible to detect a change in attitude toward the ideal of Rome as the head of the Christian church. During the

---

40. *Ep.* IV.17.1–2, to Arbogast, who also received a verse letter from bishop Auspicius of Toul (*Epist. Austrasicae* 23).

41. *Ep.* IV.1.4.     42. *Ep.* VIII.9.5, lines 20, 39.

43. *Carm.* XII.6–7.     44. *Ep.* VIII.9.3, "agis ipse iam civem."

later fifth century there was a break, at least in communication, with the pope at Rome, even among the churches in southeastern Gaul, which could by now be considered almost an extension of northern Italy. More significantly, we can see in Gaul during the fifth century the foundation and expansion of cults to local saints in the form of increased construction of churches and shrines and of the production of saints' *Vitae*. Although there would never be a total elimination of "foreign" saints, in some cases at least these new cults of local saints became rivals, and even replacements, for shrines dedicated to the outstanding saints of Rome, St. Peter and St. Paul. The significance of these local cults for all aspects of society becomes most apparent in the sixth century, a period for which there is much more information; but already in the fifth century, as local Gallic interests became important again following Rome's abandonment of most of Gaul to the barbarian kingdoms, in the same way the Christian churches in Gaul began to stress local cults and local saints.

In the early fifth century, however, this later isolation was still unforeseen, and even churches on the fringe of the empire tried to preserve links with Rome. A town like Rouen, which was not very prominent even in its own district in western Gaul, carefully acquired relics of Italian saints, and its bishop Victricius even traveled to Rome in 403 and exchanged letters with the pope in order to ensure "unanimity."[45] Yet it is apparent too that these links between Rome and such fringe towns had been stretched to the breaking point and that Victricius' appeal to Rome had represented one last attempt to maintain contact with the "old country" to the south.

This exchange of letters between Rome and Rouen is one of the few known examples of papal communication with a Gallic town outside southeast Gaul; usually only cities in Provence corresponded with Rome. These links were partially self-serving, because with the transfer of the prefectural court to Arles, Provençal cities had begun feuding over ecclesiastical primacy.[46] But as a result of these incessant requests for the pope to settle the issue, the bishops of southeastern Gaul could also pretend that they were in contact with ecclesiastical affairs in the rest of the Roman Empire, even with doctrinal controversies over Greek theology.[47] Yet these

45. Paulinus of Nola *Ep.* 18.5; Innocent I *Ep.* 2.17; and above, p. 59. For the subsequent expansion of Christianity at Rouen, see Musset (1976).
46. Griffe (1964–1966) II, 146–64.
47. Leo I *Ep.* 102–3, and Griffe (1964–1966) II, 170–3.

links were also tenuous, because even the bishops of Arles, who generally fared well, were prepared to disregard the authority of the pope when convenient and instead enforce their own prominence by the strong-arm tactics of using a private "military band" to ensure their choice of suffragan bishops.[48] After the early 460s, during the decades in which barbarian kingdoms took over the western empire, there is a gap in the extant papal correspondence up to 494.[49] During the last years of the fifth century and in the early sixth century only the councils of Provençal bishops maintained any direct contact with Roman practices and popes. The rest of Gaul had long since gone its own way.

During and after the middle of the fifth century, Gallic churches had placed increasingly greater emphasis on the cults of local martyrs or, more significantly, of local bishops, some of whom had only recently died. The two cults in Gaul about which we know the most—those of the martyr St. Julian at Brioude (in the Auvergne) and of St. Martin at Tours—were both revived and expanded in the middle of the century. Although when Sidonius had published his collected poems in 469 the cult of St. Julian was well known at Brioude,[50] this popularity was apparently a fairly recent development, because in the early fifth century the site was better known for a pagan festival of Mars and Mercury.[51] In fact, the Christians at Brioude had been confused about the celebration of St. Julian's festival until Bishop Germanus of Auxerre discovered the proper date.[52] Eventually the saint's martyrdom was written up in a *Passio*, and probably during the 470s people constructed a church in his honor.[53]

---

48. For Hilary of Arles, see Leo I *Ep.* 10.6, and Valentinian III *Nov.* 17. Several studies provide various contexts for the activities of Hilary: see Mathisen (1979a), on competition among Gallic aristocrats over episcopal sees; Heinzelmann (1976) 76–84, on feuding between Gallic and Italian aristocrats; and Griffe (1964–1966) II, 197–212, on the autonomy of Gallic churches as opposed to papal hegemony.

49. Gelasius *Ep.* 19 = *Epist. Arelatenses* 22, "praetermissum diu . . . sermonem."

50. *Carm.* XXIV.16–19; *Ep.* IV.6.2 may also refer to the shrine of St. Julian. On the publication of Sidonius' poems, see A. Loyen, Budé edition I (1960) XXX–XXXV.

51. Gregory of Tours *VJ* 5.

52. *VJ* 29.

53. *Passio Iuliani martyris* (ed. B. Krusch, *MGH*, SRM 1, pp. 879–81), dated after Germanus' discovery of the date of the saint's festival, but before the activities of Bishop Mamertus. For the church, see Gregory of Tours *VJ* 9, *HF* II.20; and Vieillard-Troiekouroff (1976) 65–70.

At Vienne we find another revival of the cult of St. Julian, along with that of St. Ferreolus, who had previously taken St. Julian's head back to Vienne. In about 470 Bishop Mamertus of Vienne built a new church for St. Ferreolus and planned to transfer to it the relics of both saints. But by this time no one knew which tomb contained the remains of the two, and only after finding a sarcophagus containing a body and an extra head were they able to complete the translation.[54]

At Tours there was a similar restoration and revival of the cult of St. Martin, motivated largely by Bishop Perpetuus. During the 460s he replaced the small building over the tomb of St. Martin—which may have been a church dedicated to St. Peter and St. Paul—with a larger church dedicated to St. Martin.[55] For the walls of this church Perpetuus commissioned a series of verse inscriptions and frescoes; he also had the poet Paulinus of Périgueux versify a collection of recent miracle stories that clearly demonstrated how St. Martin was still present to help people, whether at a distance, as when he assisted a Roman general who was being besieged by the Visigoths, or on the spot, as when he cured a paralyzed girl brought to his tomb.[56] These miracles also emphasized the isolation in which people had been left by the withdrawal of the Roman Empire, because unlike the emperors and other civil magistrates, St. Martin had not simply disappeared. Paulinus of Périgueux left no doubt of this: "You who remain with us in piety, are hardly able to abscond from our sight. . . . Words are silent, but miracles now shine. Although you have been physically taken from our sight, by your power you seem to be present."[57] The information in this poem demonstrates how the cult of a local bishop could serve as a substitute for the ceremony and the generosity that had been distinguishing features of the presence of the Roman emperors. The building of a new church, which united people in a community project, replaced imperial construction projects.[58] Ecclesiastical festivals such as Easter, which included a community pilgrimage to St. Martin's monastery of Marmoutier across

54. *VJ* 1–2; also Sidonius *Ep.* VII.1.7, and Vieillard-Troiekouroff (1976) 339–40.

55. Ewig (1961) 3. The chronology depends on the date for *Ep.* IV.18: see A. Loyen, Budé edition II (1970) 253–4.

56. Paulinus of Périgueux *de vita S. Martini* VI.111–51, 165–84.

57. *de vita S. Martini* V.865–70, "praesens virtute videris."

58. *de vita S. Martini* VI.265–90; cf. Gregory of Tours *HF* II.15, for Bishop Euphronius of Autun supplying the marble lid for the tomb.

the Loire River, replaced imperial ceremonies.[59] And accounts of saints' lives and miracles now substituted for imperial panegyrics. As a result, throughout the fifth century the reputation of the cult of St. Martin made Tours an increasingly attractive destination for pilgrimages by the citizens of Gaul.[60]

Although these are the best-documented revivals of saints' cults, we also know of others. During the later 470s Sidonius was asked to write a *Vita* of Anianus, the bishop of Orléans who had saved his city from the Huns.[61] Also in the later 470s the bishop of Lyon asked a local priest to write a *Vita* of St. Germanus of Auxerre, which was later circulated more widely by the bishop of Auxerre.[62] In addition, many building projects sprang up throughout Gaul: at Autun, a church of St. Symphorian, a local martyr, built before 456;[63] at Clermont, in the middle of the century, a cathedral with relics of Italian saints and a church of St. Stephen, and in the 470s and 480s numerous other churches;[64] at Narbonne, a new cathedral in the early 440s and a church of St. Felix in the 450s;[65] at Bourges, a new cathedral about the middle of the century;[66] at Lyon, a new cathedral about 470.[67]

This revival of local cults after the middle of the fifth century should not be taken to imply the previous absence of cults of saints in Gaul. The cult of St. Trophimus at Arles, for instance, had become prominent already in the early fifth century as a component in Arles' claim to priority among the sees of southeastern Gaul.[68] Nor does this revival necessarily imply any drastic changes in the specific functions of relic cults, although they might have taken on additional roles. The cult of St. Trophimus is also a good

---

59. *de vita S. Martini* VI.351–460.

60. Fifth-century pilgrims to Tours included Genovefa of Paris (*Vita Genovefe virgine* 45–47); a monk from the Jura (*Vita [Patrum Iurensium] Lupicini* 8); and, most notably, King Clovis (*Epist. Austrasicae* 8). Early sixth-century pilgrims included Marius of Bevons (*Vita Marii* 5).

61. Below, p. 173.

62. Above, p. 145.

63. Gregory of Tours *HF* II.15. The *Passio* of St. Symphorian (mentioned in *GC* 76) may also have been produced at this time: see Vieillard-Troiekouroff (1976) 44–45.

64. *Ep.* III.1.2–3; and Gregory of Tours *HF* II.16, 17, 20.

65. Marrou (1970); Griffe (1964–1966) III, 45.

66. *Ep.* VII.9.21; and Vieillard-Troiekouroff (1976) 59–61.

67. *Ep.* II.10, IX.3.5; and Vieillard-Troiekouroff (1976) 138–42.

68. E.g. Zosimus *Ep.* 1, 4, 5, 6 = *Epist. Arelatenses* 1, 2, 5, 3. In 450 Arles again appealed to the authority of St. Trophimus (*Epist. Arelatenses* 12), but Pope Leo, characteristically, did not take up the hint (*Ep.* 66 = *Epist. Arelatenses* 13).

example of how local cults could be manipulated in feuds between cities—yet another way, as we will see in later chapters, of
guaranteeing the more fragmented and limited horizons of Merovingian Gaul.

The significant implication of this revival is instead in terms of
the local saints who were now being honored with expanded
cults. In some cases cults of local bishops came to replace cults of
martyrs, a transition that might be directly connected with the
rise of bishops themselves to prominence in local society.[69] In
other cases, cults of local Gallic bishops replaced those of "foreigners": at Auxerre, for instance, the shrine built by Bishop Germanus in honor of the Alpine martyrs of the Theban Legion became, after his death, a shrine in honor of the bishop himself.[70]
Elsewhere, and more importantly, cults of local bishops replaced
cults of Roman saints. At Tours, as we have seen, the new church
of St. Martin replaced an earlier church probably dedicated to St.
Peter and St. Paul; as a result of this expansion of the cult of St.
Martin, in early Merovingian Gaul it became as significant for a
monk to have mystical conversations with St. Martin as with St.
Peter and St. Paul.[71] At Saintes in the later fifth century, after
Bishop Vivianus died as men returned from Rome with relics to
dedicate a new church, his body was also buried in the church.[72]
A more telling example is the case of Bishop Maximus of Riez.
After he died during the 450s his body was buried in the church of
St. Peter that he had built; but thereafter the church took the name
of this local bishop, "on account of his abundant patronage."[73]

In earlier centuries a world view that had drawn its inspiration
from the ideal of a Roman Empire, access to imperial courts, and
knowledge of the classical heritage had helped aristocrats define
themselves and their standing in their communities. But by the
later fifth century no more imperial courts survived in Gaul, or
even in Italy. Literary culture, as we have seen, still remained significant; but in addition, local aristocrats could now articulate
their present roles as well as their relationship to the past through
the Christian idiom of relic cults and holiness.[74] With regard to

69. Griffe (1964–1966) III, 237–40.
70. Above, p. 55.
71. Vita [Patrum Iurensium] Eugendi 15.
72. Vita Bibiani vel Viviani 9; and Vieillard-Troiekouroff (1976) 284–5.
73. Dynamius Vita Maximi 15.
74. At Rome, predictably enough, the cult of St. Peter and St. Paul became a
focus for concordia: see C. Pietri (1961).

the way Gauls viewed the Roman Empire, it is therefore possible to suggest a correlation between the decline of the authority of the empire and a waning of the ideal of Rome in Gaul, and the emergence of cults dedicated to local Gallic bishops or saints. This correlation was, of course, neither chronologically exact, since no transformation can be enclosed by specific dates, nor geographically inclusive, since the cults of many foreign saints, such as St. Peter and St. Paul, remained prominent in Gaul throughout the Middle Ages.[75] No social change can ever be so precisely defined, but given the sheer inertia inherent in a great traditional society, individual examples take on great significance.

Long ago Arnaldo Momigliano insisted that we would not understand the transformation of the Roman Empire in the West until we conceded that the Christian church offered an ideal, potentially all-inclusive society competing with the society developed under the Roman Empire: "Christianity produced a new style of life, created new loyalties, gave people new ambitions and satisfactions."[76] By the later fifth century a Christian Gallic society that had already absorbed the local aristocracy, its values, and its classical heritage was prepared to exist independently, rather than in dependence on Rome. Even outsiders acknowledged this new role. When the Eastern monk Abraham visited the West, he went not to Rome, but to Clermont.[77] Demons also conceded a priority to Gaul over Rome. Although a possessed girl from Toulouse was brought to St. Peter's in Rome, the demon in her insisted that he would be exorcised only by Bishop Remigius of Rheims.[78] With its cults of local saints, Gaul was even prepared to present itself as a direct rival to Rome. In a sermon delivered at Lyon in the later fifth century, the preacher stressed how St. Alexander and St. Epipodius were "indigenous martyrs" and "special patrons." According to him, these two martyrs were worthy substitutes for St. Peter and St. Paul: "We are exalting two prizes of victory, rivals to the apostolic city, and since we have our own Peter and Paul, we oppose our two patrons to that sublime see of Rome."[79] Just as the

75. Ewig (1960b), and, for cults of Eastern saints, (1964). By the sixth century the cult of St. Peter will be used by Gallic bishops in opposition to Arianism: see Ewig (1960a).

76. Momigliano (1963a) 6, emphasized again in (1979–1980).

77. *Ep.* VII.17.2; Gregory of Tours *VP* 3.1.

78. Fortunatus *Vita Remedii* 16–23.

79. "Eusebius Gallicanus," *Hom.* LV.1, 4 (ed. Fr. Glorie, *CChr. lat.* 101A [1971] 639–40).

Roman Empire had withdrawn from most of Gaul, so now Gaul was prepared to retreat behind the support offered by cults of local saints.

\* \* \*

Bishop Sidonius, however, seems not to have been caught up in the exuberance of this expansion of Christian relic cults. His attitudes can remind us that even a bishop who seems, like Germanus of Auxerre, to be an ideal example of one major trend of the period, that is, the merger between secular and ecclesiastical elites, could still be left feeling as uneasy and bewildered as Paulinus of Pella, predisposed by his ancestry and training to define himself in terms of options that no longer had the same impact as before. The rise of the Christian idiom of holiness was never as smooth as its later prominence makes it appear, and Sidonius' final years demonstrate the inability, perhaps the hesitation, of even a bishop to take full advantage of it.

After Sidonius' return to Clermont from exile, his life and writings took on a more subdued tone in contrast to the enthusiasm of his youth and the determination of his early middle age; although now only in his late forties, Sidonius wrote with the weariness of an old man, always worrying about his friends' attitudes toward Christianity.[80] Yet he had no intention of producing any theological tracts for their benefit. Years earlier, during the debate between Claudianus Mamertus and Faustus of Riez over the nature of the soul, he had managed to remain neutral, or perhaps indifferent, to the entire dispute, commenting only on their respective literary styles and knowledge of philosophy.[81] Similarly, each time he had been asked for a biblical interpretation or a theological exposition, he had politely begged off: "You might just as reasonably join the honking of geese with the song of swans."[82]

Instead, Sidonius decided that he would publish more of his letters. In them he demonstrated his deep respect for his illustrious literary predecessors, because not only did he carefully follow the proper epistolographical form, he also revised his letters to include many quotations from or allusions to the letters of the classical exemplars of epistolary writing and publishing, Pliny and (to a

80. *Ep.* IV.9.13, as dated by Stevens (1933) 167.
81. *Ep.* IV.3, IX.9.10–15; and Griffe (1964–1966) III, 380–3.
82. *Ep.* IX.2.2; cf. IV.17.3.

lesser extent) Symmachus.[83] Eventually he completed his collection in nine books, fully aware that by doing so he had matched the number of books of private letters published by both Pliny and Symmachus.[84] But the collected edition of Pliny also included, as a tenth book, his correspondence with the emperor Trajan, and the final edition of Symmachus had matched that accomplishment by publishing as his tenth book the dispatches he had sent to the emperors when he was prefect of Rome. Sidonius had also once been prefect of Rome, but he apparently never even considered publishing a similar tenth book of official correspondence.[85] Given that Sidonius was so highly respectful of the demands of the classical norms of literature,[86] such an omission is significant, and indicates the uneasiness he felt about his present situation. For in a society dominated by barbarians and cut off from its imperial past, who would want to read any correspondence between a Gallic senator and a Roman emperor?

Sidonius' attitudes toward his other literary productions in these years also show his sense of alienation. His interests increasingly focused on heroes of the church and of pagan philosophy. During his exile from Clermont he had produced another version of the *Life of Apollonius of Tyana*, one of the great wise men of the Roman Empire.[87] At some point he also decided to write hagiography and promised the bishop of Orléans that he would compose an account of Bishop Anianus and his defense of Orléans against Attila and the Huns, one of the major Roman victories over barbarians during the fifth century.[88] At another time he resolved to write poetry only about Christian martyrs, because they alone had assisted him at difficult moments.[89] Presumably this last comment was a subtle criticism of everyone who had abandoned him, the Auvergne, and southern Gaul to the Visigoths.

As far as we know, Sidonius never completed these projects.

83. Stevens (1933) 171. For arguments about the dates of publication, see Stevens (1933) 168–74, and A. Loyen, Budé edition II (1970) XI–XXIV, XLVI–XLIX.
84. *Ep.* IX.1.1.
85. Although in the first book he had included some private letters written during his tenure as prefect: *Ep.* I.9–10.
86. Cf. Courcelle (1970), on how Sidonius' respect for the classical norms of epistolography led him to conceal his own knowledge of philosophy.
87. *Ep.* VIII.3, with A. Loyen, Budé edition III (1970) 196–7, on Sidonius' possible knowledge of Greek.
88. *Ep.* VIII.15.
89. *Ep.* IX.16.3, lines 57–80.

But at least he had considered the possibilities; history, on the other hand, he flatly refused to write, for several reasons.[90] In response to one request, he replied that the friend who had made the suggestion was himself more suited to write history because he served at the court of King Euric and therefore knew more about the politics that formed the proper subject matter of history. Sidonius also claimed that he was too disillusioned and ill: "I find less reality in the present than hope in the future."[91] Again, the recognition of a profound discontinuity in his life appears. For him, Roman history had consisted of a series of exemplary tales that he could use to illustrate important virtues or past successes of the empire. But these anecdotes came from a remote past; in his surveys of Roman history in earlier panegyrics he had never gone past the early second century.[92] This truncated version of early Roman history included, significantly enough, the wars between the Gauls and Rome, the eventual conquest of Gaul by Julius Caesar, and the pacification of the Rhine frontier; in fact, in the later fourth century a Gaul who intended to write a history of his homeland had received from the Roman senator Symmachus books describing precisely those wars.[93] Presumably the conquest was no longer offensive to an aspiring Gallic historian, because as a result of it Gaul had become a part of the Roman Empire. Sidonius and his friends had even transformed Julius Caesar himself into a "Gallic hero," the greatest general ever, a man who could be considered a highly appropriate subject for a rhetorical declamation.[94] Perhaps what Gaul really needed in the later fifth century was another Roman general like Julius Caesar who would conquer Gaul again for the Roman Empire.

The Roman legions, however, had left long ago, and for Sidonius to write a history of the fifth century he would have had to describe the undoing of Caesar's conquests by charting the collapse of the empire and its replacement in central and southern Gaul by the Visigoths. The establishment of a Roman administration would have had to culminate in a barbarian kingdom, and that prospect, he claimed, meant "either suppressing the truth or inventing a lie."[95] Nor could Sidonius have brought himself to

90. Cf. *Ep.* I.2.10, III.3.9, for his insistence that he had never written history.
91. *Ep.* IV.22.4.
92. *Carm.* II.440–78, VII.55–116; and Loyen (1943) 17–20.
93. Symmachus *Ep.* IV.18, with Wightman (1975b).
94. *Ep.* VIII.6.1, IX.14.7; *Carm.* IX.239–40, "Gallicani . . . Caesaris."
95. *Ep.* IV.22.3.

write an account somehow fitting the barbarians into Roman history, even though within a few decades such chronicles and histories became fashionable, perhaps out of the necessity of educating both barbarians and Romans about the new society they now shared. In early sixth-century Italy, for instance, Cassiodorus wrote just that sort of revisionist history by proposing, as a simple but still revolutionary aim, "to make the origin of the Goths into Roman history."[96]

Sidonius never considered this possibility; at the very most, philosophy and literature might help barbarians cease to be "beasts,"[97] but nothing could make them into Romans. For Sidonius had been raised in an aristocratic milieu that had still stressed, above all, the ideals of the Roman Empire and the classical heritage. As a younger man, probably before he became bishop, he had considered it only natural that, when he and his friends were overwhelmed by the crowd at the tomb of St. Justus in Lyon, they would relax in the shade of the tomb of another local "saint," Syagrius, who had been prefect of the Gauls and consul in the early 380s.[98] But after the final abandonment of Gaul by the Roman Empire, such a conjunction of Roman and Christian heritages was unlikely. One of the more prominent Gallic aristocrats in the fifth century had been Avitus, who had even been emperor for a few months. Although he was buried at Brioude,[99] his tomb was forgotten, because people went to Brioude only to visit the shrine of St. Julian. After the fifth century men no longer told jokes and played games while sitting around the tombs of men who had made their fame as secular magistrates.[100]

Sidonius also gave one final blunt reason why he would not write the history his friend had requested: because of the work involved and the hard feelings aroused, clerics should not write history. They were simply too honest.[101] Fortunately for us, a century later at least one Gallic bishop was not afraid to be too hon-

---

96. Cassiodorus *Variae* IX.25 (*MGH, AA* 12, pp. 291–3), and Momigliano (1966a) 183: "Cassiodorus' *Gothic History* is a landmark in the history of Latin historiography and of Late Roman politics." See also O'Donnell (1979) 43–54, 272.

97. *Ep.* IV.2.4.

98. *Ep.* V.17.3–4.

99. Gregory of Tours *HF* II.11.

100. Gregory of Tours *GC* 41; the tomb of the senator Hilarius at Dijon might be an exception (see Stroheker [1948] no. 194).

101. *Ep.* IV.22.5–6.

est, and it will be the writings of Bishop Gregory of Tours that provide us with our best insight into sixth-century religion and society. But a century later men's perspectives had changed completely. Gregory would put his barbarians, the Franks, not into Roman history, but into biblical history—a precise indication of how in Gaul a Christian society had finally come to replace a Roman society.

# IV

## The Cult of Relics
## in Sixth-Century Merovingian Gaul

In sixth-century Merovingian Gaul, Christianity offered the most comprehensive system of values for influencing people's own conduct and for evaluating the conduct of others. In the previous group of chapters we saw how relic cults and the accompanying hagiography played an important role in the assimilation of Christianity to existing secular attitudes and social relationships during the later fourth and fifth centuries. Cults and hagiography had performed different functions: they helped amend the attitudes of a Christian prophet that were uncongenial to later generations; they defined the ideal of an aristocratic bishop to which other secular aristocrats might aspire; and they substituted for imperial ceremonies and panegyrics. In the sixth century, however, the roles seem to be reversed, and relic cults become the catalyst for a Christian society. The following chapters show how, in this early medieval Christian society, beliefs centered on relic cults maintained and even enhanced the prominence of local aristocratic families as well as regulated community values through the division of space and time and the imposition of notions of illness and healing. In this way these chapters also elaborate the themes of local leadership, communities, and their interaction that are central to this book.

These chapters can, however, give a misleading finale to the book, for two reasons. First, the nature of the miracle stories that form the primary evidence for these chapters allows us to complement the activities of a small elite of bishops and clergymen by investigating the significance of a religious cult for ordinary believers. In fact, because this final group of chapters can discuss in such detail both the enduring characteristics of life in small communities and the strategies aristocratic families adopted to ensure their local prominence, modern historians would probably have preferred to have it, or its equivalent for earlier centuries, at the beginning of the book, in order to provide the context within which subsequent change would take place. In that sense it is unfortunate that our richest information comes from the end of the period under investigation and that hence these chapters must come at the end of the book, because we might then wrongly conclude that an increase in the amount of literary material necessarily implies a corresponding transition point in Gallic society.

Second, it is also misleading that our information is now so overwhelmingly Christian, because these families and communities end up looking as if they had always been Christian. Even if we had had for previous centuries further information about Christianity, a major historiographical handicap would still have been the absence of adequate evidence about religious alternatives. It is never clear whether Christian relic cults were replacing the functions of pagan cults, ignoring them, or creating and satisfying new roles. Because we have so little information about life in pre-Christian or contemporary non-Christian communities, the only proper comparison we can make for the sixth century is with earlier Christian communities such as those described in chapters 4 and 5. We must always keep in mind, however, that Christian perspectives replaced, or overshadowed, pagan paradigms that had also defined the distribution of authority and prestige, the organization of sacred space and time, and the enforcement of community values, although without changing much of the structure and nature of these communities. Although the religious beliefs that motivated men's behavior and by means of which they interpreted their society had clearly changed, it can be assumed that the characteristic forms and structures of small communities still remained similar to those of the past.

# CHAPTER 9

# Early Merovingian Gaul:
# The World of Gregory of Tours

By the time Gregory of Tours wrote his books of history in the later sixth century, "Romans" were only one among the many peoples inhabiting Gaul who seemed to coexist with the Franks with little racial or ethnic animosity. In contrast with other barbarian kingdoms, Romans and Franks were free to intermarry, and they did so with apparently little tension; some of the more notable men of Merovingian times were born of such marriages.[1] Although Romans and Franks retained separate legal identities, in his writings Gregory did not insist on that juridical distinction.[2] According to him, the term *Romani* was used, most explicitly, in a religious context by Arians to designate orthodox Catholic Christians.[3] Similarly, in the early 580s, when King Chilperic showed Gregory some gold Byzantine coins bearing a slogan referring to

Two of the best books on early Merovingian Gaul are still Dill (1926), and Dalton (1927). Gregory's *Books of Histories* (more commonly known now as the *History of the Franks*) are translated by Dalton (1927) and by Thorpe (1974), whose translation is sometimes used in the following chapters. Gregory's *Books of Miracles* and other writings are translated into French by Bordier (1857–1864); selections are translated into English by W. C. McDermott, in Peters (1975) 147–218. In this chapter references to the writings of Gregory of Tours (*HF, GM, VJ, VM, VP, GC, de cursu*) omit his name.

1. E.g. note that by the early seventh century St. Medard has acquired a Frankish father and a Roman mother: [Fortunatus] *Vita Medardi* 4. For the contrasting restrictions in the Visigothic kingdom in Spain, see Thompson (1969) 58–59, and King (1972) 6, 13–14; this ban on intermarriage was finally removed by King Leovigild, c. 580.

2. Dannenbauer (1958), and Rouche (1977), although the latter's suggestion that Gregory revealed a "tranquille complexe de supériorité" toward the Franks is questionable.

3. *GM* 24, 78–79.

the "reputation of the Romans," Gregory gave no hint of identifying himself as one such Roman.[4] For by now Catholic Romans such as Gregory were concerned far more about maintaining a pure religious orthodoxy than about preserving ethnic purity. Canons from the ecclesiastical councils of the sixth century repeatedly warned against intermarrying, or even socializing, with Jews;[5] and in 576 the bishop of Clermont went so far as to "convert," in a rather heavy-handed fashion, the Jewish community at Clermont by expelling those who refused baptism.[6] Such a development represents a reversal from the thinking of Romans a century earlier, when Bishop Sidonius, for example, had avoided barbarians, but employed Jews as messengers and even recommended one to another bishop.[7] But it was also about a century earlier that Christians had again begun to concentrate on these "internal" boundaries between Catholics and others without worrying about the "external" boundaries between Romans and barbarians. In Gregory's historical narrative, for instance, Romans appear to have disappeared from Gaul at the end of the fifth century during the reign of Clovis. In sixth-century Gaul most free men, including the descendants of the indigenous Gallo-Romans, could now be considered Franks.[8]

Hence Gregory's books of history are more than a narrative of the successful consolidation of Frankish hegemony over most of Gaul.[9] Like many other ancient historians, Gregory emphasized military campaigns, but the battles he narrated were now extended to include "the wars of kings with hostile foreigners, of martyrs with pagans, and of the churches with heretics."[10] And in these wars, although the kings were Franks by definition, most of the churchmen were descendants of old Roman families. By now Gaul was well on its way toward the fusion of aristocracies that

4. *HF* VI.2.
5. Council of Orléans a. 533, Can. 19; Council of Clermont a. 535, Can. 6; Council of Orléans a. 538, Can. 14.
6. *HF* V.11, and the subsequent elaborated version of Fortunatus *Carm.* V.5. About fifteen years later the fugitive Jews at Marseille also had to convert: cf. Gregory I *Reg.* I.45.
7. Sidonius *Ep.* III.4.1, VI.11, VIII.13.3–4.
8. "Romani" are mentioned only in *HF* I.17, 36, 41; II.9, 11, 18–19, 33; see also Kurth (1919) I, 67–137.
9. Wallace-Hadrill (1962) 148–206, is a concise survey of early Merovingian kings; likewise (1967) is an excellent introduction to the barbarian kingdoms of early medieval Europe.
10. *HF* I, praef.

would become most apparent in the seventh century, and already we can see the alignment of Franks and Romans against foreigners and heretics, as a result of which regional or geographic designations took precedence over ethnic descriptions, and the only remaining "barbarians" were the non-Christians.[11]

From these introductory remarks it is already obvious that the world of Gregory differed greatly from the world of Sidonius. In the remainder of this section let us briefly consider, as further introductory background, how both the administration of Merovingian Gaul and Gregory's own historical outlook contributed to another contrasting aspect, that is, Gregory's parochialism and localized horizons, before going on in the following sections to investigate his idea of Christian holiness.

Much of this fusion between Franks and Romans had already appeared in the generation following the death of Sidonius, in part as different barbarian kingdoms took over the administration of various regions of Gaul, and in part because maverick Roman aristocrats such as Aegidius and Syagrius, who established their own "kingdom" in north-central Gaul, were apparently accepted by some Franks as "kings."[12] The rise of Clovis in the later fifth century contributed most to this fusion of civil authority, since in addition to becoming king of all the Frankish tribes, Clovis was compared by bishops to Roman magistrates, and after his victory over the Visigoths in 507 he even assumed some of the ceremonial trappings of an emperor.[13]

At some point Clovis also converted to Christianity and acquired the patronage of St. Martin in his campaign against the Visigoths. The support given him then by the bishops and congregation of Tours remained strong,[14] because although writing two generations later, Gregory was still deeply impressed by what he knew of the king,[15] and as he described Clovis' baptism he ex-

11. Ewig (1958).
12. *HF* II.12, 27, "rex Romanorum"; see also Priscus, frag. 30 (*FHG* IV, p. 104), and Paulinus of Périgueux *de vita S. Martini* VI.111–51.
13. *HF* II.38; *Epist. Austrasicae* 2; and Avitus *Ep.* 46. The chronology of Clovis' reign is notoriously debatable; see, e.g., Van de Vyver (1936, 1937), (1938); and Lot (1938).
14. Courcelle (1964) 238–50, on the support of the Catholic clergy for Clovis.
15. Too impressed according to some critics, such as Halphen (1925), who thinks that Gregory made Clovis into a saint; Graus (1965) 393–4, is a more realistic interpretation.

plicitly referred to him as "a new Constantine."[16] With this recognition Clovis and the establishment of Frankish rule in Gaul could conveniently be fitted into Gregory's interpretation of the course of history. Because his historical account began with biblical history and can more properly be seen as a history of Christianity in Gaul than as a history of the Franks, for Gregory the great historical turning points revolved around conversion to Christianity— whether by a Roman emperor or a barbarian king—rather than around the fate of the Roman administration in Gaul.

Thus, despite a passing reference to the universal leadership of Rome,[17] Gregory's knowledge about current events at Rome was noticeably slight, derived mostly from a deacon who had once visited the city.[18] For Gregory, the Roman Empire marked merely a transient phase in the history of Gaul, whose emperors provided only a convenient means of dating events: in Gregory's list of the bishops of Tours, for instance, the first four bishops were linked to the reigns of specific emperors, two from the mid-fifth century were associated with no political events, and one in the later fifth century was finally associated with King Clovis.[19] As we have seen, it was precisely in the later fifth century that most of Gaul had been abandoned, not only by the imperial administration and army but even by the patron saints of Rome. At least according to the mythology of Gregory, St. Peter was thought to have conceded that the Huns had invaded Gaul in accordance with God's will, and he and St. Paul had also supposedly said that Metz would have to be destroyed.[20] Although at the time men had been prepared to compensate for these discouraging opinions from the saints of Rome by promoting their own local relic cults, by the later sixth century they no longer had to regret this lost past, because Gregory and his contemporaries had created alternatives for themselves that could stand defiant comparison with the attractions of Rome. When the Italian poet Fortunatus visited Nantes, he not only found that its bishop had supervised a huge construction project for detouring a river, he also conceded that the

16. *HF* II.31; cf. II.30, in which Gregory clearly modeled Clovis' vision before his victory over the Alamanni after Constantine's vision before his victory at the Milvian Bridge. Ewig (1956) 26–29, is a perceptive discussion of the use of "the tradition of Constantine" in this instance.

17. *HF* V, praef.

18. *HF* X.1, although O. Chadwick (1948) argues that this chapter is an interpolation and that Gregory of Tours' deacon was in fact in Rome during the 580s.

19. *HF* X.31.

20. *HF* II.5–6.

bishop's reputation had made his city into a "new Rome"—and this in Armorica, a region that, under the Roman Empire, had always been seen as peripheral, noted most of all for delectable oysters and unsavory bandits![21] Similarly, after a pilgrim on his way to Rome witnessed a cure by Hospicius of Nice, he knew that he needed to travel no further: "I was on my way to St. Peter, I was going to St. Paul and St. Lawrence and all the others who have glorified Rome with their blood; I have found them all here, in this very spot I have discovered them."[22]

Gregory's horizons had shrunk so considerably that his history was almost entirely centered on Christianity in Gaul.[23] Sometimes this involved a virtual reinterpretation of past Roman history. The first Roman emperor, for instance, became Julius Caesar, the conqueror of Gaul; Augustus was only his successor, who happened to be emperor at the time of two important events: the birth of Jesus Christ and the foundation of Lyon.[24] Of all the emperors of the fourth century who had campaigned on the Rhine frontier, the most memorable was apparently the usurper Magnus Maximus, "the emperor at Trier," who was noteworthy because he had met both Martin of Tours and Bishop Illidius of Clermont.[25] A further limitation was that Gregory based his historical narrative largely upon events in the Touraine and the Auvergne. These were the two regions of Gaul most familiar to him, and just as his account of early Christianity in Gaul was derived largely from the registers and local traditions of Tours and Clermont, so the later books of his histories emphasized his own activities in the same two cities.[26]

The parochialism of Gregory is apparent also in his books of

21. Fortunatus *Carm.* III.8, 10.
22. *HF* VI.6, trans. Thorpe (1974). Note also *VP* 8.6: a deacon traveling from Rome, where he had honored the tombs of "Eastern martyrs" (in this instance, perhaps St. Peter and St. Paul?), was equally impressed by the crowds at the tomb of Nicetius of Lyon, a "Gallicanus confessor"; and *VM* 4.12: a woman who was cured in a shrine near Le Mans dedicated to St. Peter and St. Paul still insisted that St. Martin had healed her.
23. On the chronology of the composition of the *HF* and its sources, see Monod (1872) 45–49, 73–108, and Oldoni (1972). Although Averil Cameron (1975) suggests a possible written source behind Gregory's account of events in the eastern empire, Baynes (1929) 231–3, is more convincing on Gregory's limited knowledge of foreign affairs.
24. *HF* I.18–19.
25. *HF* I.43, 45, V.18; *VJ* 4; *VP* 2.1.
26. For instance, Gregory knew very little about Provençal saints (see Carrias [1970]), or even about such recent and important Provençal bishops as Caesarius of Arles (see Prinz [1965] 89–90).

miracles.[27] In them he most often referred either to shrines from the regions of Gaul he knew best, or to saints who lived near Tours and Clermont or who were relatives and acquaintances. Two special "friends" dominated his miracle stories, St. Julian, the patron saint of Auvergne, whose shrine at Brioude Gregory often visited as a young man, and, to an even greater extent, St. Martin.[28] Gregory's books of the miracles of St. Martin were effectively a diary of the correct relationship between a bishop and his patron saint, and because he recorded the contemporary miracles in proper sequence (even noting a cure for a headache caused by the anxiety of waiting for another miracle to happen!), it is possible for us to deduce a fairly precise chronology for them.[29]

Gregory did most of his writing while a bishop, and given the nature of his works (not all of which are extant) we can easily get the impression that he was laboring on them during all his spare time. At least one later medieval writer commented on Gregory's diligence and curiosity, which seemed always to put him on the right "scent" of miracles.[30] But it is also essential to keep in mind the restrictions on both his subject matter and, more importantly, his experiences. Gregory was a true man of his times, and the parochialism in his writings was also an accurate indication of the contracted horizons that now narrowed men's perspectives and concerns.

As Gaul had come progressively under the control of the Franks since the end of the fifth century, cities had become the most important administrative units. The sons of Clovis in 511 (Theuderic, Chlodomer, Childebert, and Chlothar) and the sons of Chlothar again in 561 (Charibert, Guntram, Sigibert, and Chilperic) divided the cities of Gaul into kingdoms among themselves. These kings and their households usually had only intermittent contact with many of the cities nominally under their control; instead, the administration of Gaul resembled a "segmentary" form of state, in which regions and cities peripheral to the royal courts became largely autonomous, even though they technically remained within

27. See Monod (1872) 41–45, on the chronology of composition.
28. Wallace-Hadrill (1962) 52: "The cult of St. Martin seems to have coloured all that Gregory ever did, and all that he wrote."
29. VM 2.60. For the chronology of the miracles in the VM, see the important conclusions of Schlick (1966).
30. Heiric of Auxerre Miracula S. Germani I.41 (ed. Duru [1850–1863] II, 134), "miraculorum curiosus indagator ac studiosissimus editor."

the defined sphere of influence of a particular king.[31] Although several Frankish kings now ruled in sixth-century Gaul, their influence was still limited and, like that of the old Roman emperors, heavily dependent on their actual presence. Yet in each city a Frankish king might enter, he found competitors with local authority, men such as counts (who were often local landowners promoted into the royal administration), bishops, abbots, and saints. During Gregory's tenure as bishop Frankish kings came to Tours either as hostile invaders or as respectful pilgrims, and they simply avoided residing in a town so completely dominated by St. Martin.

For men who now served at the Frankish courts or in what passed as the royal administration, advancement in a career took almost the opposite course from a career in the old imperial administration.[32] Then a man had usually started out governing in the provinces and might eventually be promoted to serve in the imperial retinue. In the Frankish kingdoms, however, the count of each city was probably the most influential civil official, since he performed almost all administrative functions, such as dispensing justice, collecting taxes, and calling up and often also commanding the military levies.[33] Even the organization of the civil administration, then, handicapped most men from thinking about allegiances beyond their own cities.

Furthermore, within each city several different obligations competed for people's loyalties. At the most immediate level there were kinsmen,[34] as well as large landowners to whom men might be bound through ties of labor, debt, or other forms of servitude. Bishops and abbots were also prone to feuding with other local leaders. Since the ecclesiastical diocesan structure was based on the old Roman division of city territories, the spheres of influence of bishops and counts overlapped. Potential animosity was therefore inherent in the civil and religious administration, as Gregory eventually found to his peril in his quarrels with Count Leudast over preeminence in Tours.[35]

31. Southall (1967); also Ewig (1976a) and (1976b) 383–9.
32. Ewig (1976b) 367–8.
33. Claude (1964).
34. On feuds, see Wallace-Hadrill (1962) 121–47, and the excellent survey in Marc Bloch (1961) 123–42. *VM* 1.30 is an example of a conflict between bishop and kin over an inheritance.
35. *HF* V.47–49, and below, pp. 213, 216.

Despite the wars and local feuds, in the sixth century the landscape of Gaul still suggested the illusive tranquillity of an oriental
tea garden. Situated in a valley of opulent farms and magnificent
scenery, Dijon, for instance, seemed to be the image of prosperity.
Yet, although impressed by such delightful serenity—as well as
by the excellence of the local wine—Gregory also hinted at a more
repressive feature of the city, because in the squat stone walls surrounding it there were only four gateways;[36] and it was within
similar narrow constraints on men's thinking that, as we will see,
relic cults came to be influential.

Dijon also evoked memories about a distant past, because "the
ancient authorities say that it was built by [the third-century em-
peror] Aurelian." Almost everywhere men looked in Gaul they
might be confronted by the remains of the past being used in different ways, such as a cave in which men had hidden from the barbarians that was now turned into a hermit's cell, or a hilltop fortress
transformed into a church.[37] In more ways than one, Christianity
had built a new society out of the rubble of the past.

But if men in sixth-century Gaul were always aware of the past
through its visible remains, it was not the loss of the Roman Empire that they most regretted. In his writings Gregory had carefully inserted the history of the Franks not into Roman history,
but into biblical history. Hence the past for which he mourned
was the truly Christian one, and the Paradise he had lost was the
original one at the creation of the world. Gregory began his history with an account of Adam and Eve, but not merely to establish his chronology on a firm basis. Adam had been a "type" of
Christ, who had founded the church with his death; Adam and
Eve had lived in "the place of angels" and, perhaps most important, "among the delights of Paradise they had been happy."[38]
In many ways the activities of the Merovingian church were designed to regain that original Paradise. Now, in the later sixth
century, people lived again in "Christian times," and they again
found happiness in the presence of saints' relics: for genuine relics were those that "the martyr has confirmed with the miracles of
Paradise."[39]

36. *HF* III.19.
37. *HF* IX.12 and *VP* 11.1; also *HF* V.7, VIII.34; *VP* 1.3, 13.1, 15.1.
38. *HF* I.1; also Fortunatus *Carm.* II.4.9, on Eve: "ut paradyssiaco bene laeta-
retur in horto."
39. *HF* V.14, *VJ* 41. For other saints in Paradise, cf. *ILCV* 1062 = LeBlant II,
no. 516, and Sidonius *Ep.* VI.17.2.

*   *   *

When Gregory wrote the preface to the first book of his history he had two concerns: to apologize for his literary gracelessness, and to confess his Catholicism. This confession is important, because although Gregory never presented any systematic theology of his own, the miracles that he described could make sense only in the context of orthodox Catholicism. Since in Merovingian Gaul Catholicism still faced opposition from Judaism or Arianism (which also had political overtones, since the Visigoths and the Sueves in Spain were still Arians for most of the sixth century), Gregory's thinking tended to stress one general issue, the problem of the proper relationship between God the Father and Jesus Christ his Son within the divine Trinity. Most of Gregory's debates with Arian Visigoths or with Jews were about the correct theological formulation of this problem, and his usual conclusion was that only if God himself had appeared as a man in Jesus Christ could men be reconciled again to the Father.[40]

In less argumentative terms, what Gregory's theology allowed was a specific doctrine of the communication of grace, at the heart of which was the Incarnation, God becoming man: "The Lord of the heavens descended . . . for the redemption of the world."[41] In a modern theological perspective, "The Incarnation is the antecedent of the doctrine of Mediation, and the archetype both of the Sacramental principle and of the merits of Saints."[42] Gregory's friend Fortunatus stressed the significance of the Incarnation more succinctly than Gregory himself could have: "Unless a man correctly believes in Christ he cannot have a Father in heaven, just as the Arians, Jews, and Manichees . . . have no Father . . . ; but we, who rightly confess that the Son [was] in the world, have a Father in heaven."[43]

Gregory was not a sophisticated theologian, and in his debates he was content merely to weave together biblical passages or to browbeat opponents into submission: one went "insane with rage" after having to listen to these platitudes; another just remained silent.[44] But his insistence on orthodox Catholicism also had im-

40. *HF* VI.5; cf. V.43, VI.40.
41. *VP* 2, praef.
42. J. H. Newman, *An essay on the development of Christian doctrine* (New York, 1949) 86, quoted by Pelikan (1978) 158.
43. Fortunatus *Carm.* X.1.13.
44. *HF* V.43, VI.5.

portant implications for the way men could live, because arguments over theology were more than disputes over the correct verbal formulation of the Trinity: "Religious patterns . . . thus have a double aspect: they are frames of perception, symbolic screens through which action is experienced; and they are guides for action, blueprints for conduct."[45] Belief systems such as Arianism, Judaism, or other variations, including one that denied that God could ever feel human emotions such as anger,[46] opened up a gap between divinity and humanity, between heaven and earth, that had never been crossed since Adam had enjoyed God's presence in Paradise. In contrast, with its insistence on the full and simultaneous divinity and humanity of Christ, orthodox Catholicism held out the possibility that this chasm could be spanned again; because it had a correct doctrine about the Person of Christ, orthodox Catholicism could also have a correct perspective on the work of Christ, his church, and his saints. Hence it emphasized activities and beliefs that demonstrated the efficacy of the sacraments of the church as well as, more notably, the divine power of holy relics.

An example can serve to introduce the power of relics.[47] In one of the churches at Clermont was a small sarcophagus that no one could identify. One day when a man sat down, it cracked down the middle and toppled the man off. Gregory was a witness and drew two conclusions: first, that although no one knew who was in the sarcophagus, it contained "something divine"; and second, that the man must have done an "improper crime" to have been rejected in this way.[48] From this example two general themes emerge. One involves both the potential ubiquity but also the limitations of holiness. Given the possibility that almost anyone, anything, or any place might be holy, the problem was always how to locate genuine holiness. In many Gallic towns by the sixth century men had no problem finding holy relics and holy shrines; at Tours, for instance, we have already noted the growth of the cult of St. Martin during the fifth century. But other cults began with far more difficulty, because some tombs were found buried be-

---

45. C. Geertz (1968) 98.
46. *HF* I.4.
47. Marignan (1899) vol. II, *Le culte des saints sous les Merovingiens*, is a thorough and still useful survey of the literary sources; Brown (1977) and (1981) offers stimulating interpretations.
48. *GC* 35.

neath the pavement of new churches, while others lay forgotten beneath thorns and briers, or as in one instance, overgrown by a vineyard.[49] Near Tours was one sarcophagus, overgrown by weeds but said to be the tomb of a bishop, the lid of which a man stole in order to cover his dead son. Disaster followed, until finally, in a dream, a man dressed as a bishop claimed this tomb as his own.[50] Other saints also disclosed the location of their tombs through visions; as Gregory explained, "It is not silly to believe that often the Lord deigns to reveal in visions how saints are to be honored."[51]

The second theme is the comprehensiveness of beliefs in the working of divine power. People consistently allowed these beliefs to overflow into all aspects of their lives, thus enabling them to interpret uncommon—and common—events in a particular way. Let us consider briefly some characteristics of relic cults in Merovingian Gaul.

First, relic cults helped Christianity to consolidate and expand its position in society. Gregory stressed specifically this purpose in the preface to one of his books of miracles: "It is necessary for me to investigate, write up, and speak about those things which build up the church of God." So he began this particular book with an account of miracles worked around relics of the saint who had actually founded the Catholic church, the most important "martyr" of all: Jesus Christ.[52] In this ecclesiastical context the miracles performed around relics became dramatic enactments of the biblical message, as shown most clearly by Gregory's copious biblical citations. Miracles likewise provided conclusive arguments in favor of Catholic theological positions. In the cathedral at Bazas, for example, three crystalline drops hanging from the ceiling, when caught in a silver dish, merged into a single jewel—proof, according to Gregory, against the Arian heresy.[53] Furthermore, because Catholic theology permitted the intervention of divine power into daily life in ways that Arian theology discounted, Catholic clergy could work miracles while Arians could not. A Catholic deacon could plunge his hand into a pot of boiling water and find it cold; an Arian who did the same was burned to the bone. Actions and beliefs therefore vindicated each other, so that the miracles worked around relics were consistent with Catholic theology but not with Arianism. Thus it is understandable why the

49. E.g. *GM* 56, *GC* 51, 79.
50. *GC* 17.      51. *GC* 39; cf. *GC* 18.
52. *GM*, praef., 1–2, 5–7.      53. *GM* 12.

king of the Arian Visigoths, on the verge of converting, should first concede that only Catholic bishops could perform miracles, and then accept their theology.[54]

Second, beliefs about relics and miracles provided not only explanations for specific events, but also a framework within which to evaluate them. At Paris a soldier trying to steal the golden dove from the church of St. Dionysius (St. Denis) slipped and stabbed himself in the side; Gregory had a ready explanation: "No one doubts that this happened not by chance, but by the judgment of God."[55] When Gregory visited Radegund at her convent in Poitiers, he adored her relic of the True Cross, but then, noticing one lamp that was dripping oil, criticized her for not replacing the container. No, no, Radegund insisted, this lamp was simply bubbling over with oil: "It is the power of the holy cross which you see." Gregory wrote: "I watched in silence, and then confessed the power of the adored cross."[56]

Third, in the shimmering presence of relics, people attempted to resolve uncertainties in daily life and thereby avoid such unsettling alternatives as violence or long feuds. Many swore oaths before relics and tombs. When a dispute between a man and his neighbors at Bourges could not be settled, city magistrates insisted that both parties take public oaths before the relics of St. Stephen. In the presence of these relics doubt was eliminated, because the accuser was suddenly thrown to the pavement; Gregory added a sharp comment: "The power of the saint revealed all."[57] An archdeacon accused of adultery wanted to clear himself with an oath before the tomb of St. Maximian at Trier. Approaching the crypt, he went down some steps and passed through one door; but at the next door he stopped, too frightened to go on, and instead confessed his guilt.[58] Before these relics and tombs a shining light seemed to probe and illuminate even men's private thoughts, an exposure that some found overpowering: in one church "there was the fear of God, and also a great brightness." So it was with the celestial jewel at Bazas, which could distinguish between the innocent and the guilty: "To one man it appeared to be opaque, but to another it was crystal clear."[59]

54. HF II.3, IX.15, GM 80; also VM 1.11, for an Arian king conceding that divine cures happen only after a confession of Catholic theology.

55. GM 71.      56. GM 5.      57. GM 33.

58. GC 91; cf. GM 60.

59. HF II.16, and GM 12. For the complementary practice of sortes biblicae, cf. HF IV.16, V.14, and Courcelle (1953).

Finally, although beliefs in the efficacy of divine power sometimes seemed more threatening than reassuring, men also acquired personal patrons who could intercede for them in daily life
as well as, more importantly, in heaven. In many cities saints had
been designated as civic patrons who even offered protection
from invasions. In the early sixth century, after King Theuderic
surrounded Clermont, he was troubled by bad dreams, which his
duke explained to him: "Behold, the walls of this city are very
strong and huge fortifications surround it. So that your magnificence may clearly understand, I am speaking about the saints
whose churches surround the walls of this city; and furthermore,
the bishop of this city is considered to be influential in the presence of God."[60] King Theuderic accepted his hint and withdrew.
Individuals too could acquire saints as patrons, whose favors and
intercessions might make even ordinary people secure against the
final judgment.[61] In this sense the relationships people established with their saints evolved largely within the traditional expectations of the informal patronage that had provided the adhesive for personal relationships under the Roman Empire. Now
a saint could confront a thief and claim of himself, "I am a man
who has many friends in different regions"; and everyone knew
that one of those regions was heaven itself.[62] On Judgment Day
Gregory, for one, hoped that the angels in heaven would say,
"This is the man on whose behalf St. Martin petitions."[63]

But the location and the applicability of holiness in Merovingian society was more ambiguous than these examples may suggest, because holiness could also be found elsewhere than at holy
relics and holy shrines commemorating dead saints. Living people
might also be seen as *sancti*, "holy men" who had taken on the
characteristics of "living relics": "Although placed in a body this
monk was thought somehow already to shine with heavenly
powers."[64] The ambiguity appears most clearly with the seem-
ingly paradoxical application of notions of life and death.

Most people conceded that the saints represented by relics had
never really died, since they continued to "live" in heaven.[65] The
remains of some saints never became cold, but continued to be so

60. *VP* 4.2.
61. *GM* 106.
62. *GM* 91, with de Ste. Croix (1954).
63. *VM* 2.60, modeled after Sulpicius Severus *Vita Martini* 7.6.
64. *Vita [Patrum Iurensium] Eugendi* 19.
65. *HF* X.13.

"hot" that the snow that fell on their tombs simply melted; the remains of others never decayed, and their bodies seemed to be merely sleeping.[66] Gregory often implicitly underlined the peculiarity that holy men merely sank into the "big sleep," by describing a deathbed scene.[67] A saint's bed therefore became a prized relic, almost like another tomb. The bed of one bishop was carefully reconstructed by a successor who covered it with a shroud and burned candles before it; naturally enough, since it was treated exactly like a tomb, "The bed was adorned with many outstanding miracles."[68] Miracles happened at the bed of a holy man both while he was alive and after his death. At the spot where St. Martin had slept at Candes a woman was healed; then, abandoning her own husband, she refused to leave the saint's bed.[69]

One obvious effect of this ambiguity in ideas about life and death was to emphasize all the more clearly the common perception of holy men and saints as people with the kind of power that was not confined within ordinary limitations. One abbot, for instance, had healed people during his lifetime; after his death, "His many miracles show that he continues to live in eternity."[70] Gregory's story about the apostle John at Ephesus was even more explicit, because he had had himself buried in his tomb while he was still alive, and would not die until Judgment Day—that is, only after people no longer needed celestial patrons.[71] From the opposite viewpoint, however, many holy men appeared to be dead while they were still alive. In order to forestall his selection as bishop one monk tried to hide, appropriately enough, in a graveyard.[72] Tucked away in their cells monks and hermits might as well have been entombed. One monk at Vienne had not left his cell in forty years, "so that no one knew what he looked like; they only heard his voice." Another ascetic at Nice lived in a tower and could be approached only through a window; while alive he was infested with worms, which disappeared immediately after he died. Another monk lived in a tomblike cell furnished only with a stone bench, chair, and bed.[73] In fact, some monks were simply buried where they had lived, their cells becoming their tombs.[74]

66. GC 71, 79.

67. HF X.13, "mortis somno," and LeBlant II, no. 628 = ILCV 149, line 2: "leti hic sopor altus"; cf. VP 15.4, 20.4.    68. VP 8.8.

69. VM 3.22; other examples in Vieillard-Troiekouroff (1976) 387.

70. GC 15.    71. HF I.26, GM 29.    72. Vita Caesarii I.14.

73. Vita [Patrum Iurensium] Eugendi 5; HF VI.6; VP 14.1.

74. VP 12.3, 20.4.

In sixth-century Gaul death was very much a part of life, a sentiment of inevitability that the poet Fortunatus used as consolation: "Sooner or later that same misfortune rolls over everyone."[75] Although people knew what normally happened after death, when their bodies decayed and were eaten by worms and vermin, Gregory liked to make sure that they would not forget. One man who offended a saint became feverish, started to smoke, and produced an unbearable stench; the body of another dying man who had previously feuded with a bishop "became as black as if it had been placed on glowing coals and roasted."[76] A priest who had had to share a sarcophagus with an old corpse never forgot the trauma. "Years afterwards he used to describe the fetid stench which clung around the dead man's bones. . . . If he stuffed his cloak into his nostrils he could smell nothing as long as he held his breath; but whenever he removed his cloak, for fear of being suffocated, he inhaled the pestilential odour through his mouth and his nose and even, so to speak, through his ears!"[77] But with holy people these ordinary expectations were, again, turned upside down. After a nun at Poitiers died ("with a smile," no less), her body was "whiter than linen"; when saints were exhumed even many years after their burials, their bodies still produced fragrant scents.[78] Like an abbot who came back to life after being mistakenly laid out on a funeral bier and who could then describe the sweet splendors of heaven, living holy men appeared to fluctuate between heaven and earth, life and death, somehow surviving "without death."[79] As far as other people were concerned, the significant disjunction in the lives of holy people was not their physical death, but rather the "social death" they experienced when they renounced daily life and began to live as ascetics. For holy people, physical death was a "relatively unimportant event"[80] that apparently had no impact at all on their influence and authority.

*       *       *

These beliefs about the role of saints and living holy men in mediating access to holiness can often seem, to us, to have been only abstract doctrines or ideas. Such an interpretation would fail

75. Fortunatus *Carm.* IV.26.155.        76. *HF* V.36, *VJ* 17.
77. *HF* IV.12, trans. Thorpe (1974).
78. *HF.* VI.29, and *VP* 10.4, *GC* 83.
79. *HF* VII.1, and *VP* 7, praef.; Fortunatus *Carm.* IV.8.4.
80. Pelikan (1978) 182.

to recognize that these beliefs were neither standards against which people mechanically evaluated behavior, nor academic rationalizations intended to explain prior events. Rather, even as they were created by people's needs and expectations, these beliefs defined the nature of communities and of leadership in them. In short, we need always to remember a fundamental equation: holiness was power. Not only did beliefs about holiness clarify the availability of and the means of access to divine power, they also reshuffled the limits and exercise of power between men. Because of the holiness others had seen them to possess, saints had in addition been men "who did not respect a man's civil power but rather feared only God."[81] With living holy men the application of such divine power became more immediate, but it was also more disconcerting to others who were influential. Within cities, for instance, a bishop could help his own family force a rival aristocratic family into disgrace;[82] within kingdoms a barbarian king insisted that his fearful trembling in the presence of an abbot was really due to an earthquake![83] In this sense miracles were not only manifestations of divine power, they were also warnings to kings, magistrates, and local aristocrats: "Listen to this tale, all you who exercise civil power!"[84]

In the historical narrative, miracle stories, saints' lives, and poems of Gregory and his friend Fortunatus we therefore see men who were not cowering before unpredictable flashes of divine power, but who were actively manipulating and evaluating holiness in order to affect the distribution of prestige and authority in their communities. Catholic bishops such as Gregory had two essential concerns about the role of holiness in society. One was a theological stress on its proper source; by emphasizing that holiness came originally only through Jesus Christ, Catholic theology was able to prevent heresies and paganism from sponsoring any genuine divine power. The second concern was a more practical consideration about its proper location and availability. Bishops and abbots may have preferred holiness to be available only at the relics and shrines that were under their supervision, but, as we have seen, holiness was also a quality that could be bestowed by communities on living holy men, not all of whom were safely

81. VP 17.1. Prinz (1973) is an excellent survey, although he sometimes overstates the authority of bishops in their cities.
82. VP 4.3, with Kurth (1919) I, 200–3.
83. VP 1.5.        84. VM 1.29.

dressed in clerical robes or monastic habits. And although access to holiness provided an advantage in some feuds over prestige, arguments over genuine holiness generated still other rivalries. People in Gaul could have great respect for the remote stylite saints of Syria, but when a man began to live on his own pillar near Trier, the local bishops pointedly warned him that he had set out on the "wrong road" and then forced him into a monastery.[85] Gregory himself rebuked one monk for being deluded by diabolical cleverness, and he criticized another for allowing his holiness to become "vanity."[86]

Before we investigate in the following chapters other implications of the functioning of holiness in Merovingian society, three further general qualifications are necessary. First, to repeat an earlier point, this survey of the behavior arising from beliefs about holiness in early Merovingian Gaul is not meant to imply that they were either new or unique in the sixth century. Pagan cults had presumably filled some of the same functions; Christian holy men were already active during the fourth century, about as far back as we can meaningfully trace the history of the early Gallic church; and although many men respected relic cults in Gaul by the early fifth century, others already complained about them. Nor can we analyze whether there was any increase in the intensity of these beliefs, for the simple reason that the literary sources are of uneven quantity and character, although we can guess that the number of relic cults increased after the end of the fifth century and that, with the disappearance of the ideal of the Roman Empire in Gaul, they came to play additional roles in people's lives. Instead, the identifying characteristic of the sixth century, as contrasted with the fourth and fifth centuries, is that we can, for once, see religious beliefs and behavior in a more thickly textured context.

The second qualification is that the following chapters can give a misleading impression of the internal coherence and clarity of beliefs in relics and saints. Despite all the underlying connections, latent functions, and unconscious logic that we might discover, people in Merovingian Gaul still often thought and behaved in "illogical" ways. Relics, cults, and holy places displayed a variety of forms and origins: one place, for instance, became

85. *HF* VIII.15. For the reputation of stylite saints in Gaul, see *GC* 26; *Vita Genovefe virgine* 27; and Elbern (1966).
86. *VP* 15.2, 20.3.

holy after relics stayed there for only one night.[87] The same variety can be seen with holy men, because holiness had not yet been "disciplined" into exclusive association with specific ecclesiastical offices, forms of asceticism, or social groups.

In contrast, as Gregory and his friend Fortunatus described it, the pervasiveness of beliefs in miracles, relics, and saints gives the impression of a remarkable unanimity that seems to have transcended the geographical and social distinction between northern and southern Gaul that modern scholars use to analyze the differing fates of aristocratic families, and that they also extend into a more general cultural opposition between barbarian Gaul and Roman Gaul.[88] Although Gregory lived all his life in central, Roman Gaul, through his friends and his own travels he was familiar with parts of barbarian Gaul, such as the Seine basin and the old Belgian provinces. At different times he visited not only such southern cities as Bordeaux, Saintes, and Vienne, but also Rheims, Soissons, Metz, and Paris,[89] and he knew stories about relics and miracles in Trier and Maastricht. In all these northern cities Gregroy seems to have found the same beliefs about holiness as in his more familiar central and southern Gaul.

These beliefs were furthermore apparently effective among all types of people, and in the presence of relics and holy men rich and poor were put on the same footing.[90] Even the Frankish kings accepted these beliefs and therefore conceded much influence to the Catholic church and its churchmen.[91] Kings controlled the cities, spent the taxes, and fought wars, but the church was responsible for theology and ethics. Kings who thought otherwise were put firmly in their place. When King Chilperic proposed some unorthodox views on the Trinity, Gregory simply refused to listen, insisting that the king should instead be content with Catholic theology, especially since he was already baptized.[92]

By now Frankish kings had become "Catholic kings" who owed

87. GM 47.
88. Stroheker (1948) 110–11, and Riché (1962) 220–6.
89. Monod (1872) 36–37. See also Vieillard-Troiekouroff (1976) 454–5, although VM 3.60 probably refers to Chalon-sur-Saône and not Cavaillon, despite the reference in the next anecdote to Bishop Veranus of Cavaillon.
90. VP 4.5.
91. HF X.16; also the Edict of Guntram, a. 585 (MGH, Capitularia 1, p. 11), in which the king recognizes a distinction between his own region and "the authority of a supreme majesty that rules over the universe."
92. HF V.44.

success to their acceptance of the orthodox Trinity; in the opinion of Gregory, a good king was one "who ruled his kingdom justly, respected his bishops, was generous to the churches, helped the poor, and distributed many benefits."[93] Not all kings lived up to that ideal, and bishops had strong preferences (one whose city was transferred from one kingdom to another complained that he had fallen from heaven into hell!),[94] but usually, when confronted by the divine power of relics or holy men, the kings backed down.[95] For the Frankish kings seem already to have adopted an Old Testament perspective of themselves as ruling over God's people with the aid of church "prophets," in this case, saints or living holy men who, according to Gregory, were specific reincarnations of Old Testament figures, "the Israel of our times," "a new Moses," "a new Elijah."[96] Hence the obligations between kings and saints (or their representatives, such as bishops) were meant to reenact an ideal relationship from the biblical past.[97] In Gregory's books of history a survey of the Israelites and their kings became a natural prelude to the history of Gaul under Roman emperors and barbarian kings.

The final qualification is, however, a warning against taking such beliefs and behavior for granted, because to do so would be to postulate an inevitability or compulsion that was alien to those people's own thinking. Despite the apparent ubiquity and comprehensiveness of beliefs about relics, even in the later sixth century relics and saints still always had to "prove" themselves. Thus Gregory accepted that a silk robe had once been wrapped around the True Cross only after the water in which it had been washed began to work cures, and a friend of Gregory conceded the power of a martyr only after his relics made a dry spring bubble with water.[98] Sometimes men confronted relics and made demands of them. A bishop at Agde, when threatened by a count, went to a church, smashed the lights, and said that they would not be lit again until God avenged him; another bishop in a similar situation at Aix-en-Provence went to the tomb of St. Mitrias, insisted that no more candles be lit or psalms sung, threw brier thorns on top of the tomb, and shut the doors of the church. In this latter

93. *HF* III.25; cf. III, praef.    94. *HF* VI.22.
95. E.g. *HF* IV.2, IX.30.
96. *VJ* 7, *VM* 3.22, *VP* 3.1; cf. Fortunatus *Vita Paterni* 24–25.
97. *HF* II, praef., and III, praef.; for discussion, see Graus (1965) 304, 344–5.
98. *GM* 5, 36.

case the bishop had conducted a ritual almost directly the opposite to that involving the discovery of a tomb, so that this ineffective shrine was now to be demoted from its state of Paradise
and forgotten.[99]

In the face of such beliefs about relics and holy men, even
given these qualifications, modern historians are often bewildered that a society could invest so much in what seems to be
such a naive world view. Historians frequently refer to the credulity of the age,[100] or they attempt to offer scientific, empirical explanations for miracles, or they quietly avoid any talk of the supernatural. Yet in many ways the depths of another society's
credulity are merely an inverted reflection of the heights of historians' scepticism. Modern historians often come to resemble the
unbelievers in Merovingian Gaul for whom orthodox Catholicism
and its implications about the mediation of divine power through
holy relics were incomprehensible. One Arian king, for example,
simply could not accept that the springs of Osen (in Spain), which
miraculously filled with water each Easter, represented a "miracle
of God." One year he locked the church and posted guards; another year he dug a trench to discover any concealed pipes. Gregory added a telling comment: this Visigothic king died "because
he dared to investigate the secret of divine power; in that place
there were relics of St. Stephen."[101] We modern historians ought
to take this warning seriously too, and, although conceding that
we cannot fathom all aspects of early Merovingian mentality, at
least respectfully realize that beliefs in Christian relics offered a
logical system capable of organizing and finding sense in society.
The holiness of relic cults and saints was not only something to
believe in, it was also useful to think with. Hence, like other world
views, beliefs about holiness attempted to seize a unity underlying apparent diversity or a regularity underlying apparent disor-
der. They allowed men to increase the range of their own understanding and to make causal connections between disparate events
and ideas; they also encouraged a sense of intrinsic obligation and
thus influenced people's behavior. "This demonstration of a mean-
ingful relation between the values a people holds and the general

99. GM 78, GC 70.
100. Even the finest scholars are susceptible; cf. Delehaye (1925) 320, on Gregory of Tours: "Il accueillait tout, sans passer au creuset certains alliages sus-
pects qui brillaient à ses yeux comme du métal de prix."
101. GM 24.

order of existence within which it finds itself is an essential element in all religions, however those values or that order be conceived."[102] A system of beliefs and behavior oriented around Christian holiness was therefore one perfectly plausible way not of controlling daily events and contingencies, but rather of thinking about, understanding, and coping with them.

The difficulties involved in reconstructing such a "historical anthropology" are obvious, and they become even more complex because of the limitations of our literary sources, which tend to encourage a fragmented perspective. Gregory is our primary source of information for the sixth century, and although other authors such as Bishop Caesarius of Arles and the poet Fortunatus offer much valuable supplementary information, any discussion of sixth-century Gaul is largely an analysis of the world of Gregory of Tours. But Gregory's world was not only a restricted one, in one sense it was perhaps also unique to himself, because so much of our information comes directly from his writings and is therefore filtered through his own preconceptions. In other words, the following chapters rest upon an assumption that many other historians of early Merovingian Gaul often take for granted, that is, that the range of meanings that the cult of relics evoked for Gregory was characteristic also of his Christian contemporaries. This methodological presupposition must simply be stated as clearly as possible, because although other literary sources seem to fit with Gregory's outlook, although Gregory seems to be accurately reporting the behavior, words, and reactions of others, and although Gregory himself was shaped by the perspectives of the Christian community, it is still only an assumption, even if it does make possible the more generalized interpretations in the following chapters.

Furthermore, Gregory's world was geographically confined largely to central and eastern Gaul, and his references to the many relic cults in Gaul seem to suggest, again, splintered parochialism. Throughout Gaul many saints had cults, shrines, and relics. This was largely due to restrictions on the extent of any particular cult, because people thought that relics and shrines ought to have once been in direct contact with the original saints. Hence, al-

---

102. C. Geertz (1975a) 127. See also Walter (1966), for a challenging insistence upon understanding Gregory's belief in miracles within the context of his historiography and his society; and Horton (1970), for an important discussion of traditional religious thought.

though the cult of St. Martin was the most widespead in Gaul, Gregory still had to accept some apocryphal stories about Martin's travels in Gaul to account for its distribution; likewise he came up with a story about a Gallic woman who had been present at the execution of John the Baptist and could therefore collect some of his blood to deposit in the cathedral at Bazas.[103] And although relics were sometimes traded or used as gifts, a further restriction on the spread of a cult might be that a relic itself would refuse to be moved or divided.[104]

In other words, questions also arise about our tendency to use all the available miracle stories in a homogeneous way, because although beliefs and behavior focused on relics were widespread in Gaul, the relics and cults of particular saints were not. A good contrast is with the society of the Byzantine Empire, where a cult of icons based on the idea of resemblance eventually developed separately from relic cults. Given the eminence of a few saints such as Christ and the apostles, it then became possible for everyone, everywhere, to share in their powers; all people needed were the appropriate icons, duly sanctified by bishops. In this way minor local cults might be replaced and large areas unified under the veneration of particular saints—almost as a form of national identity.[105] In the medieval West, however, where the idea of direct contact with the saint was predominant and even icons strictly remained relics,[106] regionalism, localism, and multiplicity of relic cults and saints were common. And even though Gregory tried to insist that, because saints were merely the conduits through which the one same God revealed his power, the various relic cults did not have to lead to a fragmented society,[107] in fact, as we will see in the next chapter, the rivalries inherent in secular society were duplicated by rivalries among saints.

One way out of this fragmentary tendency would be to associate saints with specialized functions rather than with specific regions or cities; but although there is a hint of this possibility in sixth-

103. GM 11, GC 5.
104. E.g. GM 13, 54.
105. Grabar (1946) II, 343–57, is an outstanding discussion of this point.
106. On icons in sixth-century Gaul see Markus (1978), although his theory of the diffusion of Byzantine influences does not help us understand the functions of icons in Gallic society.
107. VM 4.12.

century Gaul,[108] its full development came later. We can be grateful that Gregory became bishop at Tours, the center of the most influential cult in sixth-century Gaul, because it is therefore safer to assume that the attitudes and behavior that he described were probably common throughout Gaul. But any discussion of Merovingian Gaul based primarily on the writings of Gregory of Tours will resolutely reflect his own parochial world.

108. Marignan (1899) II, 21–22.

# CHAPTER 10

# Relic Cults,
## Literary Culture,
## and the Aristocracy

During the middle of the sixth century Nicetius of Trier emerged as one dominating bishop in Gaul. Here was a man clearly in command of all situations: even while relieving himself in the bushes he had enough presence of mind to frighten off a ghost by making the sign of the cross! Given his self-confidence it is not surprising to discover that he was obstinate even toward Frankish kings, and that he feuded with no fewer than five of them during his episcopate.[1] Nicetius was also one of the few bishops in sixth-century Gaul with an international reputation: "We have heard about the notable fame of your holiness," wrote an abbot from north Italy, "which people everywhere talk about."[2] This was a particularly impressive achievement for a bishop from northern, "barbarian" Gaul, and Nicetius allowed his fame to turn his head. In one instance he sent a blunt letter to the Byzantine emperor Justinian, attempting to dissuade him from some Eastern heresies (on which the bishop was apparently badly informed) and telling him to stop persecuting orthodox Catholics: "Justinian, who has so deceived you?" In another instance he wrote to a Frankish princess married to the king of the Lombards and insisted that she convert her husband to Catholicism.[3] What an old emperor or a young Italian princess made of this advice is

---

1. Gregory of Tours *VP* 17, and *Epist. Austrasicae* 11. On Nicetius see Ewig (1954) 97–106, and Gauthier (1980) 172–89. (References to the writings of Gregory of Tours hereafter omit his name. See Chapter 9, unnumbered note.)

2. *Epist. Austrasicae* 6.

3. *Epist. Austrasicae* 7–8; and note the anathemas of the Council of Orléans a. 549, Can. 1, at which Nicetius had been present.

not known, but from another letter we know that Nicetius was also capable of offending even his neighboring bishops.[4]

Nicetius was, however, an effective bishop for his own congregation, and deserved the compliment of Fortunatus: "With you as shepherd no wolf has ever stolen any lambs from your flock, and people feel quite secure in your sheepfold." In fact, the bishop's most impressive accomplishment was this "sheepfold," a huge castle built on a hill overlooking the Moselle River. Although Nicetius had indulged himself by sending away for craftsmen from Italy, his castle was now the most secure building in the region, fortified by thirty towers, a catapult, and holy relics against all enemies, including Frankish kings.[5]

Nicetius was furthermore known for his intimate connection with divine power. On another occasion the abbot from north Italy requested his assistance again, this time with St. Ambrose of Milan: "You," he wrote to Nicetius, "have frequent dealings with people in heaven."[6] Nicetius himself once claimed that, in a dream, an angel had revealed to him God's own assessment of each Frankish king.[7] And at the end of his life he announced that he had received a personal invitation from no less than St. Paul and John the Baptist to join them in heaven. Gregory found none of this surprising; in fact, he expected nothing less. "From the moment of his birth [it was obvious] that Nicetius was destined to be a monk. When he was born, his head was seen to have almost no hair, as is common among infants, except that a few wispy strands were arranged in a faint circle, so that one might suppose these hairs to have formed the tonsure of a monk."[8]

As we investigate the prominent aristocratic families of sixth-century Gaul, we can see that in many cases their members had also apparently been destined from birth (or, perhaps better, by birth) to become abbots and bishops. The family of Gregory of Tours provides an excellent case study, not least because even before Gregory was elevated to the see of Tours, some of his ancestors had been bishops. Whether born with the distinctive monastic hairstyle or not, members of his family were destined for prominence in the church: this was another of what Godefroid

4. *Epist. Austrasicae* 11.
5. Fortunatus *Carm.* III.11–12, and *Epist. Austrasicae* 21.
6. *Epist. Austrasicae* 5.
7. *VP* 17.5.     8. *VP* 17.1, 6.

Kurth called "mitred families."[9] Hence, when Florentinus, Gregory's great-grandfather, was chosen for the see of Geneva, his wife was able to talk him out of accepting with a telling argument. "Beloved husband, do not . . . seek to become bishop of Geneva. I have conceived a child by you, and I am now pregnant with a bishop."[10] Florentinus' wife knew what she was talking about, because the baby was Nicetius, later bishop of Lyon.

The family of Gregory of Tours opens up for us the geographical strongholds of the late Gallo-Roman aristocracy. The Rhone River valley, central Gaul and Burgundy, and the basin of the Loire River were the areas in which Gregory's family was prominent, and which, along with Aquitania and some northern outposts such as Trier, had always been conspicuous for notable local aristocrats. Significantly, these were also what we might call "interface" regions, in the sense that during the later fifth and early sixth centuries they had once served as buffer zones between rival barbarian kingdoms. Perhaps it was because of their geographical position on the "frontier" that local aristocrats from these regions continued to assert their traditions and authority for so long, providing thereby a necessary link between Classical Antiquity and early medieval society. Thus K. F. Stroheker was able to conclude what is still the finest study of the late Gallic aristocracy by pointing out that some of the last literary references to "senators," always one of the proudest status titles in the Roman world, come in the seventh century from the Auvergne.[11]

Gregory's family is also a valuable example of how many of these aristocrats never stood still but instead adapted themselves to a changing society in ways that had been impossible for Sidonius during the previous century. In the following sections of this chapter let us investigate, first, the family of Gregory as a paradigm for the development of the Gallic aristocracy in early Merovingian society, emphasizing in particular its consequential intimacy with relic cults, especially those of St. Julian and St. Martin; and second, the current role of one previously influential factor in the self-definition of local aristocracies, that is, knowledge of the

9. Kurth (1919) I, 251. Krusch (1951) is a concise introduction to Gregory and his family.
10. *VP* 8.1.
11. Stroheker (1948) 135–6. On the debate between Kurth (1919) II, 97–115, and Stroheker (1965) 192–206, over Gregory's use of the title "senator," see Gilliard (1979).

classical heritage. As we will see, with his reliance on Christian relic cults and his inadequate skills in classical learning, Gregory turns out to be the exact opposite of Sidonius.

*    *    *

On his father's side Gregory's family was closely associated with Clermont and the Auvergne. His grandfather Georgius was a descendant of a senatorial family who married a woman from another prominent family that claimed Vectius Epagathus as an ancestor.[12] This man had been one of the famous martyrs at Lyon in the late second century, all of whom, according to Gregory, had been translated directly to heaven after their deaths.[13] Hence, in contrast to other Gallic aristocrats of the fifth century, who were still claiming descent from great men out of Roman history,[14] Gregory's ancestors had by then developed a Christian pedigree.[15]

Georgius' sons were Gallus and Florentius, both born probably during the reign of Clovis. Gallus was the older, and although his father tried to find an appropriate aristocratic wife for him, Gallus instead fled to a monastery near Clermont.[16] His decision is another pointed example of transformations in the Gallic aristocracy. Because prominent families apparently preferred marrying among themselves, at certain times huge fortunes were concentrated among a few families; but in the long run this tendency also entailed a gradual narrowing of candidates for inheritance. Furthermore, since Christianity now presented chastity as a respectable option even within marriage, there was a much higher probability of families simply dying out.[17]

The chief beneficiaries were Catholic churches and monasteries, which by the sixth century had already accumulated vast amounts of land.[18] These donations came from many different people, not only from kings, queens, and aristocrats, but also from smaller landowners who had no children[19] or who passed over their own relatives in order to designate a church as heir.[20] In

12. VP 6.1, with Stroheker (1948) no. 175.
13. GM 48; cf. HF I.29.
14. Sidonius Ep. IV.14.1–2, VIII.3.3, Carm. XXII.163–8.
15. If not already earlier: cf. HF I.31, on Leocadius of Bourges.
16. VP 6.1, with Stroheker (1948) no. 171.
17. As illustrated in the story of the "Two Lovers," HF I.47, GC 31.
18. Lesne (1910) 143–278.
19. VM 4.11.
20. E.g. VM 1.30, with VM 1 capitula 30.

other cases people simply felt that churches offered security for their possessions against exploitation by others.[21] In fact, churches and monasteries acquired so much land and wealth that Frankish kings felt threatened enough to cancel wills that left property to churches; as one king said, "My treasury is always empty, because all my wealth has fallen into the hands of the churches. Only bishops now rule like kings. No one respects me; all honor has been transferred to the bishops in each city."[22]

Becoming bishop of a see, and therefore administrator of its lands,[23] was thus a prize apparently worth scheming over. When Bishop Quintianus of Clermont died in 525, some citizens met at the house of the priest Inpetratus, who was an uncle of Gallus. He encouraged his nephew's ambition to become bishop and suggested that he go directly to King Theuderic; hence, when a delegation from Clermont arrived at the royal court, Gallus had already been chosen. During the sixth century such royal approval became an additional component in the procedure for selecting new bishops, sometimes even replacing election by clergy and congregations. Bribery was consequently widespread; when, for instance, the see of Bourges became vacant, candidates showed up at the court of King Guntram with "gifts."[24] The delegation from Clermont, in contrast, was treated to a banquet by King Theuderic; hence men could claim that "the largest bribe given for Gallus' bishopric was a small gold piece to the cook who served the meal."[25]

By becoming bishops some aristocrats acquired an advantage over other aristocrats who were otherwise of similar status. At Clermont, for instance, a priest who insulted Gallus was forced to bow down at the bishop's feet in public, even though the priest was a member of a senatorial family and the son of a count.[26] In the introduction to the *Vita* of Gallus, Gregory had suggested that some men could rise above the "apex of worldly nobility" in favor of "heavenly concerns": "They are just like birds soaring out of

21. *Epist. Austrasicae* 22; cf. *GM* 96.
22. *HF* VI.46, with the comments of Wallace-Hadrill (1971) 65, on royal honor. Merovingian taxation is reexamined by Goffart (1982), esp. p. 17: "What seems to have been ultimately at stake was not a tax so much as a conception of personal or corporate dignity."
23. Lesne (1910) 63–69, 279–89.
24. *HF* VI.39; also Gregory I *Reg.* V.58, and Claude (1963) 59, 65–66.
25. *VP* 6.3.
26. *VP* 6.4, with Stroheker (1948) no. 139, on Evodius.

snares and flying up into the sky."[27] But according to Gregory's own account Gallus seems not to have soared very high after all, because the old aristocratic concern over prestige remained a powerful obsession, even if it was now articulated in a Christian context.

One innovation of Bishop Gallus and his brother Florentius (Gregory's father) was to expand the cult of St. Julian at Brioude and, more significantly, specially associate their family with it. When in 543 a plague threatened Clermont, Bishop Gallus instituted an annual pilgrimage during Lent to the church of St. Julian at Brioude;[28] in addition, every year on August 28, Florentius took his entire family on another pilgrimage to Brioude for the festival of St. Julian.[29] Although Florentius had apparently died when Gregory was an infant, he left his son more than his personal reliquary;[30] like him, Gregory seems also to have considered himself uniquely attached to the cult of St. Julian. Even though the saint's church was some distance from his native city of Clermont, Gregory still referred to him as a "martyr of Clermont" and insisted that the cult of St. Julian had become his "private" possession.[31] So he called himself an *alumnus*, a foster son of St. Julian, and prayed for the saint's patronage.[32] Here we see, then, a prominent aristocratic family from the Auvergne first updating and then forming an exclusive attachment with a local cult that happened to be the most important one in the region. As we will see, association with the cult of St. Julian will be important when Gregory becomes bishop at Tours.

Florentius had followed the common tendency of Gallic families and married Armentaria, who belonged to a prominent family that in turn represented the unification of two other important families. Armentaria's father (who was not named) came from a

27. *VP* 6 praef.
28. *HF* IV.5, *VP* 6.6; still observed by his successor Cautinus, *HF* IV.13.
29. *VJ* 24–25.
30. *VP* 14.3, *GC* 39, and Stroheker (1948) no. 163. For the chronology, cf. *GM* 83: after Florentius' death his wife wore his reliquary; years later she gave it to their son Gregory, who described himself as still a young man.
31. *HF* II.11, *VJ* 1; and the readings in *MGH*, SRM 7, p. 737, on 562, 1: "Incipit liber propriae in gloria sancti martyris Iuliani peculiaris patroni nostri," and p. 741, on 584, 12: "Explicit liber de gloria sancti martyris Iuliani peculiaris patroni nostro [sic]"—both considered genuine by Krusch (1951) XIII n. 4. Note also Marignan (1899) II, 28: "On voit ainsi combien était égoiste le culte rendu aux saints."
32. *VJ* 2, 50.

family that was influential around Autun and Langres. His father Gregorius (Gregory's great-grandfather) had been count at Autun for forty years (and was possibly also a friend of Sidonius) until the early sixth century, when, upon the death of his wife, he became bishop of Langres and Dijon.[33] At some point during his episcopacy he founded a cult of his own, because after learning in a dream that a sarcophagus honored as a pagan shrine at Dijon was really the tomb of a martyr, he decided to rebuild its crypt. But the ceremony in which the saint's sarcophagus was transferred to this reconstructed crypt was as much a glorification of Bishop Gregorius as of the saint. When three yoke of oxen could not budge the huge sarcophagus, Bishop Gregorius, "spotlighted by candles," simply picked it up with the assistance of two priests and carried it inside; his audience considered this a "fantastic performance." Years later Gregorius acquired a *Passio* of the saint and then also built a church over the tomb.[34] As we will see in the next chapter, these were the usual ways to enhance a cult, and it is not difficult to imagine who took credit for the new church and who presided at services in it.

In the aristocratic competition over prestige, special association with a cult had become an additional influential factor that might even single men out for selection as bishops. In the middle of the fifth century, for instance, one priest built a church to St. Symphorian of Autun; later he became bishop of Autun.[35] In the middle of the sixth century a deacon had a nocturnal revelation, as a result of which he discovered the long-neglected tomb of the first bishop of Clermont. Thereafter people properly respected the tomb, as well as this deacon, because he became archdeacon and, when Gallus died in 551, was able to succeed him as bishop of Clermont even though initially a priest had the support of most other bishops.[36] In this way the fortunes of individuals and families fluctuated directly with the prominence of the cults with which they were specially associated. The epitaph of Perpetuus, the fifth-century bishop at Tours who had expanded the cult of St. Martin by building a new church over the saint's tomb, expressed

33. *VP* 7.1–2, with Stroheker (1948) no. 182. Gregorius was a correspondent of Sidonius if he can be identified with the addressee of *Ep.* V.18, sent to a count of Autun named Attalus; since one of Gregorius' grandsons was named Attalus (*HF* III.15), we know the name was common in the family. *PLRE* II, pp. 179–80, now makes this identification.

34. *GM* 50.    35. *HF* II.15.    36. *HF* IV.5–7; cf. *GC* 29.

this relationship most succinctly: "Perpetuus did not build such a grand tomb for St. Martin alone, he also constructed it as a memorial for himself."[37]

Some sees therefore came to be dominated by particular families. After Gregorius died in about 540, his son Tetricus (Gregory's great-uncle) became bishop at Langres and promoted a new cult of his own. Gregorius' body had been buried in a corner of the church at Dijon: "But there was just not enough space for people to approach as their reverence demanded." So Tetricus built a larger apse where people were healed before the saint's tomb. Like so many other Merovingian bishops, Tetricus too had founded a cult, but with one important difference: it was a cult to his father, for whom the heavens had been seen to open when he was buried.[38] Veneration for the new saint implied respect for Bishop Tetricus, who was the son of a man now seated among "the starry hosts."[39] Nor was this the end of the family's association with Langres and Dijon. One of Tetricus' immediate, although short-lived, successors as bishop was a relative; and Gregory's brother Petrus, who had been a deacon at Langres, was buried at Dijon next to St. Gregorius.[40] According to Fortunatus, for Gregorius and Tetricus the cities of Langres and Dijon had been *patriae sedes*, a family see.[41] As we will see again with Tours, however, this was only one among many family sees in Gaul.

The mother of Armentaria (who is also not named) came from a family that had been prominent in Burgundy, particularly around Geneva and Lyon, the region to which Armentaria herself retired after the death of her husband.[42] Florentinus, the grandfather of Armentaria, was from a senatorial family and almost became bishop of Geneva; his brother, the appropriately named Sacerdos, became bishop of Lyon. Before Sacerdos died in 552 he was able to convince King Childebert to nominate his nephew, Florentinus' son Nicetius (another of Gregory's great-uncles), as his successor.[43] As bishop, Nicetius may have quarreled with the count, but

---

37. Epitaph of Perpetuus, lines 11–12 (*PL* 58.756), although considered a later forgery by Havet (1885) 222–4.
38. *VP* 7.4–6, with Stroheker (1948) no. 385.
39. Fortunatus *Carm.* IV.2.6, an epitaph for Gregorius.
40. *HF* V.5.
41. Fortunatus *Carm.* IV.3.2, an epitaph for Tetricus.
42. Cf. *VM* 1.36, 3.60 (referring probably to Chalon-sur-Saône).
43. *VP* 8.3, with Stroheker (1948) nos. 161, 259, 337.

he also continued to live similarly to other Gallic aristocrats: "He gave his full attention to the construction of churches and houses, to the sowing of his fields and the planting of his vines." The difference, according to Gregory, was that none of these activities distracted him from prayer; that, and the fact that after his death miracles happened at his tomb.[44]

Nicetius' brother Gundulf served at the royal court before being made a duke by King Childebert.[45] His appointment is a good example of another important characteristic of the sixth-century aristocracy: not only were members of prominent families prepared to serve at the barbarian courts, but secular service could coexist with ecclesiastical service within a single family. As studies of the early Merovingian aristocracy have shown, in Aquitania, the Auvergne, and central Gaul many of the known counts and dukes had Roman names and therefore came from old Roman families (as did some with German names).[46] To take one specific example, during the sixth century in the Auvergne almost all the known counts were from Roman families, and most of these Roman counts were from only four prominent families.[47] One was the family of Gregory's mother, and even a man who married into the family could share in its eminence; hence, the husband of Gregory's niece was successively count of Clermont, duke of Clermont, a general of King Guntram, and patrician in Provence.[48] Roman aristocrats serving Frankish kings either as counts and dukes or as functionaries at the royal courts during the sixth century were thus one important factor in the eventual fusion of Frankish and Roman aristocracies.

Clearly Gregory's family possessed great prominence in central and eastern Gaul, and from this background we come finally to Gregory himself. As he grew up during the 540s and 550s he was taught by his great-uncle Nicetius, later bishop of Lyon, visited by his uncle Gallus, bishop of Clermont, and then educated by Avitus, later bishop of Clermont.[49] This was an impressive array of

44. *HF* IV.36, and his epitaph in LeBlant I, no. 25 = *ILCV* 1073, lines 13–14; for the miracles see *VP* 8.5–12, and *Vita Nicetii* 15.

45. *HF* VI.11, 26, with Stroheker (1948) no. 184.

46. Kurth (1919) I, 169–81, on the backgrounds of sixth-century counts; I, 122–30, on Roman and German names.

47. Kurth (1919) I, 183–203, on the Auvergne; I, 205–25, on the Touraine.

48. Stroheker (1948) no. 260.

49. *VP* 2 praef., 2.2, 8.2.

relatives and supporters. Gregory's father had once been introduced to a blind abbot as the son of a senator;[50] we can well imagine how Gregory would have been introduced as a young boy. In fact, as he was growing up Gregory was only too aware of his rank. Once as he was returning from Burgundy a huge thunderstorm blew up, but it passed the travelers by when he held up his reliquary. Gregory, "as impetuous youngsters usually think," decided that he and his companions had been spared a drenching on account of his own merit; whereupon he slipped from his horse and painfully learned that in fact this miracle was due to the power of the relics he was wearing.[51]

With this background it is not surprising that Gregory became a bishop, because as the poet Fortunatus wrote of another sixth-century bishop, "From both his father and his mother he inherited membership among bishops, and his episcopal see was part of the family legacy."[52] It is also not surprising that he became bishop at Tours, because his family had long had an association with both the city and with St. Martin. When a young man, his great-uncle Nicetius had once been cured after his mother prayed to St. Martin; afterwards Nicetius had the support of the saint that he would someday be a bishop.[53] Gregory had a similarly intimate relationship with St. Martin. In 563, when Gregory was about twenty-five, he came down with a severe fever that was cured only after he made a hazardous pilgrimage to St. Martin's shrine at Tours. This cure was a significant event in Gregory's life. Although on the journey he had become so ill that his friends urged him to turn back, Gregory knew that "he could not go home again." Years before, after he had been cured at the shrine of St. Illidius in Clermont, he had become a monk;[54] this time, after his cure at Tours, he became a deacon.[55] Gregory considered his introduction to St. Martin as a turning point in his life, an event that, along with his accession to the see of Tours ten years later, he went out of his way to date as precisely as possible.[56]

Furthermore, by this time Tours had become virtually a family see; as Gregory was later to assert, all but five of his predecessors as bishop had been members of his family. His immediate prede-

50. *VP* 14.3.    51. *GM* 83.
52. Fortunatus *Carm.* IV.8.7–8, on Cronopius of Périgueux.
53. *VP* 8.1.    54. *VP* 2.2.    55. *VM* 1.35.
56. *VM* 1.32–33, and 2.1, for the date of his accession.

cessor had been Eufronius, his mother's cousin. In 561, when the see became vacant, King Chlothar had wanted Cato, a priest at Clermont, to become the new bishop at Tours, although the citizens preferred the priest Eufronius. After Cato withdrew, Chlothar made inquiries about Eufronius and learned that he was a grandson of Bishop Gregorius of Langres. The king quickly changed his mind: "This is one of the noblest and most distinguished families in the land. Let the will of God and St. Martin be done: I order him to be elected bishop."[57]

Despite the prominence of his family and its connection with the see of Tours, Gregory's selection as bishop in August 573 still aroused opposition. Gregory himself was silent about the whole affair, not even recording in his books of history the death of Bishop Eufronius and his own elevation to the see. We are reduced to using inferences from other information in his writings and from a poem by Fortunatus celebrating his friend's arrival in Tours as bishop. In this dispute over Gregory's election we can also see how relic cults had come to function as a means of resolving the competition over the acquisition of ecclesiastical positions, a competition made all the more fierce because ordination into the ecclesiastical hierarchy, unlike service in the royal administration, precluded the possibility of retirement and thus limited the availability of these positions. In effect, the tensions resulting from promotions within the church could now be neutralized within the more oblique, but also more compelling, idiom of beliefs about relics and saints, and the men promoted could also acquire divine support to complement their ecclesiastical authority. The power of saints could now assist in bringing about the community consensus that was supposed to accompany the selection of new bishops;[58] for if the saints in heaven came to an agreement among themselves over the candidates and made their choice apparent, then communities could more easily reach their own consensus.

When Gregory became bishop at Tours he faced at least two immediate problems. First, Tours was apparently a see worth fighting over, and becoming bishop there would be the culmination of any man's career; once, for instance, when a prophetess informed a prominent general that he would eventually become

57. *HF* IV.15, with Stroheker (1948) no. 130.
58. On the *consensus civium* accompanying the selection of a bishop, see Claude (1963) 22–31.

bishop in a city next to the Loire River, the man was filled with pride with the expectation of presiding at Tours.[59] In 573 the archdeacon Riculf probably wanted to be promoted as bishop upon the death of Eufronius, and he may even have been supported by other bishops. For in 580, even though by then Gregory had replaced him as archdeacon, Riculf was involved in a plot to influence King Chilperic to oust Gregory from the see. He had been so sure of success that, while Gregory was away for a hearing before Chilperic, he had taken charge "as if he were bishop," with an arrogant claim: "With masterly skill I have purged Tours of those people from Clermont." Thus one problem Gregory had to face during the first years of his episcopate was that as an "outsider" from Clermont he had been promoted over an obvious internal candidate—though he himself thought this should have been no problem at all: "Riculf was a silly man, because he did not know that, except for five, all the other bishops who served at Tours were related to my family."[60]

Another problem involved the rivalry between kings over control of Tours, which occasionally included invasion of the Touraine.[61] King Sigibert had acquired the city upon the death of Charibert in 567, but his brother Chilperic always had designs on Tours. By late 573, when Gregory became bishop, Chilperic had control through his son Theudebert and persuaded Gregory to accept Leudast as count of the city. Shortly afterwards Sigibert regained control and kept it until his death in 575, when Chilperic again took over the city and Leudast again became count. Even then there was always the possibility that King Guntram might invade the Touraine. The feud with Count Leudast, who was supported by King Chilperic, was apparently one of the bishop's greatest headaches during the first years of his episcopate, and in his books of history he went out of his way to stress the servile origins and disreputable character of the man.[62] The rivalry climaxed in 580 when Leudast allied himself with Riculf in the scheme to remove Gregory from his see. One of his accusations before King Chilperic was that Gregory intended to turn Tours over to King Childebert, the son of Sigibert.

59. *HF* V.14.
60. *HF* V.49; and the discussion of McDermott (1975) 12–18.
61. Longnon (1878) 244–5, for the relationship between Tours and the sixth-century kings.
62. *HF* V.48–49.

This was, in fact, a powerful threat. For Gregory had been selected as bishop in 573 with the support of Sigibert and his queen,
Brunhild, as well as of Radegund, formerly the queen of King
Chlothar and now the founder of a convent in Poitiers; but King
Chilperic was noticeably not mentioned in Fortunatus' poem about
Gregory's accession as bishop. Gregory had also been consecrated
by Bishop Egidius at Rheims,[63] the metropolitan see of another ecclesiastical province, which was also the capital city of Sigibert's
kingdom. Technically his consecration was contrary to canon law,
which had recently specified that a bishop ought to be consecrated in the city and church that he would govern or, failing that,
somewhere else within the ecclesiastical province.[64] Gregory's irregular consecration was thus another indication of the uncertainty surrounding his appointment as bishop.[65] And because he
had been consecrated in Rheims, his sympathies would seem always to lie with the kingdom of Sigibert and his son Childebert,
rather than with that of Chilperic, who controlled Tours for most
of the early years of his episcopate.

This opposition to the appointment of Gregory is deduced
from the implications of the little that Gregory and Fortunatus
wrote and also from the assumption that resentments that smol-
dered for some years could flare up again in the plot against Gregory in 580. But by then Gregory had secured his position, and one
way he had done so was by introducing new cults to Tours. In
other words, not only did St. Julian send his foster son to St. Martin, as Fortunatus phrased it,[66] but that foster son had taken the
cult of his patron St. Julian with him to Tours, where its acceptance also ensured a better reception for Gregory as the new
bishop.

After being consecrated bishop at Rheims in late August, Gregory had returned directly to Clermont for the festival of St. Julian
at Brioude. Participation in this festival was an obligation for his
family; and while he was at Brioude, Gregory pulled some threads
from the shroud covering St. Julian's tomb, which he thought
would protect him.[67] Only then did he go on to Tours.[68] When he

63. Fortunatus *Carm.* V.3.13–15.
64. Council of Orléans a. 541, Can. 5.
65. In fact, it may also have been part of a general scheme by King Sigibert
and Bishop Egidius to encroach on bishoprics in other kingdoms: see the letters
listed under the Council of Paris a. 573, and *HF* IV.47, VII.17.
66. Fortunatus *Carm.* V.3.11–12.          67. *VJ* 34.          68. *VM* 2.1.

arrived, some monks asked him to dedicate a new church with relics of St. Julian. First, however, Gregory secretly placed these relics in the church of St. Martin, where another man then saw a flash of light from heaven. This bolt of lightning proved the power of St. Julian, and the relics were then placed on the altar. After overnight vigils they were brought to the new church, and while they were being transferred, a possessed man began to shout that St. Martin had joined himself to St. Julian.[69] Given the parochialism of relic cults, this was a startling admission, because often when relics arrived at a place where the saint was unfamiliar, men complained that the relics had been brought to a region not "indebted" to that saint.[70] But this possessed man was insisting that St. Martin had actually appealed for St. Julian to come to Tours. The implication is clear: not only had St. Martin accepted St. Julian, "the martyr of Clermont," but now Tours should accept St. Julian's foster son, the new bishop from Clermont. In other words, asserting that saints had accepted each other was now one strategy for people to resolve competition over bishoprics.[71]

Gregory missed few opportunities in quickly founding many new cults at Tours. During the first year of his episcopate he dedicated an oratory in the cellar of the church house next to the cathedral, in the altar of which he placed relics of St. Martin, St. Julian, St. Saturninus (an early bishop and martyr at Toulouse), and St. Illidius (an early bishop of Clermont, at whose tomb Gregory had once been healed). In this instance Gregory has given us a description of the dedication ceremony: "Many bishops and clerics clothed in white were present, and also a distinguished group of illustrious citizens and a crowd of other people. I held aloft these exceptionally beautiful holy relics, and I came to the door of the oratory."[72] In other words, the ceremony of dedication, in which the entire community participated, was as much an exaltation of Bishop Gregory, the "master of the ceremonies," as of the relics themselves, particularly since it was Gregory alone who could offer a convincing explanation for the terrifying flash of light that had greeted the arrival of the relics.

69. *VJ* 34–35.
70. Cf. *VJ* 32, "cur regionem tibi non debitam adgrederis?"
71. For a similar case, note how in 591 Plato, the archdeacon of Tours, was deliberately passed from St. Martin to St. Hilary to become bishop of Poitiers: Fortunatus *Carm.* X.14.3–4, with *VM* 4.32; cf. *HF* V.49.
72. *GC* 20.

Gregory never let people forget that he had the support of both St. Julian and St. Martin, as well as of a whole "family" of saints inherited from his ancestors. At Artannes he repaired the roof of an oratory containing the relics of, among others, St. Martin, St. Julian, and, significantly, his great-uncle St. Nicetius of Lyon.[73] Gregory also dedicated another church near Tours with relics of St. Julian and St. Nicetius of Lyon, and in an oratory at Tours deposited relics of St. Benignus, whose cult had been invented many years earlier at Dijon by his great-grandfather Gregorius.[74] Hence, Gregory was now establishing at Tours cults in honor of members of his family or their patron saints, and we can probably surmise that the acceptance of family cults at a city implied the acceptance of the family also.[75]

By 580, when Gregory had to face a hearing before King Chilperic over the accusations of Riculf and Count Leudast, he had become self-assured enough to ignore suggestions that he take part of the cathedral treasures and simply retire to Clermont.[76] During the hearing local citizens demonstrated on his behalf, and after he was cleared of the charges Gregory seems finally to have been supported by King Chilperic, who exiled Leudast, and by other bishops, who ordered Riculf to be committed to a monastery.[77] Gregory could now enjoy his own prominence. In 585 he and other bishops came to Orléans to see King Guntram. The king sarcastically criticized bishops who he thought had not supported him, but with Gregory he shared a drink during a courtesy call. Later he confided to Gregory that in his dreams he sometimes saw St. Tetricus of Langres and St. Nicetius of Lyon, two of Gregory's illustrious ancestors; even in his sleep the king could not escape the haunting influence of this family that was so influential in his kingdom of Burgundy.[78]

To his inherited family prominence Gregory had, by now, added many new "friends." One was the Virgin Mary, whose relics Gregory carried with those of St. Martin in a gold cross;[79] another was St. Medard, whose staff Gregory owned.[80] With the

73. Fortunatus *Carm.* X.5, 10.
74. *HF* X.31, *VJ* 50, *VP* 8.8.
75. Although cf. *VJ* 47: at least one woman did not know that relics of St. Julian were available in Tours.
76. Just as in 577 he had ignored King Chilperic's threats to mobilize the citizens of Tours against him: *HF* V.18.
77. *HF* V.49.       78. *HF* VIII.5, 8.
79. *GM* 8, 10.       80. *GC* 93.

support of St. Medard Gregory had widened his authority considerably, because his cult was centered at Soissons, where King Chlothar and his son Sigibert had built a church in his honor.[81] Yet it was Chilperic who had inherited the kingdom of Soissons when Chlothar died in 561; now, in his distrustful relationship with Chilperic, Gregory could also lean on the staff of the kingdom's most important saint.[82]

By 585, after the death of Chilperic, King Guntram was claiming hegemony over most of Gaul. But Gregory could be confident when he spoke with him too. While pleading on behalf of two men, Gregory asserted that he was mandated by his *dominus*; and to Guntram's surprise Gregory identified his "lord" not as another king, but as St. Martin. Gregory had become a man with a mission, a prospect that he relished this time "with a chuckle."[83] As the bishop who sat on "the sacred throne of St. Martin,"[84] he could now consider even acting independently of kings.

This discussion of one particular aristocratic family in sixth-century Gaul requires qualifications. First, there was never a complete overlap between bishops or abbots and local aristocrats from old Roman families, even in southern and central Gaul, because in the sixth century the holiness appropriate for promotion into the clergy could still be found in men who were not from aristocratic families. In this sense the earlier bishops at Tours who were not relatives of Gregory are the more interesting, even if, with the obvious exception of St. Martin, we cannot precisely pick them out. Among Gregory's predecessors we find men who, before their promotions, had been wood-carvers, court functionaries, or even members of poor families.[85] In other words, access to holiness could still promote men from outside local Roman aristocracies into positions of authority and prestige; the most obvious consequence would be the rise of barbarian aristocracies that also depended on associations with relic cults.

Second, ownership of or control over land and over the people who worked the land remained the most enduring basis for local influence. Despite the strictures of church councils, which for-

---

81. *HF* IV.19, 21, 51.
82. For St. Medard and his cult, see *HF* IV.19, *GC* 93; Fortunatus *Carm.* II.16; the *Vita Medardi* attributed to Fortunatus; and King Chilperic's own hymn to the saint, below, p. 220.
83. *HF* VIII.6.        84. Fortunatus *Carm.* VIII.15.3, 10.
85. *HF* III.17, IV.1, 3, and X.31, a list of all his predecessors.

bade clerics from acquiring such manifest tokens of the aristocratic lifestyle as hunting hawks and guard dogs,[86] with their control over churches' estates bishops too were great landowners.
The contrast to earlier periods was therefore that promotion to a
see now led to further internal differentiation within an already
small landowning elite. Even acquiring a civil magistracy was not
as advantageous, as the protocol set down by canon law made explicit: "If a secular official meets a cleric of even the lowest rank,
he is to bow his head; if both the secular official and the cleric are
on horseback, the secular official is to tip his hat and say hello; if
the cleric is on foot and the secular official on horseback, he is to
dismount and pay his respects to the cleric."[87]

Some bishops might go so far as to challenge royal prestige.
Leontius of Bordeaux once exposed his pretensions by sending a
priest to Paris to announce the decision by which he tried to expel
a bishop favored by King Charibert: "Hail glorious king. The
apostolic see sends the warmest greetings to your majesty." But
Charibert deflated the messenger with contrived misunderstand-
ing: "What? Have you been to Rome, so that you bring me greetings from the pope?"[88]

Hence a third qualification on this discussion about aristocracy
and relic cults is that we can already see how kings, in order to
maintain their authority, needed to acquire their own direct access to holiness. Thus Fortunatus, for instance, explicitly compared one Merovingian king to Melchizedek, the Old Testament
figure who had been both a king and a priest.[89] But this particular
analogy also represented an intrusion into the conceptual categories of early Merovingian society, because Fortunatus had grown
up in a Ravenna that had become a "sacred fortress" of the Byzantine Empire. There, in the architecture of the new churches, in the
mosaics covering their walls and domes, and in the liturgy celebrated in them, he had learned how Christian theology could absorb and even enchance the theocratic pretensions of Byzantine
emperors.[90] His ideas of authority were consequently derived
from the classical political theories about Roman emperors, which
had by now been restated in a Christian, Byzantine context.

In sixth-century Gaul, however, such a fusion was ahead of its
time. Frankish kings were only secular rulers, and even treated

86. Council of Epaone a. 517, Can. 4; Council of Mâcon a. 585, Can. 13.
87. Council of Mâcon a. 585, Can. 15.        88. HF IV.26.
89. Fortunatus Carm. II.10.21–22.        90. von Simson (1948) 23–39.

other rulers as such. They dealt with Byzantine emperors as equals, perhaps secure in the realization that the emperors needed their assistance in attacking, or at least distracting, first the Ostrogoths and later the Lombards in Italy.[91] In fact, Frankish kings had so little respect for the pretensions of the Byzantine emperors that they were prepared to substitute their own likenesses for the emperor's on his gold coins.[92]

Likewise, and in contrast to Fortunatus, Gregory was quite prepared to cut Byzantine emperors down to the size of the Frankish kings with whom he was familiar. Byzantine emperors may well have had unique access to relics such as the nails from Christ's cross; but to Gregory's way of thinking, their behavior, their greediness or their generosity, proved that they were no better, or worse, than the Frankish kings.[93]

In the writings of Gregory we therefore find few hints of sacred kingship. Only one king attained anything resembling a subsequent cult. At Agaune the Burgundian king Sigismund had been associated with the local saints after his "martyrdom" in 523, and people who had masses sung "on his behalf" (which he desperately needed, because he had also murdered his own son) were cured.[94] Even the miracles performed by the threads from King Guntram's cloak provide only another preview of sacred kingship. Not only was this account of the healing powers of King Guntram's cloak doubly unique, the only story about royal healing in the writings of Gregory and the only story about royal healing in France before the eleventh century,[95] it was also presented in a very specific context. Gregory had just mentioned in the same chapter how the king had helped a congregation near Lyon against the plague: "Guntram was so anxious about the people that he might have been taken for one of our Lord's bishops rather than for a king." In other words, only when a king acted "like a good bishop" was it possible for a royal healing to occur.[96] In sixth-

---

91. See Goubert (1955), and Goffart (1957), on Byzantine and Frankish diplomacy. For the Byzantine perspective, Agathias is a valuable source: see Averil Cameron (1968), esp. 136–9.

92. Note Procopius *Bell. Goth.* VII.33.5–6, for the indignant remarks of a loyal Greek.

93. *HF* IV.40, V.19, *GM* 5, with Wallace-Hadrill (1975) 96–103, and Reydellet (1977) 194–205, for Gregory's evaluations of Frankish kings.

94. *HF* III.5 and *GM* 74, with Graus (1965) 396–8.

95. Marc Bloch (1924) 33–36.

96. *HF* IX.21.

century Gaul miraculous power was linked exclusively with saints or their representatives, such as bishops, and the holiness of a king remained only a metaphor that enhanced the dichotomy between the divine power of saints and the secular royalty of kings.[97]

A final qualification is that special relationships with relic cults enhanced the status of cities as well as of individuals and families. In the early sixth century, for instance, the cult of St. Dionysius (St. Denis) was expanded in Paris as a component in the rivalry between the Frankish capital and the Ostrogothic city of Arles.[98] During the sixth century the most influential Gallic cults were located in Tours and Poitiers, or near Clermont. None of these cities was ever a royal residence, which may have made it easier for the old Roman aristocracies to dominate the cults and to use them as one way of enhancing their own influence. In the seventh century, however, relic cults at cities serving as royal capitals became more influential, presumably because the Frankish kings supported them. King Chilperic, for instance, dignified cities such as Paris and Soissons in the same way a Roman emperor once had, by building amphitheatres, but he also composed a poem in honor of St. Medard, the patron saint of Soissons.[99] The relationship between cults and cities or families could work both ways: just as cults contributed to the influence of families or the prestige of cities, so the authority of families and cities affected the popularity of particular cults. Hence, in the seventh century the declining influence of the cult of St. Martin seems to have coincided with the emergence of an aristocracy from Neustria and Burgundy that favored the competing cult of St. Dionysius at Paris, the capital of a Francia then supposedly unified under King Chlothar II and his son Dagobert.[100]

*    *    *

In the preceding section we examined how association with relic cults had become an effective means of enhancing the prestige of individuals, families, and cities. Other differentiating factors

97. As a brief selection from the vast literature on cults of medieval rulers, see Kantorowicz (1946) 56–64, and the outstanding survey of Graus (1965) 303–437. Riché (1976) discusses how Carolingian palaces came to resemble Paradise.

98. Levillain (1933).

99. *HF* V.17, and *Ymnus in solemnitate S. Medardi* (ed. K. Strecker, *MGH*, Poetae latini aevi carolini 4.2 [1914] 455–7 = *PL* Suppl. IV.1464–5).

100. Ewig (1961) 9–10.

were also available, among them knowledge of the classical heritage. In previous chapters we have seen that during the fourth century, Christian communities had sometimes had difficulties integrating educated men, while in the later fifth century Gallic aristocrats, including Bishop Sidonius, had revived their classical heritage in order to distinguish themselves within an increasingly barbarian world. By the sixth century, however, small Christian communities were no longer threatened by educated men, and Gallic aristocrats had lost the sense of urgency over preserving their links with the Roman Empire. It is therefore worthwhile to trace briefly the ambivalent role of the classical heritage in this Christian and barbarian society; as a contrast between the attitudes of Fortunatus and Gregory demonstrates, knowledge of the classical heritage had become, so to speak, a true "relic" in early Merovingian society, worthy of admiration when available but otherwise irrelevant and unnecessary.[101]

When Gregory was growing up during the 540s and 550s he received what was a common education then available in southern Gaul. As a young man he was taught to read and write by his great-uncle Nicetius, then a priest at Lyon who ran a "choir school";[102] later he was taught by Avitus at Clermont, where he read first the Psalms, then the Gospels, the Acts of the Apostles, and the Letters of St. Paul.[103] For with the disappearance of municipal schools young men were educated either within their families, or in church schools that stressed ecclesiastical and biblical literature: in Pierre Riché's phrase, "Knowing how to read meant knowing the Psalter."[104] Because of his father's death the young Gregory did not receive an education at home; instead, after being taught in church schools, he acquired a predominantly biblical education and learned little about the classical heritage.

The undisguised contrast between this restricted familiarity with classical culture and the past achievements of the Gallic aristocracy was heightened in the presence of a genuine man of letters. Such a gentleman was Gregory's friend Fortunatus, who was also a true Roman from north Italy. Born about 530, he had grown up first in Aquileia, then in Ravenna, which had been recently re-

101. Riché (1962) is a brilliantly comprehensive survey that forms the basis for further research on literary culture in early medieval Europe.

102. *VP* 8.2; cf. *GM* 75.

103. *VP* 2 praef., "eclesiastica . . . scripta."

104. Riché (1962) 516, and (1953). Note especially *HF* V.42, *VM* 1.7, *VP* 12.2, 20.1.

taken from the Ostrogoths by the Byzantine army of Justinian. There, as a resident of the Roman Empire, he received an education steeped in the traditional classical culture, to which biblical and patristic writings were only a supplement. In fact, much ecclesiastical writing was not, by his tastes, even very good literature, and later in life Fortunatus clearly preferred versions of the Bible in verse to the prose of the original.[105] But his classical education gave him the skill, already as a young man, to write poems flattering the bishop of Ravenna.[106]

About 565 Fortunatus left Ravenna. Although he never gave an explicit reason for his move, it may have been connected to the cure for his ailing eyes that he had received before an icon of St. Martin: "I will remember this as long as I live";[107] so perhaps his departure was part of a vow to make a pilgrimage to the saint's shrine at Tours. His journey to Gaul along the Danube and down the Rhine was a difficult one, not least because in the forests of Germany he met a culture that defied his comprehension. At their boisterous drinking parties his German hosts were unable to distinguish "the honking of a goose from the singing of a swan": "Instead of singing my poems I warbled a few verses."[108] For Fortunatus had approached Gaul by way of a "back door," and so arrived in northern Gaul without having first gone through the Roman Gaul of the south. Once there, he was pleasantly surprised, because in contrast to Germany, barbarian Gaul could conjure up visions of the old classical culture: people even spoke Latin! In the presence of one new friend, Duke Lupus, Fortunatus felt almost at home: "With you as duke, Rome returns to us in this spot."[109]

Most of all, Fortunatus found himself in demand as a poet, especially at royal courts that desired a veneer of culture. His first major public performance was probably the poem celebrating the marriage of King Sigibert and Brunhild in 566, and in it he put all his talents on display by elevating the marriage firmly into the context of classical mythology: without Cupid and Venus there would have been no wedding.[110] Fortunatus now cast himself as a potential epic poet: "If a Virgil or a Homer were perhaps alive, they would be writing about the name of Sigibert."[111] With this

105. Fortunatus *Vita S. Martini* I.10–25, and Tardi (1927) 40–55.
106. Fortunatus *Carm.* I.1–2, with *MGH*, AA 4, index s.v. "Vitalis."
107. Fortunatus *Vita S. Martini* IV.700; cf. *VM* 1.15.
108. Fortunatus *Praefatio* 5.        109. Fortunatus *Carm.* VII.7.6.
110. Fortunatus *Carm.* VI.1.        111. Fortunatus *Carm.* VI.1a.5–6.

performance he ensured his literary reputation throughout Gaul, eventually becoming the touchstone against which othrs evaluated themselves. Thus when the bishop of Bordeaux sent him some verses for his comments, he politely agreed that although the bishop had discovered "new tricks" (such as additional syllables that broke the meter), the poem was still worthy of recitation at Rome.[112] And with his own verse Fortunatus could transform even Frankish kings into Roman gentlemen. In one panegyric he made Chilperic into more than a brave warrior; the king was also a judge, a man of letters, and a theologian.[113] With King Charibert he was even more generous, comparing him not only to King David and King Solomon, but also to the emperor Trajan.[114]

Poetical skills were obviously not all Fortunatus contributed to Merovingian society. As part of his training he had also inherited a world view that understood events and people in terms of classical culture, and in many of his formal poems he was clearly more at ease with classical than with biblical themes. Although there were, of course, other sides to him—he also versified the writings of Sulpicius Severus about St. Martin and wrote *Vitae* of saints in which he honestly tried to simplify his otherwise obscure style[115]—in his poems about kings, dukes, counts, and bishops Fortunatus was more likely to pay them compliments based on allusions to the classical heritage than to employ biblical traditions.

In fact, familiarity with the classical heritage was the one distinguishing characteristic Fortunatus had to offer. Unlike other prominent men in Gaul, he no longer had either a family or a homeland. Once he left Italy he never returned: "A man born in Italy, he now lives among the fields of Gaul."[116] At Poitiers, where he lived the last thirty years of his life, he was not very influential in the church until, much later, he became bishop for a few years. All Fortunatus had to support himself with was his literary talent.[117]

112. Fortunatus *Carm.* III.18, with Riché (1962) 265–7, on the literary friends of Fortunatus.

113. Fortunatus *Carm.* IX.1.105–14.

114. Fortunatus *Carm.* VI.2.77–82, and Szövérffy (1971), on Fortunatus' distinction between Roman and barbarian.

115. Fortunatus *Vita Albini* 8–9, with the nuanced discussion of Collins (1981).

116. Fortunatus *Carm.* VIII.1.12.

117. After his death, a cult of Fortunatus appeared, which honored him as much for his poetical ability as for his saintliness: see deGaiffier (1952).

In contrast, Gregory was a solid member of the ecclesiastical hierarchy, a deacon at twenty-five and a bishop at thirty-five, and he was always surrounded by his family. This is something of a surprise, because churchmen were expected to be, like Gregory's uncle Gallus, men without families: "The love of his father, the fondness of his mother, the concern of his nurses, were not able to detain him from his love of God."[118] But Gregory was never without his friends—who included his patron saints—and his family, in particular his mother. Although after Gregory's father had died his mother, Armentaria, had retired to her own family estates, she and her son remained devoted to each other, and what Gregory wrote of his great-uncle Nicetius was equally applicable to himself: "Although he loved all men with the bond of celestial love, he was so humble before his mother that he obeyed her as if he were a slave."[119] In addition, Gregory grew up with a brother and a sister, and he had at least two nieces.[120] With the security of strong backing from his family, his friends, and his saints, Gregory would presumably have felt less need to differentiate himself with references to a classical education.

Gregory was not immune, however, to the aspirations shared by late antique aristocrats, and he looked at this classical culture with heavy nostalgia, knowing that he and many of his contemporaries might never fully revive it. Because of his limited acquaintance with classical authors, Gregory himself could only contrive to parade occasional quotations and allusions, and in his writings little tags from Virgil twinkled like relics from a glorious past.[121] This classical heritage was still meant to be the exclusive birthright of old Roman families, to which barbarians, including the Frankish kings, had no claim. In contrast to Fortunatus, Gregory had a view of the Frankish kings based largely on an ecclesiastical perspective. He compared kings to emperors too: because of his antagonistic attitude to the church and its bishops, Chilperic was "the Nero of our times." Similarly, Gregory had about the same opinion of Chilperic's literary abilities as of his theology. Thus he was highly critical of the king's Latin verse, ostensibly because it

118. *VP* 6 praef., with Theis (1976).
119. *VP* 8.2.
120. Stroheker (1948) nos. 134, 208.
121. Kurth (1919) I, 1–29, and Bonnet (1890) 48–53; also Jungblut (1977), on Gregory's metrical clausulae.

did not scan;[122] but underneath it all we get the impression that Gregory thought Chilperic had gone above himself and was trying to act too much like the Roman gentleman he had no right to be.

Despite his occasional vanities, Gregory was still painfully honest about his own literary inadequacies, not least because his lack of sufficient formal education was often matched by paralyzing respect for the grandeur of the saints he described. The Incarnation, for instance, was not only a vital premise underlying beliefs in the efficacy of relics and saints' cults, as we noted in Chapter 9; as an act of self-publication it also set an intimidating standard of literary proficiency for subsequent historians: "In the beginning was the Word."[123] Gregory's own words—as he himself knew—were not equally divinely inspired. Although he mentioned the famous vision of Jerome in which the saint had been accused of being more a Ciceronian than a Christian, he never had to face the same problem; his anxieties ran instead in the other direction, that men might rightly accuse him of not knowing the classical traditions, or even Latin, well enough. Gregory worried continually about his *rusticitas*, and even candidly conceded that he confused genders, cases, and prepositions. Perhaps, he wrote, someone might accuse him of writing "like a ponderous ox exercising in the gymnasium, or like a worn-out ass charging into a ball game."[124] But Gregory continued to write because, as his mother told him, people understood him.[125] Gregory at least had the courage to make a virtue out of necessity. Others might mockingly claim that it was preferable for a deacon to be silent than to read the lessons *rustice*, in an uncultured manner; Gregory insisted in-

122. HF VI.46; for Chilperic's hymn in praise of St. Medard, see above, p. 220 n. 99. Norberg (1954) 31–40, analyzes Chilperic's poem and agrees with Gregory's negative evaluation rather than with Fortunatus' favorable opinion of the king's literary abilities.
123. GM, praef., with, in general, Beumann (1964).
124. VP 2 praef., GC praef. Bonnet (1890) 503–626, is a massive, although still sympathetic, demonstration that Gregory's self-evaluation here was accurate; the remainder of the book shows that Gregory could also have faulted his spelling, vocabulary, morphology, and style. Nevertheless, as a device for narration, Gregory's tortured Latin is superb for giving a vivid and almost vernacular representation of contemporary events: see Auerbach (1953) 77–95, and Roberts (1980), for sensitive literary appreciations. Note also Dill (1926) 350: "Who, but the pedant, cares about the Latinity, if the Latin be true, sincere, and vivid?"
125. VM 1 praef.

stead that God preferred simplicity: "God has chosen ordinary people, not philosophers."[126]

For over a century the Gallic church had been developing a perspective on literary culture that worried less about "slips of speech than about mistakes in living."[127] In the later fifth century Julianus Pomerius had made a careful distinction between the contrasting intentions of flamboyant rhetoricians and Christian teachers: "The bishop's language should be simple and straightforward; though this may mean his Latin is less good, it should be restrained and dignified so that it prevents no one, however ignorant, from understanding it."[128] At Arles one of Pomerius' students was the future bishop Caesarius, who put these ideas into practice by preaching in a "common vernacular" comprehensible to everyone.[129] In one of his sermons he explicitly justified his practice: "Because the uneducated and simple folk cannot rise to the level of the learned, let the learned deign to lower themselves to their ignorance. The learned can understand what has been said to the simple, but the simple will in no way be able to understand preaching directed to the learned."[130]

A long tradition therefore stood behind Gregory's own apology that he would write in a "rustic" Latin, although with one important distinction. Because of their deep training in the classical heritage, men such as Pomerius and Fortunatus had consciously to affect a more "rustic" Latin, and their support for a popular and vernacular style was also a way of reminding themselves to tone down their own speaking and writing. Like earlier bishops, they always had the capacity to switch between a simple style in the presence of ordinary people and a highly eloquent style before an audience of learned men.[131] Gregory, on the other hand, did not face this dilemma, because his Latin was just naturally rustic; he had no alternative to his humble style.

Men such as Gregory, however, were now also prepared to live without the classical heritage. One man even begged a king not to send him as bishop to Avignon, because he could not put up with

126. *VM* 1 praef., 2.1.

127. *Vita Caesarii* I.2. For the traditional concern over *sermo humilis*, see Auerbach (1965), and MacMullen (1966a).

128. Julianus Pomerius *de vita contemplativa* I.23–24.

129. *Vita Caesarii* II.1.

130. Caesarius *Serm.* 86.1.

131. *Vita Hilarii* 14. On Hilary, see above, pp. 155–56; and on his literary abilities, see Cavallin (1948), and Valentin (1977) 29–36.

"the boredom of having to listen to sophisticated senators and counts discussing philosophy."[132] Instead he became bishop at Le Mans—a telling example of a man preferring a see in northern, barbarian Gaul over one in southern, Roman Gaul. For many men the classical heritage had become insufficient as a means for interpreting their society; instead, they now found in the Bible both a perspective with which to understand events and the language to articulate them. When Gregory supplied an interpretation for contemporary events he often used an analogy with biblical stories, or he quoted a verse or two: "What David sang [in the Psalms] was true of this man."[133] For clarification or consolation he now consistently looked to the Bible, and in particular to the Psalter: "Wherever opened it provided a verse of comfort."[134] Gregory even wrote a commentary on the Psalms, of which only a few stray fragments survive.[135] In his interpretations the Psalms were essentially prayers prefiguring the life of Jesus Christ and instructing people how they might live devout lives in order to inherit the heavenly Jerusalem. Yet these were not the abstract musings of an intellectual; for because the Psalms comprised most of the canticles sung during the liturgy, they too had now become "rustic," accessible to everyone. Hence, after people ceased to be afraid of the unexpected (in this case, another miracle of St. Martin), they found relief, as well as a means of glorifying God, in the communal recitation of a Psalm.[136]

From the seventh century on Latin slowly became a written or recited language with steadily less correspondence to spoken Romance languages.[137] But already for both Gregory and Fortunatus the classical heritage, like the language itself, had been molded into a new syntax of meanings. Fortunatus attempted to incorporate both Romans and barbarians into classical traditions, even if this was a task that he often seems to have performed with little real sensitivity. Gregory may have continued to admire men of letters,[138] but, in contrast to his friend, he was prepared to live

132. *HF* VI.9.
133. *HF* IV.11. On Gregory's use of biblical quotations and allusions, see Bonnet (1890) 54–61, and Antin (1963) and (1967).
134. *HF* V.49.
135. *MGH*, SRM 1.2, p. 877, with Salmon (1959) 135–6, on the *tituli*.
136. *GC* 20, with Leclercq (1963) 127: "La source principale de la formation biblique des hommes du moyen âge était la liturgie."
137. Norberg (1966).
138. Cf. Fortunatus *Carm.* IX.6–7, for correspondence with Gregory on the finer details of metrics.

without letters himself. Above all, the focal point of his life was the Christian church and, more specifically, the cult of St. Martin; and if a Latin corroded by "the rust of vulgar barbarisms"[139] was more comprehensible, Gregory was satisfied to use it.

With this attitude he reveals the humility and unpretentious simplicity that made him such an attractive personality to his medieval biographer.[140] Most of this later medieval *Vita* was based on the autobiographical passages in Gregory's own writings, but at the end the biographer added two apocryphal anecdotes. One had clearly been too tempting to pass up: in it Gregory went to Rome to be received by his contemporary, Pope Gregory the Great. While Gregory was praying, the pope pondered how a man who was so short had acquired such heavenly grace. As if having read the pope's mind Gregory had a ready answer: "The Lord made us and not we ourselves; the same Lord who made tall men also made small men."[141] In the same spirit Gregory lived with his shortcomings as a Latinist, subordinating himself to his concern for the Catholic church and fired by his zeal for St. Martin: "Which of these miracles can my littleness properly narrate? . . . Only love for my patron St. Martin compels me."[142] According to the second anecdote in the biography, although Gregory's own self-effacing instructions had directed that after his death his body be buried in a public place so that people could walk on his grave, eventually they instead built a proper tomb for his remains next to the tomb of St. Martin.[143] Such respect provides a model for modern historians too; for although it is easy to trample on Gregory for his deficient Latin and his limited literary culture, without his writings the cult of St. Martin and much of early Merovingian society would be incomprehensible.

*     *     *

In these ways old Roman aristocrats continued to maintain their standing in society. Although partially deprived of that classical culture about which they still had pretensions, they acquired a

139. Sidonius *Ep.* II.10.1.

140. As well as to other medieval writers: cf. Sigibert of Gembloux *de scriptor. eccles.* 49: "Gregorius Turonensis episcopus, vir magnae nobilitatis et simplicitatis, scripsit multa simplici sermone" (quoted in Monod [1872] 111). Latouche (1963) is a sympathetic appreciation of Gregory.

141. [Odo of Cluny] *Vita Gregorii* 24 (*PL* 71.126).

142. *VM* 2.40, "mea parvitas."

143. [Odo of Cluny] *Vita Gregorii* 26 (*PL* 71.128).

new culture in the Catholic church. There they discovered also a biblical outlook that, in addition to interpreting daily events, put even Frankish kings into a perspective in which they were expected to listen to God's prophets, the bishops. Most of all, in the beliefs focused on relic cults they found a new ideology of prestige and authority that allowed them to preserve their influence, at least through the sixth century, at the same time as it began to define a new aristocracy. For by the seventh and the eighth centuries it was the newly emerging Frankish, or rather Romano-Frankish, aristocracies that used these same methods of supporting monasteries and churches, patronizing relic cults, and, most significantly, having hagiography written about themselves or their relatives in order to promote the "self-sanctification" of their own families.[144]

144. See Prinz (1965) 489–503, (1967), and (1975).

# CHAPTER 11

# Sacred Space:
# The Cult and Church of
# St. Martin at Tours

When Gregory became bishop of Tours in 573, the dominant building within the city walls was the cathedral in which St. Martin
himself had once celebrated mass. Along with other churches in
the city it had been burned in 558, and remained in ruins until
Gregory rebuilt and rededicated it thirty years later.[1] Although
people continued to celebrate important liturgical festivals such as
Christmas and Easter in it, in many respects the cathedral had
also become a "museum" to the memory of St. Martin. Among its
treasures were relics that Bishop Ambrose had supposedly presented to St. Martin, as well as a goblet given to the saint by the
usurper-emperor Magnus Maximus. In one small cell a poem by
Fortunatus commemorated Martin's generosity to a beggar at that
very spot; more than anything else the poem resembles a placard
describing an exhibition on a museum tour.[2] And on the walls of
the cathedral visitors could still see the miraculous activities of St.
Martin, depicted in a set of frescoes.[3]

Yet it is also possible that many travelers, even local residents,
went infrequently into the old walled city, because by the sixth
century its suburbs had become the most important part of Tours.
The cultural demarcation between urban and rural represented by
the city walls was beginning to break down too, because after a
contraction in the size of cities during previous centuries, the at-

For surveys of the individual buildings at Tours and all literary references, see
Lelong (1965), and Vieillard-Troiekouroff (1976) 304–29. (References to the writings of Gregory of Tours omit his name. See Chapter 9, unnumbered note.)

1. *HF* X.31.
2. *HF* X.31, *GM* 46, *VM* 4.10; Fortunatus *Carm.* I.5 = LeBlant I, no. 165.
3. Fortunatus *Carm.* X.6.89–92, with Sauvel (1956).

traction of the churches and shrines founded in the suburbs had led to the growth of small settlements nearby, and the urban center of each city was less concentrated than in the past. Now the most impressive fortifications for cities were not their walls but their churches, access to which was controlled by "holy doorkeepers," that is, by saints and bishops.[4] In other words, admission to Christian churches now determined the application of old prejudices about urbanity and rusticity, and the people most susceptible to being labeled "countryfolk" were non-Christians. Conversely, given the portability of relics, these sacred fortifications could also surround more area and more people than the old city walls ever had. Sometimes, in fact, they enclosed an entire city territory: in the middle of the sixth century, for instance, the citizens of Rheims protected themselves from the plague by putting the shroud that covered the tomb of St. Remigius on a wagon and dragging it around the city and all the villages in its territory.[5]

As people approached Tours at the end of the sixth century, particularly from the west and the south, the "fortifications" of churches and monasteries began to fill the landscape already more than one-half mile from the city walls. Dominating everything, in importance as well as in size, was the complex—actually almost a small village—centered around the church of St. Martin.[6] In addition to the church itself, this cluster of buildings included a baptistery built by Gregory; some rooms or apartments connected to the church; and at least two courtyards, one containing another baptistery, a bell tower, and a convent, and the other accommodating a "poor house," which provided organized relief for those who could get themselves registered.[7] At the focus of the complex in the eastern end of the church, as everyone knew, was the tomb of the saint: "More sublime and more fortunate than all other places is the spot so gloriously adorned with the tomb of St. Martin's most holy body."[8]

4. Note Avitus *Hom.* 24, "plus haec basilicis quam propugnaculis urbs munitur"; and Fortunatus *Vita Germani* 38–39: shortly before becoming bishop, Germanus sees himself in a dream receiving the keys to the city's gates. For discussion, see Lestoquoy (1953), and Hubert (1977) 3–32.

5. GC 78.

6. L. Pietri (1976). In the eleventh century this settlement was in fact known as "Martinopolis": see Gasnault (1961) 65–66.

7. On the *matricula*, see Marignan (1899) I, 300–2, and Lesne (1910) 380–9.

8. *Sermo in laudem S. Martini* 4, with Peebles (1961), for discussion of this sixth-century sermon.

The church of St. Martin would have been noticeable from a distance, and not merely because of its size. After it too had been burned in 559—"a misfortune that I recall with a deep sigh," Gregory wrote—King Chlothar had assisted in its restoration by ordering its roof to be covered with tin.[9] Furthermore, the dome or large tower at the east end of the church over the altar and St. Martin's tomb might already have been gilded: according to a tenth-century sermon, the dome then "glittered in the sun like a mountain of gold."[10] From its brilliant reflection men were able, even at a distance, to pinpoint the location of the tomb, and perhaps also to remember how Martin himself had once appeared in Gaul as a "new sun" rising from the East.[11]

But if the church and tomb of St. Martin remained the goal of people's pilgrimages, once there men could easily be distracted by the spectacle. In part because of the attraction of the cult of St. Martin, in part because of its location on the Loire River and on important roads, many dignitaries passed through Tours, among them kings, queens, and Visigothic princesses.[12] Sometimes royal magistrates came to Tours to bestow favors or collect taxes;[13] other times they came to seek asylum in the church of St. Martin.[14] On the great festival days of St. Martin ecclesiastical dignitaries came to Tours[15] along with many other pilgrims who were as interested in the bazaars and the merrymaking (stimulated, perhaps, by the distribution of free wine) as in the religious ceremonies.[16] A century earlier Sidonius had described his own impressions as a pilgrim at a festival in Bordeaux, politely turning up his nose at the smoky kitchens, the damp inns, and the drunken singing.[17] During the sixth century, festival days remained great riotous celebrations, but not everyone was as priggish as Sidonius had once

9. *HF* IV.20, which also helps determine the chronology: King Childebert died at the end of 558 (Krusch [1920] 487–8); the church of St. Martin then caught fire, hence probably in 559; the city, and the cathedral, had been burned during the previous year, probably 558.

10. Odo of Cluny *Serm.* 4 (*PL* 133.733).

11. *VM* 1.3; cf. *HF* I.39.

12. *Epist. Austrasicae* 8; *VM* 1.12; Fortunatus *Carm.* VI.5.229–30.

13. Fortunatus *Carm.* X.17; *HF* IX.30, *VM* 4.6–7, and Fortunatus *Carm.* X.12.

14. *HF* IV.18, V.14, VII.21–22, 29.

15. E.g. *VM* 2.12; Fortunatus *Vita Radegundis* 33, *Vita Germani* 80–82; Baudonivia *Vita Radegundis* II.7; Jonas of Bobbio *Vita Columbani* 22 (*MGH, SRM* 4, pp. 95–96).

16. *VM* 2.49, *VP* 3.1.

17. Sidonius *Ep.* VIII.11.3.

been: one man, for instance, went to Brioude five days before the festival of St. Julian "to enjoy the laughter and the good times at his hotel."[18] In fact, the religious ceremonies may occasionally have become secondary in this environment, which openly encouraged people to celebrate; in the early sixth century one bishop finally had to reprimand his congregation for gossiping when they ought to have been praying and singing the Psalms.[19] Even King Childebert once tried to do something about the frivolities: "A complaint has been made . . . that people spend night vigils in drunkenness, debauchery, and singing, and that even on the holy days of Easter, Christmas, other festivals, and Sundays, dancers circulate through estates. We allow none of these actions that offend God to continue."[20]

Attempts to impose order and decorum had little chance of success. During festivals so many people crowded into the churches that Gregory could compare the scene at one saint's tomb to "swarms of happy bees clustering around their usual beehive."[21] Other churches were filled with the animals—even bulls—that had been dedicated to them.[22] The courtyards of churches were also littered with beggars (some of whom seem to have followed a regular festival circuit)[23] and ill people, such as a boy so deformed he resembled a monster, a mute man who imitated the cries of a beggar by clicking together wooden tablets, or another boy who was blind, deaf, dumb, and paralyzed.[24] Even then there was more to distract pilgrims' attention, because Tours was also now filled with outlandish Christian ascetics, among them a monk named Winnoch who took to drink and finally had to be confined to his cell as a raving lunatic.[25]

Although this short survey of the churches, the festivals, the visitors, and the sights reveals the outward aspects of an early Merovingian city, we need also to evaluate more implicit meanings and interconnections by investigating, in this and the following chapters about illness and time, the values of small communities and the ways they were now guaranteed by Christian beliefs. We can begin by considering the physical settings, because the buildings offered more than a backdrop; they also mirrored and

18. *VJ* 15.
19. Caesarius *Serm.* 72.1; cf. *Vita Caesarii* I.19.
20. Praeceptum a. 511/558 (*MGH*, Capitularia 1, pp. 2–3).
21. *VJ* 28, *VP* 8.6.     22. *VJ* 31.     23. Cf. *VM* 2.24, 3.58.
24. *VM* 1.40, 2.26, 3.23, 49.     25. *HF* V.21, VIII.34.

taught the beliefs and behavior appropriate to Christian communities. In this chapter let us consider, first, the contribution made
by the church and cult of St. Martin to the preservation, transmis-
sion, and adaptation of traditions about him; second, the correspondence of the spatial layout and appearance of the church to
current beliefs about holiness and its effect on people's behavior
in and around the church; and finally, the availability of St. Martin's power, either through the foundation of shrines or through
pilgrimages.

*        *        *

After Martin died in 397 he had quickly become the center of a
cult, and citizens from both Poitiers and Tours had competed for
possession of his body and therefore also of his patronage in
heaven.[26] As we saw in Chapter 6, the model of leadership exemplified by Martin had been important for helping a rather limited
Christian perspective to become assimilated with aspects of secular society; and although the "canonical" writings of Sulpicius
Severus may seem to have transmitted an image of St. Martin
fixed by past events, in fact the traditions about St. Martin were
manipulated during later centuries to ensure the dominant position of Christianity in a changing society. In other words, the past
literally lived in the present, because although the weight of tradition was light enough to allow people to do whatever was necessary in their current situations, it was also heavy enough to provide the illusion of stability and consistency. Whatever new roles
the cult of St. Martin assumed, the implication was that nothing
had really changed; Gregory, in fact, almost gave the impression
that, because the saint was still "alive," he and Martin were contemporaries.[27] Hence, each time the cult of St. Martin was expanded or altered in response to changing circumstances during
the fifth and sixth centuries, the events described in the writings
of Sulpicius were rewritten, retold, repainted, and relived.

Although Brictio, Martin's successor as bishop of Tours, had
built a church over the tomb of Martin, it was so small as to be
embarrassing for the citizens of Tours.[28] But in the later fifth century Bishop Perpetuus expanded the cult of St. Martin, presumably as an implicit indication that Gaul was now prepared to go its

26. *HF* I.48, with Carrias (1972).
27. *VM* 1 praef.        28. Sidonius *Ep.* IV.18.5.

own way independently of the Roman Empire and its saints. Perpetuus made this new significance of the expanded cult most obvious by replacing the original small church, which may have been dedicated to St. Peter and St. Paul, with a larger one dedicated to St. Martin.[29] He also commissioned some Gallic poets, among them Sidonius and Paulinus of Périgueux, to write verses to be inscribed on the walls of this church. Since some of these verses described or referred to scenes from the New Testament and the career of St. Martin, presumably Perpetuus had also commissioned a set of frescoes to be painted on the walls of the church. And finally, Perpetuus asked Paulinus of Périgueux, who had already versified Sulpicius' *Vita* and *Dialogues* of St. Martin, to turn into verse a collection of stories about miracles that had happened after the death of the saint and which Perpetuus had already recorded in prose.[30] The revival of the cult of St. Martin in the later fifth century thus included a building project, in this case a new church; a rewriting of St. Martin's deeds, including those canonized by Sulpicius Severus, as well as those that happened after his death; and a collection of paintings to illustrate the biblical message and events from Martin's life.

These same elements reappeared when Gregory revived the cult of St. Martin in the later sixth century. Although the dilapidated condition of the churches surely necessitated repairs, Gregory also had a special incentive to associate himself with the authority of St. Martin, since we have seen in the preceding chapter the difficulties he faced with his accession to the see of Tours. Gregory rebuilt the cathedral of St. Martin and the church of St. Martin, both of which had been damaged by fire. He also began to write another collection of recent miracles performed by St. Martin, in the first book of which he mentioned the writings of Sulpicius Severus and summarized the fifth-century miracle stories versified by Paulinus of Périgueux. He also received from Fortunatus yet another verse version of the writings of Sulpicius and corresponded with him about the possibility of versifying Gregory's new collection of miracle stories.[31] And finally, he appar-

29. *HF* II.14, and above, p. 168.
30. Paulinus of Périgueux *de vita S. Martini*, prologus, and *Epist. ad Perpetuum*; cf. *VM* 1.2. For arguments over the independence of Paulinus from Perpetuus, see Delehaye (1920) 8–18, and Chase (1932).
31. *VM* 1.2; Fortunatus, *Vita S. Martini*, prol. = *Epist. ad Gregorium* 3.

ently repaired the frescoes in the church of St. Martin and (probably) commissioned new ones for the cathedral.

In these two cases we can see how a revival of St. Martin's cult could function in different contexts as a sign of Gallic autonomy, or as a means for promoting an individual's standing; but by reference to a fixed past men conjured up the illusion of continuity and harmony. It is important also to consider the various components of each revival—books, paintings, buildings—as necessarily complementary aspects that had significant didactic implications for ordinary believers. In a partially literate society such as Merovingian Gaul, this constant rewriting, repainting, and rebuilding was about as close as people could get to the homeostatic process characteristic of oral traditions in preliterate societies, whereby myths about the past are continually reshaped according to the needs and purposes of the present. A sense of historical time disappeared in the context of the miracles that happened in the presence of St. Martin's tomb or relics, because people witnessed the saint still displaying the power they could read about in his *Vita* and see portrayed in the frescoes: "If someone still does not believe . . . let him go to the church of St. Martin, and every day he will see new miracles and also the repetition of what happened long ago."[32]

In the timelessness of miracles, past and present fused together. On the one hand, present events provided verifications or guarantees for past events: "Let no one doubt St. Martin's powers in the past, since he sees the benefits of present miracles being distributed."[33] Conversely, past events provided explanations for the surprises of the present, and episodes from the *Vita* of St. Martin helped people understand their own situations. After a sudden flash of light in a new oratory, Gregory was quick with an interpretation: "Do not be afraid; . . . remember what is written in the *Vita* of St. Martin."[34] The constant advertising of the past power of saints informed people of the possibilities available to them in their own communities: "For it was the habit of rustic men to give greater veneration to those saints of God whose martyrdom they could read over and over."[35] In this manner Gregory explained the expansion of the cult of St. Patroclus at Troyes; once the history of his martyrdom had been verified, the local inhabitants decided to replace the small oratory tended by one monk

32. GC 6.    33. VM 1 praef.    34. GC 20.    35. GM 63.

with a church and an annual festival. And so too people learned about the potential power still available through saints and their cults. When a family in Spain needed the assistance of St. Martin, they prayed to him "because we have read about many of your deeds, both what you did when alive and what you continue to do after your death."[36]

Because many people in Merovingian Gaul could not read, however, either because of blindness or, more likely, because of illiteracy, the usefulness of the contents of books was supplemented, first, by the consequential role of the books themselves. As in other traditional societies in which literacy is restricted, a book, or even its letters, ink, or signature, might become "holy writ" and thus a source of divine power that, like relics, was immune to terrestrial disasters.[37] An anthropologist offers an appropriate comparison: "The prestige of such [literary] works comes in part from their strangeness, in part from their being in written form. From the point of view of the villagers, these two qualities are really one, since they are things and statements which the villager has not made and which come to him, as it were, from an extraordinary, supernatural world, ready made."[38] Hence a blind deacon at Autun, having placed the *Vita* of St. Nicetius on his eyes, was cured by "the power of this book"; only then did he actually read the volume. One man was cured after licking Bishop Germanus' signature on a letter; another young man was healed after he embraced a book describing the great deeds of St. Martin, in which "immeasurable grace shines from his miracles."[39]

Second, for the many people who were unable to read, realization of the potential power of saints would have come more frequently and with greater comprehension from visible symbols, such as paintings or church buildings. The association between frescoes and books was in fact an intimate one. When a woman at Clermont wanted to decorate a new church, "She held in her lap a book from which she read stories of events that happened long ago, and she instructed the workmen what she wanted painted on the walls."[40] In this sense the walls of churches, with their frescoes and the accompanying inscriptions, were the first "il-

36. *VM* 3.8.    37. Cf. *VM* 3.42.

38. Maurice Bloch (1968) 296.

39. *VP* 8.12; Fortunatus *Vita Germani* 155; Paulinus of Périgueux *de visitatione nepotuli sui* 34, and *VM* 1.2.

40. *HF* II.17.

luminated manuscripts" of the Middle Ages: "a page revealed on a wall," in the words of Paulinus of Périgueux.[41] At the end of the sixth century Pope Gregory the Great used similar logic when disagreeing with an iconoclastic bishop of Marseille: "Paintings are allowed in churches so that illiterate people can at least look at the walls and 'read' what they cannot read in books."[42] In other words, the frescoes in churches were neither paintings in a museum to be appreciated by connoisseurs, nor representations of past events that people could no longer experience; instead, as we will see, these frescoes generated new meanings and new behavior in the people viewing them.

Finally, the most prominent physical symbols of all, the church buildings themselves, also reinforced the basic message about the potential power of saints. The stones in churches were "alive," according to Fortunatus, and the play of light through the windows so enhanced the effect that in the cathedral at Nantes, for instance, the sunshine seemed to animate the colors of the frescoes.[43] For the purpose of transmitting and teaching correct attitudes, both the appearance and the spatial layout of churches enabled them to be as articulate as books and frescoes. In fact, Gregory once wrote that "our church of the faithful is built up whenever the deeds of saints are devoutly imitated," thus including a telling ambiguity over whether he was referring to the "edification" of the Catholic church or the construction of a specific church building.[44] Hence the many new churches in early Merovingian Gaul became more than indicators of the enormous wealth spent by churchmen on construction projects; in them space had been organized, both as a reflection of beliefs about holiness and as a model for people's behavior. We know little about the appearance or layout of most churches and even less about activities in them. But for the church of St. Martin at Tours we have information about its spatial layout, its internal appearance, and, most importantly, the miracles that happened in it. Here we can see, first, that the architecture of the church offered a spatial grid corresponding to the same categories and themes found in the contemporary literature about saints, relics, and holiness; and second, that people could make a miniature "pilgrimage" through this church to receive favors and support from St. Martin.

41. Paulinus of Périgueux *Epist. ad Perpetuum*, "pagina in pariete reserata."
42. Gregory I *Reg.* IX.208, XI.10.
43. Fortunatus *Carm.* III.7.35–40, IV.23.14.
44. *VP* 20 praef.; cf. *GM* praef.

\* \* \*

Entering a church was like entering another world. Everywhere one looked there were hanging tapestries, chandeliers, and candles burning before tombs. Some churches had tinted glass windows that supposedly made it brighter inside the church than outside; some had silk shrouds ornamented with gold and gems; some had mosaics that glistened like gold, as at Cologne where the church dedicated to the Theban Legion was called *Sancti Aurei*, "The Golden Saints."[45] During the celebration of the liturgy, bishops and clerics dressed in colorful robes, and the choir wore white gowns. This visual splendor was supplemented by the sweet perfume of burning incense and the solemn chanting of the Psalms.[46]

This was a stunning effect, heightened by the belief that it was a duplication of the atmosphere in which saints lived in heaven. In fact, saints were thought to use these same churches, especially at night. At Bordeaux an old woman who had been mistakenly locked in the church saw the doors open and a choir of saints enter; at Autun two men joined in what they thought were night vigils, until they realized that these must be saints worshipping, since everything glowed even though no lights were lit.[47] Not only did saints share the same gleaming aura as a church, they produced the same sweet fragrance of balsam.[48] Thus when people entered a church, it was possible for them to experience, even if only for brief moments, the celestial atmosphere in which saints lived all the time. In churches the lights, sounds, and scents could evoke the impression, if not the very image, of Paradise.[49]

By stressing the contrast between blissfully magnificent interiors and the harsh realities of life outside, the appearance of churches emphasized the significance of a Christianity that offered men unique access to this celestial existence. In addition, the internal decoration helped define the layout or spatial arrangement of the churches and thereby also the "message" that these churches, just like religious and domestic buildings in other societies, communicated to the people who entered them. As we

45. *GM* 58, 61, 71, with Hubert (1938) 108–66, and Vieillard-Troiekouroff (1976) 403–15.
46. Cf. *HF* II.16, for a church at Clermont.
47. *GM* 33, *GC* 72.
48. *VM* 1.9.
49. Cf. *HF* II.31, "ut aestimarent se paradisi odoribus collocari."

emphasized in the introductory discussion in Chapter 9, the exact location of true holiness, and therefore of genuine manifestations of divine power, was always somewhat ambiguous, since it might appear in shrines, relics, living holy men, or all three in combination. But the layout of a Christian church represented an implicit translation of religious categories into actual spatial ones, an emplacement into a miniature terrain in which earth, heaven, and their intersection were more precisely marked out.[50] In other words, churches had a dual symbolic significance. Not only were they set apart from communities, because their interiors conjured up, even duplicated, the nature of Paradise; they also represented within themselves carefully defined passageways between earth and heaven, between ordinary life and divine existence.

In the church of St. Martin at Tours it is possible to work out not only one specific example of this "cognitive landscape," but also the correlation between it and the attitudes and behavior expected of people. For this church we have, first, the verses that were inscribed on its walls and that served as signposts informing people where they were in its sacred geography;[51] since some of these verse inscriptions seem to have accompanied frescoes, it was unnecessary for men in the fifth and sixth centuries even to be able to read them, because the paintings communicated the same message. These inscriptions and frescoes were part of the new church built in the later fifth century by Bishop Perpetuus. Although the church had been burned in 559, most of the damage and immediate reconstruction seems to have involved the wooden rafters and roof. The walls apparently survived, and when Gregory came to repair them, he claimed that he had merely restored their earlier elegance.[52] Hence men in the later sixth century would

50. Cf. T. Hawkes, *Structuralism and semiotics* (Berkeley and Los Angeles, 1977) 134: "Even the most ordinary buildings organize space in various ways, and in so doing they signify, issue some kind of message about the society's priorities, its presuppositions concerning human nature, politics, economics, over and above their overt concern with the provision of shelter, entertainment, medical care, or whatever." Churches, of course, were so charged with religious significance that they were not ordinary buildings to begin with; for analysis of the semiotics of buildings, see the outstanding studies of Bourdieu (1973), Tambiah (1973), and Gordon (1976). Gautier Dalché (1982) is a suggestive introduction to Gregory's representation of geography in general.

51. LeBlant I, nos. 170–81, with the essential discussion of L. Pietri (1974).

52. *HF* X.31, "ut prius fuerant." The frescoes were visible by the early 580s, although it is uncertain whether this was before or after Gregory's restoration: *HF* VII.22.

have understood the layout of the church in the same way as men a century earlier when the church walls were first decorated and the verses inscribed. Second, for the later sixth century we also have Gregory's diary of the miracles performed in the church, which demonstrate that men's behavior and the expectations it presupposed still corresponded with the "directions" of the inscriptions and frescoes and the behavior they demanded. In short, as people entered the west doors of the church and moved toward St. Martin's tomb in the east apse, they were effectively making a journey from their daily terrestrial existence toward the "gateway to heaven."

Despite the best efforts of archaeologists and art historians, no one has yet come up with a satisfactory diagram of the church;[53] but fortunately, the links between beliefs, behavior, and the spatial layout of the building can be understood without the aid of precise diagrams. In contrast to later Gothic architecture, most early medieval churches were not organized according to calculated geometrical proportions or ratios; their internal space was defined instead by the directions contained in the frescoes and inscriptions on the walls in the nave and the apse, and the building itself, whatever its precise dimensions or shape, was often simply "scaffolding" for the paintings.[54] Gregory himself gave only a schematic description of the church, mentioning its measurements and the number of windows, doors, and columns; people who wanted more particulars could go see it for themselves.[55] In any case, Gregory's contemporaries were well aware of the church of St. Martin, even those who could not see: when a blind woman was healed, her first question was whether this building was the church of St. Martin.[56]

In general terms, the church was built along an east-west axis with a courtyard at each end. Outside the church to the south was a main road leading to the city; a few hundred yards to the north was the Loire River. Like another church at Lyon built about the same time in the later fifth century, this church was situated between a river and a road. But although both were surrounded by these busy thoroughfares, the avenue to heaven, "the road that leads to salvation," ran directly through the churches.[57]

53. Hubert (1977) 297–303, and Vieillard-Troiekouroff (1976) 311–24.
54. von Simson (1956) 5.      55. *HF* II.14, *VM* 1.6.      56. *VM* 2.54.
57. Sidonius *Ep.* II.10.4, "omnes quo via ducit ad salutem."

As people set out on this "way of salvation" they usually entered the church of St. Martin through the doors at the west end and advanced east toward the altar and the tomb. Just in front of these west doors, somewhere on the bell tower, was this inscription: "As you enter the church, look upwards, because a lofty faith admires the excellent entranceways. . . . This [bell] tower is security for the timid but an obstacle to the proud; it excludes proud hearts and protects the weak. That tower [or dome, over the altar and the tomb] is higher. Famous for its starry roads, it has led St. Martin to the citadel of heaven. From there he who has already journeyed to the rewards of Christ calls people; having gone on already, he has sanctified this journey through the stars."[58] Even before people entered the church this inscription, as well as two others placed near these west doors,[59] warned them that they needed the correct attitudes as determined in particular by *fides*; and according to the miracle stories of Gregory, most people did go to church because they were "compelled by faith."[60] Furthermore, this inscription explicitly promised that progression through the church involved a simultaneous vertical advancement upward to heaven. As people entered and walked through the church toward the altar and the tomb, they were also imitating St. Martin's journey up through the stars.

Over these west doors was another inscription, which accompanied a fresco portraying the New Testament story of the Widow's Mite. This inscription and fresco reiterated the necessity of performing good works in order to prove a person's faith: "If good works are lacking, then indeed faith is empty."[61] At the doors to the church people were repeatedly advised that they must have the proper disposition when they entered: those without faith would not be cured.[62] According to the example of the Widow's Mite, one way of demonstrating faith was through charity, an action that people could easily perform on the spot, given the hordes of beggars clustered around the church. Hence, when Gregory offered a comment on the death of a man who had misused charity, he employed precisely this story of the Widow's Mite to make his point.[63]

Inside the church the emphasis shifted. Here the frescoes and

58. LeBlant I, no. 170, "sidereum . . . iter."
59. LeBlant I, nos. 171–2.     60. E.g. *VM* 2.9.
61. LeBlant I, no. 173.     62. *VM* 2.49.     63. *VM* 1.31.

accompanying inscriptions presented acts of mediation between heaven and earth. One fresco showed Jesus Christ when he was a man, walking on the waves in order to save Peter from drowning; this, appropriately enough, was over the north doorway facing the Loire River.[64] Another fresco showed the church at Jerusalem in which the Holy Spirit descended upon the apostles, as well as the throne of the apostle James and the pillar on which Christ had been whipped.[65] And another fresco, or perhaps a series of them, apparently showed deeds from the life of St. Martin. Although most of the inscriptions on the walls of the church are now anonymous, we know that the author of the verses accompanying the frescoes depicting the life of St. Martin was Paulinus of Périgueux. According to him, St. Martin was a successful patron in the kingdom of heaven, from whom people could still expect assistance: "Through God's restoring power Martin renews whatever a page in the holy books reveals."[66]

Jesus Christ, the church he founded, and his saints, such as St. Martin: for Gregory and for other Christians of Merovingian Gaul these were the significant men and institutions through which divine power had once appeared on earth, and continued to do so. Thus, when Gregory mentioned some miracles that had happened on the Loire River, he insisted that in each case God had revealed his divine power through the mediation of saints, and in one instance he made a specific comparison between one of these miracles and the salvation of Peter by Jesus Christ.[67] The scene of the fresco on the church wall facing the Loire probably influenced Gregory's interpretation of this miracle, and it presumably conveyed the same message of divine mediation to other pilgrims in the church.

At the altar of the church and at the tomb of St. Martin, however, if people felt they were worthy enough to go that far,[68] they passed from earth to heaven. On the arch of the apse over the altar was this inscription based on the biblical story of Jacob's Ladder: "How this place must be feared! Indeed, it is the temple of

64. LeBlant I, no. 174.
65. LeBlant I, no. 175.
66. LeBlant I, no. 176 = Paulinus of Périgueux, *de orantibus* 17–18 (using the text in *CSEL* 16.1, p. 165, which here differs from LeBlant).
67. *VM* 1.2, representing Gregory's own comment on a story he had read in Paulinus of Périgueux *de vita S. Martini* VI.351–460; also *HF* V.49, *VM* 1.10, 2.17.
68. Cf. *VM* 1.12.

God and the gateway to heaven."[69] Three more inscriptions were placed near the tomb of St. Martin, which was in the back of the apse. One emphasized the "presence" of St. Martin: "Here Bishop Martin of blessed memory is buried; although his soul is in the hand of God, he is completely here, present, made manifest by every favor of his powers." Another stressed how St. Martin had received a crown of justice as his reward. The third described his holiness: "Confessor by his merits, a martyr by his cross, an apostle by his actions, Martin shines in heaven and here in this tomb. May he remember [us], and by washing away the sins of our miserable life may he conceal our crimes under his merits."[70] The characteristic layout of an early Christian church often resembled that of the great assembly hall in which emperors had once held court while enthroned in the apse. In this church, however, the saint's tomb was in the apse, and St. Martin was now praised for his reassuring presence, justice, and patronage, which had been the laudable characteristics of emperors. But unlike the old Roman emperors, St. Martin was not about to leave Gaul. Once, as Gregory and his congregation were preparing to celebrate Christmas Eve in the church, a possessed man claimed that St. Martin had abandoned Tours and gone to Rome. The people were naturally upset, until a miraculous cure demonstrated the saint's "arrival": St. Martin was still present after all.[71] A sixth-century sermon offered explicit assurance: not only did the tomb of St. Martin ensure that Tours was the most important city in Gaul, it also made Tours the equal of Rome.[72]

The "gateway to heaven" over the altar and the tomb was near the great tower or dome at the east end of the church. Representing the intersection of heaven and earth, this was a "gravity-free" zone. St. Martin had gone up to the stars, but his presence remained; the prayers and requests of believers went up to heaven, and cures and miracles came back down; people went to church with their offerings and left with their health restored.[73] As one of the inscriptions over the west doors claimed, "The person who makes just requests returns after gaining his vows."[74] Bishop Avitus of Vienne had explicitly used the analogy of Jacob's Ladder to

69. LeBlant I, no. 177, quoting Genesis 28:17.
70. LeBlant I, nos. 178–80.
71. *VM* 2.25; cf. *GM* 89, for a saint's festival marking the *adventus sancti*.
72. *Sermo in laudem S. Martini* 4.
73. Cf. *GM* 66.          74. LeBlant I, no. 171.

describe this transaction: "The angels climb up the ladder when they present our prayers in heaven; they descend as they transmit our expectations from heaven."[75] Hence, when on one occasion a possessed man climbed up to the rafters of the dome and jumped, he floated down to the pavement and landed unhurt.[76] Given the symbolic meaning that corresponded with the spatial arrangement of the church, people could anticipate that this man would suffer no painful consequences. Surviving the leap was a miracle, but only in the sense that it was another indication of the divine power that people expected to find at saints' tombs. In the church of St. Martin the dome functioned as a huge lens, focusing divine power on the altar and the tomb; and in its intense beam men were made whole.

Whatever meaning the interior arrangement of this church may therefore have acquired or lost in later centuries, in early Merovingian Gaul we find a close correlation between its spatial layout, as defined by its frescoes and the accompanying inscriptions, basic Christian beliefs about holiness and divine power, and their potential impact on daily affairs. A church was a saint's "huge and private house"[77] in which he entertained his guests among the delights of Paradise: "The miracles proceeding from the saint's tomb prove that he lives in Paradise."[78] Within a church, not only did people find that the spatial arrangement and interior decoration confirmed their cosmological beliefs and theology, they also had the opportunity to share in a heavenly existence in the "new Jerusalem, built in heaven and transferred to this spot," as Avitus expressed it.[79] Like saints who lived that way all the time, they too might briefly experience a life "free from the cares of this world."[80]

As it has been described, the spatial layout of this church can appear to be completely static, a timeless emplacement of a cosmological theology about the possibilities of mediation between divine power and human existence. Gregory gave a long and precise account of the translation of the body of St. Martin to this church, emphasizing that the sarcophagus had been deliberately

---

75. Avitus *Hom.* 17.    76. *VM* 1.38.
77. *GM* 91, "domus magna atque secreta."
78. *GC* 52; cf. *VM* 1.5, "Paradise again receives St. Martin, who is happy with the saints."
79. Avitus *Hom.* 22–23.
80. Cf. LeBlant I, no. 171.

moved both at the right time (July 4) and to the correct spot: "With the assistance of the Lord it was brought to the place where it is now adored." The anticipated consequences naturally followed: "From that day many miracles happened in that spot."[81] In fact, everything in the church of St. Martin seems to have had its correct place: when a priest tried to move a sacred stone on which St. Martin had once sat, he "offended" the saint, became ill, and died.[82]

But the church was not simply a static model, because in Merovingian Gaul people knew that, just like the beliefs it replicated, this church was alive. Paulinus of Périgueux pinpointed this vitality in verses inscribed on the walls of the church: "No page is able to embrace such powers; although this concrete and these stones are covered with inscriptions, an earthly building cannot enclose what the kingdom of heaven takes up and what the stars inscribe in fiery gems."[83] As we will see in the next two chapters, people consistently "enacted" their beliefs exactly where we would expect within this sacred space. Another way of energizing this static landscape was through the celebration of the liturgy, by means of which men synchronized themselves with celestial time; in fact, it is possible that the inscriptions about St. Martin in the apse were inspired by liturgical prayers.[84] Within the church people's behavior therefore often corresponded with expectations about sacred space and liturgical time: for instance, at the correct time, during the celebration of mass, a lame man lying in the correct spot, before the tomb, was healed and walked to the altar to participate with the congregation.[85]

This discussion of the church of St. Martin requires two qualifications. First, this church is unique in Merovingian Gaul because of the amount of information still available; not only can we use the inscriptions (and the implied frescoes) that were displayed on the walls, we also have in Gregory's diary of the miracles of St. Martin an account of how people acted in this church. In all of Merovingian Gaul, at the church of St. Martin in Tours during the later sixth century we come the closest to understanding the intimate interaction between beliefs and behavior. Yet, although other

81. *VM* 1.6.
82. *GC* 6.
83. LeBlant I, no. 176 = Paulinus of Périgueux, *de orantibus* 5–8.
84. LeBlant I, p. CVII, and (1892) 457–8.
85. *VM* 2.47.

Christian churches no doubt also transmitted symbolic significance, it is difficult to generalize, since the internal appearance
and layout of the church of St. Martin were not necessarily typical of churches in Gaul. Some churches had a cruciform design or
a double altar; in others relics were kept in subterranean crypts;
still others, perhaps only in southeastern Gaul, apparently had
icons.[86] Presumably these modifications affected the way people
understood the layout of their church and its relationship to their
Christian beliefs; but without more information, it remains difficult for us to understand why the people of Narbonne, for instance, could not bear to look at an icon (or a fresco) in their cathedral that showed the crucified Jesus Christ wearing only a linen
undergarment.[87]

The second qualification is that a modern analysis of the church
of St. Martin can be overly schematic, and hence misleading. Not
only are modern historians merely critical observers and not en-
thusiastic participants,[88] but Merovingian men themselves did not
always act in accordance with the expectations of this symbolic
terrain. Like a rule of etiquette, the spatial grid of the church of
St. Martin conceded the possibility of misbehavior. Some people
never journeyed through the interior of the church at all; a priest
who arrived late one night, for instance, found himself locked out
and had to make do with praying behind the apse and collecting
some holy dust there.[89] Other people clustered around "the feet of
St. Martin," which often meant that they gathered outside the east
apse in which the tomb was located. Some stayed there for years;
many were eventually cured, one man after praying in the courtyard, another after touching the shroud hanging on the outer wall
of the apse.[90] In these ways people could bypass the expectations
of the interior of the church and approach the tomb directly, from
the rear. But as we will see, ill and possessed people occupied an

86. E.g. *GM* 32–33.
87. *GM* 22. The Christological controversies of the time offer one appropriate
context for interpretation: see Pelikan (1971) 266–77.
88. Cf. P. Bourdieu, *Outline of a theory of practice* (English trans., Cambridge,
1977) 116–17: "To speak . . . of overall resemblance and uncertain abstraction, is
still to use the intellectualist language of representation—the language which an
analyst's relation to a corpus spread out before him in the form of documents
quite naturally forces on him—to express a logic which is acted out directly in
the form of bodily gymnastics without passing through the express apprehen-
sion of the 'aspects' selected or rejected, of the similar or dissimilar 'profiles.'"
89. *VM* 4.25.
90. *VM* 2.42, 50.

ambiguous, almost holy, status in the community, and they may have been privileged to take a direct detour around the sacred space of the church.

Inside the apse there was also, somewhere, one more inscription, composed by Sidonius, in which he had claimed that Perpetuus' new church was the equal of Solomon's temple. His poem ended with a weak pun on the bishop's name that neither he nor other poets could overlook: "May the high walls of Perpetuus last perpetually."[91] In fact, despite the fire in the middle of the sixth century and the Norman invasions and other fires in the ninth and tenth centuries, the church of St. Martin survived well into the Middle Ages, and the saint's cult, even though it was eventually challenged and surpassed by the influence of other cults, continued to guarantee the prominence of Tours. In the late eighth century Alcuin pointedly contrasted the size of the city with the importance of its patron saint: "Why do I speak of you, city of Tours, you who are small and despicable with regard to your walls, but important and praiseworthy because of the patronage of St. Martin?"[92]

By the later Middle Ages, however, although we have further information about the appearance and layout of the church, our understanding of its symbolic meaning is far more limited, largely because we do not have sufficient information about people's behavior in it. Another handicap is that after a fire in the early tenth century, the interior of the church was redecorated in a far more lavish manner. In addition to an expansion in its width to accommodate the large crowds of pilgrims who came to Tours on festival days or passed through on their way to the shrine of St. James in Compostela, builders grafted an ambulatory around the apse containing the tomb of St. Martin and added a transept (although the latter may have been built already before the tenth century).[93] Although at the very least there was still a close correlation between the layout of the church and the formal celebra-

91. Sidonius *Ep.* IV.18.5 = LeBlant I, no. 181; cf. Paulinus of Périgueux *de vita S. Martini* VI.506.

92. Alcuin *Vita Willibrordi* 32 (*MGH*, SRM 7, p. 139); note also *Vita Eligii* I.32, II.68 (SRM 4, pp. 688, 734), for Tours as "the city of St. Martin" in the early seventh century.

93. For the later history of the church of St. Martin see Hersey (1943), Lesueur (1949), and Vieillard-Troiekouroff (1961). Note also Odo of Cluny *Serm.* 4, "De combustione basilicae beati Martini," and 5, "In festo S. Martini" (*PL* 133.729–52); and Vieilliard (1963) 60.

tion of liturgy, as seen, for instance, in the penitential ceremony of the "humiliation" of saints and monks during the eleventh and twelfth centuries,[94] in many of these modifications to the building, purely practical and aesthetic considerations seem to have taken precedence.

\* \* \*

Other holy places were, of course, also associated with the cult of St. Martin, and most were dignified with a relic or two. Many of these shrines were near Tours, such as at Candes, where Martin had died, and at Marmoutier, his monastery. At both places the saint's bed was a venerated object; but remembering that saints were thought not to die but only to fall asleep, we can compare these beds to St. Martin's final resting place, his tomb. About his cell at Candes, Gregory wrote that "in other circumstances one can hardly call it a bed, except that Martin slept on the pavement on a layer of cinders with a stone as his pillow." So visitors went to Candes expecting to find there the same sort of assistance that they could obtain at the saint's tomb in his church.[95]

During the sixth century Marmoutier was still a functioning monastery, so devoted to the memory of its founder that at least one monk used a copy of his *Vita* as a pillow.[96] Already by the later fifth century part of the festivities of Lent included a pilgrimage to the monastery where St. Martin had lived "like an angel." There people followed the "footsteps of St. Martin," weeping over the places where he had prayed, fasted, and sung Psalms; there they also visited the cell where the saint had slept, in which an inscription described the gravelike appearance of his bed.[97] During the sixth century pilgrims still followed a fixed route, and they even took home mementoes of their visit.[98] At Marmoutier, then, "stations" marked with inscriptions traced the monastic life of St. Martin, and by visiting them pilgrims could relive the saint's life.[99]

Within Gaul, St. Martin, and in particular his miracles, had become a common topic of conversation. On his travels to various cities in Gaul, Gregory was continually hearing more stories about him. For instance, at Saintes: "While we were talking about the

94. Geary (1979).

95. *VM* 3.22; Fortunatus *Vita Radegundis* 34; Baudonivia *Vita Radegundis* I.14.

96. *VM* 3.42.

97. LeBlant I, no. 169; also Paulinus of Périgueux *de vita S. Martini* VI.90, 351–68, and *VM* 1.2.

98. *VM* 2.39.    99. LeBlant I, nos. 166–9.

miracles of St. Martin over dinner, one of the local citizens told this story, which the others verified." Or at Ligugé, St. Martin's first monastery outside Poitiers: "I asked the abbot whether the Lord had revealed any miracle there"; the abbot of course had many stories to tell.[100] Sometimes Gregory heard about the miracles from visitors to Tours, or he received letters from bishops in whose cities the relics of St. Martin had preformed miracles.[101] Everyone in Gaul seemed to have his own story, even a boatman at Trier. When he learned that an abbess had visited the saint's church at Tours, he was only too eager to tell her how St. Martin had once helped him too.[102]

But these references to scattered manifestations of St. Martin's power, and even more, the extravagant claims of Gregory and Fortunatus about the cult's worldwide diffusion[103] can give a misleading impression of its availability. In fact, a map plotting the shrines of St. Martin known from the sixth century shows that, despite an expected scattering in remote areas, the cult was concentrated in the vicinity of Tours.[104] The diffusion of even the most important cult of sixth-century Gaul remained limited, confined largely to central Gaul.

The limited extent of the cult can be confirmed by investigating the origins of the pilgrims who traveled to Tours. Gregory, who had a vested interest, again gave the impression that the cult appealed to a worldwide audience.[105] Some pilgrims, coming from Spain or Italy, did travel far. But of all pilgrims with known origins, just over one-quarter came from Tours and its territory, and of the remaining pilgrims, almost nine-tenths came from within 125 miles of Tours.[106] In this respect the origins of pilgrims closely correspond with the diffusion of shrines to St. Martin.

Nor was the cult of St. Martin without competition. Even at

100. *VM* 4.30–31.
101. E.g. *VM* 4.7–8. Gregory was prepared to listen to anyone tell about a miracle of St. Martin. As he wrote the story of Abbot Guntharius, whose horse had refused to move until the abbot had prayed at an oratory dedicated to St. Martin, Gregory would have preferred to hear confirmation straight from the horse's mouth: "O horse, if the Lord were to open your mouth, I would like you to say what you saw." (*GC* 8).
102. *VM* 4.29; cf. 2.16.
103. *VM* 1.16; 4 praef.
104. Vieillard-Troiekouroff (1976) 448–52 (map at p. 448), and Ewig (1961).
105. *VM* 2.53.
106. Lelong (1960), esp. his map at p. 233, with the qualifying comments of L. Pietri (1977).

Tours people were healed by other saints; a woman with a fever, for example, was healed at the monastery of St. Venantius, which was just outside the complex surrounding the church of St. Martin.[107] In another case a blind woman lying before the tomb of St. Martin was told, in a dream, to seek the assistance of St. Julian instead.[108] Within the larger catchment area of the cult, as defined by the diffusion of shrines and the origins of pilgrims, there were also other important religious centers, such as Poitiers, Orléans, Auxerre, and, above all, Paris. And at the fringes there were additional cult centers, such as Brioude, the center of the cult of St. Julian. The influence of his cult was more restricted, and therefore perhaps more typical. Although at and near Tours there were shrines to St. Julian (due to the influence of Gregory, who had a special attachment to the cult), most of his shrines were near Brioude, and most pilgrims came from Clermont, in whose territory the village of Brioude was located, or from cities such as Limoges, which were marginal to the cult of St. Martin at Tours.[109] Hence, although the cult of St. Martin may have exerted the strongest attraction during the sixth century, many smaller local saints' cults survived at its edges, or even closer to its center.

As we have seen, the existence of so many local cults could easily lead to rivalries between their various supporters, or even between cities. Given this competition to the cult of St. Martin (which, for us, is disguised by the dominance of the writings of Gregory during this period), it is not clear whether a fully developed idea of pilgrimage was already associated with Tours. Although eventually it became a confirmed destination for pilgrims, even a rival of Rome, as a medieval poem claimed,[110] during the sixth century Tours was merely the location of the most popular and illustrious cult in Gaul, and not a city to which men felt obligated to go. If they could obtain what they wanted at another local cult, their journey was over; thus a blind man on his way to the church of St. Martin, after being healed instead at the church of St. Hilary in Poitiers, never completed his trip to Tours.[111]

The idea of a church's "sacred space" also has, in another per-

107. *GC* 15; cf. *VP* 16.4.
108. *VJ* 47.
109. *VJ* 28, 41, 45, for pilgrims from Limoges.
110. Theodulf *Carm.* 61 (*MGH*, Poetae latini aevi carolini 1 [1881] 555); in general see Delaruelle (1963).
111. Fortunatus *de virtutibus Hilarii* 17–19.

spective, significant implications for our conception of early medieval pilgrimages. Eventually the pilgrimage, the *iter* or *peregrinatio*, came to suggest a long, arduous expedition, at the end of which people received forgiveness or a blessing. In the sixth century we already find this literal sense, since many people did make long trips to the shrine of St. Martin.[112] The annual pilgrimage from Clermont to Brioude to celebrate the festival of St. Julian was also considered an *iter*; and since during these pilgrimages people such as Gregory and his brother might become so ill that they could hardly continue, their blessing upon arrival was to receive a cure.[113]

The idea of pilgrimage had wider symbolic significance, however, and thus it could generate parallel associations of meaning in people's minds. A pilgrimage was essentially a journey from a familiar setting to a sacred spot or goal, a journey that furthermore distinctly separated people, either permanently or only temporarily, from full involvement in the norms of communities. So the notion of *iter* sometimes also referred to the "journey" people made within a church as they moved from the west doors toward the altar and the tomb at the east end; we have already seen this application in the church of St. Martin at Tours, in which an inscription near the west doors reminded people that, as they entered, they were setting out on a *sidereum iter*, the same excursion through the stars that St. Martin had already completed.

The idea of an *iter* was often also applied to people's lives after they became monks or clerics. In eastern Gaul, for instance, two men on the verge of becoming ascetics were tempted to give up "the journey they had begun." At Poitiers a nun dreamed that, as she was setting out on a "journey," she had been assisted by a man who guided her to the spring of living water; as a result, she had herself bricked up in a cell.[114] The analogical relationships between these various notions of *iter* can be carried further. Once people started such journeys they were expected to finish them. Ten years before he became bishop, Gregory had set out on a pilgrimage that he had vowed to make to Tours, and although he became so ill that he could scarcely continue, he insisted that he must complete the journey before he returned home.[115] In the same manner people who undertook the "journey" of asceticism

112. E.g. *VM* 3.32, 38.      113. *VJ* 24.
114. *HF* VI.29, *VP* 1.1.      115. *VM* 1.32, "votivum iter."

were expected to continue it throughout their lives. In a letter sent to Radegund when she founded her convent at Poitiers, bishops pointed out that St. Martin was her guide for the journey that she and the other nuns were now committed to completing, because, the bishops also stated, a nun could leave the convent only "like Eve expelled from Paradise."[116]

To begin a pilgrimage was to undertake an expedition along the same "road of righteousness" that Old Testament heroes, the apostles, and the holy martyrs had once followed all the way to the kingdom of heaven, and the vital requirement was the renunciation of all secular impediments.[117] By setting out on these journeys, whether a pilgrimage to Tours or an ascetic life, people were voluntarily separating themselves from their communities and from normal social relationships, no longer acknowledging their homes and families, depending instead upon the unpredictable hospitality of strangers. Gregory described the consequences very concisely: "Holy men become exiles when they wish to follow the celestial life even though still in their own homeland, as well as when they seek foreign places across the seas."[118] Thus one woman abandoned her family in order to make an *iter* to Tours; although her husband brought her back home, she set out again on another *iter* to Tours and this time stayed as a nun. The different notions of pilgrimage blended together and, as in this example, some who set out on occasional journeys ended up as "professional" travelers by becoming living holy men or women who could then act as tour guides for others.[119] When a lame priest was cured by an old man he met on the road, he was also guided on his way to the cathedral at Langres: "Priest, do you know who has restored your health? It is St. Martin of Tours."[120]

These analogical associations between the various notions of *iter* have two important implications. First, "journeys" have now been harnessed as an obedient component of Christian life. During the sixth century we find no revivalist movements such as the one once associated with Priscillian and his supporters, in which

116. *HF* IX.39, "dux iteneris."
117. *VJ* 1, "via iustitiae"; cf. [Orientius] *Explanatio nominum Domini* 138 (*CSEL* 16.1, p. 249).
118. *VP* 3, praef.
119. *VP* 19.2, with van Gennep (1960) 184–5, and Turner (1973) 211–22, on the sacredness acquired by pilgrims, and Ladner (1967), on overlapping medieval ideas about "alienation" as both pilgrimage and monasticism.
120. *GC* 11.

the image of an *iter* had represented people's new lives; nor do we find any living holy men as mobile as Martin of Tours and Germanus of Auxerre had been. Instead, such potentially threatening "nomadism" had been channeled into professional asceticism, trips to specific shrines, and, most significant, simply entering churches in order to approach saints' tombs; "journeys" were now a part of normal, institutionalized Christian society.

Second, these analogies also imply accessibility and total participation, because even ordinary people, merely by entering and by traveling through a church such as that of St. Martin in Tours, could share in the happiness that living holy men enjoyed all the time during their ascetic lives and that others found upon completing long journeys to Tours. One of the inscriptions at the entrance to the church of St. Martin explicitly reminded people that, as they were about to travel along an abbreviated "road of righteousness," they not only needed to demonstrate the correct attitudes, they could also expect the same rewards, because at the end of their journeys they would meet St. Martin, who had acquired his "crown of righteousness" from God himself.[121] Setting out on a pilgrimage of any sort meant entering into a state of holiness, even if only for the duration of the journey. By adopting the proper attitudes of faith and reverence and by completing a miniature pilgrimage along this "road of righteousness" through the church to St. Martin's tomb, ordinary people too could thereby approach the "gateway to heaven."

\*     \*     \*

For us, the combination of the inscriptions from the sanctuary walls with Gregory's stories of the many miracles that happened in the church makes the church of St. Martin at Tours the best example during the period of the close relationship between the organization of sacred space and Christian beliefs and behavior. For the people of early Merovingian Gaul, however, the church was a living symbol of Christian society, both a descriptive model of their basic beliefs and a prescriptive model for correct behavior. Since within the sacred space of this church they could make miniature pilgrimages to the tomb of St. Martin, many of these pilgrims, including the ones who came from elsewhere to Tours, had a specific purpose similar to that of later pilgrims to Canterbury:

121. LeBlant I, nos. 171, 179.

The holy blisful martir for to seke
That hem hath holpen whan that they were seke.

As we will see in the next chapter, the notion of illness often implied that people had infringed on these essential Catholic beliefs and had misbehaved; and many pilgrimages to, as well as within, the church of St. Martin were thus designed to seek cures and to restore people to a wholeness in their communities that they had lost.

# CHAPTER 12

# Illness, Healing, and Relic Cults

As Gregory diligently recorded the significant events for each year, his recollection of the epidemics that appeared with monotonous regularity exposed his deepest emotions: "And so we lost the little children who were so dear and sweet to us, whom we had hugged to our bosoms."[1] Throughout Gregory's lifetime, regional epidemics plagued Gaul; in fact, the final entry in his history described an epidemic at Tours and Nantes in 591 that affected domestic cattle and wild animals as well as people.[2]

While contemplating these disasters Gregory also revealed the contradictory feelings of anyone facing harshly inevitable realities. As he wrote about the children who died, he had to wipe the tears from his eyes, but at the same time he could comfort himself only by repeating the patient words of Job.[3] In many cases men could do no more, because natural disasters, food shortages, poor nutrition, and even snakes and rats in the streets[4] conspired against them. Running through Merovingian attitudes was a fundamental uneasiness about the extent of men's control over nature. Gregory himself extolled the urban magnificence of Dijon, even though the city was distinguishable from the lush countryside only by its massive walls, and insisted that a wolf that strayed into Poitiers represented only an unnatural prodigy.[5] Even in cities men still lived in a rustic environment, and epidemics perhaps most easily stripped away the brittle veneer of urban civilization.

1. *HF* V.34. (References to the writings of Gregory of Tours omit his name. See Chapter 9, unnumbered note.)
2. *HF* X.30.
3. Likewise Monegund mourning the death of her daughters, *VP* 19.1.
4. As at Paris, *HF* VIII.33.
5. *HF* III.19, V.41.

The classification and identification of epidemics and diseases have become an important branch of modern historical studies, in particular as a means for making indirect deductions about material and social characteristics of past societies. But the study of diseases (taken in a broad sense to include disabilities as well as sicknesses), and especially of the cures that were often described as miracles, also offers historians access to people's beliefs and attitudes, not just because the prevalence of diseases deeply affected their thinking, but more significantly because categories of illnesses and healing procedures were closely related to, if not identical with, the modes of classification also found in religious beliefs. Like the space of church buildings, so the body and its malfunctions offered another idiom with which to articulate community values and the distribution of prestige and authority.

A study of diseases and of miraculous cures also raises important historiographical problems. First, we are often faced with ailments and cures that can seem, to us, to be trivial or irrelevant. Although many of the people whom Gregory described would be considered ill or physically disabled in our society too, other cases were more peculiar, involving, for instance, a woman with a leg paralyzed due to some unknown anxiety, a slave who suffered recurrent bouts of paralysis whenever his master put him back to work, or a man who was cured of his alcoholism each time he took the pledge before the tomb of St. Martin.[6] To us, such ailments do not necessarily require miraculous cures, but for Gregory, miracles that led to the alleviation of anxieties, the resolution of community disputes, or the healing of the blind and paralyzed were all as significant a corroboration of the working of divine power as a miracle involving the elimination of a fly buzzing around the dinner table.[7]

Second, a more restricted empirical knowledge of human physiology already indicates one aspect of the different mental world within which medieval miracles are to be understood. Even in a strictly biological sense the basic differentiation between life and death, for instance, seems often to have introduced confusion. Not only did Merovingian writers compare ill people with

6. *VM* 1.22, 2.11, 53. As a result, St. Martin eventually became a patron saint for drunkenness: see v. Kraemer (1950) 38–42.

7. *GM* 106; but cf. Fortunatus *Vita Germani* 79, for a demon appearing "in the guise of a fly."

the dead,[8] but in at least one case an abbot who went into a fever coma was treated as dead by the weeping monks who prepared his body for burial. Perhaps their tears had blinded them, but fortunately the abbot awoke before the funeral reached its conclusion.[9] Noting this fundamental uncertainty over life and death is not to be taken as an attempt to explain away any miracles involving the resurrection of the dead;[10] instead, it only makes pointedly obvious the importance of including ignorance as one contextual factor in our understanding of cures in past societies.

Yet we have also seen in Chapter 9 how an ambivalence over life and death was also vitally important to the articulation of Christian beliefs about holiness and its accessibility in saints and relics. Hence the third and most important problem we face is to include ideas about diseases and cures within the history of attitudes and beliefs. Three modern tendencies can thus be avoided. One is to adopt an attitude of polite but condescending scepticism, an attitude already taken in Merovingian Gaul by some, in particular heretics, toward miraculous cures. Bishop Nicetius of Trier simply ridiculed such hesitation in reply: "Perhaps some [Arians] say that they only pretend that those who seem to have been blind from birth were really blind. But why do they say that, when there at Tours we see these blind people healed, and we see them return with the grace of God as healthy men to their own families?"[11] Similarly, Gregory always attempted to be precise about the illnesses that were cured at shrines, because he knew that both the saints' and his own credibility were at stake. Although he may not have recorded everyone's name, Gregory tried to give an accurate description of the circumstances surrounding each cure: "When the rumor went around that the power of the blessed Bishop Martin had appeared, I would call the custodians of the church of St. Martin and learn from them what had happened."[12] And these were usually public displays of miraculous power; not only did witnesses agree that people were cured, they also agreed that they had been ill and in need of cures. Hence, when a boy's withered hand was healed at St. Martin's church, "the entire congregation witnessed the great deeds of God."[13]

8. *VM* 2.3, 18, 3.2; Fortunatus *Carm.* II.16.142.

9. *HF* VII.1.

10. Note *VM* 1.21, on the resuscitation of a man hanging on the gallows: "This display of power [by St. Martin] is not inferior to resurrecting a dead man"; cf. *VP* 2.1, for Martin's contemporary, Bishop Illidius of Clermont.

11. *Epist. Austrasicae* 8.       12. *VM* 3.45.       13. *VM* 2.55.

Another unhelpful viewpoint is to classify these illnesses as mere psychological illusions, "diseases of the mind,"[14] or "shared deceptions,"[15] with the implication that people in Merovingian Gaul were mistaken or neurotic about a reality that only we can finally perceive. The distress and cries of agony were, in fact, genuine: a woman whose face broke out in sores because she had hoed a field during a festival came running to the church of St. Martin "screaming and shouting; she remained in this torment for four months."[16] To claim therefore that either individuals or the entire age was credulous or naive is merely to handicap our understanding of that society by imposing on it our own misgivings.

The final tendency to be avoided is to rely strictly upon a scientific, rationalistic viewpoint. Even when conceding that these cures did take place, some modern historians adopt a method either of attempting to identify the diseases in modern physiological terms, or of introducing as explanations for the cures (whether the diseases are identified or not) such factors as mistaken diagnosis or prognosis, mere alleviation of the symptoms, remission, spontaneous cure, or the simultaneous use of other remedies. This method is, again, not very illuminating, in part because unknown variables such as the effects of diet raise uncertainties about the identification of past diseases in modern terms,[17] but more importantly because strictly biological explanations also introduce misleading translations of the actions and beliefs of past societies into our own categories of analysis. As we study the relationship between disease and society, the primary unit of reference ought to include more than people's physiological misfortunes: "This means looking at states of health and disease not as clinical entities in the abstract but as lived experiences of individuals, families, and communities."[18] In Merovingian Gaul people's attitudes toward diseases were as intimately concerned with community and individual values as with physical sickness and disability; and a better translation of these attitudes would instead be

14. Thomas (1971) 251; see also the dialogue between H. Geertz (1975) and Thomas (1975), on his psychological interpretation.

15. Marc Bloch (1924) 420, "des illusions collectives," 429, "une erreur collective."

16. *VM* 2.57.

17. Braudel (1973) 43–44; Biraben and Le Goff (1969) is a clarification of the plague of the early Middle Ages.

18. Fortes (1976) xviii.

in terms of social exclusion and reintegration. Rather than concentrating simply on biological "disease," we should also consider "illness," which "will be determined by the views of particular individuals or cultures—it is of a social and psychological nature."[19] In this perspective people who became ill were often seen as outside the community, as people excluded, disgraced, confined, or humiliated. For these social illnesses men needed "social cures," and hence the therapy of healing also involved a process of reintegration and acceptance by the community: "Therapy then becomes a matter of sealing up the breaches in social relationships simultaneously with ridding the patient . . . of his pathological symptoms."[20] And at the focus of this therapy in Merovingian Gaul was the cult of relics.

In small, face-to-face communities the nexus between social disturbances and individual afflictions was therefore drawn so tightly that people who became ill often thought that they had sinned or committed a crime, while others asked what they had done to "deserve" becoming ill.[21] Accidental misfortunes were also interpreted within this perspective of personal responsibility; as Gregory commented after describing how a fire had destroyed the possessions of a man who had ignored a festival, "If anyone thinks that this happened by chance, let him note that the fire damaged none of the surrounding buildings."[22]

In other words, an investigation of misfortune, illness, and healing becomes a study of the values of communities and the means at their disposal to encourage the acceptance of those values. Just as in the fourth century, as we have seen, beliefs about orthodoxy and heresy had functioned as one language to clarify tensions within communities, so in the sixth century beliefs about illnesses and their cures have become another means of preserving community norms and relationships, although with two important, and interconnected, differences. First, rather than being evaluated as heretics influenced by external, foreign ideas, community deviants are seen as ill people stricken because of their own sins. Communities are now threatened more often from

19. Lewis (1976) 90.
20. Turner (1967a) 360. Note also Skultans (1976) 190–1, who argues that "sociosomatic" is more appropriate than "psychosomatic" as a description for illnesses that have no obvious pathological causes.
21. VM 3.38.
22. GC 80.

within than from without. Second, rather than waiting to be accused of deviancy by others, people have so thoroughly merged
community values with Christian expectations that they will themselves usually know when they have "sinned" and should be ill.
Let us therefore investigate, first, the cures and techniques of
healing that were considered acceptable, since these effectively
indicated which set of beliefs, and therefore which group of
people, were now dominant; second, the interplay of illness and
cure as a gauge of community values and in particular of the regulation of infringements against them; and third, the effect of cures
upon people's standing in their communities.[23]

* * *

An example illustrating the underlying similarities between
pagan and Christian rituals of healing can introduce how acceptance of or opposition to these rites was closely associated with
the distribution of authority and prestige in communities. Near
Cologne was a pagan shrine at which local inhabitants feasted to
the point of vomiting and offered votive sculptures of whatever
part of their bodies was in pain. Presumably this was a purgative
and healing ritual, but as such it did not differ much from behavior before the tomb of St. Martin. There too people vomited, especially after swallowing some of the dust from the tomb, and there
too they attempted to touch the tomb itself, the shroud, or the
wooden barrier surrounding it. In the church of St. Martin such
behavior was acceptable; but the pagan ceremonies were so offensive to one of Gregory's uncles that he tried to burn down the
shrine.[24] In other words, pagan cures differed from Christian
cures not necessarily in techniques or even results, but rather in
the alternative they offered to the restrictions imposed by Christianity on all aspects of daily life, an alternative that bypassed
churches, bishops, and relic cults.

In fact, Gregory himself was willing to concede some value to
orthodox medical skills by recognizing the efficacy of doctors'
remedies; one of his priests, he once wrote, would have died if
doctors had not been there with their cupping glasses.[25] Apparently he had also read enough medical handbooks to be familiar

23. Marignan (1899) II, 183–212, is a thorough collection of information.
24. *VP* 6.2.
25. *HF* VI.22.

with operating techniques and medicinal herbs,[26] and he and his family were prepared to use the latter. Until she was finally cured at Tours, his mother had found relief from a stabbing pain in her leg only by drugging herself on the vapors from a fireplace or by using an ointment. Gregory too, when he suffered from one of his stomachaches, first tried the usual remedies: "I confess, I often sat in the bathtub, and I bound some hot pads to my tortured stomach, but nothing could heal my sickness"; finally he found relief at the tomb of St. Martin.[27]

Of course, the conventional techniques and remedies of doctors had the potential to go disastrously wrong: men who endured bloodletting, for instance, also risked bleeding to death.[28] But the point is not that beliefs in the efficacy of relics were to be a substitute for unsafe traditional remedies (although they could be), nor that they were beliefs of last resort; instead, these Catholic beliefs coexisted with the remedies of doctors as long as Christianity and its representatives were allowed to be preeminent and provide the underlying interpretation.[29] Gregory therefore criticized doctors, soothsayers, and prophets not because they merely prescribed bandages, potions, and charms or because their remedies were not always successful, but because they appeared not to recognize the subordination of themselves and their remedies to beliefs in the exclusive curative power of Christian relics and saints. The same was true with their patients, because Gregory conceded that some people "deserved" to be ill for not respecting the power of relics. Thus an archdeacon from Bourges who attempted to supplement the cure he had received at St. Martin's church by consulting a Jewish doctor eventually went blind: "Let this story teach each Christian that, when he has been worthy to receive a heavenly cure, he should not seek earthly remedies."[30]

In this perspective the debate over proper remedies crystallized the competition between individuals over influence. The cures available at relic shrines defined and established new personal relationships of authority and dependence, but only among men who all respected Christian beliefs about relics. More subtle,

26. *HF* V.35, *VM* 2.18–19, 3.60.
27. *VM* 3.10, 4.1.
28. Fortunatus *Vita Germani* 159.
29. Cf. *VM* 3.34: "The skill of doctors had no effect against this illness unless the assistance of the Lord was added."
30. *HF* V.6; cf. *VM* 2.1, 19.

and therefore more powerful, opposition came from men who attracted the same audience as bishops and saints, but from an alternative perspective. Pagan healers and pagan medicine also offered more than remedies or prescriptions; as a council in the early sixth century had stated, pagan phylacteries were "obligations on people's souls,"[31] and like the cures at Christian shrines they too defined relationships between people in which healers were invested with authority.

The similarities are again worth emphasizing. In 587 a man came to Tours claiming that he could work miracles by forcibly tugging on the limbs of ill people. Gregory bluntly objected: this was not healing through holiness, but delusion through black magic.[32] But an identical accusation of sorcery had once been made against a monk by the parents of a young boy who went mad in the presence of relics of St. Julian.[33] Another significant comparison involves "wise women." During the plague of 571 a woman who claimed that she knew how to cure the people of Clermont was exposed by a monk as the devil in disguise.[34] A contemporary was Monegund, who worked cures through a medicine made from vine leaves, herbs, and saliva; another contemporary was Radegund, who cured a nun by using herbs.[35] But unlike the woman exposed as a fraud, Monegund was a nun at Tours who was eventually honored as a saint, and Radegund was the highly respected founder of a convent at Poitiers.

Despite the superficial similarities, orthodox Christians therefore contrasted these different healers: some could recognize true illnesses and offer proper remedies, while the others offered only a sham. In the same manner in which the ability to distinguish between orthodoxy and heresy had once bolstered the position of bishops, so the imposition of these vital distinctions between proper and improper cures was again an indication of who would have authority in communities.[36]

---

31. Council of Agde a. 506, sententiae 21, "obligamenta animarum."
32. *HF* IX.6.
33. *VJ* 45.
34. *VP* 9.2; and *HF* V.14, VII.44, for other "false prophetesses."
35. *VP* 19.3 and *GC* 24; Fortunatus *Vita Radegundis* 78.
36. Cf. Thomas (1971) 227: "In the last resort the only means of telling whether a cure was magical or not was to refer it to the authorities—the Church, the Law, and the Royal College of Physicians. If they permitted its employment, then no scruples need be felt by laymen."

\*     \*     \*

Before bishops and living holy men could offer their cures, however, other people had first to admit that they were ill, and such confessions take us again into the dynamics of small communities. To repeat, however, this discussion is not directly concerned with sickness and disability as physical afflictions, and it does not provide physiological (or even sociological) explanations for all the miraculous cures that Gregory and his contemporaries recorded. Some cures may have been due, in a strictly biological sense, to mistaken diagnosis, normal remission, or ignorance about physical health; others continue to bewilder us. But by considering these afflictions and their alleviations as social illnesses and social healings, we can complement discussions of physiological aspects by recreating a context in which notions of shame, disgrace, guilt, and exclusion became the catalyst for behavior.

Many of the main themes converge in one introductory example, which illustrates in particular the prominent role of the community of Tours. A man named Ursulf became blind because, by repairing a fence on the first day of Lent, he had infringed a community convention about the regulation of work time. Although he was in Tours for two months, he received his cure only at a precise time, during mass on Easter Sunday, and at a precise place, in the church of St. Martin. As a blind man Ursulf had been excluded from the community, unable to work and forced to live on charity; without someone guiding him he could not participate in the liturgical festivals. Once cured, however, he reintegrated himself into the community by walking unassisted to the altar and receiving the Eucharist with everyone else. And during this healing process he acquired a new "master" in St. Martin to replace the old master who had ordered him to work on the fence.[37]

Most frequently, people came down with social illnesses because they did the wrong thing at the wrong time, particularly on Sundays or festival days; grinding wheat, baking bread, making keys on Sundays—all these activities could lead to paralysis or blindness.[38] Sometimes men became ill because of others' misbehavior. A man stricken with paralysis learned in a dream that his affliction was an indication of the sinfulness of other people

37. VM 2.13.
38. Below, pp. 285–87.

and that before he could be cured he had to become an itinerant preacher warning against perjury, usury, and failure to attend mass on Sundays.[39] Other people were struck down for infringing on sacred property; a man who tried to eat some grapes belonging to a church, for example, developed a paralyzed hand. In this instance Gregory could not resist his own little joke, because although the man was a court jester, under the circumstances he had nothing funny to say![40]

Significantly, the symptoms of these illnesses were often directly related to the nature of the infringements. A man who threatened to make shoes from a bishop's cloak had his feet burned; another who washed his feet in a silver vessel belonging to a church was crippled.[41] Men who made false oaths felt pain in the fingers of the hand with which they had sworn, or found their tongues stiffening up.[42] An accused arsonist who made a false oath felt himself burning up.[43] As Gregory summarized after one man's threats against an abbot, "The mouth that had said it would seize the field from the church was tongue-tied, the eyes that had lusted were blinded, the hands that had grasped were paralyzed."[44] The nonconformity of these people was made painfully public: they became "lepers," a comparison that Gregory used for another man covered with sores and that became a powerful image of social exclusion in the later Middle Ages.[45]

The consequence of these illnesses was an inability to participate in the normal life of a community. Occasionally expulsion from a family resulted, so that a man who lost his voice was ejected from his ancestral home by his brothers, who claimed that he had also lost his mind and could not inherit any property.[46] The most common illnesses were blindness and paralysis, which communities used as ready explanations to account for social deviance or reluctance to share their values.[47] Thus a blind woman lamented that her social illness openly declared her unsuitability to celebrate Easter: "Woe to me, because I am blinded by my sins and I do not deserve to see this festival with the other people."[48] As a result, these people, now disgraced and shunned, could

---

39. *VM* 2.40.      40. *VM* 4.7.      41. *GM* 84, *VP* 8.5.
42. *GC* 32, 67.      43. *HF* VIII.16.      44. *GC* 78.
45. *VM* 2.58, with Moore (1976).      46. *VM* 3.23.
47. Cf. Sigal (1969) 1527, who computes that 40 percent of the miracles in the *VM* refer to cases of paralysis.
48. *VM* 2.28; cf. 2.46.

only loiter in the compound surrounding the church of St. Martin. There they had to live on private charity or the rapidly increasing wealth of the church.[49] And until they were cured, these people were also excluded from the normal activities and aspirations of the community.

Although the status of ill people was therefore structurally marginal, it was also special: giving alms to the poor and ill was one positive recommendation for people about to enter the church of St. Martin. The needy were in fact needed by others who wished to demonstrate their charity, as a bishop once argued in a sermon: "The Lord wished that poor people exist so that the rich might have a means of atoning for their sins; God could have made everyone rich, but he wished to provide the wealthy with a means of charity."[50] In this structurally liminal niche the standing of ill people differed little from that of possessed people, imprisoned people, or, most revealingly, living holy people. In fact, these different categories of people living outside the normal activities of communities often overlapped. One young man claimed that a bishop who predicted his successor was talking like a madman.[51] When the Lombards saw a holy man at Nice who wore iron chains and lived in a stone tower with no entrances, they thought he was a murderer.[52] A monk in the Jura lived such an ascetic life that, "as if crippled by paralysis," he could hardly walk or even straighten himself out.[53] At Tours a priest took to drink, was possessed by a demon, and had to be chained in his cell; by the time he died he had been a holy man, a possessed man, and an imprisoned man.[54]

Possessed and ill people consequently often acquired the same insights into the workings of their communities as did living holy

49. For churches providing hospitals, hotels, asylums, and poor houses, see Lesne (1910) 333–412; MacGonagle (1936) is a general survey.

50. Caesarius *Serm.* 30.1; and *Vita Caesarii* I.20. For Gregory's own aristocratic perspective on the poor, see Schneider (1966).

51. *HF* II.1.

52. *HF* VI.6.

53. *Vita [Patrum Iurensium] Lupicini* 4.

54. *HF* VIII.34, with Lesne (1910) 390–1, for the monastery as a place of confinement, and Turner (1969) 80–118, for an outstanding discussion of the dialectic between liminality and community structure. It is also most revealing that E. Goffman, *Asylums: Essays on the social situation of mental patients and other inmates* (Garden City, N.Y., 1961) 3–124, could use the Rule of St. Benedict to great effect in his comprehensive analysis of such "total institutions" as asylums, army camps, prisons, and monasteries.

men. Like holy men, or like ill people who made pilgrimages, possessed people were also fellow travelers making "a long journey."[55] Ill people often had dreams in which saints visited and talked with them, and not only could possessed people make observations that ordinary people failed to see, but because of their transitional position outside ordinary protocol they could publicly announce their insights with impunity. They knew whether the power of a saint was in fact present, or whether people were celebrating a festival on the correct date.[56] They alone dared to articulate the realities of a covert struggle over personal authority. When Bishop Nicetius of Trier confronted King Theudebert with the sins of his supporters, a possessed boy began to shout out the powers of the bishop and the misdeeds of the king; many thought that this boy had been a messenger from God.[57] Some men even attempted unscrupulously to misuse the proclamations of possessed people; so one man wishing to discredit the bishop of Clermont bribed a woman to act as if possessed and to cry out that the bishop was a thief.[58]

Such open commentary was necessary when the relationship between divine power and secular affairs was potentially so uncertain. Saints did not always make their intentions and support obvious: everyone knew that they broke protocol by not responding to letters.[59] Thus one way of acquiring certainty was to listen to the possessed and ill people who publicized a saint's power; possessed men, as Gregory explained, could "conjure up the saints of God in people's minds."[60] But like illness, demonic possession was an ambiguous condition. A false prophet who proclaimed himself to be Christ and his female companion to be Mary was simply a madman and a bandit, according to Gregory; but a woman who predicted a fire at Paris was not, as some claimed, a fortune-teller, a vain dreamer, or possessed by an evil demon, because she had had a vision of a saint.[61] As with the resolution of other ambiguities, here too the ability to impose a decision about genuine insight and mere fakery has implications about the location of authority in communities.

But although there were structural similarities between the roles of the ill, the possessed, and living holy men, there were

55. Fortunatus *Vita Germani* 53.
56. GM 89, VM 3.39.    57. VP 17.2.    58. HF IV.11.
59. HF V.14.    60. VJ 30.    61. HF VIII.33, X.25.

also fundamental differences. Holy men were thought to have assumed their marginal status voluntarily and permanently; the ill and the possessed, in comparison, became social outcasts involuntarily and, they hoped, only temporarily. For all except holy people, becoming social outcasts exacted a huge penalty, because the price these people paid for ignoring the etiquette and conventions of their communities was a life of misery. Furthermore, they became firmly attached to a particular spot, generally near a shrine where there were relics. At Tours most of these people congregated in the complex around the church of St. Martin, where they were "acceptably" ill or mad. This courtyard became their home, and on one occasion these beggars and madmen even violently protested a bloody brawl on the premises.[62]

Concentrating these outcasts around the religious focal point of a community marks a striking contrast to the later Middle Ages. Then ill people would be secluded in hospitals and possessed people would be placed in asylums, or madmen would be put on ships and allowed to drift between cities that rejected them. For Gregory, the church was also a ship, prefigured by Noah's ark, which had sailed serenely among the evil hazards of the world; in fact, when Gregory described the ark as one of the seven wonders of the world, he portrayed it as somewhat similar to the long, narrow architecture of a typical basilica, complete with doors and windows.[63] Given the large crowd of ill and possessed people huddled in their courtyards, Merovingian churches can be seen as "ships of fools," with the vital distinction that they were not sailing anywhere. Although structurally marginal, ill and possessed people, like living holy men, were situated precisely at the center of Christian communities.

The differentiation between holiness, madness, and illness poses some of the same questions that arise from discussions of witchcraft and sorcery. Historians of early medieval Christianity also face "the difficult task of establishing which aspects of such beliefs and behaviour are institutionalized and which represent deviancy. . . . To what extent, then, is a witch or a madman an unsuccessful prophet? To what extent is a prophet a socially approved deviant?"[64] A further important difference was that holiness, a fairly permanent state, was thought to have control over

62. HF VII.29.     63. HF I.4, de cursu 2.     64. Beidelman (1970) 354–5.

illness and madness, which were usually only temporary states. Hence it was possible for the ill and the possessed to be cured at shrines in a process of healing that involved reintegration into the community.

Often people first publicly confessed their misdeeds before they were healed. Three madmen who were "confessing their crimes and praying that St. Martin heal them" were suddenly cured during a festival; a woman's paralyzed hand was healed after she promised never again to do anything improper on a Sunday; a man unable to approach the altar and celebrate mass confessed that he had sinned and was then forgiven by the bishop.[65] Often too, after being cured, these people participated in the liturgy. A paralyzed girl walked to the altar; a mute woman recited the Lord's Prayer during mass; a lame man stood up to receive communion; a woman whose blindness had prevented her from participating in the litanies now joined people for mass.[66] Following their cures many people reentered the community by sharing a meal or by going back to work; after one blind woman was healed, she married and had children.[67]

Accounts of people being rescued from prisons can also be considered as miracles of "healing." In one instance Gregory made an explicit comparison: when a woman was healed, it was "as if a load of chains fell from her limbs to the ground."[68] In another case a girl unjustly imprisoned wept because she could not participate in a festival; suddenly her shackles fell away, and she joined everyone else at the church of St. Martin.[69] Many saints' tombs were littered with piles of broken chains, because there in the presence of relics prisoners, madmen, and the ill were all cured.[70] In each case the result was the same, since people returned to their families and communities. One inscription on the wall of the church of St. Martin promised that "a man will enter in tears but leave in happiness";[71] the common refrain at the conclusion of many of Gregory's miracle stories demonstrates the fulfillment of that promise: "The person was happy and went home."

The drama surrounding these miracles of healing was an enactment of the same beliefs about the potential intersection of

65. *VM* 2.34, 3.55; Fortunatus *Vita Marcelli* 37–38.
66. *VM* 2.14, 30, 47; Fortunatus *Vita Germani* 96.
67. *VM* 1.19.      68. *VJ* 9; cf. Fortunatus *Vita Paterni* 35.
69. *VM* 3.41.      70. *GC* 92; cf. 65, 93.
71. LeBlant I, no. 176 = Paulinus of Périgueux, *de orantibus* 22.

heaven and earth that animated the cults of saints. At the church of St. Martin in Tours these beliefs had acquired a spatial emplacement, as we have seen, and hence many cures at the church commonly happened in the expected spot near the altar and tomb of St. Martin. In the central nave of the church, people read on the wall an inscription describing the potential power of St. Martin: "You who kneel and dip your face to the dusty ground and press your tearful eyes to the hard earth—lift your eyes, with fearful gaze imagine his miracles and entrust your cause to a distinguished patron." At least one man received his cure after carefully following the directions specified in this inscription; standing before the altar at the "gateway to heaven," he raised his arms, looked up, and was healed.[72]

In this drama of healing many cures happened at specific times, in particular during the celebration of mass on one of the festivals of St. Martin or on other festival days: "Only seldom does a festival happen at which the saint does not show his power here."[73] These cures were reenactments of the healings that had been performed by Martin during his lifetime and that were now depicted in the frescoes on the walls of the church. In these frescoes people could see how Martin had once healed the blind, the lame, and the mad.[74] Now, according to Gregory, St. Martin was still "preaching": "Although he cannot reveal himself openly to the people, he continually shows himself in his obvious powers when he illuminates the blind, cures the paralyzed, and restores other ill people to their original health."[75] From Gregory's records we know that people thought that Martin's displays of power in the past were precedents for the present. Before one blind woman was healed in the church of St. Martin she said, "I have faith that the man who could heal a poor leper with a kiss can restore light to my eyes"; likewise at Poitiers a paralyzed woman, after recalling how St. Martin had once raised a dead man there, asked to be healed in the same way.[76] During the celebration of mass on the two annual festivals of St. Martin at Tours, readings from his Vita were substituted for some of the lessons from the Bible. These were the climax of the ceremony, and it was during these readings that many were healed.[77]

72. LeBlant I, no. 176 = Paulinus of Périgueux, de orantibus 1–4, with VM 1.7.

73. GC 88.

74. LeBlant I, no. 176 = Paulinus of Périgueux, de orantibus 13–14, 18–20.

75. VM 2.40.          76. VM 1.19, 4.30.          77. VM 2.14, 29, 49, 3.48.

In the therapy of healing, individuals and communities regained an original wholeness and health, and also a pristine happiness. After a man who had been born lame was eventually healed at St. Martin's tomb, Gregory claimed that the man had been born again; similarly, a woman healed of her paralysis at Poitiers became an "aged infant" and, as if the cure were her birth, asked for milk.[78]

Most of our evidence about these rituals of healing comes from Tours, where Gregory was bishop. Only there do we still have sufficient information to construct an elaborated model of how illness and healing could serve as a means for coping with social deviance and breaches in community values; only there do we have the additional set of inscriptions, and the frescoes that accompanied some of them, that allow us to investigate the relationship between an emplacement and an enactment of the beliefs that determined community etiquette. We can guess, however, that other relic cults functioned in similar ways. Since Gregory also provides a series of miracle stories about the shrine of St. Julian at Brioude, we can use them as a brief recapitulation of social illnesses and rituals of healing.

Men who came to the shrine of St. Julian had become ill after having infringed community conventions; a man who plowed on Sunday, for instance, found that his hand was paralyzed.[79] These ill people were consequently excluded from community activities: when the saint asked a woman in a dream why she was not at a vigil, she replied that her paralysis prevented her from walking.[80] But after a public confession people were cured. A man who went blind in his one good eye because he sought revenge on the man who had put out the other eye was healed after confessing his sins before the saint's tomb and forgiving the man who had wounded him; a man paralyzed after making a false oath made a public confession after his voice was restored.[81] These cures commonly occurred during the festival of St. Julian, during the celebration of mass, or during a Sunday vigil.[82] And the divine power of St. Julian was contrasted with the remedies proposed by soothsayers, who offered solutions that bypassed relic cults, thus also bypassing Bishop Gregory, who was a "foster son" of St. Julian. Against such men Gregory let his bitterness show, and he became almost too austerely dismissive as he contrasted a slave who de-

78. VM 1.40; Fortunatus *de virtutibus Hilarii* 26–29.
79. VJ 11.        80. VJ 9.        81. VJ 10, 19.        82. VJ 9, 16, 47.

servedly died after treatment by a soothsayer with a slave who lived after swallowing holy dust.[83]

As we have seen in Chapter 6, appropriating the ideology and functions of doctors had been one way of clarifying the position of Christian leaders. But these new "spiritual doctors"[84] offered more than medicine for physical ailments, because in the presence of holy relics people could request both cures for diseases and forgiveness for sins.[85] St. Martin was a *medicus* to be sure, but the kind of doctor who, when he healed a blind man, illuminated in addition the eyes of his heart so that the man could truly see.[86] Under these conditions, after conceding the demands expected by Catholic beliefs, men were healed and could again participate fully in the community and its activities. As Gregory concluded after being cured of yet another stomachache by swallowing dust from St. Martin's tomb, "Unharmed, I went and had a meal."[87]

*    *    *

A further aspect of the ritual of healing is equally notable. Not only did healing involve a cure and the possibility of reintegration into the community, it also carried an implication of judgment and pardon. Like prisoners, ill people thought they had committed crimes and did not "deserve" to participate in festivals or services with others. Thus one woman knew precisely why her withered hand had not been healed: "I did not deserve to receive what I sought because my sins were in the way."[88] Because people who were ill or mad were supposedly bound by the power of demons, often they requested not a cure, but release; at the tomb of St. Martin one ill man shouted, "My lord Martin, free me!"[89] And when ill people were healed, it was because they had been "found worthy" of the cure and of forgiveness for their sins.

In this context of divine judgment St. Martin and other saints were also "advocates" who pleaded the cases of their "foster children" before the tribunal of God. As such, they had even more authority than civil judges: one saint, for instance, actually reached out from his tomb to embrace and protect a grave robber from a

83. *VJ* 46a.
84. Caesarius *Serm.* 5.5; and *Vita Caesarii* I.15, 17; cf. *GM* 30, "caelestis medicus."
85. *VM* 4 praef.
86. *VM* 2.13.     87. *VM* 2.1.     88. *VM* 2.56.
89. *VM* 2.26; cf. 3.53, for an identical plea from a convicted thief.

judge![90] Before the tombs of saints people discovered the difference "between the just and the unjust, those who fear God and those who do not serve him."[91] When they were cured, they were also declared to be "not guilty" and forgiven for their sins; no longer did they have to be confined in "that infernal prison" like other sinners waiting with trepidation for the Last Judgment.[92] Thus there was even some advantage for people in becoming ill and being cured, since then, in contrast to people who had always been healthy, they had a permanent record that they had at least once been favorably judged by a saint. Nicetius of Lyon, for instance, carried on his face the scar from a childhood illness as obvious evidence of St. Martin's favor. Gallus, Gregory's paternal uncle, once had his foot healed by St. Julian; later he showed the scar, "insisting that here was the power of the holy martyr."[93]

In this context too it becomes understandable why Gregory himself seems to have been ill so often. His medieval biographer found especially noteworthy both his constant ill health and the numerous cures he received from St. Martin: "Each time Gregory was ill, he ran to his own St. Martin and was quickly cured; this happened often."[94] Like most people in Merovingian Gaul, Gregory suffered from frequent stomachaches, fevers, dysentery, and headaches; but his aches and pains also presented the opportunity to assure himself, and others, of the support of saints: "Whenever my head aches and my temples pound, whenever my ears ring, my eyes become tired, or my joints ache, as soon as I bring the afflicted part of my body into contact with St. Martin's tomb or with the shroud draped over it, I immediately regain my health."[95] In his diary of the contemporary miracles of St. Martin, Gregory carefully began and concluded each book with accounts of his own cures, not so much to demonstrate his own infirmities as to prove that he enjoyed the favor of the saint. St. Martin was now his "private" patron, a "friend of God" to whom Gregory was in debt: "May my worthless ability permit him to be honored

90. GC 61; cf. VJ 50, "advocatus in causis alumni proprii coram Domino adsistens."
91. VJ 46a.
92. HF X.13, VM 4.26.
93. VP 8.1, VJ 23. Brown (1981) 108–113, discusses the similar judicial overtones of the ritual of exorcism.
94. [Odo of Cluny] *Vita Gregorii* 14 (PL 71.122).
95. VM 3 praef.

as is appropriate for a friend of God who, when so many illnesses burdened me, so often restored me to health."[96] Gregory was likewise careful to record the cures he had received from other saints as proof that he had acquired favors from them too.[97]

The ritual of healing changed people's lives by putting them into a state of grace from which they were not meant to fall again. At Poitiers, for example, two lepers became clerics after being judged and healed: "They properly chose to bear the yoke of that Lord who had freed them from their punishment."[98] Other cured people also entered into an intimate relationship with their patron saints, because they too had become "debtors" and were expected to return each year to the shrines at which they had been cured.[99] Such debt bondage took precedence over all other ties; a woman cured of paralysis, for instance, thereafter vacillated between health and illness depending upon whether she remembered her vows or lived with her husband.[100] A man who later became a bishop celebrated the anniversary of his cure by annually offering candles to St. Hilary: "In debt for his life he paid back what he owed to his doctor."[101] Hence, in a society in which most people were now Catholic Christians, this ritual of healing may have acquired even more significance than baptism, because cures now had the additional result of differentiating among people who were already members of the church.

Finally, the acceptance of these beliefs about illness and healing was also a public indication of socialization, of people's internalized acquiescence with the social expectations of Christian communities. Nowhere does this acquiescence become more obvious than in the common idea that the most powerful medicine saints could offer was some of the dust from their tombs; in fact, the sarcophagi of some saints had been scratched so often that holes had been worn through.[102] To us it may seem peculiar to select dust as the most effective curative agent, as opposed to, for example, the water used to wash the tombs, lamp oil, or even a holy man's spittle, all of which were cherished as relics and which also might have more obvious medicinal qualities. Such rationalist considerations again indicate only our distance from the world of Gregory, because the idea of sacred dust was integrated instead

96. VM 4 praef.    97. GM 50, GC 43.
98. Fortunatus de virtutibus Hilarii 11–14.    99. GC 101.
100. Vita Marii 17.    101. Fortunatus de virtutibus Hilarii 6–10.
102. E.g. GC 35, 52, 73.

into a logic that defined the essence of acceptable behavior in Christian communities. Geertz concisely summarizes the paradoxical coherence of religious logic: "Such [religious] symbols render the world view believable and the ethos justifiable, and they do it by invoking each in support of the other. The world view is believable because the ethos, which grows out of it, is felt to be authoritative; the ethos is justifiable because the world view, upon which it rests, is held to be true. . . . Seen from inside, it appears as simple fact."[103]

Our modern difficulty in accepting these "simple facts" about the communities of Merovingian Gaul is similar to the scepticism of a Jew who tried to dissuade a pilgrim from going to Tours: "St. Martin will be of no assistance to you because the earth covering him has made him earthen; you go to his church in vain, because a dead man cannot give medicine to living men."[104] Gregory pointedly disagreed. For him, it was precisely holy dust, the most obvious reminder of men's daily existence, that had the most potent celestial qualities: "O heavenly purgative! This dust overwhelms the subtleties of doctors, surpasses sweet aromas, and is more powerful than all strong ointments; . . . most important of all, it eliminates the stains of conscience."[105]

Since swallowing dust, even holy dust, was not one of the usual remedies prescribed in medical handbooks, the attitude of Gregory shows all the more clearly that it was not the strictly curative qualities of holy dust that made it popular and effective. To some extent there was a theological doctrine at the basis of his attitude, because it was closely linked to the belief in a final bodily resurrection. Although man was a "creature of mud" and might even be pulverized, nevertheless, like the mythical phoenix he would breathe again when the millennial trumpets sounded.[106] A man who disbelieved in the final resurrection might try to quote the words of the Bible, "You are dust and you will return to dust"; Gregory argued in reply that God could resurrect men even if their dust were scattered by the wind.[107] In this sense a belief in the healing qualities of holy dust became an implicit affirmation of

103. C. Geertz (1968) 97.
104. *VM* 3.50.
105. *VM* 3.60; cf. *VP* 8.5: the most precious legacy a bishop could leave his church was "the dirty lump of his body."
106. *de cursu* 12; cf. *HF* I.1: God created man from "a lump of fragile mud."
107. *HF* X.13.

a theological doctrine about the ultimate resurrection of the body.

In the last resort, however, statements stressing the superiority of holy dust over conventional medicines remained paradoxical, but only to those who were alienated from Christian communities and their values. People who were fully socialized had become so identified with the paradoxes inherent in their beliefs and actions that they no longer perceived them as paradoxes. Drinking a potion made from holy dust represented the ultimate act of abasement, a total acceptance of the distinctively Christian ethos that regulated community values and that was now so comprehensive that it could also, as we will see in the next chapter, determine the "timing" of people's lives.

# CHAPTER 13

# Sacred Time:
# Liturgy and the
# Christianization of Time

Divine power came by way of saints living in heaven, and to men of early Merovingian Gaul, relics of the saints were souvenirs left behind during visits to earth. As usual, Gregory and his family demonstrate clearly the attitude that relics were mementoes from heaven: for Gregory, the handkerchief of his great-uncle, Bishop Nicetius of Lyon, was a *munus caeleste*, a gift from heaven; for his sister, the leaf she picked up at a shrine in Besançon turned out to be another gift from heaven, which cured her husband of a fever.[1] Relic cults were now dotted on the landscape of Gaul to form a great constellation, so that although Jesus Christ and the church were symbolized by the great lights in the sky—the sun and the moon—saints were the "stars" of Merovingian society.[2]

Comparisons of relics to gifts from heaven or of saints to shining stars should be taken as more than figures of speech, however, because they also reveal, again, the importance of establishing links between mundane daily life and the divine power available from heaven. As we have seen in Chapter 11, the internal appearance and layout of churches represented one way of precisely visualizing and locating these points of contact. But churches appeared to be static models; and to prevent them from becoming inert, unable to keep up with the stately rhythms of the stars, they had to

1. *VP* 8.8, *GM* 70. (References to the writings of Gregory of Tours omit his name. See Chapter 9, unnumbered note.)

2. *GM* 51, *VM* 1.12, *VP* 18 praef., *GC* 37. Note also, most explicitly, Eucher of Lyon *Formulae* II (*CSEL* 31, p. 10): "Sol dominus Iesus Christus, quia fulgeat terris. . . . Luna ecclesia, eo quod in hac mundi nocte resplendeat. . . . Stellae sancti sive docti . . . interdum et angeli."

be energized. The celebration of liturgy provided one form of dynamism by effectively transforming churches into

> an image of the moving heavens, a log-book of the
> sun's journey and the moon's.

In consequence, during the celebration of mass or in the observance of the liturgical year, people synchronized themselves with the rhythms of heaven and harmonized with the activities that saints were performing in their heavenly Paradise. Gregory's account of Venantius, a fifth-century abbot at Tours, is an example of how seriously men took these tasks: "The Lord deigned to reveal to Venantius the secrets of the mysterious heavens. One Sunday after Venantius had completed his prayers and was returning from the churches of the saints, in the courtyard of the church of St. Martin he leaned on his staff and stood for a long time, not moving, his eyes and ears turned toward heaven. Finally he stirred and began to groan and sigh. When friends asked what was wrong, that he should tell them if he had seen something divine, he replied, 'Woe to us who are lazy and slow. Behold, in heaven mass is being celebrated, but we sluggish people have not yet begun to celebrate this sacrament. Indeed, I tell you that I heard the voices of angels in the heavens, singing the *Sanctus* in praise of the Lord.' After he said this, he ordered that mass be immediately celebrated in his monastery."[3] In other words, the celebration of the liturgy and the observance of holy days were attempts to replicate what was happening in heaven; Catholic liturgy was meant to be both in time and in tune with a score composed in heaven and transcribed in the stars.

Rather than add to the excellent research already available on the forms and content of early liturgy, we can instead complement it by concentrating on the attitudes of the participants and the implications of liturgy for daily living. "The hardest thing of all," one of the best historians of liturgy has argued, "is to assess [the effects of changes in the liturgy] upon the ideas and devotions of the vast unlearned and unliterary but *praying* masses of contemporary christian men and women . . . whose salvation is . . . of the very purpose of the church's existence."[4] In the following sections let us discuss, first, masses and their correspondence to the activities of saints; second, the liturgical day and week and the

3. *VP* 16.2.
4. Dix (1945) 303.

ways in which people might "misbehave" on festival days; and third, the liturgical year and its potential dissonance with the agrarian calendar. In each case a discussion of the various components making up liturgical time leads back, once again, to the dynamics of behavior in small communities.

*    *    *

From scattered references in the writings of Gregory and other sixth-century authors it is possible to construct the outline of an "ideal" public mass.[5] In general, the first part of mass, which was open to everyone, included a mixture of antiphons (usually Psalms) and hymns, prayers, readings of biblical lessons, and a homily or sermon. The second part was the actual celebration of the Eucharist, and included the presentation of the elements as well as more antiphons and prayers. Within this schematic outline there was considerable variation, although the general shape of individual masses was probably similar, as ecclesiastical councils tried occasionally to ensure.[6] More significant, however, was the motivation behind this uniformity; when in the later fifth century one council suggested that, at least within an ecclesiastical province, men ought to follow the same sequence of Psalms and the same order for the minor ceremonies, the rationale was not merely to achieve conformity, but rather to ensure correspondence with the oneness of the Trinity: "If there are variations in our services, they might seem out of tune."[7] Liturgical services, in other words, were meant to be imitations, if not actual enactments, of celestial behavior, and not simply perfunctory performances from missals.

A letter attributed to Bishop Germanus of Paris makes these expectations explicit. Although many scholars now date the letter to the seventh or even the eighth century,[8] it can still be used as comparative information to help interpret the services over which

---

5. Beck (1950) 134–50, and Jungmann (1952–1958) I, 74–78, for additional information.

6. Council of Agde a. 506, Can. 30.

7. Council of Vannes a. 461/491, Can. 15; cf. Council of Epaone a. 517, Can. 27.

8. Quasten (1934); for the dating, see A. Wilmart, *DACL* VI (1924) 1049–1102, although the debate continues as van der Mensbrugghe (1962) argues again for a sixth-century context. For other descriptions of the celebration of mass during the sixth century, see *Vita Caesarii* II.35, and Fortunatus *Carm.* II.9.21–71.

bishops such as Germanus himself once presided. For the author of this letter, the celebration of mass was a facsimile of the joining of heaven and earth. "As the clerics sing the Psalms the bishop enters, with the appearance of Christ; he comes from the sacristy as if from heaven into the treasury of the Lord, his church, so that as much by his warnings as by his exhortations he might nourish good deeds in the people and extinguish evil deeds." The choir of clerics was his heavenly host, which sang "in the manner of angels." And the celebration of the Eucharist was a reenactment of the death, burial, and triumphant resurrection of Christ, because as the bishop broke the bread, "then the celestial is mixed with the terrestrial, and during the bishop's prayer the heavens are opened."

Gregory of Tours readily sympathized with this allegorical interpretation, which stressed the immediate and practical rather than the historical or strictly theological significance of mass. He also thought that during the celebration of the liturgy the entire Christian community acquired direct access to divine holiness. A ceremony of public baptism, for instance, not only reaffirmed the significance of participation in the Eucharist, it also conjured up recollections of a great moment from the early church when divine power had been granted to all believers. Thus in the mid-sixth century at Clermont, after many Jews converted to Christianity, the public celebration of their baptism on Pentecost became, according to Gregory, a reenactment of the original Pentecost.[9] This comparison was a particularly apt one for Gregory to make, because, as we noted in Chapter 11, a fresco depicting the original Pentecost decorated one wall of his church of St. Martin at Tours.

Furthermore, saints themselves sometimes attended these services. Once while Abbot Venantius was celebrating mass in the church of St. Martin at Tours, he claimed to see an old man dressed like a monk climbing down a ladder from one of the windows in the apse and coming to the altar to bless the elements.[10] When we recall that St. Martin's tomb was in the apse, it is apparent that the congregation was about to communicate with bread and wine blessed by the saint himself. At Angers a paralytic dreamed that a man told him to enter the church when he heard the bell ringing for mass, because then St. Albinus and St. Martin

9. *HF* V.11.
10. *VP* 16.2.

would also be present. When the bell tolled, the man approached St. Albinus' tomb, and as the choir began to sing, a sweet fragrance filled the church and the man was cured.[11] Sometimes saints also participated directly in the services. Near Bordeaux, for instance, as the choir sang the Psalms during mass, two saints buried against opposite walls joined in the antiphons: "So sweet is this singing that it often soothes the ears of those listening."[12]

For ordinary members of the community, perhaps the most important feature of mass was that they could sing along, or "communicate," with saints. During the second part of mass, the celebration of the Eucharist when most of the drama took place around the altar, the audience became the actors. Often the elements were offerings from the congregation; one woman, for instance, presented some superb wine for the celebration of a series of requiem masses for her husband.[13] During the prelude to communion the congregation chanted the *Sanctus* during the canon of prayers and recited the Lord's Prayer, sometimes again in harmony with the saints.[14] Finally, at the distribution of the elements, the congregation approached the altar.[15] One bishop emphasized this communal participation by having these verses inscribed on the silver chalice: "From this cup the congregation drinks life from the holy blood that flowed from the wound of the eternal Christ."[16] In the Catholic liturgy the equality of the participants at this point was emphasized by the fact that there was no separate chalice for royalty, as there was in the Arian liturgy;[17] hence, celebrating the Eucharist meant sharing a common meal at which everyone, including kings, bishops, ordinary people, and saints, feasted together.

The idea that the celebration of mass was an opportunity for ordinary believers to share with the men they recognized as leaders—whether bishops or saints—in "the mystery of the body and the blood"[18] was not new to the sixth century; we have seen in Chapter 4 how our initial information about Christianity in Gaul already indicated the importance of liturgical feasts as a means for defining common values. The transition from opportunity to obligation was also not new, because attendance at mass had long

11. GC 94.      12. GC 46.      13. GC 64.
14. *VM* 2.14, *VP* 16.2.
15. Council of Tours a. 567, Can. 4.
16. Remigius of Rheims, *apud* Hincmar *Vita Remigii* 2 (*MGH*, SRM 7, p. 262).
17. *HF* III.31.      18. *VM* 2.25.

served as a demonstration of fellowship. Many people came to the church for the first part of mass, among them kings, aristocratic ladies, and once even an assassin who stabbed a bishop during Easter mass.[19] But before the celebration of the Eucharist all except full members had to leave. Thus, although King Theudebert once complained when Bishop Nicetius of Trier refused to continue the mass in the presence of his companions, he relented when he heard them accused of incest, murder, and adultery.[20]

Because participation in the Eucharist was now a public "character reference," it also took on judicial overtones, just as we have already seen with the notion of healing; for often after people had been cured, they attended mass and thereby further demonstrated their innocence. In one instance, a man who was rumored to have murdered his own mother still walked up to receive the Eucharist on the feast day of St. Julian at Clermont. The bishop, conceding that God and St. Julian would judge the issue, only warned the man of the consequences: "God will be looking into the deepest confines of your heart."[21] Even though Gregory still was not convinced of the guiltlessness of this man, presumably participation in the Eucharist was a firm trial by ordeal by means of which men could prove their innocence. As Gregory commented in another context, "Although we are polluting ourselves in the very act, we approach the altar of the Lord and dare to receive his holy body and blood—an act of judgment rather than an attempt to seek forgiveness."[22] For men with guilty consciences the alternative to rash participation was to stay away from mass, which in small communities was almost an open admission of guilt.

In these ways participation in mass expressed more than the mystical unity of the Christian Body of Christ, because it also now played an important role in creating and preserving the nature of small Gallic communities. By synchronizing and harmonizing themselves with the activities of saints in heaven, people also enforced and transmitted the day-to-day values and expectations of their own communities. Gregory lived among men who were intent upon letting the rhythms of the stars govern the tempo of the liturgy as well as their daily lives. In some cases they even selected lessons at random in order to learn about future events;

19. *HF* VIII.31; cf. VIII.7, IX.9.
20. *VP* 17.2.        21. *HF* X.8.        22. *GM* 85.

and although these improvised liturgical readings were suspiciously similar to astrology or fortune-telling, for Gregory they were manifestations of divine power, "prophecies of the saints."[23] The celebration of mass was a performance of the music of the spheres, and its rhythms even spilled over into daily life.

\* \* \*

The structure of a liturgical day varied throughout Gaul. On Sundays and other festival days bishops (and sometimes priests) celebrated public mass at the third hour, about mid-morning. At various times of the year (Advent and Lent) masses were also held in the late afternoons of weekdays; and masses may also have been celebrated in the early morning of almost every day. Shorter services (offices) were celebrated at various times of the day, including lauds at daybreak (then known as matins) and vespers in the evening. These services commonly consisted of canticles from the Psalms and readings from the Bible. At night, or sometimes in the very early morning when it was still dark, people celebrated vigils, in particular on nights preceding festival days.[24]

However a liturgical day may have been structured—and daily observance of the entire sequence of offices was probably normal—it was different from our usual notion of a day, in that a liturgical day was apparently measured from sundown to sundown and its nighttime preceded its daytime.[25] The darkness of nighttime became a preparation for the brightness of light-time, as one council insisted: "Let us spend the night that brings us to the blessed light in spiritual vigils and let us not sleep, . . . but let us pray and keep watch so that we might be considered worthy to become heirs in our Saviour's kingdom."[26] As we might expect, ideas of healing corresponded with this awareness of a daily liturgical sequence from darkness to light, with the result that ill people were frequently healed during vigils and thus enabled to attend mass at dawn.[27]

Attendance at certain vigils was apparently obligatory,[28] and at

23. *HF* II.37, IV.16; and Council of Orléans a. 511, Can. 30, Council of Auxerre a. 561/605, Can. 4, for interdictions on fortune-telling.
24. Beck (1950) 108–25, on the offices, and 127–34, on the varieties and frequency of masses.
25. *VM* 3.31.       26. Council of Mâcon a. 585, Can. 1.
27. *VJ* 9, 11; cf. *GM* 50.
28. See Lupus of Troyes and Euphronius of Autun *Epist. ad Talasium* (*CChr. lat.* 148, p. 140).

Tours people who failed to observe Christmas Eve faced excommunication.[29] Christmas Eve vigil was kept in the cathedral, after which the congregation moved on to the church of St. Martin to celebrate morning mass.[30] Predictably, vigils were tiring: Gregory himself slipped off for a quick nap during one Christmas Eve;[31] other men, after keeping vigils, went to a monk's cell to refresh themselves with wine.[32] But the sequence of a liturgical day also reinforced the underlying Christian message of access to divine holiness. Just as the sun at dawn brightened the darkness of the night, so the divine power of saints could illuminate people's lives. The many stories describing the miraculous combustion of candles during the night or the perpetual burning of lamps before saints' tombs show that for saints it was always daytime.[33]

But if the sequence of a liturgical day was straightforward, in that night was a preparation for daylight, its rhythms were flexible. According to the Roman system of measuring the time of day, both daylight and darkness were divided into twelve equal hours. But Gregory and his contemporaries also knew that because of the differences in the length of days and nights between the seasons, the hours were of uneven duration throughout the year; because of this seasonal fluctuation, people had to take special care to remain synchronized with the celestial rhythms. A council at Tours in 567 tried to account for this fluctuation by indicating how many antiphons and Psalms ought to be sung at matins in the various months.[34] Gregory also explained the correspondence between the regular movement of the stars, the times at which the bells were to be rung for the celebration of nocturnal offices, vigils, and matins at daybreak, and the number of Psalms that could be sung during each service. For him the stars were the timepieces of nature, "witnesses of divine power . . . which never grow old, never suffer any accident and are never diminished by any fall so long as the Lord does not order the world to be destroyed." Through careful observance of the movements of the stars, the liturgical day could be synchronized with the fluctuations of the celestial day: "In this discussion [of the movements of the stars] I am neither teaching astrology nor expecting to foretell the future. Instead I am suggesting how the [liturgical] cycle in praise of God might reasonably be carried out, and at what hours

29. VP 8.11.    30. VM 2.25.    31. GM 86; cf. VM 1.33.
32. VJ 36.    33. E.g. GC 68.    34. Council of Tours a. 567, Can. 19.

a man who wishes attentively to fill the offices ought to rise and pray to the Lord."[35] As people celebrated the daily (and nightly) liturgy, they continued to time themselves with the rhythms of the stars in heaven.

Within the liturgical week the primary emphasis was on the feast days, which could be either the festival days of saints or Sundays. Sunday was the first day of the week, a commemoration of the appearance of light on the first day of creation and of the resurrection of Jesus Christ at Easter; as such, in contrast to the "private days" of the rest of the week, it was a "holy day."[36] One council attempted to ensure that everyone would attend the celebration of public mass on Sunday: "On every Sunday all men and all women are to present to the altars an offering of bread and wine, so that they are freed from their accumulated sins."[37] Conversely, people were allowed to do little else on feast days except attend mass and pray; on Sundays, Gregory declared, all "public work" was prohibited.[38] Various sixth-century councils made the same point more emphatically and specifically. One council insisted that people were not to perform any agrarian activities "so that all the more easily they might come to church and be free for praying"; another council claimed that Sunday was "a day of perpetual rest": "With their bodies and their souls let everyone be intent on singing hymns and praising God." In another canon this same council insisted that everyone was to respect Easter and Holy Week by "praising our creator and regenerator evening, morning, and noon."[39] Other councils further specified what people could not do on festival days. They could not travel, prepare food, ornament either their homes or themselves, or do any work in their fields or vineyards; nor could they hold judicial hearings or harness their oxen.[40] Given these exhortations and prohibitions, as well as the fact that they were backed up by royal edicts,[41] there

35. *de cursu* 9, 16.
36. *HF* I.23, X.30, and Council of Mâcon a. 585, Can. 1.
37. Council of Mâcon a. 585, Can. 4.
38. *HF* X.30.
39. Council of Orléans a. 538, Can. 31; Council of Mâcon a. 585, Can. 1–2 (and note the sequence of the day).
40. Council of Orléans a. 538, Can. 31; Council of Mâcon a. 585, Can. 1; Council of Narbonne a. 589, Can. 4; Council of Auxerre, a. 561/605, Can. 16.
41. Cf. Edict of Guntram a. 585 (*MGH*, Capitularia 1, pp. 11–12), referring to Council of Mâcon a. 585, Can. 1.

was apparently nothing for people to do on festival days other than to go to church services and pray.

Nevertheless, as we would expect, many people did "insult" festival days.[42] The actual offenses are sometimes predictable, sometimes unexpected. A man who plowed his field on Sunday found that he was unable to drop the handle of the plow because his right hand was paralyzed; another who hoed his vineyard during a saint's festival twisted his neck; another who picked fruit on Easter went blind.[43] A man who tried to collect his recently mown hay on a Sunday had a sore foot; another who ground wheat on Easter had a paralyzed hand; another who brewed beer on a saint's festival watched his house burn down.[44] Men who repaired fences on Sundays or on Easter developed paralyzed hands; a man who made a key on Sunday developed paralyzed fingers.[45] Women who baked bread on Sunday night were crippled or paralyzed; a girl developed a contracted hand for sewing on Sunday.[46] A woman who gave birth to a deformed baby later conceded that she had conceived the child on a Sunday night.[47] A girl who combed her hair on Sunday was paralyzed; another who washed her face on Good Friday was excluded from the presence of the Lord after her death; a man who laced his boots on Sunday developed paralyzed hands and feet.[48]

As a result of these offenses people contracted the kinds of social illnesses that made their misdeeds obvious to everyone else and left them as social outcasts until they were cured. According to one council, these people had acted "in a rash and disrespectful manner"; and the afflictions described by Gregory made it only too clear what happened to reckless people who ignored the proper *reverentia*. The same council also defined acceptable behavior: "Let your hands and your eyes be engaged with God for the entire

42. *HF* X.30, "ob dominici diei iniuriam."
43. *VJ* 11, *VM* 2.57, *GC* 97; Fortunatus *Vita Germani* 140.
44. *VM* 3.3, 4.45, *GC* 80.
45. *VM* 2.13, 3.7, 29, 45, *VP* 15.3; Fortunatus *Vita Germani* 138.
46. *GM* 15, *VM* 3.31, 56; Fortunatus *Vita Germani* 50.
47. *VM* 2.24.
48. *VP* 7.5, *GC* 5; Fortunatus *Vita Germani* 102. To complete the list, note also *VM* 2.40 (perjury and usury on Sunday), 3.55 (working on Sunday), 4.45 (collecting hay on Sunday); Fortunatus *de virtutibus Hilarii* 24–25 (woman carrying water for her own use on Sunday), *Vita Germani* 46, 156 (working on Sunday), 136 (loading a horse on Sunday); and, although not from the later sixth century, *Vita Genovefe virgine* 37, 55 (working on Sunday). For similar restrictions in a modern Greek village, see Du Boulay (1974) 63–65.

day." In fact, as we have seen, people who infringed the conventions of the community most often were blinded or paralyzed.[49]

The infringements themselves require more explanation, but a pattern begins to emerge only when we cluster them together. Then we can detect an analogical relationship between combing hair, having sex, plowing and hoeing the ground, fencing in a field, making a key for a lock, lacing boots, grinding grain, or baking bread. All of these activities can be taken as indications of a civilized culture in which men prefer cooked over raw food or wish to tame the ground and control its production rather than let it grow wild. But by acting in a civilized manner, people violated nature. Either they united what nature divides (by having sex, sewing, lacing boots, brewing beer), or they separated and cut what was naturally united (by enclosing fields, making keys, harvesting). The activities considered "inappropriate" to festival days[50] were all signs of culture, in opposition to that natural state characteristic of Paradise: according to Gregory's account, for instance, Eve conceived a child only after she and Adam had been ejected from Paradise.[51] The implication seems to have been that, on Sundays and on saints' festivals, people were to deny their normal, civilized way of life and live instead in conformity with nature. Thus one woman, after being cured of the paralysis she had suffered for baking on Sunday, vowed that thereafter she would never again work on Sundays, but instead only pray.[52]

Such a natural lifestyle would have raised people to a state of holiness, even if only for the day. Most holy men lived far more in conformity with nature, and their "natural" lives were in explicit opposition to the lives of ordinary people. One hermit who lived in the forest near Clermont "had a tiny garden that he moistened with rainwater, and from which a vegetable always refreshed him. He had no companion apart from the assistance of God, and his neighbors were wild beasts and the birds who visited him every day as if he were a servant of God."[53] Wild animals posed no problems for this holy man: in his presence a wild boar became as tame as a lamb, while another ascetic found that his power could domesticate sparrows to eat crumbs from his hand.[54] Some holy men apparently ate nothing but "health foods." The founding fa-

49. Council of Mâcon a. 585, Can. 1; and GM 84–88, on *temeritas*.
50. Cf. VM 3.55, "huic diei . . . incongruum."
51. HF I.1–2.      52. GM 15.      53. VP 12.1.      54. VP 12.2.

thers of monasticism in the Jura Mountains lived on herbs and vegetable roots; others ate only bread, although the loaves were never baked in their own cells, and they drank only water, perhaps sweetened with honey, instead of wine and cider.[55] At least one monk drank nothing at all: whenever he was thirsty, he simply soaked up water through his fingertips![56] Such a diet was apparently the opposite of normal expectations (although perhaps not realities) about food. A young servant who abandoned her mistress because she could not put up with an ascetic diet of barley bread and water made her intentions clear: "I would rather eat the food of this world and have enough to drink!"[57] Holy men furthermore dressed in clothes made from animal skins, and some never cared for their hair or beards.[58] On feast days, therefore, ordinary people not only harmonized their activities with those of the saints during the celebration of mass, but by living this natural life they were also imitating living holy men who spent their time in prayer.

Such demands involved a peculiar notion of the significance of time. When Gregory wrote about the woman who confessed that she had conceived a monstrous child on Sunday night, he commented that "the other days are sufficient for the satisfaction of sexual desire, but on Sunday one must remain pure and spend the day praising God."[59] His attitude was an indication of one of the fundamental paradoxes in the teachings of Christianity: "Look at the birds in the sky, . . . think of the flowers growing in the fields; . . . set your hearts on his kingdom first."[60] Such a recommendation was a denial of future time, in that people were not to worry about what might happen to them on the next day. Predictably, holy men alone lived in this state of perpetual present time. One hermit, for instance, lived strictly off charity; he never prepared his own food because others offered it to him "whenever the necessity arose."[61]

In this context we can also understand the injunctions of Gregory against usury and greediness, because usury was a practice and greediness an attitude implying excessive concern about the future. Men who tried to accumulate money through sharp busi-

55. HF V.10, VI.8, X.8, VP 1.1; Fortunatus Vita Paterni 27.
56. VP 1.2.     57. VP 19.1.     58. HF IV.32, VP 20.3.
59. VM 2.24.     60. Matthew 6:26–33; cf. VP 15.1.
61. HF VI.8; cf. VM 1.17, VP 13.3, 14.1.

ness dealings eventually lost all their profits; likewise men who worked their land on festival days were being greedy and might ultimately forfeit "the celestial mystery of our redemption."[62] In contrast, the proper attitude toward money and wealth involved generosity and charity, which implied no restrictions in daily life because they did not construct any web of dependent social relationships and did not entail any expectations about future obligations between the people involved. Charity was instead a pure and simple act that exposed the disposition of people's hearts, and men even gave away their entire supply of grain with the full confidence that someone else would support them in turn.[63]

But the expectation that, even though only on Sundays and festival days, all people were to live like holy men, in strict conformity with nature and a timeless present, also generated problems. While one monk refused to accept a gift of fields and vineyards from King Chilperic of Burgundy, claiming that it was not proper for monks to work, and requested instead that they be given wine, grain, and gold,[64] other people still had to work these fields and produce the surplus that could then endow this monastery. And it was precisely in terms of the agrarian cycle that conflicts with the liturgical cycle might appear, because sometimes the two cycles did not synchronize well. The man who repaired his fence on Easter did so because he saw a herd of cows grazing in his corn field and worried that he might lose "the rewards of a year's labor"; the man who wanted to collect his recently mown hay on a Sunday was worried that he might otherwise lose it in a rainstorm.[65] The unpredictability of the weather left men apprehensive, and sometimes outraged. In 584 a disastrous sequence of frost, storms, and drought ruined vineyards and crops; men were so "angry with God" that they irrationally destroyed what was left of their vines.[66] Hence men could easily face a dilemma in which the demands of the liturgical cycle conflicted with worries that they might lose a crop unless they did something, even on a Sunday or a festival day. Although both annual cycles were related to the movements of the heavens, the agrarian cycle, unlike the liturgical cycle, was often unpredictable.

---

62. *VM* 3.29; cf. *GM* 57, *GC* 110, and Council of Orléans a. 538, Can. 30. Le Goff (1980) 29–42, is a stimulating discussion of the contrast between "merchant's time" and "Church's time."

63. *Vita Caesarii* II.8–9; also *HF* VII.1.    64. *VP* 1.5.

65. *VM* 4.45, with *HF* IV.34; *VP* 15.3.    66. *HF* VI.44.

*   *   *

In the world of Late Antiquity most communities lived on a subsistence level. Agricultural techniques were primitive: in the whole of his writings Gregory rarely mentioned a plow. This is more likely a reflection of reality than of the constraints of his subject matter, since he did include several stories about men working in fields or even using water mills. Instead, the standard tools for working the land were an axe and a hoe. Often we forget how much of early Merovingian Gaul was still covered with forests and therefore how much hard effort was required first to clear the land and then to prevent it from going back to scrub.[67] In many ways, of course, people had learned how to use the forest and its products as integral parts of their livelihoods; in it men grazed animals, hunted, and gathered wood to make charcoal.[68] But it often presented a serious handicap to the exploitation of the soil; hence, even a reclusive hermit going off into the forest had the sense to take an axe and a hoe.[69] So too when a duke died, Gregory praised him for the villas he had founded *a novo*, which we might translate here as "from scratch."[70]

Once established, however, the agrarian cycle was tied to definite rhythms of its own. From scattered references in the writings of Gregory and Fortunatus we can obtain hints of the rhythms men expected. Spring was noted for excessive rain and sometimes even snow. Then men could only wait for the "more delightful spring breezes" that would make travel possible again.[71] In late spring and early summer men gathered in one harvest; the remaining stubble was used as fodder for the herds.[72] Summer was notorious above all for its heat; produce matured, but nothing germinated. During the summer the weather was generally dry.[73] Men gathered fruit from the trees and mowed hay.[74] In the late summer there was another harvest.[75] Grapes matured on the vines in September, and wine was usually available in October. Men also sowed their fields in late autumn.[76] Winters were very

67. Note Marc Bloch (1966) 5: "Man's most formidable obstacle was the forests"; and Higounet (1966) 386: "un 'âge de la forêt.'"
68. *VP* 12.2, with Etienne (1978); *GC* 30.     69. *VP* 9.2.
70. *HF* VI.20.       71. *HF* IX.16, 39–40.       72. *HF* IV.42, *VP* 4.4, 15.3.
73. *HF* VIII.9, "tempus sterile," 23, *VP* 5.1.
74. *HF* VI.44, VIII.8, 40, *VM* 4.45.
75. Fortunatus *Carm.* VIII.10.7–8.       76. *HF* V.33, VI.45, IX.5, *VJ* 36.

cold, with storms and, in the north, perhaps three or four feet of snow.[77]

In later centuries, when men were better prepared to exploit the land, a more coercive attitude toward natural resources led to a customary association of particular agrarian activities with specific months, as is seen most clearly (and probably at its earliest) in Carolingian calendars.[78] But even wishful iconography could not eliminate the fickleness of the agrarian cycle. Harvests were frequently threatened by storms.[79] A drought during late spring might leave no fodder for the herds; rivers might flood so badly in September that people could not complete the autumn sowing of winter corn.[80] Famine and starvation were always probable. In the later fifth century people in the Jura Mountains had only fifteen days' supply of corn left for the three months remaining until harvest; in 585 almost all of Gaul suffered a great famine and many people were reduced to nibbling at flower seeds, roots, or grass, or even to selling themselves into slavery.[81] This general famine was apparently as catastrophic as Gregory made it sound, because at Tours in subsequent years more people than usual had to be freed from unjust slavery or debt.[82] And even though many famines in Gaul were only regional, the difficulties in transportation prevented adjacent regions from helping. During a famine in Burgundy in the later fifth century, for instance, a wealthy senator found it easier to bring starving people to his estate than to transport grain to them.[83]

The importance of the agrarian cycle cannot be overemphasized, because people's survival depended on it. But with the introduction of Christianity, and even more with the systematic ordering of the liturgical year during the fifth century in Gaul, another annual cycle also became important. This was the liturgical year, whose rhythm determined the observance of festivals, vigils, and fasts.

For Tours we have a document of major importance. In the catalogue Gregory gave of all his predecessors as bishop of Tours, he

77. *HF* III.37, VIII.23, X.19, *GC* 18, 71, 75; Marius of Avenches *Chron.* s.a. 566.

78. See Stern (1955) 141–66, on Carolingian miniatures depicting the labors of the months.

79. *Vita Genovefe virgine* 50; *Vita Hilari* 1.

80. *HF* V.33, *VP* 4.4.

81. *Vita [Patrum Iurensium] Lupicini* 3, and *HF* VII.45.

82. *VM* 3.41, 46–47.     83. *HF* II.24.

included both the regulations that Bishop Perpetuus had drafted in the later fifth century for the observance of vigils and fasts, and another list that, although it suggested only where vigils were to be held, can be used as an indication of the important festival days in Tours, since these were usually the ones preceded by vigils.[84] The first half of the list referred to the general festivals such as Christmas and Easter, the second half to more local festivals commemorating, in addition to former bishops of Tours, St. Symphorian of Autun and St. Hilary of Poitiers. Although the festivals were scattered throughout the year, the greatest concentration was in high summer, late summer, and winter, with the celebration of Lent and Pentecost taking up most of spring, early summer, or both, depending upon the date of Easter. Although on the list the longest gaps between festival days occurred for seven weeks during the middle of the summer and for two months during autumn, by the later sixth century the gaps may have been longer. Gregory was not explicit as to whether Perpetuus' schedule was still being observed a century later, since he wrote only that "today" he still had a copy of the list. And he made no reference to the celebration of some of these festivals at Tours. In his diary of St. Martin's miracles the prominent feast days were, in addition to Sundays in general, Christmas, Epiphany, the Easter season, and, especially, the two festivals of St. Martin on July 4 and November 11.

In some respects there was a correspondence between the annual liturgical cycle at Tours and the agrarian cycle. The season of Easter, although movable, in general coincided with the advent of spring, the budding of trees and flowers, and the late spring harvest; hence, during Lent people decorated the doors of their homes and the altars of churches with fresh flowers.[85] In the middle of the summer, "when the sun burns everything with its heat and dries out even more robust bodies with its intensity," the festival of St. Martin provided a refreshing break, "desirable" to the people.[86] About the time of the late summer harvest was the festival of the Passion of St. John on August 29, whose vigils were observed in a baptistery, a building that conjured up images of rebirth into the Christian community. During the periods of most agricultural ac-

84. HF X.31.
85. Fortunatus Carm. VIII.7; cf. II.9, IX.3.
86. VM 2.34, VP 5.1; Fortunatus Carm. VII.8.1–30.

tivities, the spring harvest and the grape-picking and sowing of autumn, there were usually the fewest festivals.

The calculation of the date of the one movable festival, Easter, supposedly also demonstrated some natural flexibility in the liturgical year. Depending upon a complicated calculation of full moons, Easter could occur any time between the middle of March and the end of April. In fact, the calculation was apparently so complex that, although the schedule drawn up by Victorius of Aquitania in 457 was still being used in the sixth century,[87] it did not solve all problems, because in some years there were still discrepancies over the date.[88] Thus Gregory tried to claim that the date of Easter instead corresponded with a purely natural event, the flowing of the Spanish springs, or with the spontaneous filling of a baptismal pool at Embrun.[89] In this way a correlation between the annual liturgical cycle of festivals and the annual ecological cycle seemed to appear, similar to the correspondence between the times of celebrating liturgical hours and the fluctuation in the length of the hours of days throughout the year.

Members of the ecclesiastical hierarchy were furthermore not isolated from agrarian activities. Bishops meeting in a council at Tours in 567 knew what to do about behavior that they had decided to prohibit: "Although the undergrowth polluted by evil has been cut once, it is to be pruned again with the knife of faith and ripped out by the roots."[90] Gregory likewise seized upon agrarian metaphors to confirm the resurrection of the Lord, comparing it to trees that regained their leaves or to seeds that sprouted in the furrows.[91] Both the liturgical cycle and the agrarian cycle emphasized the ideas of death and decay, rebirth and resurrection. During the winter the predominant aspects of the year were the cold, dampness, and darkness, but during the spring and summer the emphasis was on heat, dryness, and light.

In fact, however, these annual cycles often conflicted with each other. Sometimes the power of the saints directly interfered with the ecological cycle, so that wine was available in May or flowers bloomed out of season.[92] These events were seen as miracles, in-

---

87. See Pope Hilarus *Ep.* 2, and Victorius of Aquitania *Cursus paschalis* (both ed. Thiel [1867] 130–7, and *PL* Suppl. III.380–6). For its use in the sixth century, see *HF* I praef., X.23, and Council of Orléans a. 541, Can. 1.
88. *HF* V.17, X.23.      89. *HF* V.17, VI.43, *GM* 23–25, *GC* 68.
90. Council of Tours a. 567, Can. 10.
91. *HF* X.13, *de cursu* 11.      92. *GM* 90, *VJ* 36.

terventions of divine power; on the other hand, sometimes the cycle of weather was so irregular that prodigies and omens just "naturally" happened.[93] Occasionally, of course, the liturgical cycle admitted some innovations of its own, as happened at Vienne in the later fifth century when Bishop Mamertus instituted the penitential rogations as a reaction to a series of appalling prodigies such as earthquakes, fires, and packs of wild animals inside the city, none of which seemed to have respect for the celebration of Easter.[94] At the time his innovation may have been an attempt at synchronizing liturgical and ecological time again; but once established, the rogations were merely another fixed annual ceremony that men were expected to observe.[95]

Far more important was the potential conflict between the fixed character of the liturgical cycle and the indeterminate nature of the agrarian cycle. All the different components of the liturgy, although allowing some flexibility, were still expected to happen at fixed times or on fixed dates. People were to imitate the saints, who always knew the correct time: the body of St. Martin, for instance, refused to be moved until it was precisely his festival day.[96] Hence, when a possessed man announced that the congregation at Bessay had celebrated a festival a day early, people had to keep vigils that night and celebrate mass again the next day.[97] In short, services were celebrated at the proper hours each day; every Sunday was a festival day; all festival days were tied to specific dates, including Easter, once its date had been calculated. Bishop Nicetius of Lyon therefore seized control of his life by carefully regulating his celebration of both night and day services "at fixed times, according to a definite law."[98] In contrast, no agrarian cycle could be set according to definite laws or predictable patterns. Every day, every week, and every month the demands of the liturgy could, for many people, conflict with the demands of working the land.

93. *HF* VI.44, VII.11.
94. See *HF* II.34; Avitus *Hom.* 6, "In rogationibus"; and the contemporary observations of Sidonius *Ep.* V.14, VII.1. For other rogations established in response to a natural disaster such as the plague, see *HF* IV.5 and *VP* 6.6 (Clermont), *HF* IX.21 (Marseille), *HF* X.30 (Tours and Nantes).
95. Cf. Avitus *Hom.* 7, "nobis annuum quoddam iter . . . currentibus."
96. *VM* 1.6. Note also how holy men know precisely when they will die, as if ensuring that their subsequent festival will be on the correct day: e.g. *VP* 6.7, 10.4, 13.2, 20.4; Fortunatus *Vita Germani* 206.
97. *GM* 89.          98. *Vita Nicetii* 5.

\* \* \*

Despite its superficial correlation with ecological or agrarian time, liturgical time was an artificial construct conforming to the needs of communities. Given the contrived quality of liturgical time we might expect to find some implicit correlations between its various components, such as the liturgical day and the liturgical year. During the liturgical day, for instance, we have seen how the vigils of the preceding night became a preparation for the services during the daylight hours; likewise in the celebration of the liturgical year the winter vigils on Christmas Eve signified the unanimity of the community, thereby ensuring that people "lived through the cycle of this year with peace."[99] Easter marked the conclusion to "the cycle of a departing year"[100] and generally coincided with the period in which there was more daylight than darkness. The periods of fasting were reduced as people had more food after the spring harvest, just as during the early daylight hours of a feast day people shared a common meal during the celebration of mass. In both the liturgical day and the liturgical year darkness and fasting gave way to light and feasting.

The correlations within the liturgical cycle, however, and between it and the agrarian year, are still not comparable to those anthropologists have formulated for the societies they analyze. This is largely a result of the nature of the material at historians' disposal. Many of the comments here about the liturgical year, for instance, are based on localized material from Tours, while some of the supplementary interpretation of the liturgy and most of the information about the agrarian year come from scattered references to other regions of Gaul. But the liturgical cycle at Tours defined what was probably a unique year, since the festivals of its own local saints were not common throughout Gaul.[101] Its liturgical practice may also have been unique, because Gregory once mentioned that at another town matins were celebrated differently.[102] We know too that there was a wide variation in agrarian rhythms throughout Gaul, which makes it difficult to focus on particular regions and to assume that all the fragmentary references can be conflated into a homeostatic picture of agrarian life in early Merovingian Gaul.

99. *VP* 8.11.      100. *GM* 23.
101. Beck (1950) 95–107, 311–14.      102. *VM* 3.38.

Nevertheless, at the most general level of analysis, agrarian time and liturgical time were based on fundamentally conflicting premises. Seasonal or ecological time-reckoning does not involve an abstract notion of time; instead, although events happen in a logical order, it is their own sequence that determines the "measuring" of time. Liturgical time-reckoning, in comparison, introduces a precise and abstract measure of the passage of time with which people must synchronize their activities. Under ecological, agrarian time-reckoning the activities themselves take precedence, and their relationship to one another determines the passage of time; under liturgical time-reckoning the emphasis is reversed, and artificial fixed points or units of time determine the moments at which activities must be performed.

Merovingian Gaul was now living simultaneously with both systems of determining time, which had several important consequences. First, at least two different groups of people were created: those who could or would live according to liturgical time, and those who had to live according to agrarian time. Most commonly, only churchmen or monks could live according to the new liturgical demands. Bishops had, in general, long ago given up all ordinary "work": "A bishop is to be engaged only in reading, praying, and preaching the word of God."[103] Although in the later Middle Ages some monastic rules emphasized that monks were to work as well, in early Merovingian Gaul there were few monks or clerics who had to work the land and probably even fewer who both worked and diligently observed all the daily services.[104] Holiness may well have resulted from abstinence, but unfortunately, excessive fasting often meant that some monks could not work even when they were expected to.[105] One monk, because he was a recluse, had to grow his own food, although he also maintained his prayers; interestingly enough, his neighbors thought that his combination of working and praying was ridiculous.[106] Hence, although some monks in sixth-century Gaul "worked with their own hands and raised crops with the sweat from their brows,"[107] they too were increasingly freed from such labor. Max Weber summarized the development most succinctly: "The monk is the first human being who lives rationally, who works methodically and

103. *Statuta ecclesiae antiqua* 3(XX) (*CChr.* lat. 148, p. 166).

104. Although *Vita Eutropii*, pp. 56–57, is one example; see Prinz (1965) 532–40.

105. *VP* 11.1, 15.2.       106. *VP* 10.1.       107. *VP* 18.1.

by rational means toward a goal, namely the future life. Only for him did the clock strike, only for him were the hours of the day divided—for prayer."[108] But these practitioners of "virtuoso religion" still needed more than prayer alone to live on, and men who worked the land ultimately supported the religious specialists. Councils called such support tithes or offerings, but the result was the same: "Without the impediment of work, churchmen can be available for the spiritual ministry at the legitimate hours."[109]

Second, the contrast between liturgical time and agrarian time coincided with other divisions in society. Liturgical time could easily become urban time, since the great churches and the clerics who celebrated the services were often in or near cities, while agrarian time tended to reflect rural time. A city may have tried to maintain a close religious symbiosis with its dependent territory by insisting, for instance, that major festivals were to be celebrated with the bishop in the city.[110] But throughout Antiquity there had always been a latent contrast between urban life and rural life, and now an insistence on the superiority of liturgical time over agrarian time and injunctions giving priority to services in cathedrals over those in parish or villa churches were attempts to reinforce this dichotomy again in favor of urban life.

In another, perhaps more basic, sense the contrast between these two ways of marking time also seems to correspond with the contrast between leisured time and unleisured time, between those who lived on a surplus and those who worked to produce it. In general, people without leisure time were those who lived in the countryside; a peasant near Clermont might rise before daylight, but only to collect wood from the forest.[111] But this correspondence was not exact, since even in cities men might not have time to fulfill the proper liturgical expectations. On the other hand, some rural dwellers made great efforts to attend matins, even traveling a mile a day through winter storms.[112] Presumably also landowning aristocrats living on their estates may have had the time but not the corresponding inclination to perform all the liturgical obligations; hence, again, church councils repeatedly insisted that the important festivals could not be celebrated in private oratories or at villas.[113]

108. M. Weber (1927) 365.     109. Council of Mâcon a. 585, Can. 5.
110. Council of Clermont a. 535, Can. 15, with Wood (1979).
111. GC 30.     112. Fortunatus *Vita Germani* 8.
113. Council of Agde a. 506, Can. 21; Council of Orléans a. 511, Can. 25.

Finally, the fundamental dichotomy was between churchmen and everyone else, and an insistence on the priority of liturgical time was also a claim for the expanded authority of Christianity and its hierarchy. The impact of liturgical time thus supports the argument of Jacques Le Goff: "These were religious schemata in the full sense, which destructured the traditional images of society organized according to social functions and remodeled them along the lines of vocations subordinated to religious needs."[114] Although in the later Middle Ages this dichotomy led to the appearance of a class of professional Christians, such as monks, who devoted all their time to observing the liturgy, in Merovingian Gaul the full impact of liturgical time still extended to everyone. Thus, although the monks at Tours had their own schedule of annual fasts, a similar schedule was apparently applicable to everyone else.[115]

How ordinary people spent their time had become a concern of the church. Celebrating the festival of Janus on the first day of January, for instance, was considered a waste of time.[116] Instead, people were expected to attend public mass on Sundays, on the important festivals, and even on the festivals of minor local saints, however they may have felt about the saints' claims to holiness. At Evaux a villager decided not to attend the festival of an eccentric hermit: "Do you really think . . . that a man who fell from a tree when he was after fruit is now in the company of the angels, so that he should be respected as a saint? It is better to do what needs to be done at home than to honor such a saint." So he stayed home—only to watch all his possessions burn up.[117] Perhaps more than anything else it was men's attitudes toward the pervasive disposition of liturgical time that ensured the dominant role of Christianity in shaping the values and relationships of communities.

114. Le Goff (1980) 91. Note also Harrison (1976) 137, for the conclusion to an extended discussion of the fate of the pagan luni-solar calendar: "Practical, then, among barbarians, it could not survive for long in an age when Christianity and letters were virtually inseparable."
115. Council of Tours a. 567, Can. 18, with *HF* X.31, the schedule of Perpetuus.
116. Council of Tours a. 567, Can. 23, and *Vita Hilari* 2, with the detailed discussion in Arbesmann (1979).
117. *GC* 80.

*    *    *

By its very nature close analysis of a society, whether by historians or by anthropologists, seems to impose a pressing regularity and uniformity that the members of that society often did not feel themselves. In fact, these ideas about the organization of time, space, and personal relationships of authority and dependence instead liberated people to go on with the necessities of daily life. Hence the imposition of Christian ideas about time must not be viewed in a negative perspective; in their own way these ideas generated many of the characteristics that anthropologists appreciate in the small, traditional communities in which they have lived and worked, including "an intensely poetic quality in everyday life and thought, and a vivid enjoyment of the passing moment"[118]—aspects of life that we have often lost. Festivals and church services offered a welcome relief to the drudgery of ordinary work, and attendance at these celebrations was one way of reaffirming basic community values. Most of all, synchronizing with liturgical time was another way for ordinary people to participate in the divine rhythms of heaven. According to Gregory, saints were actually dancing in heaven, just as virgins or monks were sometimes thought to dance during the church services as the choir sang Psalms.[119] Such comments emphasize that one of our problems with understanding ancient liturgy is that we can no longer hear it in context, and hence cannot sense its addictive rhythms in the same way that its participants could.

One distinctive architectural feature of early medieval churches in Gaul was the towers or domes containing the bells that tolled out the liturgical hours: "When the bells sounded, people got up and met together in the cathedral."[120] But these bells not only enabled people to synchronize with the divine rhythms of heaven, they also ensured harmony and conformity within communities. Thus a sixth-century preacher could conjure up the happiness that people felt on a festival of St. Martin by stressing this correlation between the celestial music of the saints and the unanimity of communities. For during this festival, both "the faithful on earth"

118. Horton (1970) 170.
119. *VJ* 50, "victor saeculi in caelo trepudiat"; Fortunatus *Carm.* VIII.3.3–4.
120. *HF* VI.25, *VM* 3.23; Fortunatus *Carm.* II.9.43–44; and Vieillard-Troiekouroff (1976) 398–401.

and "the saints in heaven" gathered and celebrated together: "This is the day on which the holy Catholic church rejoices and dances together."[121]

121. *Sermo in laudem S. Martini* 1, "haec est etenim dies in qua sancta ecclesia catholica . . . multiplici exultatione tripudiat." In contrast, Christians insisted that pagan festivals were characterized by "disordered dances," and hence to be avoided: see Leclercq (1949) = *PL* Suppl. IV.973–5.

# Epilogue

# CHAPTER 14

# The Fates of
# Ausonius and Paulinus
# of Nola

At the end of the period under investigation, we are still left with the fundamental transition from a pagan, Roman Gaul to a Christian, medieval Gaul. This transition can be, in fact must be, studied from many different angles, because no single theme or topic can provide one continuous narrative thread with which we can adequately tie together the loose ends. As one way of reviewing aspects of this transformation in brief, however, let us consider two aristocrats whose families together encompass Late Antiquity in Gaul. Ausonius is the best-known example of a fourth-century Gallic aristocrat who took advantage of the proximity of an imperial court in northern Gaul to promote his and his family's prestige. Paulinus of Nola, in contrast, is an example of a contemporary aristocrat who initially served in the imperial administration, but in the early fifth century finally became a bishop in Italy; and eventually members of a collateral branch of his family become, during the sixth century, successive bishops at Bordeaux. The careers of Ausonius and Paulinus of Nola and the fates of their families have already been used in several excellent historical studies to illustrate such important topics as the impact of access to imperial courts upon local Gallic aristocracies and the metamorphosis of secular aristocrats into Christian bishops. This book has touched on the same topics, although trying also to illuminate them from different perspectives, in particular by evaluating the transformation of Gallic society against the resilient characteristics of local leadership and of life in small communities. As we look at these two men and their families it may also be useful to summarize some of the primary concerns of this book and to suggest topics for further consideration.

*    *    *

First of all, Ausonius' family illustrates the local influence that other aristocratic families shared. Already in the middle of the third century, as far back as Ausonius himself knew, his mother's family had been prominent in eastern Gaul, probably near Autun. In the confusion of the later third century, however, this family had been one victim of feuding between local aristocrats and had had to move to Dax in southwestern Gaul. There its fortunes revived, and within a few generations it had also extended its influence into Bazas and Bordeaux.[1]

Although members of the family achieved prominence as doctors, professors, and, of course, landowners, there was nothing particularly outstanding about it in comparison with other locally influential families. Instead it was able to benefit from an intrusion into traditional Gallic society, that is, the presence of the imperial court. Because the emperor Valentinian had taken up residence at Trier, and because he furthermore wanted his young son Gratian to become a cultured gentleman, in 367 he invited the noted professor Ausonius to enter "the golden palace of the Augustus" and become his son's tutor.[2] Once there, the older professor was able to influence more than just the education of the teenage emperor, particularly during the years after the death of Valentinian in 375. Then Ausonius himself became prefect of the Gauls in 378 and consul in 379; his relatives and his friends held other high imperial magistracies; and his family became one of the few "consular" ones in Gaul.[3] At the height of his influence he was able to promote the career of one of his students, Paulinus of Nola, who became suffect consul and then governor of Campania about 381. This is an excellent, and undisguised, example of the network of patronage and influence that now radiated out from Ausonius, and Paulinus himself conceded that he owed his honors to his former teacher, whom in a later letter he still acknowledged as "my patron."[4]

1. On Ausonius and his family, see Matthews (1975) 69–76.
2. Ausonius *praef.* 1.24–27.
3. Symmachus *Ep.* I.25.
4. Paulinus of Nola *Carm.* X.93–96; on Paulinus, see Frend (1969).

But although the lives and reputations of these two men began in a similar fashion, they ended quite differently. Already during his governorship Paulinus had come under the influence of another "patron," St. Felix of Nola. Impressed by the miracles at the saint's tomb, he had the road to Nola repaired, along with some of the buildings at the shrine.[5] After his governorship, Paulinus and his new wife began to take the demands of Christianity more seriously by selling their possessions; in the opinion of one Christian contemporary, they were now "dead," no longer interested in the world and its attractions.[6] Ausonius was baffled. When Paulinus no longer answered his letters, he lamented that their friendship was coming to an end: "We are shattering our yoke, Paulinus."[7] Ausonius went on to reminisce about the "old Paulinus" whom he used to know, and he insisted that his loyalty and respect for his "old friend" remained unchanged. Nor could he understand why Paulinus was breaking up the "kingdoms" of his estates: "I do not [want to] weep over a mangled and plundered house, or over the kingdoms of the old Paulinus scattered among a hundred landlords, or over [hearing that] you . . . confide in foreign friends and forget your old friends."[8] In the polite society of Gallic aristocrats Paulinus had done the unforgivable: he had not kept up his side of a correspondence, he had ignored his friends, and he had even abandoned his native city in favor of a new allegiance to Nola. And although in his letters Ausonius had, probably unwittingly, echoed the language of Christians by conceding that Paulinus was now a "new man" who no longer resembled his "old friend,"[9] he would have agreed with those Italian aristocrats who felt that Paulinus had indeed ruined both himself and his family by "migrating" from the Senate.[10]

These changes in the life and attitudes of Paulinus, as well as Ausonius' reactions, emphasize two general points we need to re-

5. Paulinus of Nola *Carm.* XXI.367–94.

6. Eutropius *Ep.* 2 (*PL* 30.48); on Eutropius, see Courcelle (1964) 303–17.

7. Ausonius *Ep.* 27.1, with Fabre (1949) 156–71, on their friendship.

8. Ausonius *Ep.* 27.115–18.

9. Ausonius *Ep.* 27.31–32, 104–5. Some scholars have identified the *vetus Paulinus* mentioned by Ausonius here with the grandfather of Paulinus of Nola (Maillé [1959] 76 n. 5), or with his father (Lienhard [1977] 25). But the other passages from *Ep.* 27, as well as *Ep.* 28.33–34, make it clear that by using *vetus* Ausonius was referring to Paulinus and his past. See also Paulinus of Nola *Carm.* X.131–46, for his own description of his "new mind"; and Lienhard (1977) 33–51, on Paulinus' idea of conversion.

10. Ausonius *Ep.* 27.58, with Ambrose *Ep.* 58.1–3 (*PL* 16.1178–9).

member as we evaluate the transformation of Gallic society. First, the transition from a pagan society to a Christian one cannot be taken for granted; instead, it ought to evoke in modern historians as much surprise, perplexity, and even discomfort as Ausonius felt when he contemplated the new life of his former student. Even Paulinus apparently felt uneasy over the implications of his conversion, and he thus left Gaul for Spain before finally settling in Italy. As we have seen in Parts I and II, neither the abiding local influence of Gallic aristocrats, which appeared most clearly whenever the imperial court was absent, nor the inadequacies of Christian ideology through the fourth century gave much indication of the future prominence of Christianity. Even if Ausonius had been prepared to accept Paulinus' rejection of a civil career in order to return to the leisured life of local aristocrats, he could never have acknowledged his student's further decision to commit himself to such a self-limiting cult. In order for us to understand how two former friends could eventually feel so misunderstood and unappreciated by each other, we need more studies that are prepared to struggle with the hesitations, ambiguities, and paradoxes of the process, to struggle, that is, with the intangible and half-articulated habits, sentiments, and prejudices of ordinary men.

The need for this further research is all the more apparent when we consider that, second, much of this transformation took place in people's minds. Although during the process we pass from pagan, Roman Gaul to Christian, barbarian Gaul, the change was marked less by men's outward styles of life than by the ways they could now think about and give meaning to their daily lives. During the fourth century the ideal of service at imperial courts or within the Roman administration had been added, as we have seen, to loyalties to native cities. Ausonius provided a typical summary: "Bordeaux is my native city, but Rome surpasses all native cities; I love Bordeaux, I venerate Rome; I am a citizen in Bordeaux, a consul in both."[11] Paulinus, in contrast, not only turned his back on the expectations of his past heritage and on his budding civil career, he also moved to Italy to take up residence near the shrine of St. Felix in what he now considered to be his true native city: "I have not abandoned Hebromagus [his ancestral estate in Aquitania] in order to cultivate a little garden; instead of my inheritance and my native city I have preferred the Garden of

11. Ausonius *ord. urb. nob.* 20.39–41.

Paradise. My truer home is my eternal one there, and my truer native city is there where I have my first country and my chief dwelling."[12] Paulinus' friend Sulpicius was another exile who had left his native city (which we do not even know) in order to live in a monastic community in southern Gaul. In 400 Paulinus wrote and commended Sulpicius for having sold most of his estates and retreated into a monastery: "You are a foreigner to your native city, so that you have become an inhabitant of Paradise and a citizen of your original native city."[13] In order to understand both the motives that led men ostensibly to abandon their heritage and native cities and the transformation of transcendent ideals whereby the roads in Gaul eventually seem to have led more often to Paradise than to Rome, we also need research that is better equipped to apply the models and insights that anthropologists, sociologists, and historians of other periods have developed to study people's mental worlds.

Ausonius, of course, had neither the opportunity to take advantage of modern studies of psychology and sociology, nor the foresight to match our historical hindsight. Instead, even though the overthrow of the emperor Gratian by the usurper Magnus Maximus had forced him, his relatives, and his friends to retreat to their estates in Aquitania, he could continue to have high hopes for his grandsons. For one of them he composed a little book in which he urged the lad to work hard at his studies and, more importantly, to consider the many honors of his grandfather and uncle, for he hoped that his grandson might imitate them and someday become consul himself.[14]

In the opinion of Ausonius and other senators of the later fourth century, the family of Ausonius was destined for future successes, while the family of Paulinus of Nola appeared to be ruined. Yet precisely the opposite happened during the fifth and sixth centuries. Ausonius had another grandson named Paulinus (of Pella) who was the brother (or half-brother) of the young boy to whom Ausonius had addressed the exhortation to study hard

---

12. Paulinus of Nola *Ep.* 11.14. Note that according to a later apocryphal tradition, Paulinus once supposedly passed himself off to a barbarian prince as a gardener: Gregory I *Dial.* III.1 (ed. A. deVogüé, trans. P. Antin, *SChr.* 260 [1979] 260).

13. Paulinus of Nola *Ep* 24.3; and note Fortunatus *Vita Marcelli* 13, "natus Parisii sed civis paradisi."

14. Ausonius *Ep.* 22.99–100.

and aspire to a consulship. By his own description Paulinus had been raised just that way; but after the barbarian invasions during the winter of 406/407 he had lost both his local influence and his estates. Two of his sons had tried to make their way in these new times, one by serving the Visigothic king at Bordeaux, the other by becoming a Christian priest. But when Paulinus died about 460, the family of Ausonius came to an end. During the fifth century, so far as we know, no one else in Gaul claimed descent from or connection to the family of Ausonius. No one, apparently, was inclined to take up his own broad hint: "Let many derive their names, as the fashion is, from my house."[15]

Paulinus of Nola, however, remained an influential man even after his conversion, a man who prepared his family for "the coming age" by acquiring "nobility" within the Christian ecclesiastical hierarchy.[16] While living at Nola, Paulinus found St. Felix to be even more influential than Ausonius, because the saint was an eternal patron, "without limit," whose influence was not subject to the hazards of usurpations or the appearance of new dynasties. In contrast to Ausonius' connections at an imperial court, St. Felix had introduced Paulinus to "the friends of the celestial Lord."[17] As a result, in about 410 Paulinus became bishop of Nola, as well as, after the pope, the most prominent Christian leader in Italy. At his funeral in 431 everyone, not just the Christians, mourned that they had lost a patron, a defender, and a teacher.[18]

Although Paulinus of Nola had no surviving children, his family continued to flourish in Gaul through such collateral lines as that of Pontius Leontius. During the middle and later fifth century this man and his son Paulinus were two of the most prominent local aristocrats in Aquitania, whose position of eminence was enhanced by their huge villa that, with its high walls, tall towers, barns, and Christian chapel, resembled a medieval castle. Like other Gallic aristocrats of the fifth century, the Pontii Leontii lived in a hilltop fortress and continued to be "lords of the hills."[19]

15. Ausonius *praef.* 1.9–10, as trans. by Green (1978) 25–26. The speculation of Twyman (1970) 485–6, is so tenuous that it is negligible even if correct.

16. Prudentius *c. Symm.* I.558–60, and Jerome *Ep.* 118.5; cf. Sulpicius Severus *Vita Martini* 25.4–5, for Martin's high opinion of Paulinus.

17. Paulinus of Nola *Carm.* XXI.344, 453–5, XXVII.147; more examples in Fabre (1949) 350 n. 6.

18. Uranius *Ep.*, 9 (*PL* 53.863); and, for Paulinus' prominence in Italy, *Coll. Avell.* 25 (*CSEL* 35, p. 71).

19. Sidonius *Carm.* XXII. For other Gallic aristocrats living now in fortresses, see Sidonius *Ep.* IV.15.3, V.14.1; and Marrou (1954).

Even into the sixth century, after Aquitania had been incorporated into the kingdom of the Franks, members of this family retained their local influence, although now, significantly, they became bishops themselves. During the middle and later sixth century two, perhaps three, generations of this family held the see of Bordeaux, thus enhancing the antiquity of their family with ecclesiastical "nobility."[20] Yet these new ecclesiastical aristocrats also continued to maintain links with their traditional secular heritage, because in addition to their patronage for Christian shrines they still feuded with other aristocrats (among them, by now, Frankish kings), and they still enjoyed their estates near Bordeaux: neither the family nor the "kingdoms" of Paulinus had been ruined after all.[21]

This contrast between Ausonius, Paulinus of Nola, and the fates of their families is, admittedly, slightly unfair, since in fact neither family survived with direct descendants. Yet it remains significant that after the middle of the fifth century, not only did no one apparently want to claim descent from Ausonius, but no one knew much about him either. Sidonius, for instance, may have remembered that Ausonius had been a notable poet,[22] but he had actually visited the estate of the Pontii Leontii. In the later sixth century Gregory of Tours never mentioned Ausonius. Instead, he considered Paulinus of Nola the finest exemplary figure from the past, because Paulinus had overcome what were now seen as the handicaps of wealth and education in order to become a bishop and finally a saint in the Christian church.[23] By the sixth century the men to remember and admire from the fourth and fifth centuries were not the imperial magistrates, but the Christian leaders.

A summary of these two men and their families cannot be left, however, as a simple contrast between aristocratic world views. In part, concentrating on the topic of aristocracies is inadequate; although we may know more about aristocrats, the transformation of late antique Gallic society also extended to others. The

20. On Amelius, Leontius I, and Leontius II, see Fortunatus *Carm.* I.15, IV.9–10; and Maillé (1959) 73–97.

21. Fortunatus *Carm.* I.6, 8–13, for the shrines; I.18–20, for the estates.

22. Sidonius *Ep.* IV.14.2, if *ausonios* really refers to Ausonius. In the catalogue of writers and teachers whom he was not going to elaborate upon, a survey that included people from prehistoric mythology to the middle of the fifth century, Sidonius never mentioned Ausonius: *Carm.* IX.211–317.

23. Gregory of Tours *GC* 108.

leaders—whether emperors, bandits, bishops, or saints—may attract our attention, but in fact they had acquired their prominence only because of attitudes and ideals shared with their supporters or the communities in which they lived. As Geertz explains in an excellent discussion of leadership, "It is not . . . standing outside the social order in some excited state of self-regard that makes a political leader numinous but a deep, intimate involvement . . . in the master fictions by which that order lives."[24] For late-antique men, leaders therefore embodied common values. At one time individual emperors were seen as the personifications of shared ideals and imperial authority.[25] In Part III of this book we have seen how these secular ideologies were applied to Christian bishops and saints in order to fit them into Gallic society, so that by the middle of the fifth century the best representation of "charity itself" had become a portrait of a bishop's face.[26] Styles of leadership, whether secular or ecclesiastical, cannot therefore be understood in isolation from the aspirations of communities and supporters.

Finally, by emphasizing the nature of local leadership and of life in small communities we can also define some fixed points against which to measure significant contrasts and transitions. Hence, discussion of the transformation of a great traditional society like late antique Gaul involves the study of changes in the midst of underlying stability. But it is our own language that turns out to be most inadequate here, for as we investigate this paradoxical transformation our major problem is not the nature or amount of information available, but rather the inability of models of historical analysis to discuss durability and change simultaneously, yet without becoming schematic or simply resorting to metaphors. Even at the end of the period under investigation, which was discussed in Part IV of this book, the new coherence of meaning available through Christian beliefs about holiness, relics, and saints drew upon a lexicon of older significations, with the result that early Merovingian communities still viewed their leaders in traditional terms. One final example points out clearly both the discontinuity and the continuity of the history of late antique Gaul, as well as the sheer indifference of those people to the pagan, Roman, Christian, or medieval aspects of their lives that

24. C. Geertz (1977) 171.
25. *Pan. lat.* VII(6).4.3–5, 20.2.
26. Hilary of Arles *Sermo de vita Honorati* 26.

modern historians tend to emphasize. Their preference was rather for the commonplace, everyday emotions and concerns that make them, like us, difficult to understand, but that also allow us to sympathize with them. During the sixth century, many people were unaware of the novelty of saints' cults, and one woman instead expressed her own relationship with her new patron saint in a stunningly conventional way, in terms of true romance. For after seeing St. Julian in a vision and being cured of her paralysis, the woman fell in love with the saint: "The woman always said that the man was tall, well dressed, and exceptionally eloquent. On his face was a smile, and his blond hair was streaked with some grey. He moved gracefully, and he spoke openly and most pleasantly. His skin was whiter than shiny lilies. And out of the thousands of men she often saw, there was no one else like him."[27]

27. Gregory of Tours *VJ* 9.

# SELECT EDITIONS OF ANCIENT AUTHORS

Agroecius of Sens *de orthographia*   H. Keil, *Grammatici latini* VII (Leipzig, 1880) 113–125

Ambrose *Epistolae*   *PL* 16.875–1286

Ammianus Marcellinus   J. C. Rolfe, Loeb, 3 vols. (1935–1939)

Augustine *contra Felicem*   J. Zycha, *CSEL* 25.2 (1892) 801–852

   *contra Fortunatum*   J. Zycha, *CSEL* 25.1 (1891) 83–112

   *contra mendacium*   J. Zycha, *CSEL* 41 (1900) 469–528

   *Epistolae*   *PL* 33

   *de haeresibus*   *PL* 42.21–50

Aurelius Victor *Caesares*   F. Pichlmayr and R. Gruendel (Leipzig, 1966) 77–129

[Aurelius Victor] *Epitome*   F. Pichlmayr and R. Gruendel (Leipzig, 1966) 133–176

Ausonius   H. G. Evelyn-White, Loeb, 2 vols. (1919–1921)

Avitus of Vienne   R. Peiper, *MGH, AA* 6.2 (1883)

Baudonivia *Vita Radegundis*   B. Krusch, *MGH, SRM* 2 (1888) 364–395

Caesarius of Arles *Sermones*   G. Morin, *CChr. lat.* 103–104 (2nd ed., 1953)

*Carmen de providentia Dei*   M. P. McHugh (Washington, D.C., 1964)

Claudian   M. Platnauer, Loeb, 2 vols. (1922)

Claudianus Mamertus   A. Engelbrecht, *CSEL* 11 (1885)

Concilia Galliae   C. Munier, *CChr. lat.* 148 (1963), and C. de Clercq, *CChr. lat.* 148A (1963)

Consentius *de barbarismis et metaplasmis*   H. Keil, *Grammatici latini* V (Leipzig, 1868) 386–404

Constantius *Vita Germani*   W. Levison, *MGH, SRM* 7 (1920) 247–283; and R. Borius, *SChr.* 112 (1965)

*CTh = Codex Theodosianus*   Th. Mommsen and P. Krueger, (Berlin, 1905)

*Digest*   Th. Mommsen and P. Krueger, *Digesta Iustiniani.* Corpus Iuris Civilis I (Berlin, 13th ed., 1920)

(Cassius) Dio   E. Cary, Loeb, 9 vols. (1914–1927)

Dynamius *Vita Maximi*   *PL* 80.33–40

Egeria *Itinerarium*   H. Pétré, *SChr.* 21 (1948)

Ennodius of Pavia *Vita Epiphani*   F. Vogel, *MGH, AA* 7 (1885) 84–109; and G. M. Cook (Washington, D.C., 1942)

*Epistolae Arelatenses*   W. Gundlach, *MGH*, Epistolae 3 (1892) 5–83
*Epistolae Austrasicae*   W. Gundlach, *MGH*, Epistolae 3 (1892) 111–153
Eucher of Lyon   C. Wotke, *CSEL* 31 (1894)
Eunapius of Sardis   C. Müller, *FHG* IV (1851) 7–56
Eutropius *Breviarium*   H. Droysen, *MGH*, AA 2.2 (1879) 8–182
*Expositio totius mundi et gentium*   J. Rougé, *SChr.* 124 (1966)
Faustus of Riez   A. Engelbrecht, *CSEL* 21 (1891)
Filastrius of Brescia *diversarum hereseon liber*   F. Marx, *CSEL* 38 (1898)
Firmicus Maternus *Mathesis*   W. Kroll and F. Skutsch, 2 vols. (Leipzig, 1897–1913)
Fortunatus   F. Leo and B. Krusch, *MGH*, AA 4 (1881–1885)
Gennadius of Marseille *de scriptoribus ecclesiasticis*   *PL* 58.1059–1120
[Gennadius of Marseille] *Liber ecclesiasticorum dogmatum*   C. H. Turner, *J. Theol. Studies* 7 (1905) 89–99
[Pope] Gregory I *Registrum epistolarum*   P. Ewald and L. M. Hartmann, *MGH*, Epistolae 1–2 (1891–1895)
Gregory of Tours   W. Arndt and B. Krusch, *MGH*, SRM 1 (1885); new edition of HF by B. Krusch and W. Levison, *MGH*, SRM 1.1 (1937–1951)
> HF   *Libri historiarum ('Historia Francorum')*
> GM   *Liber in gloria martyrum*
> VJ   *Liber de passione et virtutibus S. Iuliani martyris*
> VM   *Libri I–IV de virtutibus S. Martini episcopi*
> VP   *Liber vitae patrum*
> GC   *Liber in gloria confessorum*
> de cursu   *De cursu stellarum ratio, qualiter ad officium implendum debeat observari*
Herodian   C. R. Whittaker, Loeb, 2 vols. (1969–1970)
Hilary of Arles *Sermo de vita Honorati*   S. Cavallin, *Vitae sanctorum Honorati et Hilarii* (Lund, 1952) 49–78; and M. D. Valentin, *SChr.* 235 (1977)
Hydatius *Chronica*   *Chron. Min.* II, 13–36; and A. Tranoy, *SChr.* 218–219 (1974)
[Pope] Innocent I *Epistolae*   *PL* 20.463–612
Jerome *adversus Iovinianum*   *PL* 23.211–338
    *contra Vigilantium*   *PL* 23.353–368
    *de viris illustribus*   *PL* 23.601–720
    *Epistolae*   I. Hilberg, *CSEL* 54–56 (1910–1918)
Jordanes *Getica*   Th. Mommsen, *MGH*, AA 5 (1882) 53–138
Julian   W. C. Wright, Loeb, 3 vols. (1913–1923)
[Pope] Leo I *Epistolae*   *PL* 54.593–1218
Libanius *Julianic orations*   A. F. Norman, Loeb I (1969)
*Liber pontificalis*   L. Duchesne, I (Paris, 1884–1886)
Marcellus *de medicamentis*   G. Helmreich (Leipzig, 1889)
Marius of Avenches *Chronica*   *Chron. Min.* II, 232–239
Merobaudes   F. Vollmer, *MGH*, AA 14 (1905) 1–20
*Notitia Dignitatum*   O. Seeck (Berlin, 1876)
*Notitia Galliarum*   *Chron. Min.* I, 584–612
*Novellae*   P. Meyer (Berlin, 1905)
[Odo of Cluny] *Vita Gregorii*   *PL* 71.115–128
Olympiodorus   C. Müller, *FHG* IV (1851) 57–68
Orosius   C. Zangemeister, *CSEL* 5 (1882)

Palladius *Historia lausiaca*   C. Butler (Cambridge, 1904)

*Panegyrici latini*   E. Galletier, Budé, 3 vols. (1949–1955); and R. A. B. Mynors, OCT (1964)

Paulinus of Nola   G. de Hartel, *CSEL* 29–30 (1894)

Paulinus of Pella *Eucharisticos*   H. G. Evelyn-White, Loeb *Ausonius* II (1921) 304–351; and C. Moussy, *SChr.* 209 (1974)

Paulinus of Périgueux   M. Petschenig, *CSEL* 16.1 (1888) 17–165

Julianus Pomerius *de vita contemplativa*   *PL* 59.415–520

Priscillian of Avila   G. Schepss, *CSEL* 18 (1889) = *PL* Suppl. II (1960) 1391–1483

Procopius   B. H. Dewing, Loeb, 7 vols. (1914–1940)

Prudentius   H. J. Thomson, Loeb, 2 vols. (1949–1953)

*Querolus* or *Aulularia*   R. Peiper (Leipzig, 1875)

Rutilius Namatianus *de reditu suo*   J. W. Duff and A. M. Duff, Loeb *Minor Latin poets* (1935) 753–829

Salvian   F. Pauly, *CSEL* 8 (1883); and G. Lagarrigue, *SChr.* 176, 220 (1971–1975)

*Sermo in laudem S. Martini*   *PL* Suppl. IV (1968) 602–604; cf. Peebles (1961)

Severus of Minorca *Epistola de Iudaeis*   *PL* 20.731–746

SHA = Scriptores Historiae Augustae   D. Magie, Loeb, 3 vols. (1921–1932)

Sidonius Apollinaris   W. B. Anderson, Loeb, 2 vols. (1936, 1965); and A. Loyen, Budé, 3 vols. (1960–1970)

[Pope] Siricius *Epistolae*   *PL* 13.1131–1194

Socrates *Historia ecclesiastica*   *PG* 67.29–842

Sozomen *Historia ecclesiastica*   J. Bidez and G. C. Hanson, *GCS* 50 (1960)

Strabo   H. L. Jones, Loeb, 8 vols. (1917–1932)

Sulpicius Severus   C. Halm, *CSEL* 1 (1866)

Symmachus   O. Seeck, *MGH*, AA 6.1 (1883)

Victricius of Rouen *de laude sanctorum*   *PL* 20.443–458

Vincentius of Lérins *Commonitorium*   *PL* 50.637–686

*Vita Bibiani vel Viviani*   B. Krusch, *MGH*, SRM 3 (1896) 94–100

*Vita Caesarii*   B. Krusch, *MGH*, SRM 3 (1896) 457–501

*Vita Eutropii*   P. Varin, *Bulletin du Comité historique des monuments écrits de l'histoire de France*, Histoire-sciences-lettres 1 (1849) 53–64

*Vita Genovefe virgine*   B. Krusch, *MGH*, SRM 3 (1896) 215–238

*Vita Hilari*   *Acta Sanctorum* Oct. XI (1864) 638–639

*Vita Hilarii*   S. Cavallin, *Vitae sanctorum Honorati et Hilarii* (Lund, 1952) 81–109

*Vita Lupi*   B. Krusch, *MGH*, SRM 7 (1920) 295–302

*Vita Marii*   *PL* 80.25–32

*Vita Nicetii*   B. Krusch, *MGH*, SRM 3 (1896) 521–524

*Vita Orientii*   *Acta Sanctorum* Maius I (1866) 62–63

*Vita Patrum Iurensium Romani, Lupicini, Eugendi*   B. Krusch, *MGH*, SRM 3 (1896) 131–166; and F. Martine, *SChr.* 142 (1968)

[Pope] Zosimus *Epistolae*   *PL* 20.642–686

Zosimus *Historia nova*   L. Mendelssohn (Leipzig, 1887)

# BIBLIOGRAPHY

Abel, A. (1966). "Aspects sociologiques des religions 'manichéennes.'" In *Mélanges offerts à René Crozet*, ed. P. Gallais and Y. J. Riou, vol. I, pp. 33–46. Poitiers.

Agache, R. (1975). "La campagne à l'époque romaine dans les grandes plaines du Nord de la France d'après les photographies aériennes." In *Aufstieg und Niedergang der römischen Welt*, vol. II.4, ed. H. Temporini, pp. 658–713. Berlin.

Albertini, E. (1912). "Les étrangers résidant en Espagne à l'époque romaine." In *Mélanges Cagnat*, pp. 297–318. Paris.

d'Alès, A. (1936). *Priscillien et l'Espagne chrétienne à la fin du IVᵉ siècle*. Paris.

Alföldi, A. (1952). *A conflict of ideas in the late Roman Empire*. English translation: Oxford.

Alföldy, G. (1971). "Bellum desertorum." *Bonner Jahrbücher* 171, pp. 367–376.

———. (1973). "Der heilige Cyprian und die Krise des römischen Reiches." *Historia* 22, pp. 479–501.

———. (1974). "The crisis of the third century as seen by contemporaries." *Greek, Roman and Byzantine Studies* 15, pp. 89–111.

Amit, M. (1965). "Les moyens de communication et la défense de l'empire romain." *La parola del passato* 20, pp. 207–222.

Anderson, P. (1974). *Passages from Antiquity to feudalism*. London.

Antin, P. (1963). "Notes sur le style de Saint Grégoire de Tours et ses emprunts (?) à Philostrate." *Latomus* 22, pp. 273–284.

———. (1964). "La mort de Saint Martin." *Revue des études anciennes* 66, pp. 108–120.

———. (1967). "Emplois de la Bible chez Grégoire de Tours et Mgr Pie." *Latomus* 26, pp. 778–782.

Applebaum, S. (1972). "Roman Britain." In *The agrarian history of England and Wales*, vol. I.2, ed. H. P. R. Finberg, pp. 1–277. Cambridge.

Arbesmann, R. (1979). "The 'cervuli' and 'anniculae' in Caesarius of Arles." *Traditio* 35, pp. 89–119.

Arce, J. (1980). "La 'Notitia Dignitatum' et l'armée romaine dans la *diocesis Hispaniarum*." *Chiron* 10, pp. 593–608.

Arnheim, M. T. W. (1972). *The senatorial aristocracy in the later Roman Empire.* Oxford.

Athanassiadi-Fowden, P. (1981). *Julian and Hellenism: An intellectual biography.* Oxford.

Audin, A. (1952–1953). "L'acropole de Lugdunum." *Bulletin de la Société nationale des antiquaires de France,* pp. 87–88.

———. (1953). "Pourquoi Lugdunum fut-it abandonné?" *Revue archéologique de l'Est et du Centre-est* 4, pp. 61–65.

Auerbach, E. (1953). *Mimesis: The representation of reality in Western literature.* English translation: Princeton.

———. (1965). "Sermo humilis." In *Literary language and its public in Late Latin Antiquity and in the Middle Ages,* pp. 25–66. English translation: London.

Babut, E. Ch. (1909). *Priscillien et le priscillianisme.* Paris.

———. (1910). "Paulin de Nole et Priscillien." *Revue d'histoire et de littérature religieuses,* n.s. 1, pp. 97–130, 252–275.

Bachrach, B. S. (1967). "The Alans in Gaul." *Traditio* 23, pp. 476–489.

———. (1969). "Another look at the barbarian settlement in southern Gaul." *Traditio* 25, pp. 354–358.

———. (1973). *A history of the Alans in the West.* Minneapolis.

Baer, Y. (1961). *A history of the Jews in Christian Spain,* vol. I. English translation: Philadelphia.

Balil, A. (1960). "Mosaico de Bellerofonte y la Quimera, de Torre de Bell-lloch (Gerona)." *Archivo Español de Arqueologia* 33, pp. 98–112.

———. (1966). "Su gli spettacoli di anfiteatro." In *Mélanges d'archéologie et d'histoire offerts à André Piganiol,* ed. R. Chevallier, vol. I, pp. 357–368. Paris.

Barbero de Aguilera, A. (1963). "El priscilianismo: ¿herejía o movimiento social?" *Cuadernos de historia de España* 37–38, pp. 5–41.

Bardy, G. (1949). "Pèlerinages à Rome vers la fin du IVᵉ siècle." *Analecta Bollandiana* 67, pp. 224–235.

———. (1950). "Constance de Lyon, biographe de saint Germain d'Auxerre." In *Saint Germain d'Auxerre et son temps,* pp. 89–108. Auxerre.

Barnes, T. D. (1972). "Some persons in the Historia Augusta." *Phoenix* 26, pp. 140–182.

———. (1974). "Merobaudes on the imperial family." *Phoenix* 28, pp. 314–319.

———. (1975). "Constans and Gratian in Rome." *Harvard Studies in Classical Philology* 79, pp. 325–333.

———. (1976). "Imperial campaigns, A.D. 285–311." *Phoenix* 30, pp. 174–193.

———. (1978). *The sources of the Historia Augusta.* Brussels.

———. (1982). *The new empire of Diocletian and Constantine.* Cambridge, Mass. and London.

Barruol, G. (1976). "La résistance des substrats préromains en Gaule Méridionale." In *Assimilation et résistance à la culture gréco-romaine dans le monde ancien,* ed. D. M. Pippidi. Travaux de VIᵉ Congrès international d'études classiques, pp. 389–405. Bucharest and Paris.

Bartelink, G. J. M. (1967). "Les démons comme brigands." *Vigiliae Christianae* 21, pp. 12–24.

Baynes, N. H. (1929). Review of F. Lot, *La fin du monde antique et le début du Moyen Age* (1927), and other books. *Journal of Roman Studies* 19, pp. 224–235.

———. (1948). Review of W. Seston, *Dioclétien et la tétrarchie*, vol. I (1946). *Journal of Roman Studies* 38, pp. 109–113.

Beck, H. G. J. (1950). *The pastoral care of souls in south-east France during the sixth century*. Rome.

Beidelman, T. O. (1970). "Towards more open theoretical interpretations." In *Witchcraft confessions and accusations*, ed. M. Douglas, pp. 351–356. London.

van Berchem, D. (1955). "Aspects de la domination romaine en Suisse." *Schweizerische Zeitschrift für Geschichte* 5, pp. 145–175.

———. (1956a). *Le martyre de la légion thébaine*. Basel.

———. (1956b). "Du portage au péage: Le role des cols transalpins dans l'histoire du Valais celtique." *Museum Helveticum* 13, pp. 199–208.

Berger, A. (1953). *Encyclopedic dictionary of Roman law*. Philadelphia.

Beumann, H. (1964). "Gregor von Tours und der Sermo rusticus." In *Spiegel der Geschichte: Festgabe für Max Braubach*, ed. K. Repgen and S. Skalweit, pp. 69–98. Munster.

Bialor, P. (1968). "Tensions leading to conflict and the resolution and avoidance of conflict in a Greek farming community." In *Contributions to Mediterranean sociology*, ed. J. G. Peristiany, pp. 107–126. Paris and The Hague.

Bidez, J. (1930). *La vie de l'empereur Julien*. Paris.

Biraben, J. N. and J. Le Goff (1969). "La peste dans le haut Moyen Age." *Annales: é.s.c.* 24, pp. 1484–1510.

Blagg, T. F. C. (1981). "Architectural patronage in the western provinces of the Roman Empire in the third century." In *The Roman West in the third century: Contributions from archaeology and history*, ed. A. King and M. Henig. BAR International Series 109, pp. 167–188. Oxford.

Blázquez, J. M. (1974). "Der Limes im Spanien des vierten Jahrhunderts." In *Actes du IXᵉ Congrès international d'études sur les frontières romaines*, ed. D. M. Pippidi, pp. 485–502. Bucharest.

Bloch, Marc (1924). *Les rois thaumaturges*. Strasbourg and Paris.

———. (1961). *Feudal society*. English translation: London.

———. (1966). *French rural history*. English translation: Berkeley and Los Angeles.

Bloch, Maurice (1968). "Astrology and writing in Madagascar." In *Literacy in traditional societies*, ed. J. Goody, pp. 278–297. Cambridge.

Blockley, R. C. (1972). "The panegyric of Claudius Mamertinus on the emperor Julian." *American Journal of Philology* 93, pp. 437–450.

Blok, A. (1969). "Variations in patronage." *Sociologische Gids* 16, pp. 365–378.

Blumenkranz, B. (1960). *Juifs et Chrétiens dans le monde occidental, 430–1096*. Paris.

Bolton, B. M. (1973). "Mulieres sanctae." In *Sanctity and secularity: The church and the world*, ed. D. Baker. *Studies in Church History* 10, pp. 77–95. Oxford.

Bonnet, M. (1890). *Le Latin de Grégoire de Tours*. Paris.

Booth, A. D. (1978). "Notes on Ausonius' *Professores*." *Phoenix* 32, pp. 235–249.

Bordier, H. L. (1857–1864), ed. and trans. *Les livres des miracles et autres opuscules de Georges Florent Grégoire évêque de Tours*. 4 vols. Paris.

Borius, R. (1965), ed. and trans. *Constance de Lyon, Vie de Saint Germain d'Auxerre*. SChr. 112. Paris.

Bourdieu, P. (1973). "The Berber house." In *Rules and meanings*, ed. M. Douglas, pp. 98–110. Harmondsworth.

Boussard, J. (1948). "Etude sur la ville de Tours du I$^{er}$ au IV$^e$ siècle." *Revue des études anciennes* 50, pp. 313–329.

Bowersock, G. W. (1973). " 'The social and economic history of the Roman Empire' by M. I. Rostovtzeff." *Daedalus* 103.1, pp. 15–23.

Braudel, F. (1972). *The Mediterranean and the Mediterranean world in the age of Philip II*. English translation: London.

———. (1973). *Capitalism and material life, 1400–1800*. English translation: New York.

Broughton, T. R. S. (1959). "The Romanization of Spain: The problem and the evidence." *Proceedings of the American Philosophical Society* 103, pp. 645–651.

———. (1965). "Municipal institutions in Roman Spain." *Cahiers d'histoire mondiale* 9, pp. 126–142.

Brown, P. (1967). *Augustine of Hippo*. Berkeley and Los Angeles.

———. (1972). *Religion and society in the age of Saint Augustine*. London.

———. (1977). "Relics and social status in the age of Gregory of Tours." The Stenton Lecture, 1976. University of Reading. Reprinted in *Society and the Holy in Late Antiquity*, pp. 222–250. Berkeley and Los Angeles, 1982.

———. (1981). *The cult of the saints: Its rise and function in Latin Christianity*. Chicago.

Bruguière, M. B. (1974). *Littérature et droit dans la Gaule du V$^e$ siècle*. Paris.

Buckley, B. (1981). "The Aeduan area in the third century." In *The Roman West in the third century: Contributions from archaeology and history*, ed. A. King and M. Henig. BAR International Series 109, pp. 287–315. Oxford.

Burdeau, F. (1964). "L'empereur d'après les panégyriques latins." In F. Burdeau, N. Charbonnel, M. Humbert, *Aspects de l'empire romain*, pp. 1–60. Paris.

Burridge, K. (1969). *New heaven, new earth*. Oxford.

Butler, R. M. (1959). "Late Roman town walls in Gaul." *Archaeological Journal* 126, pp. 25–50.


Cameron, Alan (1967). "Rutilius Namatianus, St. Augustine, and the date of the *De Reditu*." *Journal of Roman Studies* 57, pp. 31–39.

———. (1968). "Celestial consulates: A note on the Pelagian letter *Humanae referunt*." *Journal of Theological Studies*, n.s. 19, pp. 213–215.

Cameron, Averil (1968). "Agathias on the early Merovingians." *Annali della Scuola normale superiore de Pisa*, 2nd ser., 37, pp. 95–140.

———. (1975). "The Byzantine sources of Gregory of Tours." *Journal of Theological Studies*, n.s. 26, pp. 421–426.

Carrias, M. (1970). "La connaissance des saints provençaux dans l'oeuvre de Grégoire de Tours." *Provence historique* 20, pp. 317–339.

———. (1972). "Etude sur la formation de deux légendes hagiographiques à l'époque mérovingienne: Deux translations de Saint Martin d'après Grégoire de Tours." *Revue d'histoire de l'église de France* 58, pp. 5–18.

Casey, P. J. (1977). "Carausius and Allectus—rulers in Gaul?" *Britannia* 8, pp. 283–301.

Cavallera, F. (1922). *Saint Jérôme, sa vie et son oeuvre*. 2 vols. Louvain and Paris.

Cavallin, S. (1948). "Les clausules des hagiographes arlésiens." *Eranos* 46, pp. 133–157.

Chadwick, H. (1972). "Prayer at midnight." In *Epektasis: Mélanges patristiques offerts au Cardinal Jean Daniélou,* ed. J. Fontaine and C. Kannengiesser, pp. 47–49. Paris.

———. (1976). *Priscillian of Avila.* Oxford.

Chadwick, N. K. (1965). "The colonization of Brittany from Celtic Britain." *Proceedings of the British Academy* 51, pp. 235–299.

Chadwick, O. (1948). "Gregory of Tours and Gregory the Great." *Journal of Theological Studies* 49, pp. 38–49.

Chase, A. H. (1932). "The metrical lives of St. Martin of Tours by Paulinus and Fortunatus and the prose life by Sulpicius Severus." *Harvard Studies in Classical Philology* 43, pp. 51–76.

Chastagnol, A. (1973). "Le repli sur Arles des services administratifs gaulois en l'an 407 de notre ère." *Revue historique* 249, pp. 23–40.

———. (1978). "Sidoine Apollinaire et le sénat de Rome." *Acta Antiqua Academiae Scientiarum Hungaricae* 26, pp. 57–70.

Chatillon, F. (1954a). "'Un certain Prosper . . .'" *Revue du Moyen Age latin* 10, pp. 204–206.

———. (1954b). "Sur Saint Augustin et le Manichéisme médiéval." *Revue du Moyen Age latin* 10, pp. 206–208.

Claude, D. (1963). "Der Bestellung der Bischöfe im merowingischen Reiche." *Zeitschrift der Savigny-Stiftung für Rechtsgeschichte* 80, Kanonistische Abteilung 49, pp. 1–75.

———. (1964). "Untersuchungen zum frühfränkischen Comitat." *Zeitschrift der Savigny-Stiftung für Rechtsgeschichte,* Germanistische Abteilung 81, pp. 1–79.

———. (1978). "Prosopographie des spanischen Suebenreiches." *Francia* 6, pp. 647–676.

Cleland, D. J. (1970). "Salvian and the Vandals." *Studia Patristica* 10 = *Texte und Untersuchungen* 107, pp. 270–274.

Closa Farres, J. (1978). "Sermo Punicus, sermo Graecus, sermo Latinus y sermo gentilis en la carta encíclica del obispo Severo de Menorca." *Helmantica* 29, pp. 187–194.

Clover, F. M. (1971). *Flavius Merobaudes: A translation and historical commentary.* Philadelphia.

Cohn, N. (1962). "Medieval millenarism: Its bearing on the comparative study of millenarian movements." In *Millennial dreams in action,* ed. S. L. Thrupp. *Comparative Studies in Society and History,* suppl. 2, pp. 31–43.

Colin, J. (1954). "Sénateurs gaulois à Rome et governeurs romains en Gaule au IIIᵉ siècle." *Latomus* 13, pp. 218–228.

Collins, R. (1981). "Observations on the form, language and public of the prose biographies of Venantius Fortunatus in the hagiography of Merovingian Gaul." In *Columbanus and Merovingian mentality,* ed. H. B. Clarke and M. Brennan. BAR International Series 113, pp. 105–131. Oxford.

Courcelle, P. (1953). "L'enfant et les 'sorts bibliques.'" *Vigiliae Christianae* 7, pp. 194–220.

———. (1964). *Histoire littéraire des grandes invasions germaniques.* 3rd ed. Paris.

———. (1966). "Le serpent à face humaine dans la numismatique impériale du Vᵉ siècle." In *Mélanges d'archéologie et d'histoire offerts à André Piganiol,* ed. R. Chevallier, vol. I, pp. 343–353. Paris.

————. (1968). *Recherches sur les "Confessions" de Saint Augustin.* Paris.

————. (1970). "Sidoine philosophe." In *Forschungen zur römischen Literatur: Festschrift zum 60. Geburtstag von Karl Büchner,* ed. W. Wimmel, pp. 46–59. Wiesbaden.

Cramer, F. H. (1945). "Bookburning and censorship in ancient Rome: A chapter from the history of freedom of speech." *Journal of the History of Ideas* 6, pp. 157–196.

Czúth, B. (1965). *Die Quellen der Geschichte der Bagauden.* Acta Universitatis de Attila Jozsef nominatae, Acta antiqua et archaeologica 9. Szeged.

Czúth, B., and S. Szádeczky-Kardoss (1958). Summary: "Die Bagauden-Bewegung in Spanien." *Bibliotheca classica orientalis* 3, p. 140.

————. (1959). Summary: "Die Bagauden in den Alpen." *Bibliotheca classica orientalis* 4, pp. 280–281.

Dagron, G. (1978), ed. and trans. *Vie et miracles de Sainte Thècle: Texte grec, traduction et commentaire.* Subsidia Hagiographica 62. Brussels.

Dalton, O. M. (1927). *The history of the Franks by Gregory of Tours.* Vol. I, *Introduction.* Oxford.

Dannenbauer, H. (1958). "Die Rechtsstellung der Gallorömer im fränkischen Reich." In *Grundlagen der mittelalterlichen Welt,* pp. 94–120. Stuttgart.

DeClercq, V. C. (1957). "Ossius of Cordova and the origins of Priscillianism." *Studia Patristica* 1 = *Texte und Untersuchungen* 63, pp. 601–606.

Decret, F. (1970). *Aspects du Manichéisme dans l'Afrique romaine.* Paris.

————. (1979). "Les conséquences sur le christianisme en Perse de l'affrontement des empires romain et sassanide de Shâpûr I$^{er}$ à Yazdgard I$^{er}$." *Recherches augustiniennes* 14, pp. 91–152.

De Francis, J. (1950). *Nationalism and language reform in China.* Princeton.

Dekkers, E. (1953). "Les traductions grecques des écrits patristiques latins." *Sacris Eruditi* 5, pp. 193–233.

Delaruelle, E. (1963). "La spiritualité des pèlerinages à Saint-Martin de Tours du V$^e$ au X$^e$ siècle." In *Pellegrinaggi e culto dei santi in Europa fino alla 1$^a$ crociata.* Convegni del Centro di studi sulla spiritualità medievale IV, pp. 199–243. Todi.

Delehaye, H. (1920). "Saint Martin et Sulpice Sévère." *Analecta Bollandiana* 38, pp. 5–136.

————. (1925). "Les recueils antiques de miracles des saints." *Analecta Bollandiana* 43, pp. 5–85, 305–325.

Demougeot, E. (1956). "Une lettre de l'empereur Honorius sur l'*hospitum* des soldats." *Revue historique de droit français et étranger* 34, pp. 25–49.

Devos, P. (1967). "La date du voyage d'Egérie." *Analecta Bollandiana* 85, pp. 165–194.

————. (1973). "Silvie la sainte pèlerine." *Analecta Bollandiana* 91, pp. 105–120.

Dill, S. (1926). *Roman society in Gaul in the Merovingian age.* London.

Dix, G. (1945). *The shape of the liturgy.* London.

Domínguez del Val, U. (1967). "Herencia literaria de padres y escritores españoles de Osio de Córdoba a Julián de Toledo." In *Repertorio de historia de la ciencias eclesiásticas en España,* vol. 1, pp. 1–85. Salamanca.

Douglas, M. (1966). *Purity and danger.* Harmondsworth.

———. (1970), ed. *Witchcraft confessions and accusations*. London.

Drewery, B. (1972). "History and doctrine: Heresy and schism." *Journal of Ecclesiastical History* 23, pp. 251–266.

Drinkwater, J. F. (1975). "Lugdunum: 'Natural capital' of Gaul?" *Britannia* 6, pp. 133–140.

———. (1978). "The rise and fall of the Gallic Iulii: Aspects of the development of the aristocracy of the Three Gauls under the early empire." *Latomus* 37, pp. 817–850.

———. (1981). "Money-rents and food-renders in Gallic funerary reliefs." In *The Roman West in the third century: Contributions from archaeology and history*, ed. A. King and M. Henig. BAR International Series 109, pp. 215–233. Oxford.

Du Boulay, J. (1974). *Portrait of a Greek mountain village*. Oxford.

Duby, G. (1974). *The early growth of the European economy: Warriors and peasants from the seventh to the twelfth century*. English translation: London.

Duchesne, L. (1894–1915). *Fastes épiscopaux de l'ancienne Gaule*. 3 vols. Paris.

Dürig, W. (1952). "Disciplina: Eine Studie zum Bedeutungsumfang des Wortes in der Sprache der Liturgie und der Väter." *Sacris Erudiri* 4, pp. 245–279.

Duhr, J. (1928). "Le 'De fide' de Bachiarius." *Revue d'histoire ecclésiastique* 24, pp. 5–40, 301–331.

Duparc, P. (1959). "La Sapaudia." *Comptes rendus de l'Académie des inscriptions et Belles-lettres*, pp. 371–384.

Dupraz, L. (1961). *Les passions de S. Maurice d'Agaune*. Fribourg.

Dupré, N. (1973). "La place de la vallée de l'Ebre dans l'Espagne romaine: Recherches de géographie historique." *Mélanges de la Casa de Velazquez* 9, pp. 133–175.

Duru, L. M. (1850–1863), ed. *Bibliothèque historique de l'Yonne*. 2 vols. Auxerre.

Duval, P. M. (1963). "L'originalité de l'architecture gallo-romaine." In *VIII<sup>e</sup> Congrès international d'archéologie classique, Paris, 3–13 Septembre 1963*. Rapports et communications, pp. 33–54. Paris.

Elbern, V. H. (1966). "HIC SCS SYMION: Eine vorkarolingische Kultstatue des Symeon Stylites in Poitiers." *Cahiers archéologiques* 16, pp. 23–38.

Engelmann, E. (1956). "Zur Bewegung der Bagauden im römischen Gallien." In *Vom Mittelalter zur Neuzeit: zum 65. Geburtstag von H. Sproemberg*, ed. H. Kretzschmar, pp. 373–385. Berlin.

Ensslin, W. (1937). "Valentinians III. Novellen XVII und XVIII von 445." *Zeitschrift der Savigny-Stiftung für Rechtsgeschichte*, Romanistische Abteilung 57, pp. 367–378.

Etienne, R. (1962). *Bordeaux antique*. Bordeaux.

———. (1966). "Ausone et l'Espagne." In *Mélanges offerts à Jérôme Carcopino*, pp. 319–332. Paris.

———. (1978). "Ausone et la forêt." *Annales du Midi* 90, pp. 252–255.

Ewig, E. (1954). *Trier im Merowingerreich: Civitas, Stadt, Bistum*. Trier.

———. (1956). "Der Bild Constantins des Grossen in den ersten Jahrhunderten des abendländischen Mittelalters." *Historisches Jahrbuch* 75, pp. 1–46.

———. (1958). "Volkstum und Volksbewusstsein im Frankenreich des 7. Jahrhunderts." In *Caratteri del secolo VII in Occidente*. Settimane di studio del Centro italiano di studi sull'Alto Medioevo 5, pp. 587–648. Spoleto.

――――. (1960a). "Die Kathedralpatrozinien im römischen und im fränkischen Gallien." *Historisches Jahrbuch* 79, pp. 1–61.

――――. (1960b). "Der Petrus- und Apostelkult im spätrömischen und fränkischen Gallien." *Zeitschrift für Kirchengeschichte* 71, pp. 215–251.

――――. (1961). "Le culte de Saint Martin à l'époque franque." *Revue d'histoire de l'église de France* 47, pp. 1–18.

――――. (1964). "Die Verehrung orientalischer Heiliger im spätrömischen Gallien und im Merowingerreich." In *Festschrift Percy Ernst Schramm*, vol. I, pp. 385–400. Wiesbaden.

――――. (1972). "Von der Kaiserstadt zur Bischofsstadt: Beobachtungen zur Geschichte von Trier im 5. Jahrhundert." In *Die Stadt in der europäischen Geschichte: Festschrift Edith Ennen*, ed. W. Besch et al., pp. 59–73. Bonn.

――――. (1976a). "Die fränkischen Teilungen und Teilreiche (511–613)." In *Spätantikes und fränkisches Gallien: Gesammelte Schriften (1952–1973)*, vol. I, pp. 114–171. Munich.

――――. (1976b). "Résidence et capitale pendant le haut Moyen Age." In *Spätantikes und fränkisches Gallien: Gesammelte Schriften (1952–1973)*, vol. I, pp. 362–408. Munich.

Fabre, P. (1949). *Saint Paulin de Nole et l'amitié chrétienne*. Paris.

Faral, E. (1946). "Sidoine Apollinaire et la technique littéraire du Moyen Age." *Miscellanea Giovanni Mercati*, Vol. II: *Letteratura medioevale = Studi e testi* 122, pp. 567–580. Vatican City.

Fernández de Avilés, A. (1945). "El mosaico de las Musas, de Arróniz, y su restauración en el Museo Arqueológico Nacional." *Archivo Español de Arqueologia* 18, pp. 342–350.

Finley, M. I. (1958). Review of A. E. R. Boak, *Manpower shortage and the fall of the Roman Empire in the West* (1955). *Journal of Roman Studies* 48, pp. 156–164.

――――. (1973). *The ancient economy*. London.

――――. (1975). "Utopianism ancient and modern." In *The use and abuse of history*, pp. 178–192, 240–242. London.

――――. (1978). "Empire in the Greco-Roman world." *Greece and Rome* 25, pp. 1–15.

Fishwick, D. (1978). "The development of provincial ruler worship in the western Roman Empire." In *Aufstieg und Niedergang der römischen Welt*, vol. II.16.2, ed. W. Haase, pp. 1201–1253. Berlin.

Flam-Zuckermann, L. (1970). "A propos d'une inscription de Suisse (CIL xiii. 5010): Etude du phénomène du brigandage dans l'Empire romain." *Latomus* 29, pp. 451–473.

Fleuriot, L. (1974). "Sur quelques textes gaulois: Deux formules de Marcellus de Bordeaux." *Etudes celtiques* 14, pp. 57–66.

Fontaine, J. (1961). "Verité et fiction dans la chronologie de la *Vita Martini*." In *Saint Martin et son temps. Studia Anselmiana* 46, pp. 189–236.

――――. (1963a). "Une clé littéraire de la *Vita Martini* de Sulpice Sévère: La typologie prophétique." In *Mélanges offerts à Mlle. Christine Mohrmann*, pp. 84–95. Utrecht and Anvers.

――――. (1963b). "Sulpice Sévère a-t-il travesti Saint Martin de Tours en martyr militaire?" *Analecta Bollandiana* 81, pp. 31–58.

———. (1967–1969), ed. and trans. *Sulpice Sévère, Vie de Saint Martin. SChr.* 133–135. 3 vols. Paris.

———. (1968). "Hilaire et Martin." In *Hilaire de Poitiers: Evêque et docteur*, pp. 59–86. Paris.

———. (1972). "Valeurs antiques et valeurs chrétiennes dans la spiritualité des grands propriétaires terriens à la fin du IV^e siècle occidental." In *Epektasis: Mélanges patristiques offerts au Cardinal Jean Daniélou*, ed. J. Fontaine and C. Kannengiesser, pp. 571–595. Paris.

———. (1974). "Société et culture chrétiennes sur l'aire circumpyrénéenne au siècle de Theodose." *Bulletin de litterature ecclésiastique* 75, pp. 241–282.

———. (1975). "L'affaire Priscillien ou l'ère des nouveaux Catilina: Observations sur le 'Sallustianisme' de Sulpice Sévère." In *Classica et Iberica. A festschrift in honor of the Reverend Joseph M. F. Marique, S.J.*, ed. P. T. Brannan, pp. 355–392. Worcester, Mass.

———. (1976a). "Hagiographie et politique, de Sulpice Sévère à Venance Fortunat." *Revue d'histoire de l'église de France* 62, pp. 113–140.

———. (1976b). "Romanité et hispanité dans la littérature hispano-romaine des IV^e et V^e siècles." In *Assimilation et résistance à la culture gréco-romaine dans le monde ancien*, ed. D. M. Pippidi. Travaux du VI^e Congrès international d'études classiques, pp. 301–322. Bucharest and Paris.

Fortes, M. (1976). "Forward." In *Social anthropology and medicine*, ed. J. B. Loudon, pp. ix–xx. London and New York.

Fournier, P. F. (1955). "La persistance du gaulois au VI^e siècle d'après Grégoire de Tours." In *Recueil de travaux offert à M. Clovis Brunel*, vol. I, pp. 448–453. Paris.

Frayn, J. M. (1974). "Subsistence farming in Italy during the Roman period: A preliminary discussion of the evidence." *Greece and Rome* 21, pp. 11–18.

Frend, W. H. C. (1952). *The Donatist church.* Oxford.

———. (1953). "The Gnostic-Manichaean tradition in Roman North Africa." *Journal of Ecclesiastical History* 4, pp. 13–26.

———. (1961). "The Roman Empire in the eyes of Western schismatics during the fourth century A.D." In *Miscellanea historiae ecclesiasticae = Bibliothèque de la Revue d'histoire ecclésiastique*, fasc. 38, pp. 9–22. Louvain.

———. (1965). *Martyrdom and persecution in the early church.* Oxford.

———. (1969). "Paulinus of Nola and the last century of the western empire." *Journal of Roman Studies* 59, pp. 1–11.

Funke, H. (1967). "Majestäts- und Magieprozesse bei Ammianus Marcellinus." *Jahrbuch für Antike und Christentum* 10, pp. 145–175.

Gager, J. G. (1975). *Kingdom and community: The social world of early Christianity.* Englewood Cliffs, N.J.

de Gaiffier, B. (1952). "S. Venance Fortunat, évêque de Poitiers: Les témoignages de son culte." *Analecta Bollandiana* 70, pp. 262–284.

———. (1954). "La lecture des Actes des martyrs dans la prière liturgique en Occident: A propos du passionnaire hispanique." *Analecta Bollandiana* 72, pp. 134–166.

———. (1970). "Hagiographie et historiographie." In *La storiografia altomedievale.*

Settimane di studio del Centro italiano di studi sull'Alto Medioevo 17, pp. 139–166. Spoleto.

———. (1976). "Priscillien mentionné dans le martyrologe hiéronymien?" *Analecta Bollandiana* 94, p. 234.

Galletier, E. (1949–1955), ed. and trans. *Panégyriques latins*. 3 vols. Paris.

Galliou, P. (1981). "Western Gaul in the third century." In *The Roman West in the third century: Contributions from archaeology and history*, ed. A. King and M. Henig. BAR International Series 109, pp. 259–286. Oxford.

García y Bellido, A. (1959). "El elemento forastero en Hispania romana." *Boletín de la real Academia de la historia* 144, pp. 119–154.

Gasnault, P. (1961). "Le tombeau de Saint Martin et les invasions normandes dans l'histoire et dans la legende." *Revue d'histoire de l'église de France* 47, pp. 51–66.

Gaudemet, J. (1958). *L'église dans l'empire romain (IV^e – V^e siècles)*. Paris.

Gauthier, N. (1980). *L'évangélisation des pays de la Moselle: La province romaine de Première Belgique entre Antiquité et Moyen-Age (III^e – VIII^e siècles)*. Paris.

Gautier Dalché, P. (1982). "La représentation de l'espace dans les *Libri Miraculorum* de Grégoire de Tours." *Le Moyen Age* 88, pp. 397–420.

Geary, P. J. (1978). *Furta sacra: Thefts of relics in the central Middle Ages*. Princeton.

———. (1979). "L'humiliation des saints." *Annales: é.s.c.* 34, pp. 27–42.

Geertz, C. (1968). *Islam observed: Religious development in Morocco and Indonesia*. Chicago.

———. (1975a). "Ethos, world view, and the analysis of sacred symbols." In *The interpretation of cultures*, pp. 126–141. London.

———. (1975b). "Religion as a cultural system." In *The interpretation of cultures*, pp. 87–125. London.

———. (1977). "Centers, kings and charisma: Reflections on the symbolics of power." In *Culture and its creators: Essays in honor of Edward Shils*, ed. J. Ben-David and T. N. Clark, pp. 150–171. Chicago.

Geertz, H. (1975). "An anthropology of religion and magic, I." *Journal of Interdisciplinary History* 6, pp. 71–89.

Gellner, E. (1977). "Patrons and clients." In *Patrons and clients in Mediterranean societies*, ed. E. Gellner and J. Waterbury, pp. 1–6. London.

van Gennep, A. (1960). *The rites of passage*. English translation: London.

Gessel, W. (1970). "Germanus von Auxerre (um 378 bis 448): Die Vita des Konstantius von Lyon als homiletische Paränese in hagiographischer Form." *Römische Quartalschrift* 65, pp. 1–14.

Gilliard, F. D. (1979). "The senators of sixth-century Gaul." *Speculum* 54, pp. 685–697.

Girardet, K. (1974). "Trier 385. Der Prozess gegen die Priszillianer." *Chiron* 4, pp. 577–608.

Goffart, W. (1957). "Byzantine policy in the West under Tiberius II and Maurice: The pretenders Hermenegild and Gundovald (579–585)." *Traditio* 13, pp. 73–118.

———. (1982). "Old and new in Merovingian taxation." *Past and Present* 96, pp. 3–21.

Goldschmidt, R. C. (1940). *Paulinus' churches at Nola*. Amsterdam.

Goody, J. (1968). "Introduction." In *Literacy in traditional societies*, ed. J. Goody, pp. 1–26. Cambridge.

Gorce, D. (1925). *La lectio divina*. Paris.

Gordon, R. L. (1976). "The sacred geography of a mithraeum: The example of Sette Sfere." *Journal of Mithraic Studies* 1, pp. 119–165.

Goubert, P. (1955). *Byzance avant l'Islam*. Vol. II.1, *Byzance et les Francs*. Paris.

Grabar, A. (1946). *Martyrium. Recherches sur le culte des reliques et l'art chrétien antique*. 2 vols. Paris.

Graus, F. (1965). *Volk, Herrscher und Heiliger im Reich der Merowinger*. Prague.

Green, R. P. H. (1978). "Prosopographical notes on the family and friends of Ausonius." *Bulletin of the Institute of Classical Studies of the University of London* 25, pp. 19–27.

Grenier, A. (1905). "La transhumance des troupeaux en Italie et son rôle dans l'histoire romaine." *Mélanges d'archéologie et d'histoire* 25, pp. 293–328.

Gricourt, J. (1967). "Trésor de monnaies romaines de Noyelles-Godault (Pas-de-Calais). Carausius et Allectus en Gaule." *Revue des études anciennes* 69, pp. 228–254.

Griffe, E. (1956). "L'apocryphe hiéronymien 'De septem ordinibus ecclesiae.'" *Bulletin de littérature ecclésiastique* 57, pp. 215–224.

———. (1961). "Saint Martin et le monachisme gaulois." In *Saint Martin et son temps*. Studia Anselmiana 46, pp. 3–24.

———. (1964–1966). *La Gaule chrétienne à l'époque romaine*. 3 vols. Paris.

Grondijs, L. (1952). "Une église manichéenne en Espagne." *Comptes rendus de l'Académie des inscriptions et belles-lettres*, pp. 490–497.

Grosjean, P. (1957). "Notes d'hagiographie celtique: 28. La seconde visite de S. Germain d'Auxerre en Grande-Bretagne; 29. Le dernier voyage de S. Germain d'Auxerre." *Analecta Bollandiana* 75, pp. 174–185.

Günther, R. (1965). "Revolution und Evolution im weströmischen Reich zur Zeit der Spätantike." *Zeitschrift für Geschichtswissenschaft*, Sonderheft 13, pp. 19–34.

Gussone, N. (1976). "Adventus-Zeremoniell und Translation von Reliquien: Victricius von Rouen, De laude sanctorum." *Frühmittelalterliche Studien* 10, pp. 125–133.

Hahn, I. (1962). "Die soziale Utopie der Spätantike." *Wissenschaftliche Zeitschrift der Martin-Luther-Universität Halle-Wittenberg* 11, pp. 1357–1361.

Halphen, L. (1925). "Grégoire de Tours, historien de Clovis." In *Mélanges d'histoire du Moyen Age offerts à M. Ferdinand Lot*, pp. 235–244. Paris.

Harrison, K. (1976). *The framework of Anglo-Saxon history to A.D. 900*. Cambridge.

Hatt, J. J. (1965). "Essai sur l'evolution de la religion gauloise." *Revue des études anciennes* 67, pp. 80–125.

Havet, J. (1885). "Questions mérovingiennes, II. Les découvertes de Jérôme Vignier." *Bibliothèque de l'École des Chartes* 46, pp. 205–271.

Heinzelmann, M. (1975). "L'aristocratie et les évêches entre Loire et Rhin jusqu'à la fin du VIIᵉ siècle." *Revue d'histoire de l'église de France* 62, pp. 75–90.

———. (1976). *Bischofsherrschaft in Gallien*. Munich.

Hersey, C. K. (1943). "The church of Saint-Martin at Tours (903–1150)." *Art Bulletin* 25, pp. 1–39.

Higounet, C. (1966). "Les forêts de l'Europe occidentale du V^e au XI^e siècle." In *Agricoltura e mondo rurale in Occidente nell'Alto Medioevo*. Settimane di studio del Centro italiano di studi sull'Alto Medioevo 13, pp. 343–398. Spoleto.

Hilton, R. H. (1976), ed. *Peasants, knights and heretics*. Cambridge.

Hobsbawm, E. J. (1959). *Primitive rebels*. Manchester.

———. (1969). *Bandits*. Harmondsworth.

Hoepffner, A. (1948). "Les deux procès du pape Damase." *Revue des études anciennes* 50, pp. 288–304.

Holum, K. G. and G. Vikan (1979). "The Trier ivory, *adventus* ceremonial, and the relics of St. Stephen." *Dumbarton Oaks Papers* 33, pp. 113–133.

Hopkins, K. (1961). "Social mobility in the later Roman Empire: The evidence of Ausonius." *Classical Quarterly*, n.s. 11, pp. 239–249.

———. (1978). "Divine emperors or the symbolic unity of the Roman Empire." In *Conquerors and slaves: Sociological studies in Roman history*, vol. I, pp. 197–242. Cambridge.

———. (1980). "Taxes and trade in the Roman Empire (200 B.C.–A.D. 400)." *Journal of Roman Studies* 70, pp. 101–125.

Horne, P. (1981). "Romano-Celtic temples in the third century." In *The Roman West in the third century: Contributions from archaeology and history*, ed. A. King and M. Henig. BAR International Series 109, pp. 21–26. Oxford.

Horton, R. (1970). "African traditional thought and Western science." In *Rationality*, ed. B. R. Wilson, pp. 131–171. Oxford.

Hubert, J. (1938). *L'art pré-roman*. Paris.

———. (1977). *Arts et vie sociale de la fin du monde antique au Moyen Age*. Geneva.

Huizinga, J. (1924). *The waning of the Middle Ages*. English translation: New York.

Hunt, E. D. (1972). "St. Silvia of Aquitaine: The role of a Theodosian pilgrim in the society of East and West." *Journal of Theological Studies*, n.s. 23, pp. 351–373.

———. (1982). "St. Stephen in Minorca: An episode in Jewish-Christian relations in the early 5th century A.D." *Journal of Theological Studies*, n.s. 33, pp. 106–123.

Jankowski, N. (1967). "Das gallische Gegenreich (259–274 n. Chr.) und seine soziale Basis im Spiegel der Historia Augusta." *Helikon* 7, pp. 125–194.

Jones, A. H. M. (1963). "The social background of the struggle between paganism and Christianity." In *The conflict between paganism and Christianity in the fourth century*, ed. A. Momigliano, pp. 17–37. Oxford.

———. (1964). *The later Roman Empire*. Oxford and Norman, Okla.

Jullian, C. (1910). "Notes gallo-romaines, XLVII: La jeunesse de Saint Martin." *Revue des études anciennes* 12, pp. 260–280.

———. (1920a). "Notes gallo-romaines, LXXXV: Questions hagiographiques: La légion thébaine." *Revue des études anciennes* 22, pp. 41–47.

———. (1920b). "Notes gallo-romaines, LXXXVI: Castrum Bagaudarum, les origines de Saint-Maur-des-Fossés." *Revue des études anciennes* 22, pp. 107–116.

———. (1922). "Notes gallo-romaines, XCIII–XCIV–XCV: Remarques critiques sur les sources de la Vie de Saint Martin." *Revue des études anciennes* 24, pp. 37–47, 123–128, 229–235.

———. (1922–1923). "Notes gallo-romaines, XCVI–XCVII–XCVIII–XCIX: Remarques critiques sur la vie et l'oeuvre de Saint Martin." *Revue des études anciennes* 24, pp. 306–312; and 25, pp. 49–55, 139–143, 234–250.

Jungblut, J. B. (1977). "Recherches sur le 'rythme oratoire' dans les 'Historiarum libri.'" In *Gregorio di Tours*. Convegni del Centro di studi sulla spiritualità medievale XII, pp. 325–364. Todi.

Jungmann, J. A. (1952–1958). *Missarum solemnia: Explication génétique de la messe romaine*. 3 vols. Paris.

Kaden, E. H. (1953). "Die Edikte gegen die Manichaër von Diokletian bis Justinian." In *Festschrift Hans Lewald*, pp. 55–68. Basel.

Kantorowicz, E. H. (1946). *Laudes regiae: A study in liturgical acclamations and mediaeval ruler worship*. Berkeley and Los Angeles.

Kelly, J. N. D. (1975). *Jerome*. London.

King, P. D. (1972). *Law and society in the Visigothic kingdom*. Cambridge.

Koeppel, G. (1969). "Profectio und Adventus." *Bonner Jahrbücher* 169, pp. 130–194.

Kolendo, J. (1970). "La chronologie des guerres contre les Germains au cours des dernières années de la tétrarchie." *Klio* 52, pp. 197–203.

Korsunski, A. R. (1961). Summary: "Die Bewegung der Bagauden." *Bibliotheca classica orientalis* 6, pp. 82–89.

v.Kraemer, E. (1950). *Les maladies désignées par le nom d'un saint*. Societas Scientiarum Fennica, Commentationes humanarum litterarum 15.2. Helsinki.

Krusch, B. (1920). "Chronologica regum Francorum stirpis merowingicae, catalogi, computationes annorum vetustae cum commentariis." *MGH*, SRM 7, pp. 468–516. Hannover and Leipzig.

———. (1951). "Gregorii episcopi Turonensis decem libri historiarum. Praefatio." *MGH*, SRM 1.1, editio altera, fasc. III, pp. IX–XXII. Hannover.

Kurth, G. (1919). *Etudes franques*. 2 vols. Paris and Brussels.

deLabriolle, P. (1911). "Mulieres in ecclesia taceant: Un aspect de la lutte antimontaniste." *Bulletin d'ancienne littérature et d'archéologie chrétiennes* 1, pp. 3–24, 103–122.

Lacarra, J. M! (1945). "Textos navarros del Códice de Roda, k) De laude Pampilona epistola." *Estudios de edad media de la Corona de Aragón, sección de Zaragoza* 1, pp. 266–270.

Ladner, G. B. (1967). "Homo viator: Mediaeval ideas on alienation and order." *Speculum* 42, pp. 233–259.

Lagarrigue, G. (1971–1975), ed. and trans. *Salvien de Marseille, Oeuvres*. SChr. 176, 220. 2 vols. Paris.

Landsberger, H. A. (1974). "Peasant unrest: Themes and variations." In *Rural protest: Peasant movements and social change*, ed. H. A. Landsberger, pp. 1–64. London.

Langlois, P. (1969). "Les poemes chrétiens et le christianisme d'Ausone." *Revue de philologie* 43, pp. 39–58.

Latouche, R. (1963). "Quelques réflexions sur la psychologie de Grégoire de Tours." *Le Moyen Age* 69, pp. 7–15.

Lauffer, S. (1971). *Diokletians Preisedikt*. Berlin.

Leach, E. (1972). "Melchisedech and the emperor: Icons of subversion and orthodoxy." *Proceedings of the Royal Anthropological Institute*, pp. 5–14.

LeBlant, E. (1892), ed. *Nouveau recueil des inscriptions chrétiennes de la Gaule antérieures au VIII^e siècle*. Paris.

Leclercq, J. (1949). "Sermon ancien sur les danses déshonnêtes." *Revue Bénédictine* 59, pp. 196–201.

———. (1961). "S. Martin dans l'hagiographie monastique du Moyen Age." In *Saint Martin et son temps. Studia Anselmiana* 46, pp. 175–187.

———. (1963). "L'Ecriture Sainte dans l'hagiographie monastique du haut Moyen Age." In *La Bibbia nell'Alto Medioevo*. Settimane di studio del Centro italiano di studi sull'Alto Medioevo 10, pp. 103–128. Spoleto.

LeGentilhomme, P. (1943). "Le désastre d'Autun en 269." *Revue des études anciennes* 45, pp. 233–240.

Le Goff, J. (1980). *Time, work and culture in the Middle Ages*. English translation: Chicago.

Lelong, C. (1960). "De l'importance du pèlerinage de Tours au VI^e siècle." *Bulletin trimestriel de la Société archéologique de Touraine* 32, pp. 232–237.

———. (1965). "Evolution de la topographie religieuse de Tours du IV^e au VI^e siècle." *Bulletin trimestriel de la Société archéologique de Touraine* 34, pp. 169–185.

Lesne, E. (1910). *Histoire de la propriété ecclésiastique en France*. Vol. I, *La propriété ecclésiastique aux époques romaine et mérovingienne*. Paris.

Lestocquoy, J. (1953). "De l'unité à la pluralité: Le paysage urbain en Gaule du V^e au IX^e siècle." *Annales: é.s.c.* 8, pp. 159–172.

Lesueur, F. (1949). "Saint-Martin de Tours et les origines de l'art roman." *Bulletin monumental* 107, pp. 7–84.

Levillain, L. (1933). "La crise des années 507–508 et les rivalités d'influence en Gaule de 508 à 514." In *Mélanges offerts à M. Nicolas Iorga*, pp. 537–567. Paris.

Levison, W. (1904). "Bischof Germanus von Auxerre und die Quellen zu seiner Geschichte." *Neues Archiv der Gesellschaft für altere deutsche Geschichtskunde* 29, pp. 95–175.

Levy, R. (1957). *The social structure of Islam*. 2nd ed. Cambridge.

Lewin, L. (1979). "The oligarchical limitations of social banditry in Brazil: The case of the 'good' thief Antonio Silvino." *Past and Present* 82, pp. 116–146.

Lewis, G. (1976). "A view of sickness in New Guinea." In *Social anthropology and medicine*, ed. J. B. Loudon, pp. 49–103. London and New York.

Lewuillon, S. (1975). "Histoire, société et lutte des classes en Gaule: Une féodalité à la fin de la république et au debut de l'empire." In *Aufstieg und Niedergang der römischen Welt*, vol. II.4, ed. H. Temporini, pp. 425–583. Berlin.

Lienhard, J. T. (1977). *Paulinus of Nola and early Western monasticism*. Cologne and Bonn.

Longnon, A. (1878). *Géographie de la Gaule au VI^e siècle*. Paris.

Loriot, X. (1975). "Les premières années de la grande crise du III^e siècle: De l'avènement de Maximin le Thrace (235) à la mort de Gordien III (244)." In *Aufstieg und Niedergang der römischen Welt*, vol. II.2, ed. H. Temporini, pp. 657–787. Berlin.

Lot, F. (1928). "Du régime de l'hospitalité." *Revue belge de philologie et d'histoire* 7, pp. 975–1011.

———. (1929). "La *Vita Viviani* et la domination visigothique en Aquitaine." In *Mélanges Paul Fournier*, pp. 467–477. Paris.

———. (1931). "A quelle époque a-t-on cessé de parler Latin?" *Bulletin du Cange: Archivum Latinitatis Medii Aevi* 6, pp. 97–159.

———. (1938). "La victoire sur les Alamans et la conversion de Clovis." *Revue belge de philologie et d'histoire* 17, pp. 63–69.

Louis, R. (1950). "L'église d'Auxerre et ses évêques avant Saint Germain." In *Saint Germain d'Auxerre et son temps*, pp. 39–88. Auxerre.

Loyen, A. (1942). *Recherches historiques sur les panégyriques de Sidoine Apollinaire.* Paris.

———. (1943). *Sidoine Apollinaire et l'esprit précieux en Gaul aux derniers jours de l'empire.* Paris.

———. (1956). "Sidoine Apollinaire et les derniers éclats de la culture classique dans la Gaule occupée par les Goths." In *I Goti in Occidente*. Settimane di studio del Centro italiano di studi sull'Alto Medioevo 3, pp. 265–284. Spoleto.

———. (1969). "Le rôle de Saint Aignan dans la défense d'Orléans." *Comptes rendus de l'Académie des inscriptions et belles-lettres*, pp. 64–74.

MacCormack, S. (1972). "Change and continuity in Late Antiquity: The ceremony of adventus." *Historia* 21, pp. 721–752.

———. (1975). "Latin prose panegyrics." In *Empire and aftermath: Silver Latin II*, ed. T. A. Dorey, pp. 143–205. London.

———. (1981). *Art and ceremony in Late Antiquity.* Berkeley and Los Angeles.

MacGonagle, S. H. (1936). *The poor in Gregory of Tours.* New York.

MacIntyre, A. (1973/74). "Ancient politics and modern issues." *Arion*, n.s. 1/2, pp. 425–430.

MacMullen, R. (1963). "The Roman concept robber-pretender." *Revue internationale des droits de l'antiquité*, ser. 3, 10, pp. 221–225.

———. (1965). "The Celtic renaissance." *Historia* 14, pp. 93–104.

———. (1966a). "A note on *sermo humilis*." *Journal of Theological Studies*, n.s. 17, pp. 108–112.

———. (1966b). "Provincial languages in the Roman Empire." *American Journal of Philology* 87, pp. 1–17.

———. (1967). *Enemies of the Roman order.* Cambridge, Mass.

———. (1974). *Roman social relations 50 B.C. to A.D. 284.* New Haven and London.

———. (1976). *Roman government's response to crisis A.D. 235–337.* New Haven.

Maddicott, J. R. (1978). "The birth and setting of the ballads of Robin Hood." *English Historical Review* 93, pp. 276–299.

Madoz, J. (1941). "Un nueva redacción del 'Libellus de fide' de Baquiario." *Revista española de teología* 1, pp. 457–488.

Maillé, Marquise de (1959). *Recherches sur les origines chrétiennes de Bordeaux.* Paris.

Marignan, A. (1899). *Etudes sur la civilisation française.* 2 vols. Paris.

Markus, R. A. (1972). "Christianity and dissent in Roman North Africa: Changing perspectives in recent work." In *Schism, heresy and religious protest*, ed. D. Baker. *Studies in Church History* 9, pp. 21–36. Cambridge.

———. (1978). "The cult of icons in sixth-century Gaul." *Journal of Theological Studies*, n.s. 29, pp. 151–157.

Marrou, H. I. (1951/52). "Ammien Marcellin et les 'Innocents' de Milan." *Recherches de science religieuse* 40, pp. 179–190.

———. (1954). "Un lieu dit 'Cité de Dieu.'" In *Augustinus Magister*, vol. I, pp. 101–110. Paris.

———. (1965). *Histoire de l'éducation dans l'antiquité*. 6th ed. Paris.

———. (1966). "Hérétiques fantômes: Les Amétrites (sur un texte de Filastre de Brescia)." In *Mélanges d'archéologie et d'histoire offerts à André Piganiol*, ed. R. Chevallier, vol. III, pp. 1645–1651. Paris.

———. (1970). "Le dossier épigraphique de l'évêque Rusticus de Narbonne." *Rivista di archeologia cristiana* 46, pp. 331–349.

Marwick, M. G. (1965). "Some problems in the sociology of sorcery and witchcraft." In *African systems of thought*, ed. M. Fortes and G. Dieterlen, pp. 171–188. Oxford.

———. (1970). "Witchcraft as a social strain-gauge." In *Witchcraft and sorcery*, ed. M. G. Marwick, pp. 280–295. Harmondsworth.

Mathisen, R. W. (1979a). "Hilarius, Germanus and Lupus: The aristocratic background of the Chelidonius affair." *Phoenix* 33, pp. 160–169.

———. (1979b). "Resistance and reconciliation: Majorian and the Gallic aristocracy after the fall of Avitus." *Francia* 7, pp. 597–627.

———. (1979c). "Sidonius on the reign of Avitus: A study in political prudence." *Transactions of the American Philological Association* 109, pp. 165–171.

———. (1981a). "Avitus, Italy and the East in A.D. 455–456." *Byzantion* 51, pp. 232–247.

———. (1981b). "The last year of Saint Germanus of Auxerre." *Analecta Bollandiana* 99, pp. 151–159.

Matthews, J. (1971). "Gallic supporters of Theodosius." *Latomus* 30, pp. 1073–1099.

———. (1975). *Western aristocracies and imperial court, A.D. 364–425*. Oxford.

Max, G. E. (1979). "Political intrigue during the reigns of the western Roman emperors Avitus and Majorian." *Historia* 28, pp. 225–237.

McClure, J. (1979). "Handbooks against heresy in the West, from the late fourth to the late sixth centuries." *Journal of Theological Studies* n.s. 30, pp. 186–197.

McDermott, W. C. (1975). "Felix of Nantes: A Merovingian bishop." *Traditio* 31, pp. 1–24.

van der Mensbrugghe, A. (1962). "Pseudo-Germanus reconsidered." *Studia Patristica* 5 = *Texte und Untersuchungen* 80, pp. 172–184.

Meslin, M. (1964). "Nationalisme, état et religions à la fin du IVᵉ siècle." *Archives de sociologie des religions* 18, pp. 3–20.

———. (1969). "Persistances païennes en Galice, vers la fin du VIᵉ siècle." In *Hommages à Marcel Renard*, ed. J. Bibauw, vol. II, pp. 512–524. Brussels.

Millar, F. (1977). *The emperor in the Roman world (31 B.C.–A.D. 337)*. London.

Minor, C. E. (1975). "'Bagaudae' or 'Bacaudae'?" *Traditio* 31, pp. 318–322.

Momigliano, A. (1963a). "Christianity and the decline of the Roman Empire." In *The conflict between paganism and Christianity in the fourth century*, ed. A. Momigliano, pp. 1–16. Oxford.

———. (1963b). "Pagan and Christian historiography in the fourth century A.D."

In *The conflict between paganism and Christianity in the fourth century*, ed. A. Momigliano, pp. 79–99. Oxford.

———. (1966a). "Cassiodorus and Italian culture of his time." In *Studies in historiography*, pp. 181–210. New York.

———. (1966b). "M. I. Rostovtzeff." In *Studies in historiography*, pp. 91–104. New York.

———. (1972). "Popular religious beliefs and the late Roman historians." In *Popular belief and practice*, ed. G. J. Cuming and D. Baker. Studies in Church History 8, pp. 1–18. Cambridge.

———. (1979–1980). "Declines and falls." *American Scholar* (winter issue), pp. 37–50.

Monod, G. (1872). *Etudes critiques sur les sources de l'histoire mérovingienne*, vol. I. Paris.

Moore, R. I. (1976). "Heresy as disease." In *The concept of heresy in the Middle Ages (11th–13th c.)*, ed. W. Lourdaux and D. Verhelst. Proceedings of the International Conference, Louvain, May 13–16, 1973, pp. 1–11. Louvain and The Hague.

Morin, G. (1913). "Pro Instantio, contre l'attribution à Priscillien des opuscules du manuscrit de Wurzbourg." *Revue Bénédictine* 30, pp. 153–173.

———. (1928a). "Pages inédites de deux pseudo-Jérômes des environs de l'an 400, I. Deux lettres mystiques d'une ascète espagnole." *Revue Bénédictine* 40, pp. 289–310.

———. (1928b). "Pages inédites de deux pseudo-Jérômes des environs de l'an 400, II. Portion inédite de l'apocryphe hiéronymien *De septem ordinibus ecclesiae*." *Revue Bénédictine* 40, pp. 310–318.

Moss, J. R. (1973). "The effects of the policies of Aetius on the history of western Europe." *Historia* 22, pp. 711–731.

Moussy, C. (1974), ed. and trans. *Paulin de Pella, Poème d'action de grâces et Prière.* SChr. 209. Paris.

Musset, L. (1976). "De Saint Victrice à Saint Ouen: La christianisation de la province de Rouen d'après l'hagiographie." *Revue d'histoire de l'église de France* 62, pp. 141–152.

Nock, A. D. (1933). *Conversion.* Oxford.

Norberg, D. (1954). *La poesie latine rythmique du haut Moyen Age.* Stockholm.

———. (1966). "A quelle époque a-t-on cessé de parler Latin en Gaule?" *Annales: é.s.c.* 21, pp. 346–356.

O'Donnell, J. J. (1979). *Cassiodorus.* Berkeley and Los Angeles.

Oldoni, M. (1972). "Gregorio di Tours e i 'Libri historiarum': Letture e fonti, metodi e ragioni." *Studi medievali*, 3rd ser., 13, pp. 563–700.

Palanque, J. R. (1934). "La date du transfert de la préfecture des Gaules de Trèves à Arles." *Revue des études anciennes* 36, pp. 359–365.

———. (1965). "L'empereur Maxime." In *Les empereurs romains d'Espagne.* Actes du Colloque international du Centre national de la recherche scientifique, Madrid 1964, pp. 255–263, and discussion, pp. 263–267. Paris.

————. (1973). "Du nouveau sur la date du transfert de la préfecture des Gaules de Trèves à Arles?" *Provence historique* 23, pp. 29–38.

Passelac, M. (1972). "Le bronze d'applique de Fendeille." *Revue archéologique de Narbonnaise* 5, pp. 185–190.

Peebles, B. M. (1961). "An early 'Laudatio Sancti Martini': A text completed." In *Saint Martin et son temps. Studia Anselmiana* 46, pp. 237–249.

Pelikan, J. (1971). *The emergence of the Catholic tradition (100–600).* Chicago and London.

————. (1978). *The growth of medieval theology (600–1300).* Chicago and London.

Percival, J. (1969). "Seigneurial aspects of late Roman estate management." *English Historical Review* 84, pp. 449–473.

Peters, E. (1975), ed. *Monks, bishops and pagans.* Philadelphia.

von Petrikovits, H. (1971). "Fortifications in the north-western Roman Empire from the third to the fifth centuries A.D.." *Journal of Roman Studies* 61, pp. 178–218 plus map.

Pietri, C. (1961). "Concordia apostolorum et renovatio urbis (culte des martyrs et propagande pontificale)." *Mélanges d'archéologie et d'histoire* 73, pp. 275–322.

————. (1976). "Remarques sur la topographie chrétienne des cités de la Gaule entre Loire et Rhin (des origines au VII^e siècle)." *Revue d'histoire de l'église de France* 62, pp. 189–204.

Pietri, L. (1970). "La conversion en Belgique seconde d'un ancien officier de l'armée de Julien, Jovin." *Revue du Nord* 52, pp. 443–453.

————. (1974). "Les tituli de la basilique Saint-Martin édifiée à Tours par l'évêque Perpetuus (3^e quart du V^e siècle)." In *Mélanges d'histoire ancienne offerts à William Seston,* pp. 419–431. Paris.

————. (1976). "Bâtiments et sanctuaires annexes de la basilique Saint-Martin de Tours, à la fin du VI^e siècle." *Revue d'histoire de l'église de France* 62, pp. 223–234.

————. (1977). "Le pèlerinage martinien de Tours à l'époque de l'évêque Grégoire." In *Gregorio di Tours.* Convegni del Centro di studi sulla spiritualità medievale XII, pp. 93–139. Todi.

————. (1982). "La succession des premiers évêques tourangeaux: Essai sur la chronologie de Grégoire de Tours." *Mélanges de l'Ecole française de Rome, Moyen Age–Temps modernes* 94, pp. 551–619.

Pijoán, J. (1954). *Summa artis: Historia general del arte,* vol. VIII. Madrid.

dePlinval, G. (1950). "Les campagnes de Saint Germain en Grande-Bretagne contre les Pélagiens." In *Saint Germain d'Auxerre et son temps,* pp. 135–149. Auxerre.

Pounds, N. J. G. (1969). "The urbanization of the classical world." *Annals of the Association of American Geographers* 59, pp. 135–157.

Prinz, F. (1965). *Frühes Mönchtum im Frankenreich* (Munich and Vienne).

————. (1967). "Heiligenkult und Adelscherrschaft im Spiegel merowingischer Hagiographie." *Historische Zeitschrift* 204, pp. 529–544.

————. (1973). "Die bischöfliche Stadterrschaft im Frankenreich vom 5. bis zum 7. Jahrhundert." *Historische Zeitschrift* 217, pp. 1–35.

————. (1975). "Aristocracy and Christianity in Merovingian Gaul: An essay." In *Gesellschaft, Kultur, Literatur. Beiträge L. Wallach gewidmet,* ed. K. Bosl, pp. 153–165. Stuttgart.

Puech, H. C. (1949). *Le Manichéisme, son fondateur, sa doctrine*. Paris.

Quasten, J. (1934), ed. *Expositio antiquae liturgiae gallicanae Germano Parisiensi ascripta*. Munster.
———. (1950). *Patrology*. Vol. I, *The beginnings of patristic literature*. Utrecht and Antwerp.

Rebuffat, R. (1974). "Enceintes urbaines et insécurité en Maurétanie Tingitane." *Mélanges de l'Ecole française de Rome*, Antiquité 86, pp. 501–522.
Reece, R. (1981). "The third century: Crisis or change." In *The Roman West in the third century: Contributions from archaeology and history*, ed. A. King and M. Henig. BAR International Series 109, pp. 27–38. Oxford.
Reydellet, M. (1977). "Pensée et pratique politiques chez Grégoire de Tours." In *Gregorio di Tours*. Convegni del Centro di studi sulla spiritualità medievale XII, pp. 171–205. Todi.
Reynolds, R. E. (1970). "The pseudo-Hieronymian 'De septem ordinibus ecclesiae': Notes on its origins, abridgements and use in early medieval canonical collections." *Revue Bénédictine* 80, pp. 238–252.
Rice, D. T. (1965), ed. *The dark ages*. London.
Riché, P. (1953). "Le Psautier, livre de lecture élémentaire d'après les vies des saints mérovingiens." In *Etudes mérovingiennes*, pp. 253–256. Paris.
———. (1957). "La survivance des écoles publiques en Gaule au V<sup>e</sup> siècle." *Le Moyen Age* 63, pp. 421–436.
———. (1962). *Education et culture dans l'Occident barbare VI<sup>e</sup>–VIII<sup>e</sup> siècles*. Paris.
———. (1976). "Les représentations du palais dans les textes littéraires du haut Moyen Age." *Francia* 4, pp. 161–171.
Ries, J. (1957, 1959). "Introduction aux études manichéennes: Quatre siècles de recherches." *Ephemerides Theologicae Lovanienses* 33, pp. 453–482; and 35, pp. 362–409.
———. (1964). "Jésus-Christ dans la religion de Mani. Quelques éléments d'une confrontation de Saint Augustin avec un hymnaire christologique manichéen copte." *Augustiniana* 14, pp. 437–454.
Roberts, J. T. (1980). "Gregory of Tours and the monk of St. Gall: The paratactic style of medieval Latin." *Latomus* 39, pp. 173–190.
Ropert [*sic*] (1976). "Mentalité religieuse et régression culturelle dans la Gaule franque, du V<sup>e</sup> au VIII<sup>e</sup> siècle." *Cahiers de Tunisie* 24, pp. 45–68.
Rosaldo, M. Z. (1974). "Woman, culture, and society: A theoretical overview." In *Woman, culture and society*, ed. M. Z. Rosaldo and L. Lamphere, pp. 17–42. Stanford.
Rosenwein, B. H. (1978). "St. Odo's St. Martin: The uses of a model." *Journal of Medieval History* 4, pp. 317–331.
Rostovtzeff, M. (1957). *The social and economic history of the Roman Empire*, 2nd ed. Oxford.
Rouche, M. (1977). "Francs et Gallo-Romains chez Grégoire de Tours." In *Gregorio di Tours*. Convegni del Centro di studi sulla spiritualità medievale XII, pp. 141–169. Todi.
Rougé, J. (1966). "L'Histoire Auguste et l'Isaurie au IV<sup>e</sup> siècle." *Revue des études anciennes* 68, pp. 282–315.

Rousseau, P. (1976). "In search of Sidonius the bishop." *Historia* 25, pp. 356–377.
———. (1978). *Ascetics, authority, and the Church in the age of Jerome and Cassian.* Oxford.
Rousselle-Esteve, A. (1971). "Deux examples d'evangelisation en Gaule à la fin du IV$^e$ siècle: Paulin de Nole et Sulpice Sévère." In *Béziers et le Biterrois*, pp. 91–98. Montpellier.
Rousselle, A. (1974). "Abstinence et continence dans les monastères de Gaule méridionale à la fin de l'Antiquité et au début du Moyen Age. Etude d'un régime alimentaire et de sa fonction." In *Hommages à André Dupont*, pp. 239–254. Montpellier.
———. (1976). "Du sanctuaire au thaumaturge: La guérison en Gaule au IV$^e$ siècle." *Annales: é. s.c.* 31, pp. 1085–1107.

Sáinz Rodríguez, P. (1964). "Estado actual de la cuestión priscilianista." *Anuario de estudios medievales* 1, pp. 653–657.
Salmon, P. (1959). *Les "tituli psalmorum" des manuscrits latins.* Paris.
Sauvel, T. (1956). "Les miracles de Saint Martin: Recherches sur les peintures murales de Tours au V$^e$ et au VI$^e$ siècle." *Bulletin monumental* 114, pp. 153–179.
Sawyer, P. H. (1978). *From Roman Britain to Norman England.* New York.
Schlick, J. (1966). "Composition et chronologie des *De virtutibus sancti Martini* de Grégoire de Tours." *Studia Patristica* 7 = *Texte und Untersuchungen* 92, pp. 278–286.
Schmidt, K. H. (1980). "Gallien und Britannien." In *Die Sprachen im römischen Reich der Kaiserzeit*, ed. G. Neumann and J. Untermann. *Bonner Jahrbücher*, Beiheft 40, pp. 19–44. Cologne.
Schneider, J. (1966). "Die Darstellung der Pauperes in den Historiae Gregors von Tours: Ein Beitrag zur socialökonomischen Struktur Galliens im 6. Jahrhundert." *Jahrbuch für Wirtschaftsgeschichte*, Teil IV, pp. 57–74.
Schönberger, H. (1969). "The Roman frontier in Germany: An archaeological survey." *Journal of Roman Studies* 59, pp. 144–197.
Seston, W. (1940). "De l'authenticité et de la date de l'édit de Diocletien contre les Manichéens." In *Mélanges offerts à Alfred Ernout*, pp. 345–354. Paris.
———. (1946). *Dioclétien et la tétrarchie*, vol. I. Paris.
Setton, K. M. (1941). *Christian attitude towards the emperor in the fourth century.* New York.
Sigal, P. A. (1969). "Maladie, pèlerinage et guérison au XII$^e$ siècle: Les miracles de Saint Gibrien à Reims." *Annales: é. s.c.* 24, pp. 1522–1539.
Simmel, G. (1955). *Conflict.* English translation: Glencoe.
von Simson, O. (1948). *Sacred fortress: Byzantine art and statecraft in Ravenna.* Chicago.
———. (1956). *The Gothic cathedral.* Princeton.
Skultans, V. (1976). "Empathy and healing: Aspects of spiritualist ritual." In *Social anthropology and medicine*, ed. J. B. Loudon, pp. 190–222. London and New York.
Skydsgaard, J. E. (1974). "Transhumance in ancient Italy." *Analecta Romana Instituti Danici* 7, pp. 7–36.
Southall, A. W. (1967). "A note on state organization: Segmentary states in Africa

and in medieval Europe." In *Early medieval society*, ed. S. L. Thrupp, pp. 147–155. New York.

Spain, S. (1977). "The translation of relics ivory, Trier." *Dumbarton Oaks Papers* 31, pp. 279–304.

Stancliffe, C. E. (1979). "From town to country: The christianisation of the Touraine 370–600." In *The church in town and countryside*, ed. D. Baker. *Studies in Church History* 16, pp. 43–59. Oxford.

Steckmesser, K. L. (1966). "Robin Hood and the American outlaw." *Journal of American Folklore* 79, pp. 348–355.

de Ste. Croix, G. E. M. (1954). "Suffragium: From vote to patronage." *British Journal of Sociology* 5, pp. 33–48.

———. (1974). "Why were the early Christians persecuted?" In *Studies in ancient society*, ed. M. I. Finley, pp. 210–249. London.

Stern, H. (1955). "Poésies et représentations carolingiennes et byzantines des mois." *Revue archéologique*, ser. 6, 45, pp. 141–186.

Stevens, C. E. (1933). *Sidonius Apollinaris and his age*. Oxford.

———. (1957). "Marcus, Gratian, Constantine." *Athenaeum* 35, pp. 316–347.

de Stoop, E. (1909). *Essai sur la diffusion du Manichéisme dans l'empire romain*. Gand.

Stroheker, K. F. (1948). *Der senatorische Adel im spätantiken Gallien*. Tubingen. [Numbers refer to people listed in the prosopography, pp. 141–227.]

———. (1965). *Germanentum und Spätantike*. Zurich and Stuttgart.

———. (1972–1974). "Spanien im spätrömischen Reich (284–475)." *Archivo Español de Arqueologia* 45–47, pp. 587–605.

Sundwall, J. (1915). *Weströmische Studien*. Berlin.

Suys, E. (1925). "La sentence portée contre Priscillien (Trèves 385)." *Revue d'histoire ecclésiastique* 21, pp. 530–538.

Syme, R. (1958). *Tacitus*. Oxford.

———. (1971). *Emperors and biography*. Oxford.

Szádeczky-Kardoss, S. (1968). "Bagaudae." *RE* Suppl. XI, col. 346–354. Stuttgart.

Szövérffy, J. (1971). "A la source de l'humanisme chrétien médiéval: 'Romanus' et 'barbarus' chez Vénance Fortunat." *Aevum* 45, pp. 77–86.

Tambiah, S. J. (1973). "Classification of animals in Thailand." In *Rules and meanings*, ed. M. Douglas, pp. 127–166. Harmondsworth.

Tardi, D. (1927). *Fortunat. Etude sur un dernier représentant de la poésie latine dans la Gaule mérovingienne*. Paris.

Theis, L. (1976). "Saints sans famille? Quelque remarques sur la famille dans le monde franc à travers les sources hagiographiques." *Revue historique* 255, pp. 3–20.

Thevenot, E. (1950). "Médecine et religion aux temps gallo-romains: Le traitement des affections de la vue." *Latomus* 9, pp. 415–426.

Thiel, A. (1867), ed. *Epistolae Romanorum pontificum genuinae*, vol. I. Braunsberg.

Thomas, K. (1971). *Religion and the decline of magic*. London.

———. (1975). "An anthropology of religion and magic, II." *Journal of Interdisciplinary History* 6, pp. 91–109.

Thompson, E. A. (1944). "The emperor Julian's knowledge of Latin." *Classical Review* 58, pp. 49–51.

———. (1948). *A history of Attila and the Huns.* Oxford.

———. (1952a). "Peasant revolts in late Roman Gaul and Spain." *Past and Present* 2, pp. 11–23.

———. (1952b). *A Roman reformer and inventor.* Oxford.

———. (1956a). "The settlement of the barbarians in southern Gaul." *Journal of Roman Studies* 46, pp. 65–75.

———. (1956b). "Zosimus on the end of Roman Britain." *Antiquity* 30, pp. 163–167.

———. (1957). "A chronological note on St. Germanus of Auxerre," *Analecta Bollandiana* 75, pp. 135–138.

———. (1966). *The Visigoths in the time of Ulfila.* Oxford.

———. (1969). *The Goths in Spain.* Oxford.

———. (1976–1979). "The end of Roman Spain. Parts I–IV." *Nottingham Mediaeval Studies* 20, pp. 3–28; 21, pp. 3–31; 22, pp. 3–22; and 23, pp. 1–21.

———. (1977). "Britain, A.D. 406–410." *Britannia* 8, pp. 303–318.

Thorpe, L. (1974), trans. *Gregory of Tours, The history of the Franks.* Harmondsworth.

Torres, C. (1949). "Límites geográficos de Galicia en los siglos IV y V." *Cuadernos de estudios gallegos* 4, pp. 367–383.

Tranoy, A. (1974), ed. and trans. *Hydace, Chronique. SChr.* 218–219. 2 vols. Paris.

Turner, V. (1967a). "A Ndembu doctor in practice." In *The forest of symbols,* pp. 359–393. Ithaca.

———. (1967b). "Witchcraft and sorcery: Taxonomy versus dynamics." In *The forest of symbols,* pp. 112–127. Ithaca.

———. (1969). *The ritual process: Structure and anti-structure.* London.

———. (1973). "The center out there: Pilgrim's goal." *History of Religions* 12, pp. 191–230.

Twyman, B. L. (1970). "Aetius and the aristocracy." *Historia* 19, pp. 480–503.

Valentin, M. D. (1977), ed. and trans. *Hilaire d'Arles, Vie de Saint Honorat. SChr.* 235. Paris.

Van de Vyver, A. (1936, 1937). "La victoire contre les Alamans et la conversion de Clovis." *Revue belge de philologie et d'histoire* 15, pp. 859–914, and 16, pp. 35–94.

———. (1938). "L'unique victoire contre les Alamans et la conversion de Clovis en 506." *Revue belge de philologie et d'histoire* 17, pp. 793–813.

Van Sickle, C. E. (1934). "Eumenius and the schools of Autun." *American Journal of Philology* 55, pp. 236–243.

Vieillard-Troiekouroff, M. (1961). "Le tombeau de Saint Martin retrouvé en 1860." *Revue d'histoire de l'église de France* 47, pp. 151–183.

———. (1976). *Les monuments religieux de la Gaule d'après les oeuvres de Grégoire de Tours.* Paris.

Vielliard, J. (1963), ed. and trans. *Le Guide du pèlerin de Saint-Jacques de Compostelle.* 3rd ed. Mâcon.

Vogt, J. (1974). "Ecce ancilla Domini: The social aspects of the portrayal of the Virgin Mary in Antiquity." In *Ancient slavery and the ideal of man,* pp. 146–169. Oxford.

deVogüé, A. (1978). "Sur la patrie d'Honorat de Lérins, évêque d'Arles." *Revue Bénédictine* 88, pp. 290–291.

Vokes, F. E. (1966). "Montanism and the ministry." *Studia Patristica* 9 = *Texte und Untersuchungen* 94, pp. 306–315.

Vollmann, B. (1965). *Studien zum Priszillianismus*. St. Ottilien.

———. (1974). "Priscillianus." *RE* Suppl. XIV, col. 485–559. Munich.

Vollmer, F., and H. Rubenbauer (1926). "Ein verschollenes Grabgedicht aus Trier." *Trierer Zeitschrift* 1, pp. 26–30.

Wallace-Hadrill, J. M. (1962). *The long-haired kings*. London.

———. (1967). *The barbarian West 400–1000*. 3rd ed. London.

———. (1971). *Early Germanic kingship in England and on the continent*. Oxford.

———. (1975). "Gregory of Tours and Bede: Their views on the personal qualities of kings." In *Early medieval history*, pp. 96–114. Oxford.

Walter, E. H. (1966). "Hagiographisches in Gregors Frankengeschichte." *Archiv für Kulturgeschichte* 48, pp. 291–310.

Weber, M. (1927). *General economic history*. English translation: New York.

Weber, W. (1979). "Die Reliquienprozession auf der Elfenbeintafel des Trierer Domschatzes und das kaiserliche Hofzeremoniell." *Trierer Zeitschrift* 42, pp. 135–151.

Weinstock, S. (1971). *Divus Julius*. Oxford.

Wells, C. M. (1976). "The impact of the Augustan campaigns on Germany." In *Assimilation et résistance à la culture gréco-romaine dans le monde ancien*, ed. D. M. Pippidi. Travaux du VI^e Congrès international d'études classiques, pp. 421–431. Bucharest and Paris.

Whatmough, J. (1970). *The dialects of ancient Gaul*. Cambridge, Mass.

Whittaker, C. R. (1976). "Agri deserti." In *Studies in Roman property*, ed. M. I. Finley, pp. 137–165, 193–200. Cambridge.

———. (1978). "Land and labour in North Africa." *Klio* 60, pp. 331–362.

———. (1980). "Rural labour in three Roman provinces." In *Non-slave labour in the Greco-Roman world*, ed. P. Garnsey, pp. 73–99. Cambridge.

Widengren, G. (1965). *Mani and Manichaeism*. English translation: London.

Wieruszowski, H. (1922). "Die Zusammensetzung des gallischen und fränkischen Episkopats bis zum Vertrag von Verdun (843) mit besonderer Berücksichtigung der Nationalität und des Standes." *Bonner Jahrbücher* 127, pp. 1–83.

Wightman, E. M. (1970). *Roman Trier and the Treveri*. London.

———. (1975a). "The pattern of rural settlement in Roman Gaul." In *Aufstieg und Niedergang der römischen Welt*, vol. II.4, ed. H. Temporini, pp. 584–657. Berlin.

———. (1975b). "Priscae Gallorum memoriae: Some comments on sources for a history of Gaul." In *The ancient historian and his materials*, ed. B. Levick, pp. 93–107. Farnborough.

———. (1978). "Peasants and potentates: An investigation of social structure and land tenure in Roman Gaul." *American Journal of Ancient History* 3, pp. 97–128.

Williams, G. H. (1951). "Christology and Church-State relations in the fourth century." *Church History* 20.3, pp. 3–33, and 20.4, pp. 3–26.

Willis, R. G. (1970). "Instant millennium: The sociology of African witch-cleansing cults." In *Witchcraft confessions and accusations*, ed. M. Douglas, pp. 129–139. London.

Wood, I. N. (1977). "Kings, kingdoms and consent." In *Early medieval kingship*, ed. P. H. Sawyer and I. N. Wood, pp. 6–29. Leeds.

———. (1979). "Early Merovingian devotion in town and country." In *The church in town and countryside*, ed. D. Baker. *Studies in Church History* 16, pp. 61–76. Oxford.

Wormald, P. (1976). "The decline of the western empire and the survival of its aristocracy." *Journal of Roman Studies* 66, pp. 217–226.

Worsley, P. (1968). *The trumpet shall sound*. 2nd ed. London.

Wortley, J. (1980). "The Trier Ivory reconsidered." *Greek, Roman and Byzantine Studies* 21, pp. 381–394.

# INDEX

Abraham, monk, 171
*adventus*: of Constantine, 10; and presence of emperor, 21–22; of Julian, 35; of Christian relics, 59–60, 65, 215; of Constantius II, 61–62; of Martin, 125; of St. Martin, 140, 244; of Germanus of Auxerre, 144
Aegidius, Roman general, 181
Aelianus, leader of Bagaudae, 30–32
Aetius, Roman general, 46, 48, 148, 153
Agaune, 219
Agde, 197
Aix-en-Provence, 197
Alamanni, raids by, 28–29, 34
Alans: settlements of, 38, 46, 148–49; raids by, 42, 150
Albinus, St., 280–81
Alcuin, opinion of Tours, 248
Alexander, St., 171
Allectus, general of Carausius, 32
Alps, Bagaudae in, 48–49
Amandus, leader of Bagaudae, 30–32
Ambrose, bishop of Milan: ecclesiastical career of, 73; and Priscillianism, 88, 97, 103, 107, 110; as saint, 203; and Martin of Tours, 230
Amiens, 125
Angers, 280
Anianus, bishop of Orléans, 148, 169, 173
Anthemius, emperor, 160
Apollonius of Tyana: life of, by Sidonius, 173

Aquitania: as part of Armorica, 36, 42; considered remote, 37; settlement of Visigoths in, 38, 51, 148, 150–51; and Priscillianists, 98–100; beauty of, 157–58; local aristocrats of, 204, 210, 306–9. *See also* Bordeaux
Araceli, 51–52
Aravatius, bishop of Tongres, 148
Arianism, Arians: opposition of, to Martin, 125; identify Catholics as Romans, 179; of Visigoths, 187; attitude of, toward miracles, 187–90, 258; liturgy of, 281
aristocracies, local: importance of, in Gaul, 13–16, 37, 41–42; and bandits, 16–20; and local emperors, 29, 31–32; service of, in central administration, 33, 35–36; and misuse of power, 43–45; importance of, in Spain, 50–53. *See also* bishops
Arles, 111; seat of praetorian prefecture, 37, 45–46, 143, 166–67; provincial assembly at, 37, 153; Bishops Honoratus and Hilary, 155–56; cult of St. Trophimus at, 169; rivalry of, with Paris, 220. *See also* Caesarius
Armentaria, mother of Gregory of Tours, 207, 209, 224, 262
Armorica: definition of, 36; defense of, against barbarians, 39–41; Bagaudae in, 45–46; defense of, against Huns, 48; pagan priests of, 71; reputation of, 183

Brictio, bishop of Tours, 154, 234
Brioude: tomb of Avitus at, 175. *See also*
Julian, St.
Britain: support of, for Gallic Empire,
28–29; defense of, against barbarians,
39–41; appeal of, to Honorius, 40,
47–48; appeal of, to Aetius, 48; appeal
of, to Germanus of Auxerre, 143–44
Britannius, bishop of Trier: opponent of
Priscillian, 100
Brittany, 77
Brunhild, Frankish queen, 214, 222
Burgundians: settlements of, 38, 149,
161, 289; raids by, 39; cult of King Sigis-
mund, 219
Burgundy: and family of Gregory of
Tours, 204, 209–11, 216; aristocracy of,
220; famine in, 291

Caesarius, bishop of Arles, 103, 199,
226
Calahorra, 53
Candes, 192, 249
Carausius, emperor in Gaul and Britain:
stationed at Boulogne, 30, 32; criticized
as bandit and barbarian, 32–33; as leg-
endary hero, 39n
Carinus, emperor, 33
Carthage, 72
Carus, emperor, 33
Cassiodorus, 175
Catiline, image of, 98
Cato, priest at Clermont, 212
Celtic, survival of, 15–16, 23, 31, 47n
Charibert, king of Franks, 184, 213,
218, 223
Charietto, vigilante at Trier, 36
Childebert, king of Franks, 184, 209,
213–14, 233
Chilperic, king of Burgundians, 289
Chilperic, king of Franks, 184; and Greg-
ory of Tours, 179–80, 213–17, 224–
25; theology of, 196; and panegyric of
Fortunatus, 223; and St. Medard, 220
Chlodomer, king of Franks, 184
Chlothar, king of Franks, 184; selects
bishop of Tours, 212; and Radegund,
214; and St. Medard, 217; restores
church of St. Martin, 232
Chlothar II, king of Franks, 220
Circuitores, 81

Claudianus Mamertus, Gallic monk and
theologian, 164, 172
Claudius, emperor, 29
Clermont: churches and shrines at, 169,
188, 191, 237, 251; monks at, 171, 287;
conversion of Jews at, 180, 280; and
family of Gregory of Tours, 205–7,
213–14; counts of, 210; plague at, 263.
*See also* Sidonius
Clovis, king of Franks: conversion of,
181–82
Coblenz, 38
Cologne: pressured by barbarians, 28,
34; church of Theban Legion at, 239;
pagan shrine near, 261
Commodus, emperor, 18
Compostela, 248
Consentius, writer on Balearic Islands:
correspondence of, with Augustine,
111–12
Constans, son of Constantine III, 40,
50–51
Constantine I, emperor: at Trier, 9; arrival at Autun, 10; significance of
name, 39; consequences of conversion,
70, 90
Constantine III, emperor in Britain and
Gaul, 38–41; significance of name,
39, 41
Constantinople, 71
Constantius I, emperor: support of, for
Autun, 10; emperor in Gaul, 13, 33; invasion of Britain by, 32
Constantius II, emperor: arrival of, at
Rome, 61–62; sends Julian to Gaul, 34
Constantius, priest at Lyon: writes *Vita*
of Germanus of Auxerre, 144–47, 169
conversion: of Paulinus of Nola, 50,
115–16; of Jews, 67–68, 180; of emperor, 70; of educated men, 72–74; of
Sulpicius Severus, 115, 135; of Gaul,
120–22, 132–33; of Paulinus of Pella,
151; of Clovis, 181–82
Cordoba, 94
crisis: of third century, 20–21; of fifth
century, 37, 157
cults of saints and relics: in fifth-century
Gaul, 166–72; association of, with cities, 169–70, 191, 220, 231, 250–51; recall Paradise, 186, 239–40, 245, 253;
functions of, 188–93, 212; interpre-

101, 103, 105; at Trier, 122; taught by
Ausonius, 123–24, 304; and usurper
Maximus, 126, 307
Gratian, emperor in Britain, 38
Gregorius, bishop of Langres and Dijon:
ancestor of Gregory of Tours, 208–9,
212, 216
Gregory, bishop of Tours: restores cathedral at Tours, 137, 230, 235–36; illnesses of, 184, 262, 272–74; quarrels
with Leudast, 185, 213, 216; family of,
203–12, 224; selection as bishop, 212–
15; education of, 221, 224–27; humility
of, 228; constructs baptistery at Tours,
231; and doctors, 261–63, 275
—theology of, 187–88, 275–76, 293; and
St. Martin, 184, 191, 211, 217, 234–37,
249–52, 273–74; and St. Julian, 184,
207, 252, 271–72; and cult of saints,
188–95, 258; and other saints, 211,
215–17, 274; and liturgy, 280, 284,
288, 299
—parochialism of writings, 183–84,
199–201; and Manichaeism, 103; and
Romans, 179–80; and Frankish kings,
181–82, 196–97, 219–20, 224–25; and
Fortunatus, 187; opinion of Paulinus of
Nola, 309
Gregory, pope, 228, 238
Gundulf, ancestor of Gregory of Tours,
210
Guntram, king of Franks: kingdom of,
184, 213; appoints bishop, 206; and
family of Gregory of Tours, 210, 216–
17; miracles of, 219–20

hagiography: of Martin, 119–20, 135,
137, 233–37, 270; of Germanus of Aux-
erre, 144–47; of Gallic saints, 167–69.
*See also* books; cults of saints and relics
healing. *See* illness and healing
Hebromagus, 306
Hedibia, widow in Gaul, 75
Helpidius, supporter of Priscillian, 93
Hemeric, king of Sueves, 148
heresy: interpretation of, 78–79, 88–92;
peculiar examples of, 80–81. *See also*
Arianism; Donatism; Gnosticism;
Manichaeism; Montanism; Pel-
agianism; Priscillianism

Hilarus, pope, 52
Hilary, bishop of Arles: writes *Vita* of
Honoratus, 155–56; as bishop, 167n
Hilary, bishop of Poitiers: and Martin,
121, 124; cult of, 251, 274; festival of, at
Tours, 292
Honoratus, bishop of Arles, 155–56
Honorius, emperor: institutes assembly
at Arles, 37; visit to Rhine, 39; letter of,
to Britain, 40, 47–48
Hospicius, ascetic at Nice, 183
Huesca, 111
Huns, 48, 148, 169, 173, 182
Hydatius, bishop of Merida: opponent of
Priscillian, 94, 97, 100–1, 103, 107
Hydatius, Spanish bishop and historian:
on Bagaudae, 52; on Priscillianism,
108–9; as envoy, 148
Hyginus, bishop of Cordoba: opponent,
then supporter of Priscillian, 94

icons: comparable to saints' lives, 145; in
Byzantium, 200; in Gaul, 247
Illidius, bishop of Clermont, 183, 211,
215
Illness and healing: handbooks of remedies, 129–30, 275; conventional techniques of healing, 132, 261–63, 271–
72; interpretation of miraculous cures,
257–61, 274–76; causes of illness,
264–65, 286–87; consequences of illness, 265–66; illness associated with
demonic possession, imprisonment,
holiness, 266–69; miraculous cures,
269–72; healing as judgment, 272–74;
saints as doctors, 272, 274; holy dust,
274–76. timing of cures, 283. *See also*
Martin, St.
Inpetratus, priest at Clermont, 206
Instantius, bishop: supporter of Priscillian, 93–94, 103–4
Isauria, noted for banditry, 49
*iter*: used by Priscillian, 95–96, 253–54;
applied to life of Germanus of Auxerre, 145–46, 254; as pilgrimage, 252–
54. *See also* pilgrimage
Ithacius, bishop of Ossonuba: opponent
of Priscillian, 100–1; opponent of Martin, 105–7

Designer:    Lisa Mirski
Compositor:  G & S Typesetters, Inc.
Text:        11/13 Palatino
Display:     Palatino
Printer:     Thomson-Shore, Inc.
Binder:      John H. Dekker & Sons

# LATE ANTIQUE GAUL
# AND SPAIN

0                                                  300 miles

LUGDUNENSIS

Nantes

*Loire R.*

Poitier

AQUIT

Bordeaux •

Bazas •

*Garonn*

Toulouse

GALICIA

• Braga      • Astorga

*Ebro. R.*

P Y R E N E E S

TARRACONENSIS

Saragossa •

• Lerid

LUSITANIA      • Avila

Lisbon •

Tarragona •

• Toledo

• Merida

BAL

Ossonuba •

BAETICA